# Programming the IBM Personal Computer:

# COBOL

# IBM PERSONAL COMPUTER SERIES

## Programming

N. Graham    PROGRAMMING THE IBM PERSONAL COMPUTER: BASIC

N. Graham    PROGRAMMING THE IBM PERSONAL COMPUTER: COBOL

N. Graham    PROGRAMMING THE IBM PERSONAL COMPUTER: FUNDAMENTALS OF BASIC

N. Graham    PROGRAMMING THE IBM PERSONAL COMPUTER: PASCAL

W. T. Price    PROGRAMMING THE IBM PERSONAL COMPUTER: BUSINESS BASIC

R. Rouse and T. Bugnitz    PROGRAMMING THE IBM PERSONAL COMPUTER: FORTRAN 77

S. V. Pollack    PROGRAMMING THE IBM PERSONAL COMPUTER: UCSD PASCAL

R. Rouse and T. Bugnitz    PROGRAMMING THE IBM PERSONAL COMPUTER: UCSD p-SYSTEM WITH FORTRAN 77

S. V. Pollack, R. Rouse, and T. Bugnitz    PROGRAMMING THE IBM PERSONAL COMPUTER: UCSD p-SYSTEM WITH UCSD PASCAL AND FORTRAN 77

## Functions and Applications

D. Cortesi    YOUR IBM PERSONAL COMPUTER: USE, APPLICATIONS, AND BASIC

R. Crowley    USING THE IBM PERSONAL COMPUTER: VISICALC®

M. Franklin    USING THE IBM PERSONAL COMPUTER: MACRO-ASSEMBLER

CJ Puotinen    USING THE IBM PERSONAL COMPUTER: WORDSTAR™

J. Posdamer    USING THE IBM PERSONAL COMPUTER: GRAPHICS

# Programming the IBM Personal Computer: COBOL

## Neill Graham

HOLT, RINEHART AND WINSTON

New York    Chicago    San Francisco    Philadelphia
Montreal    Toronto    London    Sydney    Tokyo
Mexico City    Rio de Janeiro    Madrid

The cover illustration is The Additive Color Model from Miles Color Art, Tallahassee, Florida, prepared using the Digital Facsimiles process (patent pending), Center for Color Graphics, Florida State University, Tallahassee, Florida.

**Library of Congress Cataloging in Publication Data**

Graham, Neill, 1941–
    Programming the IBM Personal Computer, COBOL.

    Includes index.
    1. IBM Personal Computer—Programming.  2. COBOL
(Computer program language)  I. Title.  II. Title:
Programming the I.B.M. Personal Computer, COBOL.
QA76.8.I2594G725  1984     001.64'2     83-18658

ISBN 0-03-059563-0

Printed in the United States of America

Published simultaneously in Canada

4 5 6 7    039    9 8 7 6 5 4 3 2 1

CBS COLLEGE PUBLISHING
Holt, Rinehart and Winston
The Dryden Press
Saunders College Publishing

# Contents

# Introduction

COBOL—Common Business-Oriented Language—is the most widely used programming language for business data processing on large computers. Most of the bills and account statements you receive each month are produced by computers controlled by COBOL programs.

COBOL is business-oriented in four major ways. First, instructions for the computer are phrased in English-like words and sentences, which are more meaningful to business people than the algebra-like formulas required by many other languages. Second, COBOL is oriented toward file processing—organizing and storing massive amounts of data, such as information on each employee or each customer. Third, COBOL allows arithmetic to be done in the familiar decimal number system. Certain conventions of business arithmetic, such as rounding to the nearest cent, are based on the decimal system and cannot be expressed precisely in the binary number system used by many programming languages. Fourth, numeric values can be easily printed in the form expected by business people, with dollar signs, commas, decimal points, and trailing plus and minus signs.

Like most microcomputer implementations of COBOL, IBM Personal Computer COBOL—hereafter called IBM COBOL—omits certain advanced features of Standard COBOL. But in contrast to some other implementations, the omitted features are rarely used parts of the language that are seldom missed.

As if to make up for any omissions, IBM COBOL provides powerful extensions to Standard COBOL for interacting with the user. Standard COBOL is oriented toward batch processing—processing large files stored on punched cards, magnetic tapes, or disks. Microcomputers, however, need to interact with their users via the keyboard and display screen as well as process large files. To this end, IBM COBOL extends the ACCEPT and DISPLAY statements of Standard COBOL to accept input from and display output at any point on the screen. The user is prompted for the format of input data, such as how many digits appear to the left and right of the decimal point. Data not in the proper format is automatically rejected. A special Screen Section provides a convenient way of specifying the layouts of entire display screens.

The reference manual that comes with your COBOL compiler describes the technical details of each feature of the language, but it does not try to teach you how to program in COBOL. This book, in contrast, focuses on writing COBOL programs—on using the various features discussed in the reference manual to produce programs that do particular jobs. Since this book is not intended to replace the reference manual, it will not cover every feature of IBM COBOL nor does it always cover every technical detail of the features that are discussed.

Because COBOL is a fairly large and complex language, it sometimes seems unapproachable to beginners, who become inundated with technical details. Mistakes in spelling, punctuation, and the proper positioning of program constructions on typed lines cause many errors. One of the best ways to get a feel for COBOL as quickly as possible is to imitate correct programs. Enter each of the example programs into your computer, compile it, and execute it. Note that in the beginning, just typing a COBOL program in the correct format is a very useful exercise. After you have a program from the book working properly, try modifying it to do a slightly different job—to process different kinds of data, for example. After doing this for each program in a chapter, try working the exercises for the chapter, which usually call for programs similar to the ones discussed in the chapter. This approach should go a long way toward helping you get a feel for COBOL without being drowned in technicalities.

IBM COBOL is a *compiler language*—that is, the COBOL programs you write must be translated, or *compiled,* into a special coded form before they can be executed by the computer. Entering a program and getting it executed involves more steps for a compiler language than for an interpretive language such as BASIC, where no compiling is required and one need only enter the command RUN to get a program executed. Chapter 1 is devoted to using the COBOL compiler and related programs such as the linker and the runtime system. In Chapter 1 we see how to enter a COBOL program, compile it, link the compiled program with previously written routines in the COBOL library, and execute the compiled-and-linked programs.

Chapter 2 introduces the basic structure of COBOL programs. You should concentrate particularly on the proper punctuation of COBOL programs and on the way in which various constructions are positioned on program lines. Punctuation and positioning will cause much trouble later if not mastered early.

COBOL programs are frequently used to print out data in neatly formatted reports. The data to be printed usually has to be *edited* to make it intelligible to humans. For example, dollar signs, commas, and decimal points need to be inserted in numbers representing amounts of money. Chapter 3 takes up methods of editing data and arranging it properly on a printed report.

Chapter 4 takes up arithmetic in COBOL. Note that COBOL allows you to specify arithmetical calculations by either English-like sentences or algebra-like formulas. You are free to choose whichever method you wish. Persons with business backgrounds usually choose the sentences; those with scientific backgrounds often prefer the formulas.

Chapter 5 focuses on writing programs that can interact with users via the keyboard and the display screen. Most of the COBOL features discussed in this chapter are extensions to the language that are present in IBM COBOL but not in Standard COBOL.

Business data is often organized in *tables* such as tax tables and tables giving the discount for an item depending on the quantity purchased. In Chapter 6 we see how to describe and manipulate tables in COBOL programs.

COBOL allows records in files to be organized in three ways. Records in a *sequential file* can only be processed in the order in which they are stored in the file. Records in a *relative file* can be processed in any order; each record is designated by a unique record number which is used to select that record for processing. Records in an *indexed file* can also be processed in any order; each record is designated by a unique *key value* (such as a person's name or account number) which is used to select that record for processing. Chapters 7, 8, and 9 cover these three methods of organizing files.

Chapter 10 discusses methods of combatting errors, both those made by the programmer and those made by the user. Chapter 11 describes some additional features of COBOL that did not fit into any of the earlier chapters.

The material in this book applies both to systems using diskette storage and to those (such as the IBM Personal Computer XT) using fixed-disk storage; it also applies to both DOS 1.10 and DOS 2.00. Chapter 1 first describes how to compile COBOL programs using diskette storage and DOS 1.10, then gives the additional considerations needed when using fixed-disk storage and DOS 2.00. In Chapters 2 through 11, the word "disk" can refer to either a diskette or a fixed disk. The programs run the same under both DOS 1.10 and DOS 2.00.

# Programming the IBM Personal Computer:

# COBOL

# 1

# Using the COBOL Compiler

Before the computer can follow the instructions in a COBOL program, the program must be *compiled*—translated into an easy-to-process code. Writing and compiling a program involves several steps. You begin by entering the *source program*—the COBOL program that you write—and storing it on a diskette. This is done with the aid of a *text editor* such as EDLIN—the text editor provided on the DOS (Disk Operating System) diskette. Next, you use the *COBOL compiler* to translate your source program into an *object program*. The object program is incomplete in that it refers to, but does not include many *subprograms* from the COBOL program library. You use the *linker* to combine the object program with the necessary subprograms from the program library. The result is an *executable program,* which can be run, or executed, under the control of the *runtime module*. This chapter is devoted to the details of getting a program entered, compiled, linked, and executed.

## PREPARING THE DISKETTES

To compile and run COBOL programs, you will need a DOS diskette in addition to the two diskettes supplied in the COBOL compiler package.* You will also need a supply of blank diskettes for making backup copies of the compiler diskettes and for storing the COBOL programs you write.

The COBOL compiler package contains two diskettes, the COBOL diskette (which contains the COBOL compiler) and the LIBRARY diskette (which contains the COBOL library, the linker, and the runtime module). To guard against accidental damage to your diskettes, you should make two backup copies of each diskette. Put the original diskettes and one set of backup copies in a safe place, and use the other set of backup copies for compiling COBOL programs.

You will find it convenient to create a version of the COBOL diskette containing the DOS and commonly used utility programs such as FORMAT and DISKCOPY as well as the COBOL compiler. You can use this diskette to start up your computer and perform such routine chores as formatting and copying as well as to compile COBOL programs. To make the diskette, place your DOS diskette in drive A and a blank diskette in drive B. Format the blank diskette with the /S option, which causes a copy of the operating system to be placed on the formatted diskette:

```
A>FORMAT B:/S
```

(When illustrating DOS commands, I will usually include the DOS prompts A > and B >, even though they are typed by the computer instead of the user.) Next, insert the COBOL diskette in drive A and copy the five compiler files to the newly formatted diskette:

```
A>COPY A:COBOL?.* B:
```

Finally reinsert the DOS diskette in drive A and copy the utilities you think you will need onto the new diskette. For example:

```
A>COPY A:CHKDSK.COM B:
A>COPY A:FORMAT.COM B:
A>COPY A:DISKCOPY.COM B:
A>COPY A:DISKCOMP.COM B:
```

Copy COMMAND.COM, the DOS command-interpreter program, from the DOS diskette to the LIBRARY diskette. The linker may overwrite this program in memory, and your COBOL programs will always do so. Placing COMMAND.COM on the LIBRARY diskette allows it to be automatically reloaded after the linker or a COBOL program has run.

Format another diskette, which we will refer to as the *scratch diskette*. The scratch diskette will hold your COBOL source, object, and executable programs, as well as temporary work files created by the compiler and the linker. Copy the text editor that you will use to prepare COBOL programs onto the scratch diskette. If you wish to use EDLIN for this purpose, copy EDLIN from the DOS diskette to the scratch diskette.

---

*Be sure that you have the updated version of the compiler. A patch is available through dealers to allow the compiler to be used with 512K or more of memory.

## EDITING, COMPILING, LINKING, AND RUNNING

Now let's look in detail at the steps of editing (entering and correcting), compiling, linking, and running a program. We will use the very simple COBOL program shown in Figure 1.1 as an example.

### Entering the Source Program

The starting point for the entire compilation process is a COBOL source program, which you must type into the computer and store on a diskette. A program is entered with the aid of a text editor, which accepts the program that you type, allows you to display the program on the screen and correct errors in it, and stores the program in a diskette file that you designate. You can use the text editor EDLIN, which is provided on the DOS diskette, or you can purchase a more advanced text editor, which may be more convenient for writing COBOL programs. In the following instructions I will assume that you are using EDLIN.

To begin, insert your scratch diskette (which contains your text editor) into drive B and make drive B the default drive:

```
A>B:
B>_
```

We want to enter the program EXAMPLE from Figure 1.1. COBOL source files have the extension COB, so we will store the program EXAMPLE in the file EXAMPLE.COB. We invoke the text editor to create the source file EXAMPLE.COB as follows:

```
B>EDLIN EXAMPLE.COB
```

With the aid of the text editor, you can type in the program and correct any typing errors that you might make. The details of using a text editor are beyond the scope of this book. Instructions for using EDLIN can be found in the DOS reference manual. When you exit from the text editor, your COBOL source program will be stored in the file EXAMPLE.COB on the scratch diskette.

```
IDENTIFICATION DIVISION.
PROGRAM-ID. EXAMPLE.

ENVIRONMENT DIVISION.

DATA DIVISION.

PROCEDURE DIVISION.
DISPLAY-MESSAGE.
    DISPLAY "You have succeeded in compiling and running".
    DISPLAY "a program in IBM Personal Computer COBOL".
    STOP RUN.
```

*Figure 1.1*   A sample COBOL program you can use for experimenting with the editor, compiler, and linker. All but the last three lines start in column 8—that is, each is preceded by 7 spaces. The last three lines start in column 12—each is preceded by 11 spaces.

A few words need to be said about Figure 1.1 so that you can type the program in correctly. Each of the items

```
IDENTIFICATION DIVISION.
PROGRAM-ID. EXAMPLE.
ENVIRONMENT DIVISION.
DATA DIVISION.
PROCEDURE DIVISION.
DISPLAY-MESSAGE.
```

begins in the eighth character position on the line. Character positions are usually referred to as *columns,* since all the characters in a given position line up in a column on the screen or in the printout. The items listed, then, all begin in column 8. Put another way, each item is preceded by seven blank spaces. The items on the last three lines of the program begin in column 12; each item is preceded by eleven blank spaces.

To type the first line of the program with EDLIN, hit the space bar seven times and type IDENTIFICATION DIVISION. The remaining items that begin in column 8 can be aligned beneath IDENTIFICATION DIVISION. The three blank lines are optional. For the first item that begins in column 12, press the space bar 11 times and then type the item. The remaining items that begin in column 12 can be aligned beneath the first one. The format of COBOL programs is described in more detail in Chapter 2.

## Compiling

### Using the compiler

To compile the source file that you have just created, insert the COBOL diskette in drive A and enter the following command:

```
B>A:COBOL EXAMPLE;
```

Note the semicolon following EXAMPLE, which prevents the compiler from prompting you for optional file names. If you leave out the semicolon and get the prompts, just press the Enter key in response to each prompt. Once started, the compiler operates automatically. When it terminates, the scratch diskette will contain the object file EXAMPLE.OBJ.

### Error messages

If you made any typing errors when entering the program, the compiler may display one or more *error messages*. Each error message gives the number of the line in which the error occurred followed by a description of the error. The possible error messages and their explanations are given in appendix A of the COBOL reference manual.

For example, Figure 1.2 shows the program BADEXMPL, which is the same as EXAMPLE except that the word DISPLAY is misspelled in line 10. (Note that in numbering the lines the blank lines are counted too.) When we attempt to compile BADEXMPL, the following error messages appear on the screen:

```
IDENTIFICATION DIVISION.
PROGRAM-ID. BADEXMPL.

ENVIRONMENT DIVISION.

DATA DIVISION.

PROCEDURE DIVISION.
DISPLAY-MESSAGE.
    DISPLY "You have succeeded in compiling and running".
    DISPLAY "a program in IBM Personal Computer COBOL".
    STOP RUN.
```

*Figure 1.2*  This program contains an error in the third line from the bottom—the word DISPLAY is mispelled.

```
10:  UNRECOGNIZABLE ELEMENT IS IGNORED.  DISPLY
10:  UNRECOGNIZABLE ELEMENT IS IGNORED.  You have succeeeded in
```

The first message tells us that the compiler did not recognize the misspelled word DISPLY and so ingnored it. The second message represents not an error but a situation that occurs all too frequently: An error causes other, correct parts of the program to appear erroneous to the compiler. In this case the compiler, having ignored the misspelled DISPLAY command, doesn't know what to do with the message to be displayed. The message is designated as an unrecognizable element even though it contains no error.

If you receive any error messages, return to the text editor, check the lines in question with Figure 1.1, and make any needed corrections. Pay particular attention to the punctuation marks (periods, hyphens, and quotation marks), which often cause trouble in COBOL. When you have made your corrections, exit from the editor, and execute the COBOL compiler to compile the corrected program.

There are three ways in which you can get a printout of your error messages. Typing Shift PrtSc will print the error messages currently on the screen. If you anticipate more error messages than will fit on the screen, type Ctrl PrtSc before invoking the compiler. Everything displayed on the screen, including error messages, will also be sent to the printer. (Type Ctrl PrtSc again to stop displayed output from being sent to the printer.) Finally, you can have the compiler produce a *listing*—a printout that includes the text of the COBOL program (with the lines numbered) together with any error messages. We will see later in this chapter how to request the compiler to print a listing.

If no errors are found, the compiler finishes by displaying the message

```
No Errors or Warnings
```

## Linking

To link the object program, remove the COBOL diskette from drive A and insert the LIBRARY diskette. To execute the linker, enter the following command line:

```
A:LINK EXAMPLE;
```

As with the compiler, the semicolon at the end of the command line prevents the linker from prompting for optional file names. Like the compiler, the linker operates automatically once started. When the linker finishes, the scratch diskette will contain the executable file EXAMPLE.EXE. Linker error messages are rare and usually correspond to obvious oversights, such as if the object file to be linked is not present on the scratch diskette.

### Running

Once a COBOL program is compiled, we can run it by entering the name of the program in response to the DOS prompt. If (without removing either the LIBRARY diskette or the scratch diskette) we enter the command

```
B>EXAMPLE
```

the program EXAMPLE will be run, and the message in the two DISPLAY statements will appear on the screen:

```
B>EXAMPLE
You have succeeded in compiling and running
a program in IBM Personal Computer COBOL

B>_
```

Compiled COBOL programs are executed under the control of the runtime module COBRUN.EXE, which interprets the instruction codes produced by the compiler. You do not have to worry about loading and executing COBRUN—this is done automatically when you execute your COBOL program. However, COBRUN must be available on diskette. The system first looks for COBRUN on the diskette in the default drive; if COBRUN is not found, the system searches the diskette in drive A.

When you run a program you have just compiled, the copy of COBRUN on the LIBRARY diskette is used. Whenever you run a COBOL program that is on the scratch diskette, the LIBRARY diskette should be in drive A. When you are satisfied with the performance of a COBOL program, you will usually copy the executable program from the scratch diskette on to another diskette for everyday use. To make sure that the needed runtime module is available, copy COBRUN from the LIBRARY diskette to the diskette containing the COBOL program. Make sure that the program diskette is either in drive A or the default drive when the program is run.

As mentioned earlier, a COBOL program always overwrites the DOS command interpreter COMMAND.COM. Therefore, a copy of COMMAND.COM should be on the diskette in drive A whenever a COBOL program is run. (Otherwise, after the COBOL program has finished executing, the system will prompt you to insert a DOS diskette in drive A.)

### USING A BATCH FILE

We can simplify the compilation process by using a *batch file* to issue the commands that invoke the text editor, the compiler, the linker, and the executable program. A batch file is invoked just like a program. For example, in this section we will write a batch file RUN.BAT (all batch files have the extension BAT) for compiling COBOL programs. To compile and execute the program EXAMPLE, we invoke the batch file with the command line

```
B>RUN EXAMPLE
```

(note—no semicolon after EXAMPLE). EXAMPLE is a *command-line parameter* that can be passed to the commands making up the batch file. When we write the batch file, we use %1 to represent the first command-line parameter, %2 to represent the second command-line parameter, and and so on. Before each command is executed, the first parameter will be substituted for the %1, the second parameter for %2, and so on. Thus when RUN is invoked with the parameter EXAMPLE, EXAMPLE is substituted for every occurrence of %1 in the batch file.

A batch file is just a list of DOS commands with %1, %2, and so on where parameters are to be substituted. You can create a batch file with your text editor. Alternatively, you can use the COPY command to copy from the console—that is, the keyboard—to the desired batch file. Let's use this method to create the batch file RUN.BAT and store it on the scratch diskette:

```
B>COPY CON: RUN.BAT
EDLIN %1.COB
PAUSE Insert the COBOL diskette in drive A
A:COBOL %1;
PAUSE Insert the LIBRARY diskette in drive A
A:LINK %1;
%1
^Z
```

^Z, which can be entered by pressing the function key F6, signals the end of the file. The six lines between the COPY command and ^Z are stored in the batch file. When the batch file is invoked, the commands are executed one after another, with the command-line parameter substituted for %1.

For example, suppose we invoke RUN with the command line

```
B>RUN EXAMPLE
```

When EXAMPLE is substituted for %1 in the first line of the batch file, we get

```
EDLIN EXAMPLE.COB
```

which invokes EDLIN to create or edit the file EXAMPLE.COB. When you exit from EDLIN, the system goes on to the next command in the batch file.

A PAUSE command is used to request a manual operation, such as changing a diskette, and to wait until the user has completed the operation. When the command

```
PAUSE Insert the COBOL diskette in drive A
```

is executed, the following appears on the screen:

```
B>PAUSE Insert the COBOL diskette in drive A
Strike a key when ready . . . _
```

When this message appears, insert the COBOL diskette in drive A as requested, then strike a key to continue processing.

When EXAMPLE is substituted for %1 in the next command of the batch file, we get

```
A:COBOL EXAMPLE;
```

which invokes the compiler to compile the source file EXAMPLE.COB. Note that the semicolon following EXAMPLE is the same as the semicolon following %1 in the corresponding line of the batch file. The second PAUSE command

```
PAUSE Insert the LIBRARY diskette in drive A
```

prompts you to remove the COBOL diskette and insert the LIBRARY diskette containing the linker, the library, and the runtime module.

If the compiler finds errors in your program, you will want to return to the editor and correct the errors rather than continue with the commands in the batch file. When the request to insert the LIBRARY diskette appears, type Ctrl Break. The following prompt appears:

```
Terminate batch job (Y/N)? _
```

If you respond with Y, the system will discontinue processing the batch file and stand by for further commands from the keyboard. To return to the editor, reinvoke the batch file with

```
B>RUN EXAMPLE
```

If you don't terminate batch processing, but instead insert the LIBRARY diskette and press a key, the system will execute the next command in the batch file, with EXAMPLE substituted for %1:

```
A:LINK EXAMPLE;
```

This command invokes the linker to link the object program EXAMPLE.OBJ and produce the executable program EXAMPLE.EXE. After substituting EXAMPLE for %1, the last command in the batch file becomes

```
EXAMPLE
```

which runs the program that has just been compiled and linked.

## LISTINGS, PROMPTS, AND COMMAND LINES

### Listings

You can request the compiler to produce a listing of your source program—a printout of the program with each line numbered and with the error messages listed at the end of the program. Listings provide a permanent record of your source program, and are useful (in some cases almost essential) for debugging long programs containing many errors. A listing can be sent to the printer, displayed on the screen, or stored in a diskette file. When a listing is stored on diskette, the listing file is given the extension LST. Figure 1.3 shows a listing of the erroneous program BADEXMPL.

## Compiler Prompts

The compiler deals with three files—the source file, the object file, and the listing file. If you don't provide all three files in the command line, and you don't end the command line with a semicolon, the compiler will prompt you for the files not specified in the command line.

For example, suppose we invoke the compiler with

```
B>A:COBOL
```

Since no file names are provided in the command line, the compiler prompts for all three files. The exchange between the compiler and the user might go like this:

```
Source filename [.COB]: EXAMPLE
Object filename [EXAMPLE.OBJ]:
Source listing [NUL.LST]:
```

In each prompt, the compiler indicates the default file name (or part of a file name) that it will assume. The first prompt

```
Source filename [.COB]:
```

indicates that the compiler will assume the standard extension COB. Therefore, the user can enter the file name, EXAMPLE, without the extension. The next prompt

```
Object filename [EXAMPLE.OBJ]:
```

indicates that the default for the name of the object file is EXAMPLE.OBJ. If the user responds by pressing the Enter key, as was done in the example, the compiler uses the default file name. In the third prompt,

```
BADEXMPLCOB                            08:18:35    05-Feb-83    PAGE    1
Line Number Source Line    IBM Personal Computer COBOL Compiler    Version 1.00

    1           IDENTIFICATION DIVISION.
    2           PROGRAM-ID. BADEXMPL.
    3
    4           ENVIRONMENT DIVISION.
    5
    6           DATA DIVISION.
    7
    8           PROCEDURE DIVISION.
    9           DISPLAY-MESSAGE.
   10               DISPLY "You have succeeded in compiling and running".
   11               DISPLAY "a program in IBM Personal Computer COBOL".
   12               STOP RUN.
 0010:   UNRECOGNIZABLE ELEMENT IS IGNORED.    DISPLY
 0010:   UNRECOGNIZABLE ELEMENT IS IGNORED.    You have succeeded in
```

*Figure 1.3*   The listing produced by the compiler for the program in Figure 1.2. Note the line numbers to the left of the program and the error messages at the end of the listing.

```
Source listing [NUL.LST]:
```

NUL (which stands for *null*) is a special dummy file name that causes no file to be produced. If the user responds by pressing the Enter key, NUL.LST becomes the name of the listing file, and so no listing file is produced.

In the following example, the user does not accept the defaults for the object and source listing file names:

```
Source filename [.COB]: EXAMPLE
Object filename [EXAMPLE.OBJ]: EXO
Source listing [NUL.LST]: EXL
```

The compiler processes the source file EXAMPLE.COB and produces the object file EXO.OBJ and the listing file EXL.LST. Note that the extensions OBJ and LST are still assumed even when the rest of the default file name is not accepted. In our final example, the user sends the source listing to the printer:

```
Source filename [.COB]: EXAMPLE
Object filename [EXAMPLE.OBJ]:
Source listing [NUL.LST]: LPT1
```

If CON had been used instead of LPT1, the listing file would have been displayed on the screen.

## Compiler Command Lines

The command line for the COBOL compiler has the following general form:

```
COBOL Source File,Object File,Source Listing;
```

If the command line ends with a semicolon, default values are used for missing filenames; if the semicolon is omitted, the compiler prompts for missing file names.

Let's look at some examples of compiler command lines. We are already familiar with

```
COBOL EXAMPLE;
```

which compiles the source file EXAMPLE.COB producing the object file EXAM-PLE.OBJ. The default file name for the listing file is NUL.LST, so no listing is produced.

There are two possible defaults for the source listing file name. If both commas are present in the command line, as in

```
COBOL EXAMPLE,EXO,;
```

or

```
COBOL EXAMPLE,,;
```

the default for the source listing file name is EXAMPLE.LST, and the source listing is stored in a diskette file with that name. But if one or both of the commas is missing, as in our first example, the default for the source listing file names is NUL.LST and no source listing is produced. Incidentally, in the first of the two immediately preceding examples, the object file name is EXO.OBJ; in the second, the object file name defaults to EXAMPLE.OBJ.

We can also send the source listing to the printer

    COBOL EXAMPLE,,LPT1;

or to the display

    COBOL EXAMPLE,,CON;

In each case, the object file name defaults to EXAMPLE.OBJ.


## FIXED DISKS AND DOS 2.00

The procedures given so far in this chapter assume that you are using diskette storage. With fixed-disk storage, however, all the programs and files needed to compile a COBOL program can be placed on the fixed disk, eliminating the need for diskette changes and making it unlikely that you will ever run out of disk storage during a compilation. In this section, we will look at how to create, compile, link, and execute COBOL programs using a fixed disk and DOS 2.00, the version of the operating system usually used with fixed disks.

Since a fixed disk can hold thousands of files, it is impractical to include all the files in a single directory. Thus, the most important difference between DOS 1.10 and DOS 2.00 is that the latter allows more than one directory on a diskette or fixed disk. The main, or *root*, directory can contain the names of *subdirectories;* these subdirectories can contain the names of other subdirectories, and so on. We can think of the directories as forming a *tree,* with branches extending from the root directory to each of its subdirectories and from a subdirectory to each of its own subdirectories.

We designate a particular directory by means of a *path*, which gives the names of the directories that we must pass through in traveling from the root directory to the directory in question. For example, suppose that the root directory has a subdirectory LNGPROCS (language processors), LNGPROCS has a subdirectory COMPLRS (compilers), and COMPLRS has a subdirectory COBL (containing the programs and other files needed to compile a COBOL program). We designate the subdirectory COBL by the path

    \LNGPROCS\COMPLRS\COBL

The directory names are separated by backslashes. The initial backslash indicates that the path begins at the root directory. To designate a particular file in a directory, we give the path to the directory followed by a backslash and the name of the file. Thus, we can refer to the file EXAMPLE.COB in the directory COBL as follows:

    \LNGPROCS\COMPLRS\COBL\EXAMPLE.COB

Just as we can designate a default drive, which is assumed whenever no drive is specified, we can also designate a *current directory,* which is assumed whenever no directory is specified. In DOS 2.00, we use the command CD to designate the current directory. If the default drive is drive C (a fixed disk is usually designated drive C), the command line

```
C>CD \LNGPROCS\COMPLRS\COBL
```

designates COBL as the current directory for drive C. For any command that does not specify a particular directory, COBL will be assumed. Thus

```
C>DIR
```

displays the directory COBL, and

```
C>TYPE EXAMPLE.COB
```

displays the file EXAMPLE.COB in the directory COBL. We can define a current directory for each diskette or fixed-disk drive. When no drive is explicitly mentioned, "current directory" refers to the current directory on the default drive.

When we enter a command line such as

```
C>COBOL
```

DOS 2.00 searches the current directory for the program or batch file to be executed. If we want additional directories searched, we must specify them in a PATH command. For example, the PATH command

```
C>PATH C:\;C:\LNGPROCS\COMPLRS\PASCAL
```

specifies that if a program or batch file is not found in the current directory, the root directory on drive C (C:\) will be searched followed by the directory PASCAL on drive C (C:\LNGPROCS\COMPLRS\PASCAL). For example, if we enter the command line

```
C>LINK
```

the DOS will search for LINK in the current directory first, then in the root directory on drive C, and finally in the directory PASCAL on drive C.

The simplest arrangement for compiling a COBOL program is to have all files needed during the compilation in the current directory. Thus, the current directory should contain EDLIN.COM from the DOS diskette; COBOL.COM, COBOL1.OVR, COBOL2.OVR, COBOL3.OVR, and COBOL4.OVR from the COBOL diskette; COBOL1.LIB, COBOL2.LIB, and COBRUN.EXE from the LIBRARY diskette; and LINK.EXE from the DOS Supplemental Programs diskette. (Note that the DOS 2.00 version of LINK as used, rather than the one supplied on the LIBRARY diskette.) Copy all of these files from the diskettes on which they are supplied to the fixed disk, placing all of them in the directory that will be the current directory during COBOL compilations.

The COBOL compiler normally reads the overlay files (those with extension OVR) from drive A. To have the files read from drive C, we must use the parameter /CC when the compiler is invoked. (The second letter is the drive from which the overlay files will be read; thus /CD would cause them to be read from drive D, and so on.) The compiler normally creates a temporary work file on drive B; to have the temporary file created on drive C, we must use the parameter /TC when the compiler is invoked.

If the default drive is C and all the files needed for the compilation are in the current directory for drive C, the following are the command lines needed to create, compile, link, and execute the COBOL program EXAMPLE:

```
C>EDLIN EXAMPLE.COB
C>COBOL EXAMPLE/CC/TC;
C>LINK EXAMPLE;
C>EXAMPLE
```

The source, object, and executable files will be placed in the current directory for drive C.

Since EDLIN and LINK may be used by several language processors, you may wish to place them in the root directory or in a directory of utility programs rather than in the directory associated with a particular language processor. This is permissible as long as you issue a PATH command specifying the directories that are to be searched for these programs. For example, if EDLIN is in the root directory and LINK is in UTILITY, a subdirectory of the root directory, we can issue the PATH line:

```
C>PATH C:\;C:\UTILITY
```

As described earlier, the commands for creating, compiling, linking, and executing can be placed in a batch file. No PAUSE commands are needed to instruct the user to change diskettes. However, you may still want to place a PAUSE command after the command that invokes the compiler; this pause will give the user a chance to see whether the compiler produced any error messages and then decide whether to continue with linking and execution. After examining the output from the compiler, the user can press Ctrl Break to abort the compilation and any other key to continue.

The batch file can be in any directory as long as a path for reaching it has been included in a path command. Note that batch files can contain CD and PATH commands, so a batch file in, say, the root directory could select the current directory and set up the paths needed to compile COBOL programs.

When running a compiled COBOL program, the current directory must contain the runtime module COBRUN.EXE as well as all files to be processed by the program. The executable file for the COBOL program will usually also be in the current directory, but it could be in another directory if a path for reaching it has been included in a PATH command. Since COBOL programs always overwrite the command interpreter COMMAND.COM, a copy of COMMAND.COM should be in the root directory of the drive from which the system was started, which will normally be the fixed-disk drive.

In the remainder of the book, the word "disk" can refer to either a diskette or a fixed disk, and everything said applies equally well to DOS 1.10 and DOS 2.00.

## EXERCISES

**1.** Enter, compile, link, and run the program EXAMPLE given in Figure 1.1.

**2.** Create the batch file described in the text and store it on your scratch diskette as

RUN.BAT. Repeat Exercise 1 using the batch file to invoke the editor, compiler, linker, and the executable program.

3. The COBOL diskette contains two sample batch files: RUNED.BAT and RUNEC-.BAT. Instead of going through the entire compilation process as RUN does, RUNED and RUNEC run the editor and compiler repeatedly, so you can create a program, compile it to check for errors, go back to the editor to correct the errors, compile to check for more errors, and so on. Experiment with these batch files and decide whether you prefer them to RUN.

# 2

## Elements
## of
## COBOL

This chapter introduces those elements of COBOL that occur in almost all COBOL programs. Many of the elements introduced here are discussed more fully in later chapters. The many details of even fairly simple programs sometimes prove confusing to beginners. But be assured that after a bit of practice, these details will fall into place and thereafter seem to be the "obvious" or "natural" way to write COBOL programs. I strongly suggest that you work all the exercises at the end of the chapter. Exercise 1 is particularly helpful for mastering the structure of COBOL programs.

### PROGRAM FORMAT

COBOL programs are typed in 80-character lines, of which only the first 72 characters are normally used. Each part of the program must appear at a specific position or in a specific area of the typed line. To describe this positioning, we assume that character positions on a line are numbered from 1 for the leftmost position through 80 for the rightmost position. These numbered character positions are usually referred to as *columns*—the leftmost character of a line is in column 1, the next character to the right is

**15**

in column 2, and so on. To illustrate the positioning of various parts of a program, we can use a column-number scale:

```
              1   1   2   2   2   3
1......78...2...6...0...4...8...2...
          IDENTIFICATION DIVISION.
          PROGRAM-ID. EXAMPLE.
```

With the aid of the scale, we have no trouble seeing, for example, that each line begins in column 8, with columns 1 through 7 left blank.

Each line of a COBOL program is divided into five areas as follows:

| Columns | Area |
| --- | --- |
| 1–6 | Sequence number area |
| 7 | Indicator area |
| 8–11 | Area A |
| 12–72 | Area B |
| 73–80 | Identification area (ignored by the compiler) |

### The Sequence Number Area

Columns 1 through 6 can be used for a six-digit line number, or they can be left blank. Sequence numbers are most useful with punched cards, which can easily get out of order (we may drop the deck of cards on the floor). When we create our COBOL programs with a text editor, we usually leave the sequence number area blank and use the line numbers displayed by the text editor and printed on the program listing by the compiler.

### The Indicator Area

The indicator area is used to mark lines for special purposes. For example, an asterisk in the indicator area designates a line as a *comment,* intended for human readers only. The COBOL compiler ignores any line having an asterisk in the indicator area. If we use a / instead of an asterisk, the compiler will go to the top of a new page before printing the comment. Because COBOL is specifically designed to be easy to read, COBOL programs do not require nearly as many comments as programs written in other, more obscure languages. However, brief comments explaining what a program does and how it is to be used are often included near the beginning of the program:

```
              1   1   2   2   2   3   3   4   4
1......78...2...6...0...4...8...2...6...0...4...
          IDENTIFICATION DIVISION.
          PROGRAM-ID. EXAMPLE.

      *     This program displays a two-line
      *     message for the user
```

Blank lines can be used throughout a program for readability. They cannot appear after the last line of the program, however. Blank lines at the end of a program produce the error message `ILLEGAL CHARACTER`.

## Area A and Area B

The program proper appears in areas A and B. Area A consists of columns 8 through 11, and area B consists of columns 12 through 72. Column 8, the first column of area A, is the *A margin*. Likewise, column 12, the first column of area B, is the *B margin*. The specific uses of these two areas will be discussed as we take up the various parts of a COBOL program.

    Because the parts of a program that we are most interested in appear in areas A and B, and because of the importance of distinguishing between these two areas, examples will often be displayed in the following form:

```
         1   2   2   2   3
A...B...6...0...4...8...2...
IDENTIFICATION DIVISION.
PROGRAM-ID. EXAMPLE.
```

Columns 1 through 7 are not shown, and the A and B margins are specifically marked.

## The Identification Area

The compiler ignores anything typed in the identification area, columns 73 through 80. When programs are punched on cards, the name of the program is usually punched in the identification area. If the cards of two different programs get mixed up—we drop two card decks on the floor at the same time—we can use the identification area to determine which cards go with which program. This problem is unlikely to arise when programs are stored in disk files, so we will not use the indentification area. You must be careful, however, not to let a long program line extend into the identification area, since the compiler will not process any part of the line that extends beyond column 72.

## Setting Tab Stops

Because some parts of a COBOL program must begin in particular columns or areas, you will find it convenient to use the `Tab` key to move the cursor to the required column, relieving you of the need to count out a certain number of blank spaces at the beginning of each line. Most (but, alas, not all) text editors allow you to set tab stops just as you would do on a typewriter. When you press the `Tab` key, the cursor moves to the next column to the right for which a tab stop has been set.

    Different editors respond to the `Tab` key in different ways, however. Some place one space in the source file for each column passed over when the `Tab` key is pressed, while others just put in a special tab character to indicate that the `Tab` key was pressed. Still others allow you to chose either spaces or tab characters. If you have the choice, I suggest using spaces, since this method gives you the greatest freedom to set tab stops where you want them.

If your editor puts spaces in the file, I suggest that you set tab stops at the A margin (column 8), the B margin (column 12), and every four columns thereafter—columns 16, 20, 24, and so on through column 40. After you have had some experience writing COBOL programs, you can set the tab stops according to your own preference.

If your editor puts tab characters in the file, you should set the tab stops for the editor to coincide with those assumed by the COBOL compiler, so that the editor and the compiler will interpret tab characters in the same way. The compiler assumes tab stops at columns 8, 12, and every eight columns thereafter: 20, 28, 36, and so on through 68. The last tab stop is in column 73.

EDLIN presents particular problems because it puts tab characters in the file but does not allow you to set tab stops. EDLIN assumes tab stops at columns 9, 17, 25, 33, and so on. Since the compiler assumes tab stops at columns 8, 12, 20, 28, and so on, the tab stops used by EDLIN do not conincide with those used by the compiler. It is the tab stops assumed by the compiler—not those used by EDLIN—that govern the use of the Tab key. Thus you press the Tab key once to get to the A margin, twice to get to the B margin, and so on.

Because of the conflict in tab stop settings between EDLIN and the compiler, the program text will not appear the same on the screen as it does in the program listing. For example, Figure 2.1 shows a version of the program EXAMPLE prepared using the Tab key in EDLIN. Figure 2.1a was copied from the screen and shows the program as displayed by EDLIN; Figure 2.1b shows the program listing produced by the compiler. Each line except the last three was positioned by pressing the Tab key once; these lines begin in column 9 in the EDLIN display and in column 8 in the compiler listing. The last three lines were positioned by pressing the Tab key twice; they begin in column 17 in the EDLIN display and in column 12 in the compiler listing.

Using the Tab key in EDLIN is likely to confuse beginners and give a false idea of the structure of COBOL programs. For this reason, I would suggest that beginners who must use EDLIN refrain from using the Tab key and position items with the space bar. This is not as tedious as it might sound at first, since you will frequently be typing a series of items that all begin in the same column. For the first item of the series, you will have to count spaces to move the cursor to the column in which the item is to begin. For succeeding items that start in the same column, however, just hold down the space bar until the cursor is beneath the first character of the corresponding item on the preceding line.

## PROGRAMMER-DEFINED NAMES

In natural languages such as English, we frequently refer to objects by descriptions rather than by giving them individual names. Thus, we speak of "the chair by the window" or "the table next to the wall" instead of naming the chair Charlie and the table Sue. In programming languages, however, such descriptions would only confuse the compiler, so we have to make up individual names for the objects (such as files, records, and memory areas) that appear in the program.

To make sure the COBOL compiler can distinguish programmer-defined names from other parts of the language, programmer-defined names must be constructed according to the following rules:

(a)

```
 1:        IDENTIFICATION DIVISION
 2:*       PROGRAM-ID. EXAMPLE.
 3:
 4:        ENVIRONMENT DIVISION.
 5:
 6:        DATA DIVISION.
 7:
 8:        PROCEDURE DIVISION.
 9:        DISPLAY-MESSAGE.
10:            DISPLAY "You have succeeded in compiling and running".
11:            DISPLAY "a program in IBM Personal Computer COBOL".
12:            STOP RUN.
```

(b)

```
EXAMPLE COB
                                08:23:46    07-Feb-83    PAGE   1
Line Number  Source Line    IBM Personal Computer COBOL Compiler   Version 1.00

  1        IDENTIFICATION DIVISION
  2        PROGRAM-ID. EXAMPLE.
  3
  4        ENVIRONMENT DIVISION.
  5
  6        DATA DIVISION.
  7
  8        PROCEDURE DIVISION.
  9        DISPLAY-MESSAGE.
 10            DISPLAY "You have succeeded in compiling and running".
 11            DISPLAY "a program in IBM Personal Computer COBOL".
 12            STOP RUN.
```

*Figure 2.1* (a) The program from Figure 1.1 as displayed by the text editor EDLIN. Note that EDLIN numbers the lines in the same way as the compiler [compare with part (b)]. The asterisk indicates the current line—the line last changed by EDLIN. Because of the tab-stop settings built into EDLIN, the program lines begin in columns 9 and 17 rather than in columns 8 and 12 as they should. (b) The COBOL compiler assumes that the first tab stop is in column 8 and the second is in column 12, so the lines are correctly positioned in the compiler listing even though they appear to be incorrectly positioned when displayed by EDLIN.

1. Programmer-defined names are constructed from the letters of the alphabet, the digits 0 through 9, and the hyphen. Other characters, such as spaces and punctuation marks, are not allowed.

2. A programmer-defined name may not be longer than 30 characters.

3. A programmer-defined name may not begin or end with a hyphen.

4. A programmer-defined name must contain at least one letter of the alphabet. Names consisting only of digits or digits joined by hyphens are not allowed. Although there is one exception to this rule (a paragraph name can consist of digits only), the exception is almost never used.

5. A programmer-defined name must not be the same as a reserved word—a word with a preassigned meaning in COBOL. The reserved words are listed in appendix B of the COBOL reference manual. Words marked with a square block are *not* reserved in IBM COBOL; they are reserved in some other versions of COBOL, however, so you should avoid them if you expect to use your program with more than one version of COBOL. Words marked with a + sign are reserved in IBM COBOL but not in most other versions of COBOL. Appendix A of this book lists the reserved words for IBM COBOL. Note that few reserved words are hyphenated; using hyphens in programmer-defined names will help you avoid reserved words.

To help human readers understand your program, programmer-defined names should be chosen so that they describe the objects to which they refer. Usually, a programmer-defined name consists of a series of English words joined by hyphens:

```
ACCOUNTS-RECEIVABLE-FILE
INVENTORY-RECORD
1984-TAX-TABLES
END-OF-FILE-FLAG
PRINT-SALES-REPORT
```

The more descriptive you make the names you define, the fewer comments you will need to explain your program to human readers.

Why is each of the following not allowed as a programmer-defined name?

```
-REPORT-RECORD
666                              (Exception not allowed)
CHARGE-ACCOUNT REPORT
INPUT-OUTPUT
PEOPLE-WHO-HAVE-NOT-PAID-THEIR-BILLS-FILE
ACCOUNT-#
```

## LITERALS AND FIGURATIVE CONSTANTS

Literals and figurative constants represent constant data values—data items whose values are determined once and for all when the program is written.

### Numeric Literals

Numeric literals follow the usual conventions for writing numbers, with three exceptions: (1) Numeric literals cannot contain commas; (2) a numeric literal can have at most 18 digits; and (3) a numeric literal cannot end with a decimal point. The following are valid numeric literals:

```
100   -50   8.45   71.23   -175.0   -1234567890.12345678
```

The following are *not* valid numeric literals:

```
1,234,567                    (Commas not allowed)
1684.                        (Cannot end with decimal point—
                               write 1684 instead)

1234567890.1234567890        (More than 18 digits)
```

### Nonnumeric Literals

A nonnumeric literal represents a string of characters, such as a message to be printed. The characters making up the literal are enclosed in either quotation marks or apostrophes:*

---

*Be careful not to confuse the apostrophe with the grave accent `. The latter *cannot* be used to enclose nonnumeric literals.

```
"Insert the data diskette in drive B"
"Enter name of file to be processed: "
'Invalid input--please try again'
'All your data has been erased'
```

The quotation marks or apostrophes serve as *delimiters*—they are not part of the literal but indicate where it begins and ends. The length of a nonnumeric literal can range from 1 through 120 characters. The delimiters are not counted as part of the length.

Problems can arise if a literal contains a quotation mark or an apostrophe, since the compiler may be unable to distinguish the quotation mark or apostrophe that is part of the literal from the ones that delimit the literal. There are two methods for including quotation marks and apostrophes in literals. First, a literal delimited by quotation marks can contain apostrophes, and a literal delimited by apostrophes can contain quotation marks:

```
'"How can I serve you?" said the robot'
"I know I've made some very poor decisions recently"
```

Second, two delimiters in a row within a literal are interpreted as a single delimiter. Thus, within a literal delimited by quotation marks, we can represent a quotation mark by two quotation marks in a row. Within a literal delimited by apostrophes, we can represent an apostrophe by two apostrophes in a row:

```
"""How can I serve you?"" said the robot"
'I know I''ve made some very poor decisions recently'
```

A nonnumeric literal can be continued from one line to the next:

```
        1   2   2   2   3   3   4   4   4   5   5   6   6   6   7
7A...B...6...0...4...8...2...6...0...4...8...2...6...0...4...8...2
    DISPLAY "Now is the time for all good people to come to the a
-           "id of their country".
```

The literal to be continued extends through column 72 with no closing delimiter. Any unused columns at the end of the line are treated as spaces and included in the literal. On the *continuation line*—the next line of the program—a hyphen is placed in the indicator area (column 7). The continuation of the literal is preceded by a delimiter, which must be in area B. The continued literal is terminated by a delimiter in the usual way.

## Figurative Constants

A figurative constant is a literal represented by a reserved word. The most commonly used figurative constants are ZERO and SPACE. ZERO represents the numeric value zero and is equivalent to the numeric literal 0. SPACE represents a nonnumeric constant consisting of all blank spaces. Figurative constants may be written in either singular or plural form: ZERO and ZEROS have equivalent meanings, as do SPACE and SPACES. Regardless of whether the singular or the plural form is used, the context in which the figurative constant appears determines how many zeros or spaces are represented.

## DIVISIONS, PARAGRAPHS, AND STATEMENTS

In the remainder of this chapter we will look at two sample COBOL programs, discussing as we go along the various features of COBOL illustrated by the programs. We begin with the program EXAMPLE, which we saw how to compile and execute in Chapter 1, and the program listing for which is given in Figure 2.1b. We note that EXAMPLE is made up of four *divisions,* each of which begins with a *division header:*

```
IDENTIFICATION DIVISION.
ENVIRONMENT DIVISION.
DATA DIVISION.
PROCEDURE DIVISION.
```

Each division header begins in the A margin and ends with a period. All four division headers must be present, even if some of divisions (like the Environment Division and the Data Division in the example) contain no entries. The blank lines separating the divisions are recommended for readability but are not required.

### The Identification Division

#### Paragraphs

The Identification Division assigns a name to the program and contains other descriptive information. The Identification, Environment, and Procedure divisions are organized into *paragraphs*. Each paragraph begins with a *paragraph header* followed by an *entry*. A paragraph header begins in the A margin and is followed by a period. An entry is confined to area B and is terminated by a period. For example, the Identification Division of the example program consists of a single paragraph:

```
          1   2   2   2   3
A...B...6...0...4...8...2...
IDENTIFICATION DIVISION.
PROGRAM-ID. EXAMPLE.
```

#### The PROGRAM-ID Paragraph

The paragraph header is PROGRAM-ID and the entry is EXAMPLE—the name to be assigned to the program—followed by a period. The program name can be any string of characters that does not contain a period. It is often convenient to make the program name the same as the name of the file in which the source program is stored—the program EXAMPLE is stored in the file EXAMPLE.COB.

The PROGRAM-ID paragraph is the only required paragraph in the IDENTI-FICATION division. There are five other optional paragraphs, whose entries are intended for human readers and are ignored by the compiler. The following Identification Division illustrates the optional paragraphs:

```
          1   2   2   2   3   3   4   4   4   5   5
A...B...6...0...4...8...2...6...0...4...8...2...6...
IDENTIFICATION DIVISION.
PROGRAM-ID. EXAMPLE.
AUTHOR. Neill Graham.
INSTALLATION. Holt, Rinehart and Winston.
DATE-WRITTEN. 2-7-83.
DATE-COMPILED. 2-7-83.
SECURITY. May not be reproduced without permission.
```

## The Environment Division

The *environment* of a program is the computer system on which it will be used—the computer on which it will be compiled and executed, the input devices from which it will obtain data, the output devices to which it will send data, and the operating system with which it must interact. The Environment Division supplies the details of the program's environment that the compiler needs to translate the program properly. Because of its simplicity, our example program requires no entries in the Environment Division. The division header must be present, however, or the compiler will become confused.

## The Data Division

The Data Division describes the structure of the data that the program is to manipulate. Because the only data that the example program manipulates is given by nonnumeric literals, no entries in the Data Division are required. Again, however, the division header must be present.

In many cases, the Data Division is the largest part of a COBOL program. Persons writing large programs should be aware of the limits on the size of the Data Division, which are given in chapter 6 of the reference manual.

## The Procedure Division

The Identification, Environment, and Data divisions all *describe* various aspects of the program and its environment. The Procedure Division is imperative rather than descriptive—it contains the instructions that the computer is to carry out when the program is run. The instructions are contained in *statements,* of which the example program has three:

```
          1   2   2   2   3   3   4   4   4   5   5   6   6
A...B...6...0...4...8...2...6...0...4...8...2...6...0...4...
PROCEDURE DIVISION.
DISPLAY-MESSAGE.
    DISPLAY "You have succeeded in compiling and running".
    DISPLAY "a program in IBM Personal Computer COBOL".
    STOP RUN.
```

### Paragraphs

The Procedure Division is structured into paragraphs, each of which should carry out a specific, well-defined operation. Unlike the other divisions, where the paragraph names are reserved words, the paragraph names in the Procedure Division are programmer-defined names. Paragraph names should describe the operations carried out by the corresponding paragraphs. The Procedure Division of the example program contains one paragraph, `DISPLAY-MESSAGE`.

### Statements

A paragraph in the Procedure Division contains a number of statements, each of which gives a command for the computer to carry out. Each statement begins with a *verb,* which describes the action the computer is to take. The remainder of the statement provides the information necessary to carry out the action requested by the verb. Statements are named after the verbs with which they begin; thus, the statement beginning with the verb `DISPLAY` is the `DISPLAY` statement, and the statement beginning with the verb `STOP` is the `STOP` statement.

### Sentences

A paragraph is made up of one or more *sentences,* each of which ends with a period. Each *sentence* contains one or more statements. Unless there is specific reason to do otherwise, we usually write one statement per sentence, as in the example, so that each statement is also a sentence and is followed by a period.

### The `DISPLAY` statement

The `DISPLAY` statement displays one or more data items on the screen. Each of the `DISPLAY` statements in the example program displays a single data item, which is given by a nonnumeric literal. With the form of the `DISPLAY` statement shown here, the output displayed by each `DISPLAY` statement appears on a separate line. Thus the `DISPLAY` statements in the example program print the following two lines on the screen:

```
You have succeeded in compiling and running
a program in IBM Personal Computer COBOL
```

### The `STOP` statement

The statement `STOP RUN` terminates execution of the program and returns control to the operating system. Even in larger programs, the `STOP` statement normally occurs at the end of the first paragraph. Any other paragraphs are called directly or indirectly from the first paragraph.

## FILES, RECORDS, DATA NAMES, AND PICTURES

Now let's turn our attention to the program CREATE (Figure 2.2), which creates a disk file containing a price list. The program prompts the user to enter the stock number, description, and unit price for each item on the price list. The data that the user enters for each item is stored in the disk file. The user terminates the program by pressing the Esc key, the Backtab key, or a function key.

```
IDENTIFICATION DIVISION.
PROGRAM-ID. CREATE.

*     This program creates a price-list file from data
*     supplied by the user.

ENVIRONMENT DIVISION.
INPUT-OUTPUT SECTION.
FILE-CONTROL.
     SELECT PRICE-FILE ASSIGN TO DISK
          ORGANIZATION IS LINE SEQUENTIAL.

DATA DIVISION.
FILE SECTION.
FD   PRICE-FILE
     LABEL RECORDS STANDARD
     VALUE OF FILE-ID IS DOS-FILE-NAME.
01   PRICE-RECORD.
     02   STOCK-NUMBER     PIC X(6).
     02   DESCRIPTION      PIC X(20).
     02   UNIT-PRICE       PIC 999V99.

WORKING-STORAGE SECTION.
01   DOS-FILE-NAME        PIC X(15).
01   TERMINATOR           PIC 99.

PROCEDURE DIVISION.
CREATE-FILE.
     DISPLAY (1, 1) ERASE.
     DISPLAY (5, 1) "Name of file to be created? ".
     ACCEPT (LIN, COL) DOS-FILE-NAME WITH PROMPT.
     OPEN OUTPUT PRICE-FILE.
     MOVE ZERO TO TERMINATOR.
     PERFORM ACCEPT-AND-WRITE-PRICE-RECORD
         UNTIL TERMINATOR NOT EQUAL TO ZERO.
     CLOSE PRICE-FILE.
     STOP RUN.

ACCEPT-AND-WRITE-PRICE-RECORD.
     DISPLAY (1, 1) ERASE.
     DISPLAY (5, 1) "Stock number? ".
     ACCEPT (LIN, COL) STOCK-NUMBER WITH PROMPT.
     ACCEPT TERMINATOR FROM ESCAPE KEY.
     IF TERMINATOR EQUAL TO ZERO
         DISPLAY (6, 1) "Description? "
         ACCEPT (LIN, COL) DESCRIPTION WITH PROMPT
         DISPLAY (7, 1) "Unit price? "
         ACCEPT (LIN, COL) UNIT-PRICE WITH PROMPT
         WRITE PRICE-RECORD.
```

*Figure 2.2* This program creates the price-list file in Figure 2.3 from data entered by the user.

## Files

COBOL provides two sets of statements for input and output. The ACCEPT and DISPLAY statements are used to interact with the user. The ACCEPT statement obtains data from the keyboard, and the DISPLAY statement sends data to the display or to the printer. The READ and WRITE statements, on the other hand, are used to process substantial amounts of data, such as reading a disk file or printing a report.

A *file* in COBOL is any source from which data is read by a READ statement or any destination to which data is sent by a WRITE statement. Files, then, represent substantial amounts of data such as disk files or printed reports. File processing involves a certain amount of "machinery"—entries in the Environment and Data Divisions as well as additional statements in the Procedure Division—that is not required with ACCEPT and DISPLAY.

The program CREATE uses the DISPLAY and ACCEPT statements to request and obtain price-list entries from the user and the WRITE statement to store the data obtained in the price-list file. The Identification Division gives the name of the program and briefly describes the function the program performs.

## The Environment Division

The Environment Division selects a name for the file to be created and states whether the file will be sent to the printer or stored on disk:

```
          1   2   2   2   3   3   4   4
A...B...6...0...4...8...2...6...0...4...
ENVIRONMENT DIVISION.
INPUT-OUTPUT SECTION.
FILE-CONTROL.
    SELECT PRICE-FILE ASSIGN TO DISK
        ORGANIZATION IS LINE SEQUENTIAL.
```

### Sections

The Environment and Procedure Divisions can be divided into *sections,* each of which is introduced by a *section header*. Section headers, like division and paragraph headers, begin in the A margin and are followed by a period. Each section can be further divided into paragraphs. In the Environment Division, names are assigned to files in the FILE-CONTROL paragraph of the Input-Output section.

### The FILE-CONTROL paragraph

The FILE-CONTROL paragraph must contain a SELECT entry for every file the program is to use. Like all paragraph entries, SELECT entries are written in area B; normally, they begin in the B margin. PRICE-FILE is the COBOL file name for the price-list file—the name by which a file is known in the COBOL program. This is not the same as the DOS file name (such as B:PRICELST.DAT) by which the file is known to the Disk Operating System. The COBOL file name is chosen according to the rules for programmer-defined names; like all programmer-defined names, a file name should describe the file to which it refers.

The ASSIGN clause names the input or output device to which the file is assigned—the device from which the data will be received or to which the data will be sent. In IBM COBOL there are only two possible device names—DISK and PRINTER. Since we are creating a disk file, PRICE-FILE is assigned to DISK.

### Sequential files

A *sequential* file is one in which the records must be written in the order in which they are to be stored in the file and must be read in the order in which they were stored when the file was created. IBM COBOL offers two forms of sequential files —*regular sequential* and *line sequential*. Line-sequential files are in the standard format expected by DOS commands and programs—they can be displayed with TYPE, printed with COPY, and edited with EDLIN. On the other hand, line-sequential files are limited to character data—to codes that are to be interpreted as characters. Regular-sequential files can be processed only by COBOL programs (although they can be copied with COPY), but they can contain arbitrary codes that do not represent characters.

### Regular sequential and line sequential files

The ORGANIZATION clause specifies regular-sequential or line-sequential organization:

```
ORGANIZATION IS SEQUENTIAL        regular sequential
ORGANIZATION IS LINE SEQUENTIAL   line sequential
```

Regular-sequential organization is the default, so if we desire regular-sequential organization, we can omit the organization clause entirely. Both

```
SELECT PRICE-FILE ASSIGN TO DISK.
```

and

```
SELECT PRICE-FILE ASSIGN TO DISK
     ORGANIZATION IS SEQUENTIAL.
```

specify regular-sequential organization. If we want line-sequential organization, however, we must include the organization clause

```
SELECT PRICE-FILE ASSIGN TO DISK
     ORGANIZATION IS LINE SEQUENTIAL.
```

We choose line-sequential organization for CREATE so we can use TYPE to display the file created by the program. If you do not plan to process your files with non-COBOL programs, however, you will probably want to choose regular-sequential organization, which allows greater flexibility in representing the data.

## The Data Division

### The File Section

The Data Division can have four sections, two of which are the File Section and the Working-Storage Section. The File Section contains definitions associated with files, while the Working-Storage Section defines memory areas that the program will use for temporary storage.

### FD entries

For each file named in the Environment Division there must be a corresponding FD, or *file-definition* entry in the File Section of the Data Division:

```
              1    2    2    2    3    3    4    4
A...B...6...0...4...8...2...6...0...4...
DATA DIVISION.
FILE SECTION.
FD   PRICE-FILE
     LABEL RECORDS STANDARD
     VALUE OF FILE-ID IS DOS-FILE-NAME.
```

An FD entry starts with the letters FD beginning in the A margin followed by the file name beginning in the B margin. Note that there are *two* spaces between the FD and the file name.

The remainder of the FD entry, which must be in area B, provides certain additional information about the file. In IBM COBOL, all files require a LABEL RECORDS clause, and files assigned to DISK require a VALUE OF FILE-ID clause.

The LABEL RECORDS clause states whether an identifying record (such as an entry in a disk directory) is associated with a file. For a file assigned to DISK, the clause

```
     LABEL RECORDS STANDARD
```

must be used; for a file assigned to PRINTER the clause

```
     LABEL RECORDS OMITTED
```

must be used. The two clauses can also be written

```
     LABEL RECORDS ARE STANDARD
     LABEL RECORDS ARE OMITTED
```

The word ARE can be omitted, however.

For a disk file, we must specify which file on the disk is referred to by the COBOL file name. That is, we must set up a correspondence between a COBOL file name such as PRICE-FILE and a DOS file name such as B:PRICELST.DAT. Different versions of COBOL differ considerably in how this correspondence is set up. IBM COBOL uses the VALUE OF FILE-ID clause:

```
              1    2    2    2    3    3    4    4
A...B...6...0...4...8...2...6...0...4...
     VALUE OF FILE-ID IS DOS-FILE-NAME.
```

The phrase VALUE OF FILE-ID IS is followed by a specification of the DOS file name. We could have specified the DOS file name by a nonnumeric literal:

```
        1   2   2   2   3   3   4   4
A...B...6...0...4...8...2...6...0...4...
        VALUE OF FILE-ID IS "B:PRICELST.DAT".
```

However, this would restrict the program to a particular file and even to a particular disk drive. We can make the program more general by allowing the user to enter the name of the file to be created. Therefore, we specify the DOS file name by the *data name* DOS-FILE-NAME. A data name refers an area of memory that holds a particular data item. DOS-FILE-NAME refers to the area of memory that holds the DOS file name entered by the user. DOS-FILE-NAME and the corresponding memory area are defined in the Working-Storage Section.

Note that there is only one period at the end of the entire FD entry. A common error is to put a period after the file name or after some clause other than the last one.

## Records

A file is divided into blocks of data called *records*. Each record refers to a single entity such as a person or an item of merchandise. Each READ statement reads one record from a file, and each WRITE statement writes one record to a file. In our price-list file, each record contains the stock number, the description, and the unit price of one item of merchandise.

The individual data items of which a record is composed are known as its *fields*. Each record in the price-list file has three fields: a stock-number field, a description field, and a unit-price field.

## Record descriptions

For each file, a memory area is set aside to hold records read from the file or records to be written to the file. We need to describe this memory area to the system—to give the size of the memory area and state which parts of it are associated with which fields of the record. We also need to define data names for referring to the entire memory area as well as the parts associated with individual fields. We do all of this in a *record description*, which immediately follows the FD entry for the file in question:

```
        1   2   2   2   3   3   4   4
A...B...6...0...4...8...2...6...0...4...
01   PRICE-RECORD.
     02   STOCK-NUMBER     PIC X(6).
     02   DESCRIPTION      PIC X(20).
     02   UNIT-PRICE       PIC 999V99.
```

The numbers 01 and 02 are *level numbers* and indicate levels of subdivision. The level number 01 designates the entire record; 02 designates the parts into which the record is divided. The 02 level items can themselves be divided into parts, which can in turn be divided into still smaller parts, so we can have level numbers of 03, 04, and so on.

Level numbers in the range 01 through 49 are used to designate levels of subdivision (two special level numbers, 77 and 88, are used for other purposes).

PRICE-RECORD, STOCK-NUMBER, DESCRIPTION, and UNIT-PRICE are data names. PRICE-RECORD refers to the entire record, STOCK-NUMBER refers to the stock-number field, DESCRIPTION refers to the description field, and UNIT-PRICE refers to the unit-price field. (A data name that refers to an entire record is often called a *record name*.) Data names are chosen by the programmer according to the rules for forming programmer-defined names. Although not required, it is convenient to use the same name for a file and the corresponding record except that the file name ends with FILE and the record name ends with RECORD. Thus, PRICE-RECORD is the record associated with PRICE-FILE.

The level number 01 begins in the A margin and the record name begins in the B margin; note that there are two spaces between the level number and the record name. The level numbers and data names for the parts of a record must be in area B; although their exact positions are not specified, the usual practice is to follow the same pattern as for the 01 level but indent four spaces for each level of subdivision. Thus, an 02 entry begins in column 12 and the data name begins in column 16; an 03 entry begins in column 16 and the data name begins in column 20; and so on.

A data item that is further subdivided is called a *group item;* a data item that is not further subdivided is called an *elementary item*. In PRICE-RECORD, PRICE-RECORD itself is a group item, whereas STOCK-NUMBER, DESCRIPTION, and UNIT-PRICE are elementary items.

### Pictures

We describe the structure of a record by giving the size and type of data stored in each of the elementary items. We do this by providing a *picture* for each elementary item. Only elementary items have pictures; a group item is defined by the pictures of the elementary items that are subordinate to it.

With a few exceptions, there is a one-to-one correspondence between the characters in a picture and the characters making up the corresponding data item. A picture character designates a particular *kind* of character that can appear in the corresponding position of the data item. The picture character 9 represents one of the digits 0 through 9. The picture character A represents a letter of the alphabet or a blank space. The picture character X represents any of the characters listed in appendix G of the COBOL reference manual or in Appendix B of this book. The picture character A is rarely used; we use 9s for numeric data and usually use Xs for nonnumeric data.

A *picture clause* consists of the word PICTURE followed by the picture itself. PICTURE can be abbreviated to PIC and usually is. Readability is improved if all picture clauses start in the same column; which column to use depends on how long the data names are. Columns 32, 36, and 40 are good columns for starting picture clauses.

The picture clause

```
PIC XXXXXX
```

represents a six-character *alphanumeric* field. That is, the field contains six characters, each of which can be any of the characters listed in appendix G of the COBOL reference manual or in Appendix B of this book. Counting picture characters is tedious both when we write a program and when we are reading one. For this reason, COBOL allows us to write a picture character once and indicate in parentheses how many times it is to be repeated. Thus we can write X(6) instead of XXXXX, X(20) instead of XXXXXXXXXXXXXXXXXXXX, and 9(4) instead of 9999.

Numbers are stored in *numeric fields,* which can only contain the characters 0 through 9. Typical pictures for numeric fields are 9, 99, 999, 9(4), 9(5), and so on. The number of digits in a numeric field can range from 1 through 18. Only numeric fields are recognized as containing numbers and can supply values for arithmetical calculations. For example, the two-character data value 75 can be stored in a numeric field with picture 99 or in an alphanumeric field with picture XX. The contents of the numeric field represent the number seventy-five and can be combined arithmetically with the contents of other numeric fields. The contents of the alphanumeric field are just the character 7 followed by the character 5. No numerical value is associated with this two-character data item, which cannot be used in arithmetical calculations.

The decimal-point character cannot appear in a numeric field, which can only contain digits. However, a numeric field can contain an *implied* or *assumed* decimal point. An implied decimal point can be likened to the vertical line in a ledger that separates the dollars from the cents. When we make an entry in the ledger, we don't write a decimal point but instead position the digits representing dollars to the left of the vertical line and the digits representing cents to the right of the vertical line.

In the picture for a numeric item, the implied decimal point is represented by the letter V. Since the decimal point does not actually appear in the data, V is one of the few picture characters that does not represent a position in which a character can be stored. For example, the picture 999V99 represents a five-digit numeric field with three digits to the left of the implied decimal point and two digits to the right. If the data item 12345 is stored in this field, the contents of the field represent the value 123.45. Note that if 12345 were stored in a field with picture 99V999, it would represent 12.345; if the same data item were stored in a field with picture 9999V9, it would represent 1234.5.

Returning to the record description for PRICE-RECORD, we see that STOCK-NUMBER is a six-character alphanumeric field. Numbers such as stock numbers that are not to be manipulated arithmetically are often stored in alphanumeric rather than numeric fields; this gives the user the freedom to include letters or other characters in a stock number if desired. DESCRIPTION, which stores an English description such as "Typewriter" or "Conference Table", is a 20-character alphanumeric field. UNIT-PRICE is a five-digit numeric field having (like almost all fields representing amounts of money) two digits to the right of the implied decimal point.

### The Working-Storage Section

The Working-Storage Section defines memory areas that the computer will use for temporary storage while the program is running. The Working-Storage Section for the example program defines two such memory areas, DOS-FILE-NAME and TERMINATOR. DOS-FILE-NAME holds the DOS file name entered by the user for the file to be created. The contents of DOS-FILE-NAME are used in the

VALUE OF FILE-ID clause to assign a DOS file name to PRICE-FILE. A DOS file name can be up to 14 characters long and must be terminated by a blank space. We give DOS-FILE-NAME a picture of X(15) to allow room for a 14-character file name (such as A:PRICELST.DAT) and the terminating space.

TERMINATOR will be used to hold a two-digit number representing the key that the user struck to terminate the entry of a data item. By examining the value of TERMINATOR, we can determine whether the user wishes to terminate the program or to store more data in the file.

### The Procedure Division

The Procedure Division contains two paragraphs—CREATE-FILE and ACCEPT-AND-WRITE-PRICE-RECORD. Normally, the first paragraph of a COBOL program is a supervisory paragraph that controls the overall operation of the program and calls on subordinate paragraphs to perform specific operations. The example program follows this pattern, with CREATE-FILE calling on ACCEPT-AND-WRITE-PRICE-RECORD to obtain the contents of one price record from the user and store that record in PRICE-FILE.

#### The ACCEPT and DISPLAY statements

The first task of CREATE-FILE is to obtain from the user the DOS file name for the file to be created. As already mentioned, the ACCEPT statement is used to obtain information typed on the keyboard, and the DISPLAY statement is used to display information on the screen. In IBM COBOL, both the ACCEPT and DISPLAY statements have a *line-oriented form* and a *screen-oriented form*. With the line-oriented form, each DISPLAY statement displays a new line immediately below the preceding one, scrolling up the lines already on the screen if need be to make room for the new line. Likewise, line-oriented ACCEPT statements accept data from successive typed lines. The line-oriented forms of ACCEPT and DISPLAY function in what is sometimes called "Teletype mode," since the screen is used like the paper in a Teletype machine. In contrast, the screen-oriented forms allow displayed items and data typed by the user to be positioned anywhere on the screen.

The screen-oriented forms of ACCEPT and DISPLAY are distinguished by a *position specification* immediately following the word ACCEPT or DISPLAY. The position specification has the form

       ( *line-number* , *column-number* )

and specifies the position on the screen at which a displayed item or an item entered by the user will begin. The lines on the screen are numbered from 1 through 25 and the columns are numbered 1 through 80. Thus (5, 20) represents the intersection of line 5 and column 20; (12, 40) represents the intersection of line 12 and column 40; and so on. The comma between the line number and the column number must be followed by a space.

The following statements obtain the DOS file name from the user:

```
          1   2   2   2   3   3   4   4   4   5   5
A...B...6...0...4...8...2...6...0...4...8...2...6...
     DISPLAY (1, 1) ERASE.
     DISPLAY (5, 1) "Name of file to be created? ".
     ACCEPT (LIN, COL) DOS-FILE-NAME WITH PROMPT.
```

The first DISPLAY statement moves the cursor to the upper-left corner of the screen. The reserved word ERASE causes the screen to be erased from the cursor position to the end of the screen—in this case, the entire screen is erased. The DISPLAY statement types the prompt Name of file to be created? beginning on line 5 at column 1. Note the blank space following the question mark in the nonnummeric literal.

The screen-oriented form of the DISPLAY statement leaves the cursor positioned at the end of the last data item displayed (the line-oriented form moves the cursor to the beginning of the next line). After the second DISPLAY statement has been executed, the cursor is positioned immediately after the blank space at the end of the prompt. We want to accept the file name at the current cursor position, so that the file name typed by the user will immediately follow the prompt. IBM COBOL has two predefined data names, LIN and COL, whose values are the line and column of the cursor. The position specification (LIN, COL) refers to the current cursor position. The ACCEPT statement

```
     ACCEPT (LIN, COL) DOS-FILE-NAME WITH PROMPT.
```

obtains the value of DOS-FILE-NAME with the user's response beginning at the current cursor position.

The phrase WITH PROMPT causes the ACCEPT statement to display a pattern showing the form of the data to be entered. The reserved word PROMPT refers to this pattern, rather than to the English language request for data that we usually refer to as a prompt. For an alphanumeric item, the ACCEPT statement displays a period for each character to be entered. Since DOS-FILE-NAME has a picture of X(15), the displayed pattern will consist of 15 periods.

After the two DISPLAY statements and the ACCEPT statement have been exectued, but before any characters have been typed, the following appears on the screen:

```
     Name of file to be created? ................
```

The periods represent the character positions to be filled in. The cursor shows where the next typed character will appear. As the user types, the typed characters replace the periods. After part of the DOS file name has been typed, the user screen might look like this:

```
     Name of file to be created? B:PRICEL........
```

Pressing the Backspace key moves the cursor backwards replacing characters with periods. The Cursor Left and Cursor Right keys can be used to move the cursor into the already-typed part of the entry so you can type over existing characters. The user cannot backspace beyond the beginning of the 15-character field or type beyond the end of it. When the entire file name has been entered, the screen might look like this:

```
Name of file to be created? B:PRICELST.DAT.
```

When the user presses the Enter key, any unused positions in the field (one in this case) are filled with blank spaces and the data entered is stored in the memory area designated by DOS-FILE-NAME. The periods representing unused character positions are also erased from the screen, so the final prompt and response look like this:

```
Name of file to be created? B:PRICELST.DAT
```

### The OPEN statement

The remaining statements in CREATE-FILE create the desired file and terminate the program:

```
          1   2   2   2   3   3   4   4   4
A...B...6...0...4...8...2...6...0...4...8...
      OPEN OUTPUT PRICE-FILE.
      MOVE ZERO TO TERMINATOR.
      PERFORM ACCEPT-AND-WRITE-PRICE-RECORD
          UNTIL TERMINATOR NOT EQUAL TO ZERO.
      CLOSE PRICE-FILE.
      STOP RUN.
```

The OPEN statement prepares a file for processing. A file must always be opened before data is read from it or written to it. A file is opened for INPUT, OUTPUT, I-O (both input and output), or EXTEND (adding data to the end of an existing file). Since we are going to write data to PRICE-FILE, we open it for output. We must obtain the DOS file name for a file before executing the OPEN statement. If a file with the same DOS file name already exists on the disk, the existing file will be deleted and replaced with the newly created file.

The value of TERMINATOR is used to indicate whether the user wishes to enter more data. If the value of TERMINATOR is zero, the user wishes to enter more data; if the value is not zero, all the desired data has been entered and the program can terminate.

### The MOVE statement

The value of TERMINATOR must be set to zero before processing begins. We do this with a MOVE statement, a general purpose statement for storing data items in memory or moving items from one memory area to another:

```
      MOVE ZERO TO TERMINATOR.
```

Note that ZERO is a figurative constant.

### The PERFORM statement

A PERFORM statement causes all the statements in a designated paragraph to be carried out. For example,

```
      PERFORM ACCEPT-AND-WRITE-PRICE-RECORD.
```

causes all the statements in the paragraph `ACCEPT-AND-WRITE-PRICE-RECORD` to be executed, after which processing continues with the statement following the `PERFORM` statement. We can cause a paragraph to be executed repeatedly by appending to the `PERFORM` statement a clause stating how long the repetitions are to continue. Thus the statement

```
PERFORM ACCEPT-AND-WRITE-PRICE-RECORD
      UNTIL TERMINATOR NOT EQUAL TO ZERO.
```

causes the paragraph `ACCEPT-AND-WRITE-PRICE-RECORD` to be executed repeatedly until the value of `TERMINATOR` is not zero. Specifically, before each execution of `ACCEPT-AND-WRITE-PRICE-RECORD`, the `PERFORM` statement tests the value of `TERMINATOR`. If the value is zero, the paragraph is executed, after which the value of `TERMINATOR` is tested again, and so on. If the value of `TERMINATOR` is not zero, the repetitions terminate, and processing continues with the statement following the `PERFORM` statement. Since the `PERFORM` statement tests the value of `TERMINATOR` before executing the paragraph, we must set the value of `TERMINATOR` to zero before executing the `PERFORM` statement. Note that it's up to the repeated paragraph to eventually set `TERMINATOR` to a nonzero value, thus terminating the repetitions.

### The `CLOSE` and `STOP` statements

The `CLOSE` statement terminates processing of a file, assures that all data written to the file is transferred from memory to the disk, and updates the entry for the file in the disk directory. Just as files must be opened before being used, they must be closed after use. Note that `INPUT`, `OUTPUT`, `I-O` or `EXTEND` appears in the `OPEN` statement but *not* in the `CLOSE` statement.

The `STOP RUN` statement terminates the program. The computer does *not* go on to the next paragraph, as it would if `STOP RUN` was not present. The paragraph `ACCEPT-AND-WRITE-PRICE-RECORD` is executed only when called by the `PERFORM` statement in `CREATE-FILE`.

### Top-down construction

Note that when we write `CREATE-FILE`, we do not have to worry about the details of how `ACCEPT-AND-WRITE-PRICE-RECORD` does its job—we can postpone consideration of those details until we are ready to write `ACCEPT-AND-DISPLAY-PRICE-RECORD`. This method of writing a COBOL program is known as *top-down construction*. The first paragraph outlines the entire program but defers many details to subordinate paragraphs—details we don't have to worry about when writing the first paragraph. We then work out the details paragraph-by-paragraph as we write the subordinate paragraphs.

### Obtaining data from the user

ACCEPT-AND-WRITE-PRICE-RECORD has to obtain the data for a price record from the user and write the record to PRICE-FILE. The value of TERMINATOR must be set to zero if a valid record was entered and to a nonzero value if the user requested that the program be terminated. The first job is to get the stock number and set the value of TERMINATOR:

```
         1   2   2   2   3   3   4   4   4   5
A...B...6...0...4...8...2...6...0...4...8...2...
ACCEPT-AND-WRITE-PRICE-RECORD.
     DISPLAY (1, 1) ERASE.
     DISPLAY (5, 1) "Stock number? ".
     ACCEPT (LIN, COL) STOCK-NUMBER WITH PROMPT.
     ACCEPT TERMINATOR FROM ESCAPE KEY.
```

The first DISPLAY statement clears the screen, and the second requests the user to enter the stock number. The first ACCEPT statement displays the field into which the stock number is to be typed and stores the data entered in STOCK-NUMBER. After this ACCEPT statement has been executed but before the user has entered any data, the screen looks like this:

```
Stock number? ......
```

The user can terminate entry of a data item by pressing any of a number of keys. The system stores a two-digit terminator code depending on what key was used to terminate entry of the data item. COBOL can use this terminator code to decide what to do next; that is, the terminator code provides another means for the user to give instructions to the program. The terminating keys and terminator codes are as follows:

| Key | Terminator Code |
| --- | --- |
| Enter | 00 |
| Tab | 00 |
| Esc | 01 |
| F1-F10 | 02-11 |
| Backtab | 99 |

If the user terminates entry of a stock number with the Enter or Tab key (terminator code 00), the program will assume that the user has entered a valid stock number and wishes to enter the rest of the record. If the stock number entry is terminated with any other key, the program assumes that a valid stock number has not been entered and the user wishes to terminate the program.

## ACCEPT FROM ESCAPE KEY

In addition to obtaining data entered by the user, the ACCEPT statement can be used to obtain certain system data items such as the date, the time, and the current terminator code. The phrase FROM ESCAPE KEY is used to designate the terminator code. The statement

        ACCEPT TERMINATOR FROM ESCAPE KEY.

obtains the code for the key used to terminate the last data entry and stores the terminator code in the memory area designated by the data name TERMINATOR.

### The IF statement

If the value stored in TERMINATOR is zero, the program is to continue by obtaining the description and unit price from the user. If the value of TERMINATOR is nonzero, the program is to be terminated, and no further input data is to be obtained. An IF statement allows the program to take the proper action according to the value of TERMINATOR:

```
              1    2    2    2    3    3    4    4    4    5
A...B...6...0...4...8...2...6...0...4...8...2...
    IF TERMINATOR EQUAL TO ZERO
        DISPLAY (6, 1) "Description? "
        ACCEPT (LIN, COL) DESCRIPTION WITH PROMPT
        DISPLAY (7, 1) "Unit price? "
        ACCEPT (LIN, COL) UNIT-PRICE WITH PROMPT
        WRITE PRICE-RECORD.
```

The IF statement extends from the word IF through the period following WRITE PRICE-RECORD. The two DISPLAY statements, the two ACCEPT statements, and the WRITE statement are all part of the IF statement. When the IF statement is executed, the computer checks the value of TERMINATOR. If the value of TERMINATOR is zero, all the statements embedded in the IF statement are executed. If the value of TERMINATOR is not zero, the statements embedded in the IF statement are skipped over. In terms of the present example, if the value of TERMINATOR is zero, the program will obtain values for DESCRIPTION and UNIT-PRICE. If the value of TERMINATOR is not zero, the statements obtaining the value of DESCRIPTION and UNIT-PRICE are skipped over.

The statements embedded in the IF statement are indented to make the extent of the IF statement clear to human readers. The COBOL compiler, however, pays no attention to the indentation. It is the terminating period, and only the terminating period, that determines the extent of the IF statement. If the period is misplaced, the IF statement will include fewer statements or more statements than desired, and the behavior of the program will be quite different from that intended. A common error is inadvertently typing a period after one of the embedded statements (other than the last one), thereby terminating the IF statement prematurely.

If the value of TERMINATOR *is* zero, the program proceeds to get values for

DESCRIPTION and UNIT-PRICE. Since DESCRIPTION is a 20-character alphanumeric field, the prompt for its value looks like this:

Description? .....................

As usual, the characters entered replace the periods as the user types.

The prompt for the value of UNIT-PRICE looks like this:

Unit price? 000.00

The user begins by entering digits to the left of the decimal point. As the user types, the cursor remains in the same position—just to the left of the decimal point—but as each digit is entered, all previously entered digits are shifted one place to the left. For example, after the user types 1, the display looks like this:

Unit price? 001.00

If the user now types 3, we have

Unit price? 013.00

and typing 5 gives

Unit price? 135.00

Striking the decimal point key moves the cursor to the right of the decimal point:

Unit price? 135.00

The user can now key in the digits to the right of the decimal point. If the user types 9, we have

Unit price? 135.90

and typing 8 gives

Unit price? 135.98_

As with alphanumeric fields, we can use the Backspace, Cursor Left, and Cursor Right keys to make corrections. When the Enter key is pressed, 13598 is stored in the memory area designated by UNIT-PRICE. Note that the decimal point is *not* stored, since UNIT-PRICE, being a numeric item, has only an implied decimal point. The following shows all the prompts and responses just before the Enter key is pressed to terminate the unit-price entry:

Stock number? 115263
Description? Desk Calculator
Unit price? 135.98_

### The WRITE statement

The values obtained by the ACCEPT statements are stored in the fields of PRICE-RECORD. The statement

```
      WRITE PRICE-RECORD.
```

causes the data just obtained to be stored in PRICE-FILE.

### Terminating the repetition

When the computer reaches the end of the paragraph, control is returned to the PERFORM statement in CREATE-FILE. The PERFORM statement tests the value of TERMINATOR; if the value is zero, the paragraph ACCEPT-AND-WRITE-PRICE-RECORD is executed again. If the value of TERMINATOR is not zero, no further executions of ACCEPT-AND-WRITE-PRICE-RECORD take place, and the computer goes on to the statement following the PERFORM statement.

### The created file

Since PRICE-FILE was stored with line-sequential organization, we can display it on the screen with TYPE or copy it to the printer with COPY. Figure 2.3 shows a printout of a short price-list file created with CREATE. Note two things: First, there are no spaces between the fields (the description field contains spaces if the description does not completely fill the field). Second, the unit prices contain leading zeros (as in 00279) and no decimal points.

Files such as the one in Figure 2.3 are suitable for processing by COBOL programs but are hard for human readers to interpret. In Chapter 3 we will see how to translate such a file into a well-formatted report that is intelligible to human readers.

## EXERCISES

1. Type in and compile the program CREATE (Figure 2.2). This exercise will help you become familiar with the positioning, spelling, and punctuation of the various elements of a COBOL program. The inevitable typing errors will introduce you to the compiler's error messages. If the function of any element of the program is not clear to you, be sure to review the appropriate discussion in the chapter. Use the compiled program to create a short price-list file, and examine the file with TYPE or COPY.

```
115263Desk Calculator     13598
115378Cash Register       29995
129431Typewriter          47389
224635Executive Desk      38995
224845Executive Chair     27949
224962Conference Table    24995
318145Typewriter Ribbon   00279
318251Typing Element      01695
357009Diskettes, box of 1003995
```

*Figure 2.3* The price-list file created by the program in Figure 2.2. Note that there are no spaces between the fields (the spaces that do occur are within the description field); and there are no decimal points or other punctuation marks in the unit-price field.

2. Using the program compiled in Exercise 1, experiment with the data entry facilities provided by the ACCEPT WITH PROMPT statement. Try using the Back-space key to delete previously entered characters. Try making corrections by positioning the cursor over previously entered characters with the Cursor Left and Cursor Right keys and overtyping. What happens if you try to backspace beyond the beginning of a field, or move too far to the left or right with the cursor keys? What happens if you try to type more characters than a field will hold, or if you enter a letter or sign where a digit is expected?

3. Which of the following are valid programmer-defined names?

   (a)  TAX-TABLE                              (b)  ACCOUNTS PAYABLE
   (c)  X2170                                  (d)  %-INTEREST
   (e)  CALCULATE-WAGES                        (f)  PROCEDURE
   (g)  DATA-FILE                              (h)  HOURS-WORKED
   (i)  CALCULATE-COMMISSION-AND-UPDATE-TOTAL

4. Describe the fields having the following pictures and give examples of the data that could be stored in each field:

   (a)  9(5)                                   (b)  A(4)
   (c)  X(7)                                   (d)  9V9
   (e)  9                                      (f)  XX

5. Write a COBOL program to create a name-and-address file. Each record in the file will have three fields—one for the name, one for the address, and one for the city, state, and ZIP code. Each field can hold up to 30 characters. During data entry, the program will prompt for each field on a separate line. The program will terminate when the user terminates a name entry with the Esc key, the Backtab key, or a function key.

# 3

## Editing
## and
## Reports

In Chapter 2 we saw that COBOL stores data in a compressed format that is barely intelligible to human beings. Before being presented to human readers, such data needs to be *edited* to supply spaces, dollar signs, commas, and decimal points. The edited data needs to be properly labeled and arranged neatly on the printed page. In this chapter we will see how to convert the type of data file created in Chapter 2 into an easy-to-read report.

## MORE ABOUT NUMERIC FIELDS

We recall that numeric data is the only kind on which COBOL programs can carry out arithmetic operations. With the possible exception of a + or – sign, numeric data is made up of the digits 0 through 9. No spaces, commas, decimal points, dollar signs, or other characters are allowed.

Numeric data can be signed or unsigned, with unsigned numbers considered to be positive. If a field can contain only unsigned whole numbers, its picture consists only of 9s:

```
999        9        9(7)        9(4)
```

The number of 9s in the picture, and hence the number of digit positions in the field, can range from 1 through 18. Typical values of a field with picture 9(4) are

```
0035      1645      0007      0000
```

On the other hand, none of the following are acceptable values for a field with picture 9(4) or for any other numeric field:

```
bb35      1,645      $0.07      bbbb
```

(The small b's represent blank spaces. Using b's instead of actual blanks allows us to see at a glance how many blanks are present. Note that the small b notation is not a part of COBOL—b's cannot be used to represent blanks in COBOL programs or data.)

The letter V represents the position of the implied decimal point. The V does not correspond to any character in the data. However, digit positions to the left of the V represent the whole-number part of a numerical value while digit positions to the right of the V represent the decimal part. The following pictures represent unsigned fields with decimal parts:

```
9(4)V99      9V999      999V99      V999
```

For example, the picture 99V99 represents an unsigned, four-digit field with two digits to the left of the decimal point and two digits to the right. Typical values for this field are

```
0375      2491      0098      0007
```

These represent the values that would be expressed in conventional notation as

```
3.75      24.91      0.98      0.07
```

Whereas an unsigned number is always considered to be positive, a signed number contains a sign which can be positive or negative. We indicate that a field contains a sign by writing an S as the first character of the picture. Each of the following pictures describes a signed field:

```
S99V99      S9999      S9(4)V99      SV99
```

Unless we specify otherwise, the sign is not stored as a separate character, but is embedded in the rightmost digit of the data value. That is, the code for the rightmost digit represents both the rightmost digit and the sign of the entire number. With this representation, the picture character S, like V, does not correspond to a character in the data. In examples, we indicate a combined sign-digit code by writing the sign above the digit. Using this notation, the following are possible values of a field with picture S99V99:

```
     -          +          +          -
0074      5231      8431      0009
```

These represent the values that would be expressed in conventional notation as

```
-0.74      +52.31      +84.31      -0.09
```

When a data file is produced by a COBOL program, we usually use embedded signs since they save space. On the other hand, if the file is produced with a text editor or other non-COBOL program, using embedded signs may be tedious or impossible, since we must use a letter or one of the symbols { and } to represent the combined sign-digit codes (see the table in the SIGN-clause entry in the COBOL reference manual). We can avoid this problem by using a SIGN clause to specify that the sign is separate:

        PIC S99V99 SIGN IS TRAILING SEPARATE

The PICTURE and SIGN clause together specify a five-character field, some possible values of which are

        0074-        5231+        8431+        0009-

If we can also specify that the sign precedes the number instead of following it:

        PIC S99V99 SIGN IS LEADING SEPARATE

Typical values for a field with this PICTURE and SIGN clause are:

        -0074        +5231        +8431        -0009

If no sign clause is used, the sign is embedded in the rightmost digit of the data value. This is the most common situation and the one that will be assumed in the remainder of the chapter.

We will look briefly at one other picture character, P, even though it is not frequently used. We can think of each P as representing an implied zero. For example, the picture 99PPP represents a two-digit field. The program assumes, however, that the two digits stored in the field are followed by three zeros, one for each P. The implied decimal point is to the right of the rightmost P. Thus, if the field contains 32, the program will treat this as 32000, that is, as representing thirty-two thousand. If the field contains 65, the program will treat it as 65000, and so on.

Now consider the picture PP9, which represents a one-digit field. As before, the program manipulates the data as if each P represents a 0, but now the implied decimal point is to the left of the leftmost P. Thus if the field contains 3, the computer treats this as if it were 003 stored in a field with a picture of V999—that is, the 3 actually stored represents three thousandths.

The picture for a numeric field can contain only the picture characters 9, V, S, and P, used in the combinations just described. Any other picture character disqualifies the field as being numeric.

## EDITING

Editing is the process by which data values are modified so that they can be more easily read by humans. Typical editing changes include inserting dollar signs, commas, and decimal points in values representing amounts of money.

Editing takes place when the data is moved from one field to another with a MOVE statement. The field that holds the data to be edited is called the *sending field;* the field in which the edited data is to be placed is called the *receiving field*. The picture of the sending field describes the data to be edited; the picture of the receiving field describes the editing to be done.

A field whose picture specifies editing for alphanumeric data is called an *alphanumeric-edited* field. A field whose picture specifies editing for numeric data is called a *numeric-edited* field. We edit an alphanumeric value, then, by moving it from an alphanumeric field to an alphanumeric-edited field. Likewise, we edit a numeric value by moving it from a numeric field to a numeric-edited field.

### Editing Alphanumeric Data

We specify the editing that is to take place by using *editing characters* in the picture for the receiving field. For alphanumeric data, we use three editing characters:

| Character | Function |
|-----------|----------|
| B | Insert a blank space |
| / | Insert a / (slash or stroke) |
| 0 | Insert a zero |

Editing is often illustrated by means of a table giving the pictures and contents of the sending and receiving fields:

| Sending Field | | Receiving Field | |
|---------|---------|---------|---------|
| Picture | Data | Picture | Data |
| X(8) | TOGETHER | XXBXXXBXXX | TObGETbHER |
| X(3) | 495 | 00XXX000 | 00495000 |
| X(6) | 021183 | XX/XX/XX | 02/11/83 |

(Don't confuse the picture character B with the small b's used to represent blanks in examples.)

Each line in the table describes one editing operation. For the sending field we are given the data to be edited and the picture of the field containing the data. For the receiving field we are given the picture that specifies the editing to be done and the result of editing the data with the specified picture.

In the first line of the table, for instance, we have a sending field with a picture of X(8) and containing the data TOGETHER. This data is moved to a receiving field with a picture of XXBXXXBXXX. (We could also write this picture as X(2)BX(3)BX(3), but it's questionable whether doing so would make it any easier to read.) When we move the contents of the sending field to the receiving field, the data stored in the receiving field is TO GET HER, with two blank spaces inserted as specified by the picture of the receiving field.

In the second line of the table, we have a sending field with a picture of X(3) and containing the data 495. (Although the data consists of only digits, it is considered to be alphanumeric because of the picture of the sending field.) The receiving field has a picture of 00XXX000, specifying that two zeros are to be inserted before the data obtaining from the sending field and three zeros are to be inserted after. When the contents of the sending field are moved to the receiving field, the data actually stored in the receiving field is 00495000.

The third line of the table illustrates the editing character /, which is usually used for editing dates. The sending field has picture X(6) and contents 021183. The picture of the receiving field is XX/XX/XX; after the data has been moved from the sending field to the receiving field, the contents of the receiving field are 02/11/83.

B, 0, and / are sometimes referred to as *insertion characters,* since each causes one character to be inserted in the data.

## Editing Numeric Data

The editing operations that can be carried out on numeric data are more numerous and more complex than those for alphanumeric data. We will take up each of the editing operations and the picture characters used to specify each.

### Insertion characters

The insertion characters B, /, and 0 can be used to edit numeric data in the same way that they are used to edit alphanumeric data.

### Suppressing leading zeros

Leading zeros, such as in 000035 and 000007, are confusing and annoying to humans. We would like to edit data so that leading zeros are *suppressed*—replaced by blanks. We specify leading zero suppression with the picture character Z. Z plays the same role as the picture character 9 except when the corresponding digit is a leading zero. In that case, the digit is replaced by a blank:

| Sending Field | | Receiving Field | |
|---|---|---|---|
| Picture | Data | Picture | Data |
| 9(6) | 000035 | ZZZZZ9 | bbbb35 |
| 9(6) | 000007 | ZZZZZ9 | bbbbb7 |
| 9(6) | 123456 | ZZZZZ9 | 123456 |
| 9(6) | 001010 | ZZZZZ9 | bb1010 |
| 9(6) | 000000 | ZZZZZ9 | bbbbb0 |
| 9(6) | 000000 | ZZZZZZ | bbbbbb |

In the first four lines of the table, note that leading zeros are replaced by blanks, but all other digits are left unchanged. In the fourth line, note that only the *leading* zeros are replaced by blanks.

The last two lines contrast the pictures ZZZZZ9 and ZZZZZZ. The editing produced by the two pictures differs only when the contents of the sending field are all zeros. In that case, ZZZZZ9 produces a 0 preceded by five blanks, whereas ZZZZZZ produces a string of six blanks. In most cases we want at least one zero to be printed when the value of a field is zero, so pictures such as ZZZZZ9 are common.

### Comma insertion

To make large numbers easier to read, we usually set off each group of three digits with commas. In COBOL, we use commas as picture characters to specify where commas are to be inserted in the data:

| Sending Field | | Receiving Field | |
|---|---|---|---|
| Picture | Data | Picture | Data |
| 9(4) | 4397 | 9,999 | 4,397 |
| 9(7) | 7329465 | 9,999,999 | 7,329,465 |

We can use comma insertion in conjunction with leading zero suppression. If all the digits preceding a comma are replaced with blanks due to leading zero suppression, the comma is also replaced with a blank:

| Sending Field | | Receiving Field | |
|---|---|---|---|
| Picture | Data | Picture | Data |
| 9(4) | 4397 | Z,ZZ9 | 4,397 |
| 9(4) | 0275 | Z,ZZ9 | bb275 |
| 9(4) | 0000 | Z,ZZ9 | bbbb0 |
| 9(7) | 0037945 | Z,ZZZ,ZZ9 | bbb37,945 |

Note that when a zero or a comma is suppressed, it is never simply eliminated but is always replaced by a blank. Thus, the number of characters in the receiving field remains the same no matter how many zeros or commas are suppressed.

### Decimal point insertion

A decimal point in the picture of the receiving field serves two functions. First, it causes a decimal point to be inserted in the receiving field at the designated position.

Second, it causes the data moved from the sending field to be positioned in the receiving field in such a way that the implied decimal point in the data coincides with the actual decimal point in the receiving field:

| Sending Field | | Receiving Field | |
|---|---|---|---|
| Picture | Data | Picture | Data |
| 99V99 | 7318 | 99.99 | 73.18 |
| 9V9 | 25 | 99.999 | 02.500 |
| V99 | 78 | 9.99 | 0.78 |
| 9V9 | 49 | Z,ZZ9.99 | bbbb4.90 |
| 9V9 | 00 | Z,ZZ9.99 | bbbb0.00 |

Any unused positions in the receiving field are filled with zeros. If leading zero suppression is specified, as in the last two lines of the table, then leading zeros are replaced with blanks. Leading zero suppression is usually not used for positions to the right of the decimal point or even for the first position to the left of the decimal point. Therefore, pictures such as Z,ZZ9.99 are common.

### Dollar signs

A single dollar sign in the picture for the receiving field causes a dollar sign to be inserted at the corresponding position in the data:

| Sending Field | | Receiving Field | |
|---|---|---|---|
| Picture | Data | Picture | Data |
| 9(4)V99 | 174325 | $Z,ZZ9.99 | $1,743.25 |
| 9(4)V99 | 034521 | $Z,ZZ9.99 | $bb345.21 |
| 9(4)V99 | 006348 | $Z,ZZ9.99 | $bbb63.48 |
| 9(4)V99 | 000279 | $Z,ZZ9.99 | $bbbb2.79 |

Spaces between the dollar sign and the following amount are unsightly and may invite unauthorized alteration of the amount. We would like for the dollar sign always to occur immediately before the first digit of the amount regardless of how many leading zeros have been suppressed. A dollar sign positioned in this way is called a *floating dollar sign*.

In a picture such as $Z,ZZ9.99, we can obtain a floating dollar sign by replacing each Z by a dollar sign:

| Sending Field | | Receiving Field | |
| Picture | Data | Picture | Data |
|---------|------|---------|------|
| 9(4)V99 | 174325 | $$,$$9.99 | $1,743.25 |
| 9(4)V99 | 034521 | $$,$$9.99 | bb$345.21 |
| 9(4)V99 | 006348 | $$,$$9.99 | bbb$63.48 |
| 9(4)V99 | 000279 | $$,$$9.99 | bbbb$2.79 |

The first dollar sign in the picture represents the dollar sign character that is to be inserted. The remaining dollar signs in the picture represent digit positions through which the dollar sign character can float. Leading zero suppression is applied to these digit positions, just as if the dollar signs were Zs. If necessary, the inserted dollar sign is moved to the right until it is immediately precedes the leftmost digit of the amount. If the dollar sign is moved to the right, the position it originally occupied is filled with a blank. As usual, the number of characters in the receiving field remains the same regardless of the editing done.

Beginners often find pictures with floating dollar signs confusing, since the dollar sign picture character is used for two different purposes. Remember that the first dollar sign in the picture always represents the dollar sign character to be inserted. The remaining dollar signs in the picture represent digit positions through which the dollar sign character can float. The confusion mentioned shows up when students mistakenly think that every dollar sign represents a digit position and so write pictures that specify one fewer digit positions than desired.

### Check protection

The picture character * allows the amount on a check to be printed in a form that resists alteration. Each * acts like a Z except that when a leading zero or comma is suppressed, it is replaced by an asterisk instead of a blank:

| Sending Field | | Receiving Field | |
| Picture | Data | Picture | Data |
|---------|------|---------|------|
| 9(4)V99 | 174325 | $*,**9.99 | $1,743.25 |
| 9(4)V99 | 034521 | $*,**9.99 | $**345.21 |
| 9(4)V99 | 006348 | $*,**9.99 | $***63.48 |
| 9(4)V99 | 000279 | $*,**9.99 | $****2.79 |

### Signs

We have seen that the sign of a numeric data item is normally combined with the rightmost digit of the data. When the data is edited, the sign must be extracted from the rightmost digit and placed in one of the standard positions, such as preceding the leftmost digit or following the rightmost one.

Two picture characters, + and –, are available to indicate where the sign is to be inserted. If we use the picture character +, then a + sign is inserted when the value is positive and a – sign is inserted when the value is negative. If we use the picture character –, then a blank is inserted when the value is positive and a – sign is inserted when the value is negative:

| Sending Field | | Receiving Field | |
| --- | --- | --- | --- |
| Picture | Data | Picture | Data |
| S99 | $\overset{+}{45}$ | +99 | +45 |
| S99 | $\overset{-}{36}$ | +99 | –36 |
| S99 | $\overset{+}{55}$ | –99 | b55 |
| S99 | $\overset{-}{71}$ | –99 | –71 |
| S99 | $\overset{+}{64}$ | 99+ | 64+ |
| S99 | $\overset{-}{81}$ | 99+ | 81– |
| S99 | $\overset{+}{23}$ | 99– | 23b |
| S99 | $\overset{-}{35}$ | 99– | 35– |

In most cases, we want a sign printed only when the value is negative, so the picture character – is more frequently used than +.

A sign to the left of a number can be made floating, just as with the dollar sign:

| Sending Field | | Receiving Field | |
| --- | --- | --- | --- |
| Picture | Data | Picture | Data |
| S9(4)V99 | $\overset{+}{378425}$ | ++,++9.99 | +3,784.25 |
| S9(4)V99 | $\overset{-}{069312}$ | ++,++9.99 | bb–693.12 |
| S9(4)V99 | $\overset{+}{007453}$ | --,--9.99 | bbbb74.53 |
| S9(4)V99 | $\overset{-}{000261}$ | --,--9.99 | bbbb–2.61 |

As with the dollar sign, the first + or – in a picture represents the sign to be inserted; the remaining ones represent digit positions through which the sign can float.

Instead of using a sign, we can mark negative values with either CR (for credit) or DB (for debit). These are two alternate methods for designating negative numbers. We do not, as beginners sometimes suppose, mark positive numbers with CR and negative ones with DB, or vice versa. Instead, for some accounts negative values represent credits and are marked CR; for other accounts negative numbers represent debits and are marked DB. In either case positive values are not marked—for positive values, the positions reserved for CR or DB are filled with blanks:

| Sending Field | | Receiving Field | |
|---|---|---|---|
| Picture | Data | Picture | Data |
| S9(4)V99 | 583641 (+) | $$,$$9.99CR | $5,836.41bb |
| S9(4)V99 | 098245 (–) | $$,$$9.99CR | bb$982.45CR |
| S9(4)V99 | 007123 (+) | $$,$$9.99DB | bbb$71.23bb |
| S9(4)V99 | 000495 (–) | $$,$$9.99DB | bbbb$4.95DB |

## MORE ABOUT THE MOVE STATEMENT

Because the MOVE statement is so important for editing, this is a good place to look at a few more of its properties.

A MOVE statement moves data from a sending field to a receiving field. In the statement

```
MOVE FIELD-S TO FIELD-R.
```

FIELD-S is the sending field and FIELD-R is the receiving field. The sending field can be specified by either a literal or a data name, but the receiving field must be specified by a data name. We can specify more than one receiving field if we wish. The statement

```
MOVE FIELD-S TO FIELD-R-1
              FIELD-R-2
              FIELD-R-3.
```

moves the contents of FIELD-S to FIELD-R-1, FIELD-R-2, and FIELD-R-3.

The word MOVE is perhaps somewhat misleading, since a MOVE statement never changes the contents of the sending field. Rather, a copy of the value in the sending field is placed in the receiving field. If a receiving field has the same picture as the sending field, it receives an exact copy of the value in the sending field. If the picture for the receiving field differs from that of the sending field, the value from the sending field may have to be modified before it can be placed in the receiving field. Finally, as we saw in the previous section, if the picture for the receiving field contains editing characters, the value from the sending field is edited accordingly before being placed in the receiving field.

The following table illustrates some moves between alphanumeric fields:

| Sending Field | | Receiving Field | |
|---|---|---|---|
| Picture | Data | Picture | Data |
| X(7) | Johnson | X(7) | Johnson |
| X(7) | Johnson | X(10) | Johnsonbbb |
| X(7) | Johnson | X(4) | John |

In the first line of the table, the receiving field receives an exact copy of the value in the sending field. In the second line, the value from the sending field is padded with three blanks so as to fill the receiving field. In the third line, the value from the sending field is *truncated* (three characters are discarded) so as to fit the receiving field.

In the second and third lines of the table, the value from the sending field is *left justified* in the receiving field. When the value from the sending field is too small for the receiving field, it is shifted as far to the left in the receiving field as possible and is padded on the right with blanks. When the value from the sending field is too large for the receiving field, the leftmost characters are retained and as many characters as necessary are discarded on the right.

The MOVE statement left justifies data unless the Data Division entry for the receiving field contains the clause JUSTIFIED RIGHT. If right justification *is* specified, the data from the sending field is moved as far right as possible in the receiving field; any characters that must be discarded are taken from the left end of the data.

In a MOVE statement, the sending field, the receiving field, or both may be group items. When one or both of the fields are group items, the move is carried out exactly as if it were a move from one alphanumeric field to another. If the sizes of the sending and receiving items differ, padding or truncation takes place exactly as for moves between alphanumeric fields.

When data is moved from one numeric field to another, the value from the sending field is always positioned so that its implied decimal point coincides with the implied decimal point in the receiving field. The value from the sending field may have to be truncated or padded with zeros on the left, the right, or both so that it can be properly positioned in the receiving field:

| Sending Field | | Receiving Field | |
|---|---|---|---|
| *Picture* | *Data* | *Picture* | *Data* |
| 99V99 | 3752 | 99V99 | 3752 |
| 99V99 | 3752 | 999V99 | 03752 |
| 99V99 | 3752 | 99V999 | 37520 |
| 99V99 | 3752 | 999V999 | 037520 |
| 99V99 | 3752 | 9V99 | 752 |
| 99V99 | 3752 | 99V9 | 375 |
| 99V99 | 3752 | 9V9 | 75 |

Similar truncation or padding takes place when a value is moved from a numeric field to a numeric-edited field, except in that case the implied decimal point in the numeric data is aligned with the actual decimal point in the numeric-edited field. Leading zeros introduced for padding may be changed to blanks or other characters by editing.

Note that truncating numeric data on the left is almost surely a logical error, since the numerical value represented by the data is radically changed. Truncation of any kind during a move is unusual; normally, we make each receiving field large enough to hold the values that will be moved to it.

## SALES-REPORT-I

Figure 3.1 shows a monthly sales file similar to the price-list file created in Chapter 2 except that two additional fields have been added to each record—one giving the number of items of a particular kind that were sold and the other giving the income from sales of an item. The data in Figure 3.1—particularly the numeric data—is almost totally unintelligible to a human reader. We want to write a program to convert this data into an easy-to-read report. In fact, we will write three such programs of increasing complexity.

```
115263Desk Calculator      13598005067990
115378Cash Register        29995002059990
129431Typewriter           47389008379112
224635Executive Desk       38995012467940
224845Executive Chair      27949012335388
224962Conference Table     24995000000000
318145Typewriter Ribbon    00279250067950
318251Typing Element       01695009015255
357009Diskettes, box of 1003995030119850
```

*Figure 3.1*   A sample monthly sales file for processing by the program in Figure 3.2. Because we find it almost impossible to read the data in such a file (particularly the numeric data), we need programs such as Figure 3.2 that print the contents of data files as neatly formatted reports.

The first will edit the data and arrange it in columns; the second will add a title and column headings; and the third will print multiple page reports with numbered pages and with the title and the column headings printed at the top of each page.

### The Environment Division

Figure 3.2 shows the first of the three programs, SALES-REPORT-I, and Figure 3.3 shows the report it produces. Since the Identification Division is routine, we proceed at once to the Environment Division:

```
IDENTIFICATION DIVISION.
PROGRAM-ID. SALES-REPORT-I.

*     This program prints a sales report
*     from data in a disk file.

ENVIRONMENT DIVISION.
INPUT-OUTPUT SECTION.
FILE-CONTROL.
     SELECT MONTHLY-SALES-FILE ASSIGN TO DISK
          ORGANIZATION IS LINE SEQUENTIAL.
     SELECT SALES-REPORT-FILE ASSIGN TO PRINTER.

DATA DIVISION.
FILE SECTION.
FD   MONTHLY-SALES-FILE
     LABEL RECORDS STANDARD
     VALUE OF FILE-ID IS DOS-FILE-NAME.
01   MONTHLY-SALES-RECORD.
     02   MS-STOCK-NUMBER PIC X(6).
     02   MS-DESCRIPTION  PIC X(20).
     02   MS-UNIT-PRICE   PIC 999V99.
     02   MS-NUMBER-SOLD  PIC 999.
     02   MS-SALES-INCOME PIC 9(4)V99.


FD   SALES-REPORT-FILE
     LABEL RECORDS OMITTED.
01   SALES-REPORT-RECORD PIC X(80).

WORKING-STORAGE SECTION.
01   DETAIL-LINE.
     02   DL-STOCK-NUMBER PIC XBXXBXXX.
     02   FILLER          PIC X(5) VALUE SPACES.
     02   DL-DESCRIPTION  PIC X(20).
     02   FILLER          PIC X(5) VALUE SPACES.
     02   DL-UNIT-PRICE   PIC $$$9.99.
     02   FILLER          PIC X(5) VALUE SPACES.
     02   DL-NUMBER-SOLD  PIC ZZ9.
     02   FILLER          PIC X(5) VALUE SPACES.
     02   DL-SALES-INCOME PIC $$,$$9.99.

01   DOS-FILE-NAME       PIC X(15).
01   EOF-FLAG            PIC X.
```

*Figure 3.2*   This program prints a sales report such as the one in Figure 3.3 from a data file such as the one in Figure 3.1.

```
PROCEDURE DIVISION.
PRINT-SALES-REPORT.
    DISPLAY (1, 1) ERASE.
    DISPLAY (5, 1) "Name of file to be listed? ".
    ACCEPT (LIN, COL) DOS-FILE-NAME WITH PROMPT.
    OPEN INPUT MONTHLY-SALES-FILE
         OUTPUT SALES-REPORT-FILE.
    MOVE "N" TO EOF-FLAG.
    READ MONTHLY-SALES-FILE
         AT END MOVE "Y" TO EOF-FLAG.
    PERFORM PRINT-DETAIL-LINE
         UNTIL EOF-FLAG = "Y".
    CLOSE MONTHLY-SALES-FILE
          SALES-REPORT-FILE.
    STOP RUN.

PRINT-DETAIL-LINE.
    MOVE MS-STOCK-NUMBER TO DL-STOCK-NUMBER.
    MOVE MS-DESCRIPTION TO DL-DESCRIPTION.
    MOVE MS-UNIT-PRICE TO DL-UNIT-PRICE.
    MOVE MS-NUMBER-SOLD TO DL-NUMBER-SOLD.
    MOVE MS-SALES-INCOME TO DL-SALES-INCOME.
    WRITE SALES-REPORT-RECORD FROM DETAIL-LINE.
    READ MONTHLY-SALES-FILE
         AT END MOVE "Y" TO EOF-FLAG.
```

*Figure 3.2 (continued)*

```
                1   2   2   2   3   3   4   4   4   5
A...B...6...0...4...8...2...6...0...4...8...2...
ENVIRONMENT DIVISION.
INPUT-OUTPUT SECTION.
FILE-CONTROL.
    SELECT MONTHLY-SALES-FILE ASSIGN TO DISK
        ORGANIZATION IS LINE SEQUENTIAL.
    SELECT SALES-REPORT-FILE ASSIGN TO PRINTER.
```

The program uses two files: MONTHLY-SALES-FILE, the file to be listed, and SALES-REPORT-FILE, the file to which the printed report will be written. The FILE-CONTROL paragraph contains a SELECT entry for each file. MONTHLY-SALES-FILE is assigned to DISK, and line-sequential organization is specified. (The file was created with line-sequential organization so that it could be printed out to get Figure 3.1.) SALES-REPORT-FILE is assigned to PRINTER.

### The Data Division

MONTHLY-SALES-FILE

Since MONTHLY-SALES-FILE is assigned to DISK, its FD entry specifies LABEL RECORDS STANDARD and contains a VALUE OF FILE-ID clause. As in the program we studied in Chapter 2, the DOS file name is specified by the value of the data name DOS-FILE-NAME:

```
1 15 263      Desk Calculator        $135.98      5       $679.90
1 15 378      Cash Register          $299.95      2       $599.90
1 29 431      Typewriter             $473.89      8     $3,791.12
2 24 635      Executive Desk         $389.95     12     $4,679.40
2 24 845      Executive Chair        $279.49     12     $3,353.88
2 24 962      Conference Table       $249.95      0         $0.00
3 18 145      Typewriter Ribbon        $2.79    250       $679.50
3 18 251      Typing Element          $16.95      9       $152.55
3 57 009      Diskettes, box of 10    $39.95     30     $1,198.50
```

*Figure 3.3* The sales report based on the data file in Figure 3.1. Note that the data file and the sales report contain the same data, but the data in the sales report is far easier to read.

```
              1    2    2    2    3    3    4    4
A...B...6...0...4...8...2...6...0...4...
FD   MONTHLY-SALES-FILE
     LABEL RECORDS STANDARD
     VALUE OF FILE-ID IS DOS-FILE-NAME.
```

Before we can write a COBOL record description for MONTHLY-SALES-RECORD, we need an informal description of the records in MONTHLY-SALES-FILE. We can describe a record by giving the name of each field, its size, and the type of data stored in it:

| Field | Size | Type of Data |
|---|---|---|
| Stock Number | 6 | Alphanumeric |
| Description | 20 | Alphanumeric |
| Unit Price | 5 | Numeric—two decimal places |
| Number Sold | 3 | Numeric—whole number |
| Sales Income | 6 | Numeric—two decimal places |

That is, for each line in Figure 3.1, the first six characters are the stock number, the next 20 characters are the description, the next five characters are the unit price, and so on. With this information we have little trouble writing the corresponding COBOL record description:

```
              1    2    2    2    3    3    4
A...B...6...0...4...8...2...6...0...
01   MONTHLY-SALES-RECORD.
     02   MS-STOCK-NUMBER PIC X(6).
     02   MS-DESCRIPTION  PIC X(20).
     02   MS-UNIT-PRICE   PIC 999V99.
     02   MS-NUMBER-SOLD  PIC 999.
     02   MS-SALES-INCOME PIC 9(4)V99.
```

### Qualifier names

The fields STOCK-NUMBER, DESCRIPTION, and so on appear in two re-cords—MONTHLY-SALES-RECORD and DETAIL-LINE. To distinguish the fields of the two records, we prefix the fields of MONTHLY-SALES-RECORD with MS and those of DETAIL-LINE with DL. Thus, MS-STOCK-NUMBER is the stock-number field of MONTHLY-SALES-RECORD and DL-STOCK-NUMBER is the stock-number field of DETAIL-LINE.

COBOL provides a much more cumbersome method for accomplishing the same result. Suppose, for a moment, that we omit the prefixes, so that both MONTHLY-SALES-RECORD and DETAIL-LINE contain a STOCK-NUMBER field, a DESCRIPTION field, and so on. To refer to the fields of MONTHLY-SALES-RECORD, we can use

```
STOCK-NUMBER OF MONTHLY-SALES-RECORD
DESCRIPTION OF MONTHLY-SALES-RECORD
UNIT-PRICE OF MONTHLY-SALES-RECORD
NUMBER-SOLD OF MONTHLY-SALES-RECORD
SALES-INCOME OF MONTHLY-SALES-RECORD
```

Likewise, we can refer to the fields of DETAIL-LINE as

```
STOCK-NUMBER OF DETAIL-LINE
DESCRIPTION OF DETAIL-LINE
UNIT-PRICE OF DETAIL-LINE
NUMBER-SOLD OF DETAIL-LINE
SALES-INCOME OF DETAIL-LINE
```

The record name following OF is a *qualifier* name and specifies the record to which the field in question belongs. We could also write IN instead of OF. In general, qualifer names are much clumsier to use than the two-letter prefixes illustrated earlier. For example, compare

```
MOVE MS-STOCK-NUMBER TO DL-STOCK-NUMBER.
```

with

```
MOVE STOCK-NUMBER OF MONTHLY-SALES-RECORD TO
     STOCK-NUMBER OF DETAIL-LINE.
```

### SALES-REPORT-FILE

Since SALES-REPORT-FILE is assigned to PRINTER, we specify LABEL RECORDS OMITTED. SALES-REPORT-RECORD is not divided into fields, but rather is a single alphanumeric item large enough to hold an 80-character line of printout:

```
          1   2   2   2   3   3   4
A...B...6...0...4...8...2...6...0...
FD   SALES-REPORT-FILE
     LABEL RECORDS OMITTED.
01   SALES-REPORT-RECORD PIC X(80).
```

Records to be printed are set up in the Working-Storage Section and then moved to SALES-REPORT-RECORD for printing.

### DETAIL-LINE, FILLER entries, and VALUE clauses

The Working-Storage Section contains one record description:

```
          1    2    2    2    3    3    4    4    4    5
A...B...6...0...4...8...2...6...0...4...8...2...
 01    DETAIL-LINE.
       02   DL-STOCK-NUMBER  PIC  XBXXBXXX.
       02   FILLER           PIC  X(5) VALUE SPACES.
       02   DL-DESCRIPTION    PIC  X(20).
       02   FILLER           PIC  X(5) VALUE SPACES.
       02   DL-UNIT-PRICE     PIC  $$$9.99.
       02   FILLER           PIC  X(5) VALUE SPACES.
       02   DL-NUMBER-SOLD    PIC  ZZ9.
       02   FILLER           PIC  X(5) VALUE SPACES.
       02   DL-SALES-INCOME  PIC  $$,$$9.99.
```

Each line to be printed is built up in DETAIL-LINE by moving values from the fields of MONTHLY-SALES-RECORD to the corresponding fields of DETAIL-LINE. Except for the description field, the pictures for the fields of DETAIL-LINE specify editing, so the data is edited as it is moved. For example, two blanks are inserted in the stock number (separating it into parts that are presumably meaningful to human readers, such as a department number, a supplier code, and an item number). The unit price and sales income are provided with dollar signs, decimal points, and commas, and leading zeros are suppressed in the number sold.

DETAIL-LINE must have fields not only for the data items to be printed but for the spaces separating the printed items. The fields containing the spaces will not be referred to from elsewhere in the program—we will not be moving data from them or into them, for instance—so there is no need for these fields to have unique names. When we do not want to assign a name to a field, COBOL allows us to use the reserved word FILLER where the name of the field would otherwise go. All the FILLER entries in DETAIL-LINE specify spaces separating printed items.

Normally, the COBOL compiler does not store any particular value in a field. When the execution of the program begins, the field contains meaningless data—whatever was left in the corresponding memory area by the previous program that ran on the computer. In the Working-Storage Section, however, we can use a VALUE clause to request the compiler to store a particular value in a field. The initial value supplied by the compiler can be changed by the program—by moving a new value to the field, for example. However, to make programs easier to read and understand, many programmers use VALUE clauses only for fields that are to retain their initial values throughout the execution of the program.

A VALUE clause consists of the word VALUE followed by a literal or figurative constant. For example,

```
    PIC 9V99 VALUE 2.59
```

defines a three-digit numeric field with an initial value of 2.59, and

```
PIC X(12) VALUE "Sales Report"
```

defines a 12-character alphanumeric field with an initial value of `"Sales Report"`. When a figurative constant such as `ZEROS` or `SPACES` is used, the entire field is filled with the specified character. Thus

```
PIC X(8) VALUE SPACES
```

defines an eight-character alphanumeric field initially containing eight spaces, and

```
PIC X(15) VALUE SPACES
```

defines a 15-character alphanumeric field initially containing 15-spaces. In `DETAIL-LINE`, each printed field is to be separated by five spaces. The separating spaces are provided by `FILLER` items, each of which has the `PICTURE` and `VALUE` clauses

```
PIC X(5) VALUE SPACES
```

The `VALUE` clause has one important limitation—it can be used to initialize fields* only in the Working-Storage Section. For many systems, the memory areas defined in the File Section are allocated by the operating system rather than the COBOL compiler, and different areas may be used at different times to store records for the same file. The compiler has no way of storing initial values in these areas or of assuring that such values will remain the same unless changed by the program. Therefore, `VALUE` clauses used to initialize fields are not allowed in the File Section. Since we need `VALUE` clauses for formatting printed lines, records corresponding to printed lines are usually defined in the Working-Storage Section rather than the File Section.

The Working-Storage Section defines two additional data items, `DOS-FILE-NAME` and `EOF-FLAG`:

```
           1    2    2    2    3    3    4
A...B...6...0...4...8...2...6...0...
01   DOS-FILE-NAME      PIC X(15).
01   EOF-FLAG           PIC X.
```

`DOS-FILE-NAME` holds the name of the disk file corresponding to `MONTHLY-SALES-FILE`. A *flag* is a data item whose value specifies whether a certain condition holds true or whether a certain event has occurred. In COBOL, a flag is usually a one-character alphanumeric item with the value `"Y"` if the condition is true or the event has occurred and the value `"N"` otherwise. The value of `EOF-FLAG` (EOF stands for End of File) has the value `"Y"` if all the records in `MONTHLY-SALES-FILE` have been processed and the value `"N"` if more records remain to be processed.

## Procedure Division

The Procedure Division of this program is organized very much like that of `CREATE` in Chapter 2. The first paragraph, `PRINT-SALES-REPORT`, is a supervisory paragraph that repeatedly calls the second paragraph, `PRINT-DETAIL-LINE`, to print a line of the sales report.

---

*The `VALUE` clause has another use in COBOL that has nothing to do with assigning initial values to fields. This other use is allowed in both the File and Working-Storage Sections.

PRINT-SALES-REPORT

The first three lines of PRINT-SALES-REPORT (which are exactly the same as the corresponding lines in CREATE) obtain the DOS file name corresponding to MONTHLY-SALES-FILE and store it in DOS-FILE-NAME. The remaining lines control the printing of the sales report:

```
            1    2    2    2    3    3    4    4
A...B...6...0...4...8...2...6...0...4...
        OPEN INPUT MONTHLY-SALES-FILE
             OUTPUT SALES-REPORT-FILE.
        MOVE "N" TO EOF-FLAG.
        READ MONTHLY-SALES-FILE
             AT END MOVE "Y" TO EOF-FLAG.
        PERFORM PRINT-DETAIL-LINE
             UNTIL EOF-FLAG = "Y".
        CLOSE MONTHLY-SALES-FILE
              SALES-REPORT-FILE.
        STOP RUN.
```

The OPEN statement opens the files to be used by the program. As many files as need to be opened can be listed in a single OPEN statement. Each file name must be preceded by INPUT, OUTPUT, I-O, or EXTEND as appropriate. For readability, we usually list each file on a separate line. Note that the last file name listed (and *only* the last file name) is followed by a period.

EOF-FLAG is given the initial value "N" indicating that the end of MONTHLY-SALES-FILE has not been reached. We could have given EOF-FLAG its initial value with a VALUE clause in the Working-Storage Section. However, we will follow the convention of using VALUE clauses only for data items whose values will remain unchanged during program execution. Items such as EOF-FLAG whose values will change will be initialized with MOVE statements.

The READ statement

```
    READ MONTHLY-SALES-FILE
         AT END MOVE "Y" TO EOF-FLAG.
```

checks to see if the end of MONTHLY-SALES-FILE has been reached. If not, the next record in MONTHLY-SALES-FILE is read into MONTHLY-SALES-RECORD—the record associated with MONTHLY-SALES-FILE in the File Section. If the end of MONTHLY-SALES-FILE has been reached, the statement following AT END is executed. The statement in the AT END clause moves "Y" to EOF-FLAG, indicating that the end of MONTHLY-SALES-FILE has been reached.

In COBOL, an *imperative* statement is one whose action does not depend on any condition. The OPEN, CLOSE, and MOVE statements are examples of imperative statements. Statements whose actions do depend on some condition are *conditional* statements. The IF statement is conditional, as is the READ statement with the AT END clause.

Many COBOL statements have optional clauses like AT END that specify actions to be taken under certain conditions; the presence of such a conditional clause makes a statement conditional. What's more, the conditional clause itself can contain only imperative statements—it cannot contain other conditional statements. Thus, the AT END clause on a READ statement can contain imperative statements such as MOVE, but it cannot contain conditional statements such as an IF statement or another READ statement having an AT END clause.

Note that we specify a *file* name in a READ statement and a *record* name in a WRITE statement. This is because more than one type of record can be associated with a file. When the program writes a record, it knows which type of record it wants to write, and so specifies the appropriate record name in the WRITE statement. When reading from a file, however, the program has no way of knowing which type of record occurs next in the file; hence only the file name can be specified. The catch phrase "read a file, write a record" summarizes this aspect of the READ and WRITE statements.

The PERFORM statement executes the paragraph PRINT-DETAIL-LINE repeatedly—once for each line to be printed. The repetitions continue until the value of EOF-FLAG is "Y", indicating that all the records in MONTHLY-SALES-FILE have been processed. Incidentally, note that in this program we use the = sign to test whether two values are the same, whereas in CREATE we used the phrase EQUAL TO. Both = and EQUAL TO are allowed, as are the negative forms NOT = and NOT EQUAL TO.

The value of EOF-FLAG is set to "Y" when a READ statement discovers that no more records remain to be read. To prevent the program from attempting to process a record when no record was read (because the end of the file had been reached), we want the PERFORM statement to test the value of EOF-FLAG immediately after each READ statement. We can arrange this by using two READ statements—one immediately preceding the PERFORM statement and one as the last statement of the performed paragraph PRINT-DETAIL-LINE. The READ statement preceding the PERFORM statement reads the first record from the file, and the READ statement at the end of the performed paragraph reads each remaining record. Since the PERFORM statement tests the value of EOF-FLAG before each execution of PRINT-DETAIL-LINE, each execution of a READ statement is followed immediately by a test of the value of EOF-FLAG. No statements in the PRINT-DETAIL-LINE are executed after the end of MONTHLY-SALES-FILE has been detected.

When the repetitions terminate, the files are closed and execution of the program is terminated. Note that we can close both files with a single CLOSE statement.

### PRINT-DETAIL-LINE

When PRINT-DETAIL-LINE is executed, the record to be processed has already been read from MONTHLY-SALES-FILE—either by the READ statement preceding the PERFORM statement or (on the previous execution of PRINT-DETAIL-LINE) by the READ statement at the end of PRINT-DETAIL-LINE. The first job of PRINT-DETAIL-LINE is to move the data from the fields of MONTHLY-SALES-RECORD to the corresponding fields of DETAIL-LINE. The editing specified by the pictures of the fields of DETAIL-LINE is carried out during these moves:

```
MOVE MS-STOCK-NUMBER TO DL-STOCK-NUMBER,
MOVE MS-DESCRIPTION TO DL-DESCRIPTION,
MOVE MS-UNIT-PRICE TO DL-UNIT-PRICE,
MOVE MS-NUMBER-SOLD TO DL-NUMBER-SOLD,
MOVE MS-SALES-INCOME TO DL-SALES-INCOME,
```

We set up print lines in DETAIL-LINE, which is defined in the Working-Storage Section where the VALUE clause is valid. For printing, the contents of DETAIL-LINE must be moved to SALES-REPORT-RECORD, the record associated in the File Section with the print file SALES-REPORT-FILE. We could do this with two statements:

```
MOVE DETAIL-LINE TO SALES-REPORT-RECORD,
WRITE SALES-REPORT-RECORD,
```

Instead, however, we can use the FROM option of the WRITE statement to specify the record from which the contents of SALES-REPORT-RECORD are to by obtained. The statement

```
WRITE SALES-REPORT-RECORD FROM DETAIL-LINE,
```

has exactly the same effect as the two statements just given—the contents of DETAIL-LINE are moved to SALES-REPORT-RECORD, after which the contents of SALES-REPORT-RECORD are sent to the printer.

The READ statement reads the record that will be processed on the *next* execution of PRINT-DETAIL-LINE. EOF-FLAG is set to "Y" if there are no more records to be read. Since the READ statement is the last statement in the paragraph, immediately after the READ statement is executed the PERFORM statement tests the value of EOF-FLAG. If EOF-FLAG was not set to "Y" by the READ statement, PRINT-DETAIL-LINE will be executed again to process the record that was read.

SALES-REPORT-II

SALES-REPORT-II prints a sales report with a title and column headings. Figure 3.4 shows the program, and Figure 3.5 shows a report produced by it. The overall organization of SALES-REPORT-II is the same as for SALES-REPORT-I, and some parts of the two programs (the Environment Division and the File Section, for example) are identical. We will concentrate on the areas in which the two programs differ.

**Horizontal Spacing**

As shown in Figure 3.5, the sales report is to have a title and two lines of column headings in addition to the detail lines containing the data. The Working-Storage Section contains a separate record for each line to be printed (except that one record serves for all the detail lines). TITLE-LINE corresponds to the report title, HEADING-LINE-1 to the first line of column headings, HEADING-LINE-2 to the second line of column headings, and DETAIL-LINE to the detail lines.

```
IDENTIFICATION DIVISION.
PROGRAM-ID.  SALES-REPORT-II.

*    This program prints a sales report
*    with title and column headings.

ENVIRONMENT DIVISION.
INPUT-OUTPUT SECTION.
FILE-CONTROL.
     SELECT MONTHLY-SALES-FILE ASSIGN TO DISK
          ORGANIZATION IS LINE SEQUENTIAL.
     SELECT SALES-REPORT-FILE ASSIGN TO PRINTER.


DATA DIVISION.
FILE SECTION.
FD   MONTHLY-SALES-FILE
     LABEL RECORDS STANDARD
     VALUE OF FILE-ID IS DOS-FILE-NAME.
01   MONTHLY-SALES-RECORD.
     02   MS-STOCK-NUMBER PIC X(6).
     02   MS-DESCRIPTION  PIC X(20).
     02   MS-UNIT-PRICE   PIC 999V99.
     02   MS-NUMBER-SOLD  PIC 999.
     02   MS-SALES-INCOME PIC 9(4)V99.


FD   SALES-REPORT-FILE
     LABEL RECORDS OMITTED.
01   SALES-REPORT-RECORD PIC X(80).

WORKING-STORAGE SECTION.
01   TITLE-LINE.
     02   FILLER          PIC X(34) VALUE SPACES.
     02   FILLER          PIC X(12) VALUE "Sales Report".


01   HEADING-LINE-1.
     02   FILLER          PIC X VALUE SPACE.
     02   FILLER          PIC X(5) VALUE "Stock".
     02   FILLER          PIC X(38) VALUE SPACES.
     02   FILLER          PIC X(4) VALUE "Unit".
     02   FILLER          PIC X(9) VALUE SPACES.
     02   FILLER          PIC X(6) VALUE "Number".
     02   FILLER          PIC X(10) VALUE   SPACES.
     02   FILLER          PIC X(5) VALUE "Sales".


01   HEADING-LINE-2.
     02   FILLER          PIC X VALUE SPACE.
     02   FILLER          PIC X(6) VALUE "Number".
     02   FILLER          PIC X(8) VALUE SPACES.
     02   FILLER          PIC X(11) VALUE "Description".
     02   FILLER          PIC X(18) VALUE SPACES.
     02   FILLER          PIC X(5) VALUE "Price".
     02   FILLER          PIC X(9) VALUE SPACES.
     02   FILLER          PIC X(4) VALUE "Sold".
     02   FILLER          PIC X(11) VALUE SPACES.
     02   FILLER          PIC X(6) VALUE "Income".
```

*Figure 3.4*   This program prints a sales report with title and column headings.

```
01    DETAIL-LINE.
      02    DL-STOCK-NUMBER PIC XBXXBXXX.
      02    FILLER          PIC X(7) VALUE SPACES.
      02    DL-DESCRIPTION  PIC X(20).
      02    FILLER          PIC X(8) VALUE SPACES.
      02    DL-UNIT-PRICE   PIC $$$9.99.
      02    FILLER          PIC X(8) VALUE SPACES.
      02    DL-NUMBER-SOLD  PIC ZZ9.
      02    FILLER          PIC X(10) VALUE SPACES.
      02    DL-SALES-INCOME PIC $$,$$9.99.

01    INPUT-FILE-CONTROL.
      02    EOF-FLAG        PIC X.
      02    DOS-FILE-NAME   PIC X(15).

01    PRINTER-CONTROL.
      02    LINE-SPACING    PIC 9.

PROCEDURE DIVISION.
PRINT-SALES-REPORT.
      DISPLAY (1, 1) ERASE.
      DISPLAY (5, 1) "Name of monthly sales file? ".
      ACCEPT (LIN, COL) DOS-FILE-NAME WITH PROMPT.
      OPEN INPUT MONTHLY-SALES-FILE
           OUTPUT SALES-REPORT-FILE.
      PERFORM PRINT-HEADINGS.
      MOVE "N" TO EOF-FLAG.
      READ MONTHLY-SALES-FILE
           AT END MOVE "Y" TO EOF-FLAG.
      PERFORM PRINT-DETAIL-LINE
           UNTIL EOF-FLAG = "Y".
      CLOSE MONTHLY-SALES-FILE
            SALES-REPORT-FILE.
      STOP RUN.


PRINT-HEADINGS.
      WRITE SALES-REPORT-RECORD
           FROM TITLE-LINE
           AFTER ADVANCING PAGE.
      WRITE SALES-REPORT-RECORD
           FROM HEADING-LINE-1
           AFTER ADVANCING 3 LINES.
      WRITE SALES-REPORT-RECORD
           FROM HEADING-LINE-2
           AFTER ADVANCING 1 LINE.
      MOVE 2 TO LINE-SPACING.

PRINT-DETAIL-LINE.
      MOVE MS-STOCK-NUMBER TO DL-STOCK-NUMBER.
      MOVE MS-DESCRIPTION TO DL-DESCRIPTION.
      MOVE MS-NUMBER-SOLD TO DL-NUMBER-SOLD.
      MOVE MS-UNIT-PRICE TO DL-UNIT-PRICE.
      MOVE MS-SALES-INCOME TO DL-SALES-INCOME.
      WRITE SALES-REPORT-RECORD
           FROM DETAIL-LINE
           AFTER ADVANCING LINE-SPACING LINES.
      MOVE 1 TO LINE-SPACING.
      READ MONTHLY-SALES-FILE
           AT END MOVE "Y" TO EOF-FLAG.
```

*Figure 3.4 (continued)*

```
                                  Sales Report


                                        Unit        Number         Sales
   Stock                                Price        Sold           Income
   Number          Description
                                        $135.98       5             $679.90
 1 15 263          Desk Calculator      $299.95       2             $599.90
 1 15 378          Cash Register        $473.89       8           $3,791.12
 1 29 431          Typewriter           $389.95      12           $4,679.40
 2 24 635          Executive Desk       $279.49      12           $3,353.88
 2 24 845          Executive Chair      $249.95       0               $0.00
 2 24 962          Conference Table       $2.79     250             $679.50
 3 18 145          Typewriter Ribbon     $16.95       9             $152.55
 3 18 251          Typing Element        $39.95      30           $1,198.50
 3 57 009          Diskettes, box of 10
```

*Figure 3.5*   A sales report printed by the program in Figure 3.4. Note that the Description heading is left-justified in its column, while the other column headings are centered over their columns.

In writing the records corresponding to the various lines, we need to specify the spaces between the items on each line so as to arrange the printed output in a pleasing format. The title should be centered, for example, the columns should be evenly spaced across the page, and the column headings should be positioned (in most cases, centered) over the corresponding columns. There are several approaches to laying out a printed form.

The simplest case is if you have a sample printout, such as that in Figure 3.5. This could happen if you wish the printout from your program to match that produced by another computer system. Using a *forms design ruler* (available from dealers in computer supplies), you can measure the spaces between the items in each line. When the sizes of the items can vary, as in some fields of the detail line, you must decide what is the largest possible item in each column and use these largest possible items as the basis for your measurements.

If a model form is not available, you can design your own using a *printer layout form* or *print chart*. (Pads of printer layout forms are available from dealers in computer supplies.) A printer layout form consists of a grid, each block of which corresponds to a character position on the printed page. Both the rows (corresponding to lines on the printed page) and the columns (corresponding to columns of characters) are numbered. You can position the various headings and detail items on the print chart, using either trial and error or the rules used by typists (and found in typing manuals) for centering titles and laying out columns. When you are satisfied with the layout, you can easily read off the spacings between the items from the print chart.

The easiest approach, however, is to use a computer program to lay out your form. Appendix C to this book contains a forms layout program that you can use. The program is written in IBM-PC BASIC, which is familiar to most PC users. It can be adapted to pocket and portable computers that are convenient to use when laying out forms.

Before running the layout program, we should write down the desired titles and column headings as well as the pictures for the fields in the detail line. It will help to write the number of characters in each item next to the item. The size of a detail item is (almost always) the size of the corresponding picture. Here is this preliminary work, with the item sizes enclosed in brackets:

```
                      Sales Report [12]
Stock     [5]                  [0]  Unit    [4]  Number [6]  Sales      [5]
Number    [6]  Description [11]  Price   [5]  Sold   [4]  Income     [6]
XBXXBXXX [8]   X(20)          [20]  $$$9,99 [7]  ZZ9    [3]  $$,$$9,99 [9]
```

Figure 3.6 shows a run of the layout program. The program begins by asking five questions:

```
          Page width? 80
          Left margin? 0
          Number of title lines? 1
          Number of lines? 3
          Number of columns? 5
```

```
Page width? 80
Left margin? 0
Number of title lines? 1
Number of lines? 3
Number of columns? 5


Enter title widths---

              Left              Center           Right

Title line 1    0                 12                0


Enter field widths---

Columns:    1      2      3      4      5

Line 1      5      0      4      6      5
Line 2      6    -11      5      4      6
Line 3      8     20      7      3      9




Title spacings--

              Left              Center           Right

Title line 1  0                 34                34            0


Field spacings---

Columns:      1      2      3      4      5

Line 1        1     19     19      9     10      2
Line 2        1      8     18      9     10      2
Line 3        0      7      8      8     10      0
```

*Figure 3.6*  A typical run of the forms-layout program. Instructions for using the program are given in Chapter 3 and in Appendix C.

The page width is the number of characters on a line—80 if you are using an 80-column printer. The left margin is the number of blank character positions to the left of the printed area. If you enter a negative number for the left margin, the program will choose a left margin approximately equal to the spacing between columns. To provide as much room as possible for the columns and the spaces between them, we specify a left margin of 0. There is only one title line. The number of nontitle lines is 3—two lines of column headings and one detail line. The number of columns of data is 5.

The program then asks for the sizes of the items on each title line. In general, a title has a left part, which begins at the left margin, a center part, which is centered, and a right part, which ends at the right margin. For example:

```
Acme Sales            Sales Report                    Page   1
```

The program asks for the widths of the left, center, and right parts. Since no left and right parts are present in our example, we enter 0 for them. Press the Enter key after entering each number; the program will automatically place the cursor in the proper position for the next value to be entered.

After the information concerning the title lines has been entered, the program asks you to enter the widths of the fields in the heading line and the two detail lines. The entries are made in a table with the rows and columns labeled. Again, press the Enter key after each entry; the program will position the cursor for the next entry.

In Figure 3.6 we note two unusual entries for column 2. The first heading line contains no heading for column 2; hence we enter 0 for line 1 and column 2. When writing HEADING-LINE-1, we will add the number of spaces to the left and right of column 2 to get the number of spaces between the headings for column 1 and column 3.

The program normally centers column headings over their columns. However, when a short heading (such as Description) is used over a wider column of variable-length alphanumeric items (as in column 2), the heading usually looks best left justified (like the detail items in the column) rather than centered. Entering a field width as a negative number causes the field to be left justified rather than centered. In Figure 3.6, therefore, the width of Description is entered as −11.

After all the entries have been made, the program prints the title spacings and the field spacings. In the title line there are 0 spaces between the left end of the line and the left part of the title, 34 spaces between the left part and the center part, and so on. In fact, since there are no left and right parts, 34 spaces precede the center part and 34 spaces follow it. Likewise, in line 1 there is 1 space between the left end of the line and the heading in column 1, 19 spaces between the heading in column 1 and the heading in column 2, 19 spaces between the heading in column 2 and the heading in column 3, and so on. Since in line 1 there is no heading in column 2, we add the spaces on each side of column 2 to get 38 spaces between the heading in column 1 and the heading in column 3.

The records corresponding to the various printed lines are constructed directly from the desired headings and detail items and the spacing information obtained by measuring an existing form, constructing a print chart, or using the computer program. For example, Figure 3.6 informs us that the title Sales Report should be preceded by 34 spaces. Hence, we write TITLE-LINE as follows:

```
          1   2   2   2   3   3   4   4   4   5   5   6
A...B...6...0...4...8...2...6...0...4...8...2...6...0...
01  TITLE-LINE.
    02  FILLER              PIC X(34) VALUE SPACES.
    02  FILLER              PIC X(12) VALUE "Sales Report".
```

Note that the 34 spaces that *follow* Sales Report do not have to be specified in TITLE-LINE. When the contents of TITLE-LINE are moved to the SALES-REPORT-RECORD, the MOVE statement will add as many spaces as necessary to the right of the contents of TITLE-LINE so as to make up the 80-character length of SALES-REPORT-RECORD. Likewise, for the column headings and the detail line, the spaces following column 5 do not have to be included in the corresponding record descriptions.

If you use the forms layout program, you may find—after looking at the printout from your COBOL program—that a minor adjustment or two in the spacings will improve the appearance of the printout. For example, the forms layout program positions the headings Sales and Income as follows:

```
    Sales
Income
```

Aligning the two words on the left rather than the right improves the appearance:

```
    Sales
    Income
```

To move a field one space to the right, we increase by one the number of spaces preceding the field and decrease by one the number of spaces following it. To move a field one space to the left, we decrease by one the number of spaces preceding the field and increase by one the number of spaces following it. According to Figure 3.6, Income is preceded by 10 spaces and followed by 2. To move Income one position to the right, we precede it by 11 spaces and follow it by 1 space. (Since Income is in the rightmost column, the spaces following it do not actually appear in the corresponding record.)

## Other Working-Storage Items

In our previous programs such stand-alone data items as DOS-FILE-NAME and EOF-FLAG have each been defined in separate 01-level entries. However, as a guide to someone reading the program, similar data items are often grouped into records. In SALES-REPORT-II, the two data items associated with the input file, EOF-FLAG and DOS-FILE-NAME, are made fields of the record INPUT-FILE-CONTROL. LINE-SPACING, a data item used to control vertical spacing in the printout, is made a field of the record PRINTER-CONTROL. The record names INPUT-FILE-CONTROL and PRINTER-CONTROL are intended only as guides for human readers and are never referred to by the program.

## Vertical Spacing

Looking at Figure 3.5, we see that our program should triple space (skip two lines) between the title and the column headings, single space the two lines of headings, double space (skip one line) between the second heading line and the first detail line, and single space the detail lines. What's more, the title should be printed at the top of a new page.

Our tool for vertical spacing is the ADVANCING option of the WRITE statement. For example,

```
WRITE SALES-REPORT-RECORD
    AFTER ADVANCING PAGE.
```

prints the contents of SALES-REPORT-RECORD after going to the top of a new page. The statement

```
WRITE SALES-REPORT-RECORD
    AFTER ADVANCING 1 LINE.
```

prints after advancing to the next line (single spacing). Likewise, AFTER ADVANCING 2 LINES produces double spacing; AFTER ADVANCING 3 LINES produces triple spacing, and so on. AFTER ADVANCING 0 LINES causes the WRITE statement to print without advancing. The line spacing can be specified by a data name as well as a constant. The statement

```
WRITE SALES-REPORT-RECORD
    AFTER ADVANCING LINE-SPACING LINES.
```

prints after advancing the number of lines specified by the current value of LINE-SPACING.

(There is also a BEFORE ADVANCING option that causes a line to be printed *before* rather than *after* the printer is advanced. Usually, AFTER ADVANCING proves more useful than BEFORE ADVANCING. Programmers avoid using both options in the same program, since if a WRITE statement with AFTER ADVANCING is followed by one with BEFORE ADVANCING, the second line will be printed on top of the first one.)

In SALES-REPORT-II, the headings are printed by the paragraph PRINT-HEADINGS, which is performed after the files have been opened but before any input records have been processed. The following statements print the headings:

```
WRITE SALES-REPORT-RECORD
    FROM TITLE-LINE
    AFTER ADVANCING PAGE.
WRITE SALES-REPORT-RECORD
    FROM HEADING-LINE-1
    AFTER ADVANCING 3 LINES.
WRITE SALES-REPORT-RECORD
    FROM HEADING-LINE-2
    AFTER ADVANCING 1 LINE.
MOVE 2 TO LINE-SPACING.
```

The value of LINE-SPACING controls the spacing of detail lines. PRINT HEADINGS moves 2 to LINE-SPACING so the program will double space between the second heading line and the first detail line. Thereafter, LINE-SPACING is set to 1 so that the remaining detail lines will be single spaced. The following statements (in the paragraph PRINT-DETAIL-LINE) print a detail line and set the line spacing:

```
WRITE SALES-REPORT-RECORD
      FROM DETAIL-LINE
      AFTER ADVANCING LINE-SPACING LINES,
MOVE 1 TO LINE-SPACING,
```

The first time this WRITE statement is executed, the value of LINE-SPACING has been set to 2 by PRINT-HEADINGS, producing double spacing between the second heading line and the first detail line. The MOVE statement sets the value of LINE-SPACING to 1 so that all subsequent detail lines will be single spaced.

## SALES-REPORT-III

SALES-REPORT-III is almost identical to SALES-REPORT-II except that SALES-REPORT-III can print multiple-page reports with numbered pages. To get a multiple-page report from our small test file, we use small pages—only 11 printed lines each. Figure 3.7 shows the program SALES-REPORT-III, and Figure 3.8 shows a two-page printout produced by the program.

There are basically two ways to control paging. We can use a LINAGE clause to define the size of a page; the runtime system will then inform the program when the end of a page has been reached. Alternatively, the program can count the number of lines it has printed and thus determine for itself when the end of a page has been reached. SALES-REPORT-III uses the LINAGE clause; the line-counting method is illustrated in Chapter 4.

## The LINAGE Clause

The LINAGE clause defines a *logical page,* so called because it need not have anything to do with the *physical pages*—the actual sheets of paper on which output is being printed. We could, for example, print several logical pages on each sheet of paper. Alternatively, we could allow a logical page to extend over more than one physical page. In SALES-REPORT-III we define a short 15-line logical page so we can get a two-page report from a nine-record file:

```
          1   2   2   2   3
A...B...6...0...4...8...2...
FD   SALES-REPORT-FILE
     LABEL RECORDS OMITTED
     LINAGE IS 11 LINES
         WITH FOOTING AT 11
         LINES AT TOP 2
         LINES AT BOTTOM 2,
```

```
IDENTIFICATION DIVISION.
PROGRAM-ID.  SALES-REPORT-III.

*    This program prints a multi-page sales report.
*    Each page contains only 11 lines so that paging
*    can be demonstrated with a small test file.

ENVIRONMENT DIVISION.
INPUT-OUTPUT SECTION.
FILE-CONTROL.
     SELECT MONTHLY-SALES-FILE ASSIGN TO DISK
          ORGANIZATION IS LINE SEQUENTIAL.
     SELECT SALES-REPORT-FILE ASSIGN TO PRINTER.

DATA DIVISION.
FILE SECTION.
FD  MONTHLY-SALES-FILE
     LABEL RECORDS STANDARD
     VALUE OF FILE-ID IS DOS-FILE-NAME.
01  MONTHLY-SALES-RECORD.
     02  MS-STOCK-NUMBER PIC X(6).
     02  MS-DESCRIPTION  PIC X(20).
     02  MS-UNIT-PRICE   PIC 999V99.
     02  MS-NUMBER-SOLD  PIC 999.
     02  MS-SALES-INCOME PIC 9(4)V99.


FD  SALES-REPORT-FILE
     LABEL RECORDS OMITTED
     LINAGE IS 11 LINES
          WITH FOOTING AT 11
          LINES AT TOP 2
          LINES AT BOTTOM 2.
01  SALES-REPORT-RECORD PIC X(80).

WORKING-STORAGE SECTION.
01  TITLE-LINE.
     02  FILLER          PIC X(34) VALUE SPACES.
     02  FILLER          PIC X(12) VALUE "Sales Report".
     02  FILLER          PIC X(27) VALUE SPACES.
     02  FILLER          PIC X(4) VALUE "Page".
     02  TL-PAGE-NUMBER  PIC ZZ9.


01  HEADING-LINE-1.
     02  FILLER          PIC X VALUE SPACE.
     02  FILLER          PIC X(5) VALUE "Stock".
     02  FILLER          PIC X(38) VALUE SPACES.
     02  FILLER          PIC X(4) VALUE "Unit".
     02  FILLER          PIC X(9) VALUE SPACES.
     02  FILLER          PIC X(6) VALUE "Number".
     02  FILLER          PIC X(10) VALUE   SPACES.
     02  FILLER          PIC X(5) VALUE "Sales".
```

*Figure 3.7* This program produces a multipage report such as the one shown in Figure 3.8. A page number is printed in the upper right corner of each page. The program prints only 11 lines on each page so that paging can be demonstrated with the short test file in Figure 3.1.


LINAGE IS 11 LINES gives the size of the *page body*—the part of the page that will contain printing. Each page (except possibly the last) will contain 11 printed lines. LINES AT TOP 2 specifies a *top margin* of two blank lines above the page body,

```
01   HEADING-LINE-2.
     02  FILLER            PIC X VALUE SPACE.
     02  FILLER            PIC X(6) VALUE "Number".
     02  FILLER            PIC X(8) VALUE SPACES.
     02  FILLER            PIC X(11) VALUE "Description".
     02  FILLER            PIC X(18) VALUE SPACES.
     02  FILLER            PIC X(5) VALUE "Price".
     02  FILLER            PIC X(9) VALUE SPACES.
     02  FILLER            PIC X(4) VALUE "Sold".
     02  FILLER            PIC X(11) VALUE SPACES.
     02  FILLER            PIC X(6) VALUE "Income".

01   DETAIL-LINE.
     02  DL-STOCK-NUMBER PIC XBXXBXXX.
     02  FILLER            PIC X(7) VALUE SPACES.
     02  DL-DESCRIPTION  PIC X(20).
     02  FILLER            PIC X(8) VALUE SPACES.
     02  DL-UNIT-PRICE   PIC $$$9.99.
     02  FILLER            PIC X(8) VALUE SPACES.
     02  DL-NUMBER-SOLD  PIC ZZ9.
     02  FILLER            PIC X(10) VALUE SPACES.
     02  DL-SALES-INCOME PIC $$,$$9.99.

01   INPUT-FILE-CONTROL.
     02  EOF-FLAG          PIC X.
     02  DOS-FILE-NAME     PIC X(15).

01   PRINTER-CONTROL.
     02  LINE-SPACING      PIC 9.
     02  EOP-FLAG          PIC X.

01   COUNTER.
     02  PAGE-NUMBER       PIC 999.
```

*Figure 3.7 (continued)*

and LINES AT BOTTOM 2 specifies a *bottom margin* of two blank lines below the page body. The total size of a logical page is the sum of the sizes of the top margin, the page body, and the bottom margin. Thus each logical page printed by SALES-REPORT-III has 15 (= 2 + 11 + 2) lines. No additional spacing is provided between logical pages—the bottom margin of one page is followed immediately by the top margin of the next page.

The FOOTING phrase specifies the first line of a *footing area* at the bottom of the page. When a WRITE statement prints in or advances into the footing area, the program is signaled that the end of the page has been reached. The remaining lines of the footing area can be used to print a *footing* for the page—typically summary information such as totals for certain columns. Normally, the FOOTING phrase gives the line of the page body on which the last detail line of the page will be printed. If no footing is to be printed, the FOOTING phrase should specify the last line of the page body.

If the FOOTING phrase is omitted, the footing is assumed to be at the last line of the page body. If the LINES AT TOP or LINES AT BOTTOM phrase is omitted, the corresponding margin is also omitted.

```
PROCEDURE DIVISION.
PRINT-SALES-REPORT.
    DISPLAY (1, 1) ERASE.
    DISPLAY (5, 1) "Name of monthly sales file? ".
    ACCEPT (LIN, COL) DOS-FILE-NAME WITH PROMPT.
    OPEN INPUT MONTHLY-SALES-FILE
         OUTPUT SALES-REPORT-FILE.
    MOVE 1 TO PAGE-NUMBER.
    PERFORM PRINT-HEADINGS.
    MOVE "N" TO EOF-FLAG.
    READ MONTHLY-SALES-FILE
        AT END MOVE "Y" TO EOF-FLAG.
    PERFORM PRINT-DETAIL-LINE
        UNTIL EOF-FLAG = "Y".
    CLOSE MONTHLY-SALES-FILE
          SALES-REPORT-FILE.
    STOP RUN.

PRINT-HEADINGS.
    MOVE PAGE-NUMBER TO TL-PAGE-NUMBER.
    ADD 1 TO PAGE-NUMBER.
    WRITE SALES-REPORT-RECORD
        FROM TITLE-LINE
        AFTER ADVANCING PAGE.
    WRITE SALES-REPORT-RECORD
        FROM HEADING-LINE-1
        AFTER ADVANCING 3 LINES.
    WRITE SALES-REPORT-RECORD
        FROM HEADING-LINE-2
        AFTER ADVANCING 1 LINE.
    MOVE 2 TO LINE-SPACING.
    MOVE "N" TO EOP-FLAG.

PRINT-DETAIL-LINE.
    MOVE MS-STOCK-NUMBER TO DL-STOCK-NUMBER.
    MOVE MS-DESCRIPTION TO DL-DESCRIPTION.
    MOVE MS-NUMBER-SOLD TO DL-NUMBER-SOLD.
    MOVE MS-UNIT-PRICE TO DL-UNIT-PRICE.
    MOVE MS-SALES-INCOME TO DL-SALES-INCOME.
    WRITE SALES-REPORT-RECORD
        FROM DETAIL-LINE
        AFTER ADVANCING LINE-SPACING LINES
        AT END-OF-PAGE MOVE "Y" TO EOP-FLAG.
    IF EOP-FLAG = "Y"
        PERFORM PRINT-HEADINGS
    ELSE
        MOVE 1 TO LINE-SPACING.
    READ MONTHLY-SALES-FILE
        AT END MOVE "Y" TO EOF-FLAG.
```

*Figure 3.7 (continued)*

Usually, of course, we define logical pages to coincide with the physical pages on which the output will be printed. For example, the following LINAGE clause defines a 60-line page body on a standard 66-line (11-inch) page:

```
                    Sales Report                           Page   1

  Stock
  Number         Description              Unit      Number      Sales
                                          Price      Sold       Income

  1 15 263       Desk Calculator         $135.98       5        $679.90
  1 15 378       Cash Register           $299.95       2        $599.90
  1 29 431       Typewriter              $473.89       8       $3,791.12
  2 24 635       Executive Desk          $389.95      12       $4,679.40
  2 24 845       Executive Chair         $279.49      12       $3,353.88



                    Sales Report                           Page   2

  Stock
  Number         Description              Unit      Number      Sales
                                          Price      Sold       Income

  2 24 962       Conference Table        $249.95       0           $0.00
  3 18 145       Typewriter Ribbon         $2.79     250         $679.50
  3 18 251       Typing Element           $16.95       9         $152.55
  3 57 009       Diskettes, box of 10     $39.95      30       $1,198.50
```

*Figure 3.8*  A two-page report printed by the program in Figure 3.7.

```
    LINAGE IS 60 LINES
        WITH FOOTING AT 60
        LINES AT TOP 3
        LINES AT BOTTOM 3
```

If we wanted to print a two-line footing at the bottom of each page, we could use the LINAGE clause:

```
    LINAGE IS 60 LINES
        WITH FOOTING AT 58
        LINES AT TOP 3
        LINES AT BOTTOM 3
```

The last detail line will be printed on line 58 of the page body, after which the program will be signaled that the end of the page has been reached. The program can then print the two-line footing on lines 59 and 60. The footing might consist of a blank line (to separate the footing from the detail lines) followed by a line giving totals for certain columns.

## Page Numbers

We want to number each page of our report. To do so, we include a page-number field in TITLE-LINE:

```
          1   2   2   2   3   3   4   4   4   5   5   6
A...B...6...0...4...8...2...6...0...4...8...2...6...0...
    01   TITLE-LINE.
         02   FILLER            PIC X(34) VALUE SPACES.
         02   FILLER            PIC X(12) VALUE "Sales Report".
         02   FILLER            PIC X(27) VALUE SPACES.
         02   FILLER            PIC X(4) VALUE "Page".
         02   TL-PAGE-NUMBER    PIC ZZ9.
```

We want to add 1 to the page number for each page printed. However, we recall that arithmetic can be done only on numeric items—not numeric-edited items such as TL-PAGE-NUMBER. Therefore, we keep the current page number in a numeric item PAGE-NUMBER, which we classify as a *counter:*

```
01  COUNTER.
    02  PAGE-NUMBER      PIC 999.
```

PAGE-NUMBER is given the initial value 1 in the PRINT-SALES-REPORT paragraph:

```
MOVE 1 TO PAGE-NUMBER.
```

Before printing the title line, the PRINT-HEADINGS paragraph moves the current page number to TL-PAGE-NUMBER:

```
MOVE PAGE-NUMBER TO TL-PAGE-NUMBER.
```

In preparation for printing the next page, the current page number is increased by 1:

```
ADD 1 TO PAGE-NUMBER.
```

(Arithmetic statements such as ADD are discussed in detail in Chapter 4.)

### Page Control

We use EOP-FLAG (EOP stands for End of Page) to indicate whether the end of the current page has been reached. The last statement of the PRINT-HEADINGS paragraph sets EOP-FLAG to "N", indicating that the end of the page has not been reached. The PRINT-DETAIL-LINE paragraph detects the end of the page by using the END-OF-PAGE option of the WRITE statement:

```
          1   2   2   2   3   3   4   4   4
A...B...6...0...4...8...2...6...0...4...8...
    WRITE SALES-REPORT-RECORD
        FROM DETAIL-LINE
        AFTER ADVANCING LINE-SPACING LINES
        AT END-OF-PAGE MOVE "Y" TO EOP-FLAG.
```

The END-OF-PAGE option can be used only with the LINAGE clause. When a WRITE statement prints in or advances into the footing area defined in the LINAGE clause, the statement following AT END-OF-PAGE is executed. In SALES-REPORT-III, AT END-OF-PAGE is followed by a MOVE statement that sets EOP-FLAG to "Y", indicating that the end of page has been detected.

### The IF statement with ELSE part

Following the WRITE statement, the next action to be taken depends on whether the end of the page was detected. If it was, we want to perform PRINT-HEADINGS so as to go to a new page and print headings at the top. If the end of page was not detected, we want to move 1 to L I N E - S P A C I N G to assure that remaining detail lines will be single spaced. We use an I F statement with an ELSE part to carry out the desired action:

```
      1   2   2   2   3   3   4   4
A...B...6...0...4...8...2...6...0...4...
      IF EOP-FLAG = "Y"
           PERFORM PRINT-HEADINGS
      ELSE
           MOVE 1 TO LINE-SPACING.
```

If the value of EOP-FLAG is " Y ", the statement between I F and ELSE—PERFORM PRINT-HEADINGS—is executed. Otherwise, the statement following ELSE—MOVE 1 TO LINE-SPACING—is executed. In general, we can have as many statements as desired between I F and ELSE and between ELSE and the terminating period. If the condition following I F is true, the statements between I F and ELSE are executed. If the condition is not true, the statements following ELSE are executed. Note that there is only one period at the end of the entire I F statement.

## EXERCISES

1. Write a COBOL program to create monthly sales files that can be processed by SALES-REPORT-I, SALES-REPORT-II, and SALES-REPORT-III. The program will be similar to CREATE in Chapter 2. The stock number, description, unit price, and number sold for each item should be obtained from the user. The sales income for each item should be computed by the program using the MULTI-PLY statement:

```
MULTIPLY UNIT-PRICE BY NUMBER-SOLD
     GIVING SALES-INCOME ROUNDED.
```

2. SALES-REPORT-III skips a logical page before printing page 1—an action that serves no useful purpose. To avoid wasting a page, modify the PRINT-HEADINGS paragraph so that the title line for page 1 will be printed by

```
WRITE SALES-REPORT-RECORD
     FROM TITLE-LINE
     AFTER ADVANCING 0 LINES
```

and the title line for each subsequent page will be printed by

```
WRITE SALES-REPORT-RECORD
     FROM TITLE-LINE
     AFTER ADVANCING PAGE
```

*Hints*: (1) Remember the I F statement with ELSE part. (2) You may want to delay adding 1 to the page number until after the title line has been printed.

3. Modify SALES-REPORT-III to place a two-line footing at the bottom of each page. The first line of the footing will be blank; the second will consist of either

Continued or End of Report. Continued will be printed on every page except the last one; End of Report will be printed on the last page. The footing for the last page will follow the last detail line and need not be at the bottom of the page. *Hints*: After the end of the page is detected, print the footing Continued before performing PRINT-HEADINGS to go to a new page. After all records have been processed, print the footing End of Report. To provide the blank line, each footing should be printed after advancing two lines. You may position the footings horizontally as desired.

4. Write a program to print a student grade report from a file whose records are defined as follows:

| Field | Size | Type of Data |
|---|---|---|
| Student number | 6 | Alphanumeric |
| Student name | 20 | Alphanumeric |
| Course name | 10 | Alphanumeric |
| Number grade | 3 | Numeric—whole number |
| Letter grade | 1 | Alphanumeric |

If you specify line-sequential organization, you can use a text editor to produce a sample file with which to test your program.

5. Instead of specifying the size of each field of a record, we can think of the record as a typed line and specify the columns in which each field begins and ends. The size of a field is related to the first and last columns of the field by:

$$size = last\text{-}column - first\text{-}column + 1$$

Write a program to print a tax assessment report from a file whose records are defined as follows:

| Field | Columns | Type of Data |
|---|---|---|
| Property owner | 1–20 | Alphanumeric |
| Property number | 21–26 | Alphanumeric |
| Assessed value | 27–34 | Numeric—two decimal places |
| Tax rate | 35–37 | Numeric—one decimal place |

# 4

## Arithmetic and Conditions

COBOL provides five statements for doing arithmetic: `ADD`, `SUBTRACT`, `MULTIPLY`, `DIVIDE`, and `COMPUTE`. With `ADD`, `SUBTRACT`, `MULTIPLY`, and `DIVIDE`, we use English-like sentences to describe the calculation to be carried out. With `COMPUTE`, the calculation is described by formulas as in many other programming languages such as BASIC and FORTRAN. Some COBOL programmers prefer English-like sentences; others prefer formulas. We will look at both approaches, and you can choose the one that seems most natural to you.

At this point you should be familiar enough with the format of COBOL programs that examples no longer have to be accompanied by column-number scales. Remember that statements in the Procedure Division must be entirely in area B and usually start in the B margin. When, for readability, statements or parts of statements are indented beyond the B margin, they are usually indented in increments of four spaces.

## ADD, SUBTRACT, MULTIPLY, **AND** DIVIDE

### The ADD Statement

The arithmetic statements manipulate the contents of fields defined in the Data Division. In our examples, we will use FIELD-A, FIELD-B, FIELD-C, and so on as the names of fields whose contents are to be manipulated. Let FIELD-A have a picture of 999 and consider the following ADD statement:

        ADD 25 TO FIELD-A.

Suppose that before this statement is executed, FIELD-A contains the value 150. When the statement is executed, the computer obtains the contents of FIELD-A, does the addition:

$$\begin{array}{r} 150 \\ +\ \underline{\phantom{0}25} \\ 175 \end{array}$$

and stores the sum 175 back in FIELD-A. The value of FIELD-A has been increased by 25.

We can use a data name instead of a literal to specify the value to be added to FIELD-A. Suppose that FIELD-B also has a picture of 999, and the values of FIELD-A and FIELD-B are

        FIELD-A:  150      FIELD-B:  220

The statement

        ADD FIELD-B TO FIELD-A.

adds the value of FIELD-B to that of FIELD-A. Specifically, the computer obtains the contents of FIELD-A and FIELD-B, does the addition:

$$\begin{array}{r} 150 \\ +\ \underline{220} \\ 370 \end{array}$$

and stores the sum 370 back in FIELD-A. The values of FIELD-A and FIELD-B are now

        FIELD-A:  370      FIELD-B:  220

Note that the value of FIELD-B was not changed.

We can add any number of values to the contents of a field. For example, let FIELD-C and FIELD-D also have pictures of 999 and consider the following ADD statement:

        ADD FIELD-A FIELD-B FIELD-C TO FIELD-D.

Suppose that before this statement is executed, the contents of the four fields are

        FIELD-A:  370      FIELD-B:  220
        FIELD-C:  015      FIELD-D:  100

When the statement is executed, the computer obtains the values of the four fields, carries out the addition:

```
      370
      220
      015
   +  100
      705
```

and stores the sum 705 in FIELD-D. The values of the four fields are now:

```
FIELD-A:   370      FIELD-B:   220
FIELD-C:   015      FIELD-D:   705
```

Only the value of FIELD-D was changed.

When a series of data names or literals occurs in an arithmetic statement, we can separate the data names or literals with commas (each comma must be followed by at least one space). Using commas, the preceding example can be written:

```
ADD FIELD-A, FIELD-B, FIELD-C TO FIELD-D.
```

We can also write the data names or literals on separate lines, like this:

```
ADD FIELD-A
    FIELD-B
    FIELD-C TO FIELD-D.
```

### The GIVING option

The GIVING option can be used with the ADD, SUBTRACT, MULTIPLY, and DIVIDE statements. As we have seen for the ADD statement, when the GIVING option is not present, the field that receives the result of a calculation also supplies one of the data items used in the calculation. The GIVING option allows the result to be stored in a field different from any that supplied data for the calculation.

For example, consider the statement

```
ADD FIELD-A FIELD-B
    GIVING FIELD-C.
```

The values of FIELD-A and FIELD-B are added, and their sum is stored in FIELD-C. The value that FIELD-C had before the statement was executed does not enter into the calculation. For example, suppose that before the statement is executed the values of the three fields are

```
FIELD-A:   030      FIELD-B:   100      FIELD-C:   080
```

When the statement is executed, the computer adds the values of FIELD-A and FIELD-B:

```
      030
   +  100
      130
```

and stores the sum in FIELD-C:

> FIELD-A:   030        FIELD-B:   100        FIELD-C:   130

The values of FIELD-A and FIELD-B remain unchanged; the previous value of FIELD-C is replaced by the sum.

Compare the actions just described with those that would have occurred if the statement had been

> ADD FIELD-A FIELD-B TO FIELD-C.

In that case, the values of all three fields would have been added:

$$\begin{array}{r} 030 \\ 100 \\ +\ \underline{080} \\ 210 \end{array}$$

and the sum stored in FIELD-C:

> FIELD-A:   030        FIELD-B:   100        FIELD-C:   210

## The SUBTRACT Statement

When the GIVING option is not used, the field that receives the result of the subtraction also supplies the subtrahend—the value from which the other values are to be subtracted:

> SUBTRACT FIELD-A FIELD-B FROM FIELD-C.

The values of FIELD-A and FIELD-B are subtracted from the value of FIELD-C and the result is stored in FIELD-C. If the values of the three fields before the statement is executed are

> FIELD-A:   010        FIELD-B:   030        FIELD-C:   100

the values of the three fields after the statement has been executed are

> FIELD-A:   010        FIELD-B:   030        FIELD-C:   060

On the other hand, when the GIVING option is used, the value of FIELD-C is not changed, and the result is stored in the field listed after GIVING:

> SUBTRACT FIELD-A FIELD-B FROM FIELD-C
>     GIVING FIELD-D.

If the values of the fields before the statement is executed are

> FIELD-A:   010        FIELD-B:   030
> FIELD-C:   100        FIELD-D:   250

their values after the statement is executed are

> FIELD-A:   010        FIELD-B:   030
> FIELD-C:   100        FIELD-D:   060

Notice the following difference between the ADD and SUBTRACT statements. With ADD, the preposition TO is present only when the GIVING option is *not* used. When the GIVING option is used, TO is omitted. For SUBTRACT, on the other hand, the preposition FROM is present whether or not the GIVING option is used. It is ADD that is exceptional in this respect. For SUBTRACT, MULTIPLY, and DIVIDE, the preposition is present regardless of whether the GIVING option is used.

### The MULTIPLY Statement

We begin by noting an important difference between the ADD and the SUBTRACT statements on one hand and the MULTIPLY and DIVIDE statements on the other. The ADD statement allows us to add together any number of values, and the SUBTRACT statement allows us to subtract any number of values from a particular value. The MULTIPLY statement, however, allows us to multiply only two values, and the DIVIDE statement allows us to divide only two values. We can add or subtract many values with a single ADD or SUBTRACT statement, but we must write a separate MULTIPLY or DIVIDE statement for each multiplication or division to be done.

This difference aside, the MULTIPLY statement works very much like the SUBTRACT statement. For example, suppose that FIELD-A and FIELD-B have the values

        FIELD-A:  015     FIELD-B:  020

After executing

        MULTIPLY FIELD-A BY FIELD-B.

the values of the two fields are

        FIELD-A:  015     FIELD-B:  300

If we now execute

        MULTIPLY 3 BY FIELD-B.

the new value of FIELD-B will be 900. Note that in English we would probably phrase this statement as "Multiply FIELD-B by 3." This phrasing is incorrect in COBOL, however, because when the GIVING option is not used, the preposition must be followed by the name of the field in which the result is to be stored. Since 3 is not a data name, and so does not designate a field in which the result can be stored, it cannot follow the word BY. For this reason, we sometimes have to write COBOL arithmetic statements in a manner that seems backwards compared to the corresponding English phrasing.

Now suppose FIELD-A, FIELD-B, and FIELD-C have the values

        FIELD-A:  015     FIELD-B:  020     FIELD-C:  025

and we execute

        MULTIPLY FIELD-A BY FIELD-B
            GIVING FIELD-C.

After the statement is executed, the values of the fields are

<pre>
     FIELD-A:  015      FIELD-B:  020      FIELD-C:  300
</pre>

Only the value of FIELD-C is changed.
   Note that both

<pre>
     MULTIPLY 3 BY FIELD-B
         GIVING FIELD-C.
</pre>

and

<pre>
     MULTIPLY FIELD-B BY 3
         GIVING FIELD-C.
</pre>

are allowed. When the GIVING option is present, we can use literals both before and after BY. Why?

## The DIVIDE Statement

The DIVIDE statement is unique in that we can choose between two prepositions— INTO and BY. With INTO, the field preceding the preposition provides the divisor, and the field following the preposition provides the dividend. With BY, the situation is reversed: the field preceding the preposition provides the dividend, and the field following the preposition provides the divisor.
   Let's begin with the case where the GIVING option is not used. The statement

<pre>
     DIVIDE FIELD-A INTO FIELD-B.
</pre>

divides the value of FIELD-A into the value of FIELD-B and stores the quotient in FIELD-B. If the values of FIELD-A and FIELD-B before the statement is executed are

<pre>
     FIELD-A:  150      FIELD-B:  900
</pre>

their values after the statement is executed are

<pre>
     FIELD-A:  150      FIELD-B:  006
</pre>

The statement

<pre>
     DIVIDE FIELD-A BY FIELD-B.
</pre>

divides the value of FIELD-A by the value of FIELD-B and stores the quotient in FIELD-A. If the values of the fields before the statement is executed are

<pre>
     FIELD-A:  500      FIELD-B:  004
</pre>

their values after the statement is executed are

<pre>
     FIELD-A:  125      FIELD-B:  004
</pre>

   The statements

<pre>
     DIVIDE 5 INTO FIELD-A.
</pre>

and

        DIVIDE FIELD-A BY 5,

are both allowed. On the other hand, both

        DIVIDE FIELD-A INTO 5,

and

        DIVIDE 5 BY FIELD-A,

are invalid, since we cannot use a literal in place of the field into which the quotient is to be stored.

Standard COBOL allows only INTO to be used when the GIVING option is not present. The use of BY without the GIVING option is an extension provided by IBM COBOL.

When the GIVING option is used, the choice of INTO or BY still determines which field provides the divisor and which provides the dividend. However, with GIVING the quotient is stored in the field specified in the GIVING option, regardless of which preposition is chosen. Thus

        DIVIDE FIELD-A INTO FIELD-B
            GIVING FIELD-C,

divides the value of FIELD-A into the value of FIELD-B and stores the quotient in FIELD-C. The statement

        DIVIDE FIELD-A BY FIELD-B
            GIVING FIELD-C,

divides the value of FIELD-A by the value of FIELD-B and stores the quotient in FIELD-C. In each case the quotient is stored in FIELD-C, and in neither case are the values of FIELD-A and FIELD-B changed.

The DIVIDE statement computes only the quotient of a division. IBM COBOL does not provide the REMAINDER option, which would allow the (rarely used) remainder to be computed as well.

## THE ROUNDED AND SIZE ERROR OPTIONS

In general, the values manipulated by the arithmetic statements will have implied decimal points. Implied decimal points are aligned whenever necessary. When values are added or subtracted, the implied decimal points of all the values being added or subtracted are aligned. When the result of a calculation is stored in a field, the implied decimal point of the value being stored is aligned with the decimal point position in the receiving field.

After decimal points have been aligned, the value being stored can have more digits to the right of the decimal point than the field can accommodate, it can have more digits to the left of the decimal point than the field can accomodate, or both these situations can occur for the same value. We can use the ROUNDED and ON SIZE ERROR options to specify what action is to be taken when one of these situations occurs.

## The ROUNDED Option

The most common situation is for there to be more digits to the right of the decimal point than the field can accomodate. For example, suppose that FIELD-E, FIELD-F, and FIELD-G each has a picture of 99V99, the three fields have the following values:

    FIELD-E:   0325      FIELD-F:   0675      FIELD-G:   0000

and we execute the statement

    MULTIPLY FIELD-E BY FIELD-F
        GIVING FIELD-G.

In conventional notation, multiplying 3.25 by 6.75 gives 21.9375. The value to be stored in FIELD-G, therefore, is 219375, with two digits to the left of the implied decimal point and four digits to the right. But since FIELD-G has a picture of 99V99, it can only accomodate two digits to the right of the implied decimal point. When the ROUNDED option is *not* specified, the value to be stored is truncated on the right, that is, the excess digits on the right are simply discarded. Thus the value stored in FIELD-G is 2193 or, in conventional notation, 21.93.

When the ROUNDED option is used, the value to be stored is rounded to the number of decimal places that the receiving field can accomodate. Suppose that FIELD-E, FIELD-F, and FIELD-G have the values previously given and the following statement is executed:

    MULTIPLY FIELD-E BY FIELD-F
        GIVING FIELD-G ROUNDED.

Again, the product of the values of FIELD-E and FIELD-F is 219375. Now, however, the value is rounded to 2194 before being stored. After the statement has been executed, then, the values of the three fields are

    FIELD-E:   0325      FIELD-F:   0675      FIELD-G: 2194

In general, we have the following three situations with respect to rounding and truncation. We will refer to these as *options* since, by the way we write our program, we can arrange for any one of them to occur.

1. The field that receives the result of a calculation can accomodate all the decimal places produced by the calculation. Neither truncation nor rounding will take place, and the result will be the same regardless of whether or not the ROUNDED option is used.
2. The field that receives the result of a calculation cannot accomodate all the decimal places produced by the calculation, and the ROUNDED option *is not* specified. The result is truncated—the digits that cannot be accomodated are discarded without changing any of the digits that can be stored in the field.
3. The field that receives the result of a calculation cannot accomodate all the decimal places produced by the calculation, and the ROUNDED option *is* specified. In this case, the result is rounded to the number of decimal places that the receiving field can accomodate.

Only occasionally do we have to reason to use option 2, truncation. For most purposes, truncation is not acceptable, and we are reduced to options 1 and 3—make the receiving field large enough to accomodate all the decimal places resulting from a calculation, or round off the result to the number of decimal places the field can accomodate.

To apply option 1, we need to determine the number of decimal places that will result from a particular calculation. For addition and subtraction, the number of decimal places in the result is equal to the largest number of decimal places in any of the values being added or subtracted. For example, suppose we add the values of four fields with pictures of 999V9, 999V99, 99V9999, and 99V999. The sum will have four decimal places, the largest number specified for any of the fields whose values are being added.

In financial calculations, it often happens that all the fields whose values are being added or subtracted have two decimal places. The sum or difference will then have two decimal places. If the field in which the sum or difference is stored also has two decimal places, no truncation or rounding take place, and we need not include the ROUNDED option in the ADD or SUBTRACT statement.

For multiplication, the number of decimal places in the product is the sum of the number of decimal places in the multiplicand and the number of decimal places in the multiplier. For example, if we multiply the values of fields with pictures of 99V99 and 9V999, the product will have five (2 + 3) decimal places and require a receiving field with a picture of 999V99999 to avoid truncation or rounding. (Note also that the number of digits to the left of the decimal point for the product is the sum of the number of digits to the left of the decimal point for the multiplicand and multiplier. Thus the receiving field requires three (2 + 1) digits to the left of the decimal point.)

Division is the worst offender as far as the proliferation of decimal places is concerned. For example, if we divide 20 by 3, the result is 6.666666 . . ., which contains an infinite number of decimal places. Since we cannot store an infinite number of digits in any computer, option 1 is impossible. With division we must either round or (when there is specific reason to do so) truncate.

## The SIZE ERROR Option

Rounding and truncation on the right are considered to be normal mathematical operations, to be applied routinely when called for by a particular calculation. On the other hand, when a data item is truncated on the left, the numerical value it represents is changed drastically. The result of the truncation is normally meaningless and not useful for any purpose. Truncation on the left is an error condition.

COBOL provides the SIZE ERROR option for the arithmetic statements to warn when the result of an operation is too large to store in the field provided. If the result of the operation contains more digits to the left of the decimal point than the receiving field can accomodate, the value of the receiving field is not changed, and the imperative statement following ON SIZE ERROR is executed. An attempt to perform the undefined operation of dividing by zero always causes a size error. If the SIZE ERROR option is not present and a size error occurs, meaningless data (garbage) will be stored in the receiving field.

Let's look at an example. Recall that FIELD-A, FIELD-B, and FIELD-C each has a picture of 999. Suppose the values of the three fields are

FIELD-A:   050        FIELD-B:   060        FIELD-C:   040

and the statement

```
MULTIPLY FIELD-A BY FIELD-B
    GIVING FIELD-C
    ON SIZE ERROR MOVE "Y" TO SIZE-ERROR-FLAG.
```

is executed. The product of the values of FIELD-A and FIELD-B is 3000, which cannot be accomodated in FIELD-C. Therefore, the value of FIELD-C is not changed, and "Y" is stored in SIZE-ERROR-FLAG. After the statement has been executed, the three fields retain their original values:

FIELD-A:   050        FIELD-B:   060        FIELD-C:   040

On the other hand, suppose that instead the following statement is executed:

```
MULTIPLY FIELD-A BY FIELD-B
    GIVING FIELD-C.
```

No warning of error is given; after the statement has been executed, the values of FIELD-A and FIELD-B are unchanged, and FIELD-C contains a meaningless three-digit value.

## NUMERIC AND NUMERIC-EDITED FIELDS

Any field that serves as a source of data for an arithmetic operation must be numeric. It may not be numeric-edited: the COBOL arithmetic statements cannot handle the blank spaces, dollar signs, commas, decimal points, and so on that can occur in numeric-edited data. On the other hand, the result of an arithmetic operation can be stored in a numeric-edited field. The result is edited before being stored in the field, just as if it had been moved to the field with a MOVE statement. The contents of the numeric-edited field, however, cannot be used as data for any further arithmetic operations.

For example, in the statement

```
ADD FIELD-A TO FIELD-B.
```

both FIELD-A and FIELD-B serve as sources of data for the addition. Both fields, therefore, must be numeric. In particular, even though the result is stored in FIELD-B, FIELD-B also serves as a source of data for the operation and so must be numeric rather than numeric-edited.

Now consider the statement

```
ADD FIELD-A FIELD-B
    GIVING FIELD-C.
```

Since FIELD-A and FIELD-B both serve as sources of data for the addition, both must be numeric. FIELD-C only receives the result, however, so it may be numeric-edited. If it is, the sum of the values of FIELD-A and FIELD-B are edited before being stored in FIELD-C.

For example, suppose that FIELD-A and FIELD-B have pictures of 9(4)V99, and FIELD-C has a picture of $$,$$9.99. If the three fields have the values

```
FIELD-A: 070080    FIELD-B: 050060    FIELD-C: bbb$79.95
```

and the statement

```
ADD FIELD-A FIELD-B
    GIVING FIELD-C.
```

is executed, the resulting values of the three fields are

```
FIELD-B: 070080    FIELD-B: 050060    FIELD-C: $1,201.40
```

## THE COMPUTE STATEMENT

The COMPUTE statement allows us to describe a calculation by means of a formula instead of a series of English-like statements. One COMPUTE statement can take the place of a long sequence of ADD, SUBTRACT, MULTIPLY, and DIVIDE statements. When a COMPUTE statement is used for a lengthy calculation, the computer automatically allocates memory space for all intermediate results. The programmer has only to define the fields that hold the data for the calculation and the final result. If the COMPUTE statement is replaced by a sequence of ADD, SUBTRACT, MULTIPLY, and DIVIDE statements, however, the programmer must define fields in the Working-Storage Section to hold all intermediate results.

### The Arithmetic Operators

To begin, let's see how the calculations expressed by the ADD, SUBTRACT, MULTIPLY, and DIVIDE statements can be expressed with COMPUTE statements. For example, the addition specified by

```
ADD FIELD-A FIELD-B
    GIVING FIELD-C.
```

can also be specified by the COMPUTE statement

```
COMPUTE FIELD-C = FIELD-A + FIELD-B.
```

The plus sign is used, as in arithmetic, to indicate that an addition is to be performed. The addition specified on the right-hand side of the equal sign is carried out, and the result is stored in the field specified on the left-hand side of the equal sign.

Note that = and + are both preceded by a space and followed by a space. Signs such as = and + are considered reserved words in COBOL and, like any other words in the language, must be separated from adjacent words by one or more spaces. Readers familiar with other programming languages should take particular note of this requirement, since COBOL differs from most other languages in this respect.

We can specify a series of additions with a COMPUTE statement. Corresponding to the ADD statement:

```
ADD FIELD-A FIELD-B FIELD-C FIELD-D
    GIVING FIELD-E.
```

we have the COMPUTE statement:

```
COMPUTE FIELD-E = FIELD-A + FIELD-B + FIELD-C + FIELD D.
```

In both statements, the values of FIELD-A, FIELD-B, FIELD-C, and FIELD-D are added, and the result is stored in FIELD-E.

We are always free to write a long COMPUTE statement on more than one line. Thus, the preceding statement might also be written as

```
COMPUTE FIELD-E =   FIELD-A + FIELD-B + FIELD-C
                + FIELD-D.
```

or

```
COMPUTE FIELD-E =   FIELD-A + FIELD-B
                + FIELD-C + FIELD-D.
```

Subtraction is similar to addition but with minus signs in place of plus signs. For example, corresponding to the SUBTRACT statement:

```
SUBTRACT FIELD-A FROM FIELD-B
    GIVING FIELD-C.
```

is the COMPUTE statement:

```
COMPUTE FIELD-C = FIELD-B - FIELD-A.
```

Likewise, corresponding to the SUBTRACT statement:

```
SUBTRACT FIELD-A FIELD-B FROM FIELD-C
    GIVING FIELD-D.
```

is the COMPUTE statement:

```
COMPUTE FIELD-D = FIELD-C - FIELD-A - FIELD-B.
```

The hyphen and the minus sign are represented by the same character. A minus sign, however, is always preceded and followed by at least one space, whereas a hyphen is never preceded or followed by a space.

The multiplication sign used in arithmetic, ×, is not available on most computer keyboards, displays, and printers. For this reason, COBOL—like most other programming languages—uses an asterisk, *, to indicate multiplication. For example, corresponding to the MULTIPLY statement:

```
MULTIPLY FIELD-A BY FIELD-B
    GIVING FIELD-C.
```

is the COMPUTE statement:

```
COMPUTE FIELD-C = FIELD-A * FIELD-B.
```

We can specify a series of multiplications with a single COMPUTE statement, something we cannot do with MULTIPLY statements. The calculation specified by

```
COMPUTE FIELD-E = FIELD-A * FIELD-B * FIELD-C * FIELD-D,
```

would require three MULTIPLY statements:

```
MULTIPLY FIELD-A BY FIELD B
    GIVING FIELD-E,
MULTIPLY FIELD-C BY FIELD-E,
MULTIPLY FIELD-D BY FIELD-E,
```

The division sign used in arithmetic, ÷, is also not available on most input and output devices, so COBOL follows most other programming languages in using the / for division. Thus, corresponding to the DIVIDE statement:

```
DIVIDE FIELD-A INTO FIELD-B
    GIVING FIELD-C,
```

or

```
DIVIDE FIELD-B BY FIELD-A
    GIVING FIELD-C,
```

we have the COMPUTE statement:

```
COMPUTE FIELD-C = FIELD-B / FIELD-A,
```

We can also specify a series of divisions with a COMPUTE statement such as

```
COMPUTE FIELD-E = FIELD-D / FIELD-C / FIELD-B / FIELD-A,
```

which is equivalent to

```
DIVIDE FIELD-C INTO FIELD-D
    GIVING FIELD-E,
DIVIDE FIELD-B INTO FIELD-E,
DIVIDE FIELD-A INTO FIELD-E,
```

The COMPUTE statement provides one other operation, *exponentiation*, which is represented by the sign ** and used to specify repeated multiplication. For example, 2 ** 3 specifies that three 2s are to be multiplied together and is equivalent to 2 * 2 * 2. The arithmetic expression 5 ** 4 specifies that four 5s are to be multiplied together; it is equivalent to 5 * 5 * 5 * 5. The COMPUTE statement

```
COMPUTE FIELD-B = FIELD-A ** 3,
```

is equivalent to

```
COMPUTE FIELD-B = FIELD-A * FIELD-A * FIELD-A,
```

In

```
COMPUTE FIELD-C = FIELD-A ** FIELD-B,
```

the value of FIELD-B determines how many copies of the value of FIELD-A are to be multiplied together. Exponentiation is not common in business arithmetic, but it does occur in some financial calculations, such as computing compound interest.

We can specify multiple receiving fields for a COMPUTE statement:

```
COMPUTE FIELD-C FIELD-D = FIELD-A * FIELD-B.
```

The product of the values of FIELD-A and FIELD-B is stored in both FIELD-C and FIELD-D. We can also specify both the ROUNDED and SIZE ERROR options for COMPUTE statements:

```
COMPUTE FIELD-C ROUNDED = FIELD-B / FIELD-A
        ON SIZE ERROR MOVE "Y" TO SIZE-ERROR-FLAG.
```

The value of FIELD-B is divided by the value of FIELD-A. The quotient is rounded to the number of decimal places specified in the picture for FIELD-C. If the quotient is too large to fit into FIELD-C (or if the value of FIELD-A was zero), the value of FIELD-C is not changed and "Y" is stored in SIZE-ERROR-FLAG.

### Operator Priorities

When different arithmetic operators, such as + and *, appear in the same COMPUTE statement, the question arises as to the order in which the corresponding operations should be carried out. For example, in

```
COMPUTE FIELD-A = 2 + 3 * 4.
```

should the addition or the multiplication be carried out first? It's easy to see that we will get different results depending on which choice we make. If we do the addition first, we add 2 and 3 to get 5, then multiply by 4 to get 20. If we do the multiplication first, we multiply 3 by 4 to get 12, then add 2 to get 14. Since we are in trouble if we can't tell whether a calculation yields 20 or 14, we must formulate rules governing the order in which arithmetic operations will be carried out.

COBOL follows the traditional order of evaluation used in mathematics:

- Exponentations first
- Multiplications and divisions next
- Additions and subtractions last

Operations that fall in the same category (such as multiplications and divisions) are carried out from left to right as the operators appear in the expression.

We can think of the arithmetic operators as being assigned *priorities* as follows:

| | |
|---|---|
| ** | High priority |
| * and / | Intermediate priority |
| + and - | Low priority |

When an expression is evaluated, the high-priority operators are applied first, then the intermediate-priority operators, and finally the low-priority operators. Operators with the same priority are applied in left-to-right order as they occur in the expression.

Let's look at some examples, beginning with the one we started with:

```
COMPUTE FIELD-A = 2 + 3 * 4.
```

Since * has a higher priority than +, the multiplication must be done before the addition. We multiply 3 by 4 getting 12, then add 2 to get 14, which is the value the computer stores in FIELD-A. The same principle applies to the following example:

```
COMPUTE FIELD-A = 5 * 3 + 7 * 4.
```

Again, since * has a higher priority than +, the multiplications are carried out first, after which the products are added. Multiplying 5 by 3 gives 15, and multiplying 7 by 4 gives 28. Adding 15 and 28 gives 43, the value stored in FIELD-A.

Operators with the same priority are applied in left-to-right order. Thus, in

```
COMPUTE FIELD-A = 9 + 4 - 2.
```

the addition is done before the subtraction. Adding 4 to 9 gives 13 and subtracting 2 leaves 11, the value stored in FIELD-A.

The same idea applies to the following:

```
COMPUTE FIELD-A = 6 * 5 - 3 * 2 + 9 / 3.
```

Multiplications and divisions are done first, giving us the expression 30 - 6 + 3. Since - and + have the same priority, they are applied in left-to-right order. Thus, 6 is first subtracted from 30 to get 24; adding 3 gives 27, the value stored in FIELD-A.

## Parentheses

Any part of an arithmetic expression that is enclosed in parentheses is evaluated before any part of the expression that is not enclosed in parentheses. When sets of parentheses are nested one inside the other, the part of the expression in the innermost set of parentheses is evaluated first, followed by the part in the next outermost set, and so on.

Parentheses are used for two purposes: (1) to override the operator priorities, causing the operators in an expression to be applied in some order other than the one dictated by the operator priorities, and (2) to make the order in which the operators will be applied clear to someone reading the expression, even if the reader does not work with arithmetic expressions regularly and so may be uncertain of the operator priorities.

As an example of using parentheses to override operator priorities, suppose we want to add 2 and 3, then multiply the sum by 4. Neither 2 + 3 * 4 nor 4 * 2 + 3 will do the job, since for each of these expressions the operator priorities dictate that the multiplication will be done before the division. But in

```
COMPUTE FIELD-A = (2 + 3) * 4
```

the part of the expression enclosed in parentheses is evaluated first. Thus, the addition is done before the multiplication as desired, and the value 20 is stored in FIELD-A.

As an example of using parentheses to clarify an expression, let's return to the statement

```
COMPUTE FIELD-A = 6 * 5 - 3 * 2 + 9 / 3.
```

To make it clear that the multiplications and divisions are to be done before the additions and subtractions, we can enclose each multiplication and division in parentheses:

```
COMPUTE FIELD-A = (6 * 5) - (3 * 2) + (9 / 3).
```

To make it clear that the subtraction is to be done before the addition, we can enclose the subtraction in parentheses:

```
COMPUTE FIELD-A = ((6 * 5) - (3 * 2)) + (9 / 3).
```

Parentheses allow us to see at a glance the order in which the operators in a expression should be applied. With operator priorities, the correct order of evaluation is not as obvious. Some practice is required before one can look at an unparenthesized expression and see immediately the order in which the arithmetic operations are to be carried out.

## CONDITIONS

A *condition* is a declarative statement whose truth or falsity can be checked by the computer. We have already encountered conditions in IF statements and in the UNTIL option of the PERFORM statement. When a statement containing a condition is executed, the computer tests the data values referred to by the condition to determine whether the condition is true or false. The outcome of the test determines the action taken by the statement containing the condition.

### Relation Conditions

The conditions we have encountered already, such as

```
EOF-FLAG = "Y"
```

are *relation conditions*. The relation in question is that of equality, represented by the equal sign. If the relation holds—that is, if the value of EOF-FLAG is equal to "Y"—the condition is true. If the relation does not hold—if the value of EOF-FLAG is not equal to "Y"—the condition is false.

The following six relations can be used to form relation conditions:

```
IS EQUAL TO
IS NOT EQUAL TO
IS LESS THAN
IS NOT LESS THAN
IS GREATER THAN
IS NOT GREATER THAN
```

Numeric data items are compared according to their numerical values, and non-numeric items are compared according to alphabetical order. Alphabetical order is defined by the order in which the characters are listed in appendix G of the COBOL reference manual and Appendix C of this book. If 048 is the value of a field with picture 99V9 and 035 is the value of a field with picture 999, then 048 is less than 035 because 4.8 is less than 35. "JOHN" is greater than "JACK" because JOHN follows JACK in alphabetical order. If nonnumeric fields having different lengths are compared, the shorter field is extended with blanks. Thus "BILL" is less than "BILLY" since "BILL" is extended on the right with one blank, and the space character precedes "Y".

The words IS, THAN, and TO are optional, so the relations can be expressed more tersely as

```
EQUAL
NOT EQUAL
LESS
NOT LESS
GREATER
NOT GREATER
```

We can express the relations even more tersely by using symbols instead of words:

| Words | Symbols | |
|---|---|---|
| EQUAL TO | = | |
| NOT EQUAL TO | NOT = | |
| LESS THAN | < | |
| NOT LESS THAN | NOT < | (greater than or equal to) |
| GREATER THAN | > | |
| NOT GREATER THAN | NOT > | (less than or equal to) |

For example, suppose FIELD-A and FIELD-B have pictures of 999 and consider the IF statement:

```
IF FIELD-A GREATER THAN FIELD-B
    DISPLAY "YES"
ELSE
    DISPLAY "NO".
```

When the IF statement is executed, the computer compares the current values of FIELD-A and FIELD-B. If the value of FIELD-A is greater than the value of FIELD-B—the condition is true—the statement between IF and ELSE will be executed. Otherwise, the statement following ELSE will be executed. Thus if the values of the two fields are

```
FIELD-A:  152    FIELD-B:  098
```

the program will display `"YES"`. On the other hand, if the values of the two fields are

    FIELD-A:  152     FIELD-B:  160

the program will display `"NO"`.

Here's an example using the `PERFORM` statement. Suppose that `COUNT` has a picture of `99`, and a program with the following Procedure Division is executed:

```
COUNTDOWN.
    MOVE 10 TO COUNT.
    PERFORM DISPLAY-AND-DECREMENT
        UNTIL COUNT < 6.
    STOP RUN.


DISPLAY-AND-DECREMENT.
    DISPLAY COUNT.
    SUBTRACT 1 FROM COUNT.
```

The `MOVE` statement gives `COUNT` the initial value `10`. The `PERFORM` statement executes the paragraph `DISPLAY-AND-DECREMENT` repeatedly until the condition `COUNT < 6` is true. (The condition is tested prior to each execution of `DIS-PLAY-AND-DECREMENT`.) Each time `DISPLAY-AND-DECREMENT` is executed, the current value of `COUNT` is displayed, after which the value of `COUNT` is decreased by 1. `DISPLAY-AND-DECREMENT` is executed with the value of `COUNT` equal to `10`, `09`, `08`, `07`, and `06`. When the value of `COUNT` is found to be `05`, however, the condition is true, and no further executions of `DISPLAY-AND-DECREMENT` take place. The program produces the following display:

```
10
09
08
07
06
```

## Class and Sign Conditions

We can test whether or not the contents of a field is numeric or alphabetic with conditions of the following form:

        *data-name* IS NUMERIC        *data name* IS NOT NUMERIC
        *data-name* IS ALPHABETIC     *data-name* IS NOT ALPHABETIC

Note that it is the *contents* of a field—not its picture—that are tested.

The `NUMERIC` test is important when data files are created with text editors. As a result of user error, nonnumeric values—values containing spaces, letters, or punctuation marks, for example—may be entered in numeric fields. If arithmetic with these nonnumeric values is attempted, the program will be terminated with an error message. The `NUMERIC` test allows the program to check that a data value is numeric before attempting to use it in arithmetical calculations. This kind of *data validation* is discussed further in Chapter 10. Note that if the data file was created by a COBOL program, the NUMERIC test may be unnecessary, since the IBM COBOL ACCEPT statement will not allow nonnumeric data to be stored in a numeric field.

The ALPHABETIC test, like the alphabetic data (letters and spaces only) it tests for, is rarely used.

The following conditions allow us to test the sign of a numeric value as well as whether the value is zero:

```
data-name IS NEGATIVE      data-name IS NOT NEGATIVE
data-name IS ZERO          data-name IS NOT ZERO
data-name IS POSITIVE      data-name IS NOT POSITIVE
```

## Condition Names

COBOL allows us to define conditions and assign names to them in the Data Division. Conditions so defined can be referred to by name in the Procedure Division. Condition names are defined in special level 88 entries in the Data Division.

For example, consider the following entry in the Working-Storage Section:

```
01   EOF-FLAG              PIC X.
```

By following this entry with level 88 entries, we can associate condition names with particular values of EOF-FLAG:

```
01   EOF-FLAG              PIC X.
     88   NO-MORE-INPUT    VALUE "Y".
     88   NOT-THROUGH-YET  VALUE "N".
```

NO-MORE-INPUT and NOT-THROUGH-YET are condition names. The condition NO-MORE-INPUT is true when the value of EOF-FLAG is "Y" and false otherwise. In other words, the conditions NO-MORE-INPUT and EOF-FLAG = "Y" are equivalent. Likewise, the condition NOT-THROUGH-YET is true when the value of EOF-FLAG is "N" and false otherwise; the conditions NOT-THROUGH-YET and EOF-FLAG = "N" are equivalent.

Condition names can be used in statements just like any other form of condition. For example,

```
PERFORM PROCESS-A-RECORD
     UNTIL NO-MORE-INPUT.
```

executes the paragraph PROCESS-A-RECORD until the value of EOF-FLAG is "Y". Likewise, the statement

```
IF NOT-THROUGH-YET
     PERFORM COMPUTE-AND-PRINT-RESULT.
```

performs the paragraph COMPUTE-AND-PRINT-RESULT only if the value of EOF-FLAG is "N".

We can specify a series of values, each of which will cause a condition to be true:

```
01   ONE-DIGIT-NUMBER      PIC 9.
     88   ODD-NUMBER       VALUES 1 3 5 9.
     88   EVEN-NUMBER      VALUES 0 2 4 6 8.
```

The condition ODD-NUMBER is true only if the value of ONE-DIGIT-NUMBER is 1, 3, 5, or 9. The condition EVEN-NUMBER is true only if the value of ONE-DIGIT-NUMBER is 0, 2, 4, 6, or 8. Note that a VALUE clause can be introduced by either VALUE or VALUES; for clarity, we usually use the plural form when specifying more than one value.

We can also specify a range of values for which a condition will be true:

```
01   QUANTITY-ORDERED      PIC 999.
     88   SMALL-QUANTITY    VALUES 1 THRU 99.
     88   MEDIUM-QUANTITY   VALUES 100 THRU 499.
     88   LARGE-QUANTITY    VALUES 500 THRU 999.
```

The condition SMALL-QUANTITY is true only if the value of QUANTITY-ORDERED is in the range 1 through 99; MEDIUM-QUANTITY is true only if the value of QUANTITY-ORDERED is in the range 100 through 499; and so on. IBM COBOL does not allow both a range and a series of values to be specified in the same VALUE clause. We can specify either a series of values or a range of values, but not both.

Note that the use of the VALUE clause to define condition names has nothing to do with its use to initialize fields. In particular, we can use VALUE clauses to define condition names in both the File Section and the Working-Storage Section, whereas we can use VALUE clauses to initialize fields only in the Working-Storage Section.

## Compound Conditions

The conditions we have looked at so far are known as *simple conditions*. We can form *compound conditions* by combining simple conditions with the words AND, OR, and NOT. Although extremely complicated compound conditions are possible, COBOL programmers usually restrict themselves to a few simple forms that can be readily understood both by the programmer and by persons reading the program.

When simple conditions are joined by AND, the resulting compound is true only if all of the simple conditions are true. For example,

```
FIELD-A = 5 AND FIELD-B IS NUMERIC AND FIELD-C IS ZERO
```

is true only if the three simple conditions FIELD-A = 5, FIELD-B IS NUMERIC, and FIELD-C IS ZERO are all true. If any of the three conditions are false, the compound condition is false.

When simple conditions are joined by OR, the resulting compound condition is true if any of the simple conditions are true. For example,

```
FIELD-A = 5 OR FIELD-B IS NUMERIC OR FIELD-C IS ZERO
```

is true if one or more of the three simple conditions is true. The only way the compound condition can be false is if all three of the simple conditions is false.

The word NOT preceding a condition changes the condition to its negative. We never need to precede a relation, class, or sign condition with NOT, since both positive and negative forms are available for each condition. That is, instead of writing

        NOT (FIELD-A = 5)

we can use the relation NOT =:

        FIELD-A NOT = 5

We can precede a condition name with NOT. Thus the condition

        NOT LARGE-QUANTITY

is true only if the condition LARGE-QUANTITY is false. We can also precede a compound condition with NOT. The compound condition must be enclosed in parentheses:

        NOT (FIELD-A = 10 AND FIELD-B < 5 AND FIELD-C > 20)

This condition is true only if the condition in parentheses is false. The condition in parentheses is false if any of the simple conditions making it up are false. Thus, the negated compound condition is equivalent to

        FIELD-A NOT = 10 OR FIELD-B NOT < 5 OR FIELD-C NOT > 20

Likewise,

        NOT (FIELD-A = 10 OR FIELD-B < 5 OR FIELD-C > 20)

is true only if the condition in parentheses is false. The condition in parentheses is false only if all the simple conditions making it up are false. Thus, the negated compound condition is equivalent to

        FIELD-A NOT = 10 AND FIELD-B NOT < 5 AND FIELD-C NOT > 20

A compound condition made up of relation conditions can often be abbreviated. The part of a relation condition that precedes the relation is called the *subject*. Thus, in

        FIELD-A = 25

FIELD-A is the subject and = is the relation. When several relation conditions have the same subject, the subject only has to be written once. Thus

        FIELD-A = 10 OR FIELD-A < 0 OR FIELD-A > 25

can be abbreviated to

        FIELD-A = 10 OR < 0 OR > 25

When several relation conditions have the same subject and the same relation, both the subject and the relation only have to be written once. Thus

        FIELD-A = 5 OR FIELD-A = 10 OR FIELD-A = 15

can be abbreviated to

        FIELD-A = 5 OR 10 OR 15

Note that only relation conditions can be abbreviated; class and sign conditions *cannot* be abbreviated.

## PAYROLL-REPORT

Figure 4.1 shows the program PAYROLL-REPORT, which reads a file containing payroll information and produces the report shown in Figure 4.2. As usual, the pages of the report have been made small so that a multiple-page report could be demonstrated with a small test file. Each record of the input file contains an employee number, the number of hours the employee worked, and the amount that the employee is paid for each hour's work. Hours worked in excess of 40 are overtime, and employees are paid "time and a half" for overtime—each overtime hour is counted as an hour and a half. The program computes and prints each employee's regular wages (wages earned during first 40 hours), overtime wages (wages for hours in excess of 40), and gross wages (sum of regular wages and overtime wages).

### The Files

The program reads payroll records from the disk file PAYROLL-FILE and writes the payroll report to the print file PAYROLL-REPORT-FILE. The records in PAYROLL-FILE have the following form:

| Field | Size | Type of Data |
|---|---|---|
| Employee number | 6 | Alphanumeric |
| Hours worked | 3 | Numeric—one decimal place |
| Hourly rate | 4 | Numeric—two decimal places |

With this information, we can write the record description for PAYROLL-RECORD:

```
01   PAYROLL-RECORD.
     02   PR-EMPLOYEE-NUMBER        PIC X(6).
     02   PR-HOURS-WORKED           PIC 99V9.
          88   NO-OVERTIME          VALUES 0 THRU 40.
     02   PR-HOURLY-RATE            PIC 99V99.
```

To do the wage calculations properly, the program must distinguish between employees who worked overtime and those who did not. We define the condition NO-OVERTIME to be true if the value of PR-HOURS-WORKED is in the range 0 through 40. NO-OVERTIME is thus true for workers who have not worked overtime and false for those who have.

The output file is PAYROLL-REPORT-FILE. The associated record, PAYROLL-REPORT-RECORD, is an 80-character alphanumeric item corresponding to one printed line. As usual, the lines to be printed will be moved to PAYROLL-REPORT-RECORD from records in the Working-Storage Section.

```
IDENTIFICATION DIVISION.
PROGRAM-ID. PAYROLL-REPORT.

ENVIRONMENT DIVISION.
INPUT-OUTPUT SECTION.
FILE-CONTROL.
     SELECT PAYROLL-FILE ASSIGN TO DISK
          ORGANIZATION IS LINE SEQUENTIAL.
     SELECT PAYROLL-REPORT-FILE ASSIGN TO PRINTER.

DATA DIVISION.
FILE SECTION.
FD  PAYROLL-FILE
    LABEL RECORDS STANDARD
    VALUE OF FILE-ID IS DOS-FILE-NAME.
01  PAYROLL-RECORD.
    02   PR-EMPLOYEE-NUMBER        PIC X(6).
    02   PR-HOURS-WORKED           PIC 99V9.
        88   NO-OVERTIME           VALUES O THRU 40.
    02   PR-HOURLY-RATE            PIC 99V99.

FD  PAYROLL-REPORT-FILE
    LABEL RECORDS OMITTED.
01  PAYROLL-REPORT-RECORD          PIC X(80).

WORKING-STORAGE SECTION.
01  TITLE-LINE-1.
    02   FILLER                    PIC X(14) VALUE "Payroll Report".
    02   FILLER                    PIC X(59) VALUE SPACES.
    02   FILLER                    PIC X(5) VALUE "Page ".
    02   TL-PAGE-NUMBER            PIC Z9.

01  TITLE-LINE-2.
    02   FILLER                    PIC X(13) VALUE "Ajax Products".
    02   FILLER                    PIC X(59) VALUE SPACES.
    02   TL-MONTH                  PIC 99.
    02   FILLER                    PIC X VALUE "/".
    02   TL-DAY                    PIC 99.
    02   FILLER                    PIC X VALUE "/".
    02   TL-YEAR                   PIC 99.

01  HEADING-LINE-1.
    02   FILLER                    PIC X(8) VALUE "Employee".
    02   FILLER                    PIC X(6) VALUE SPACES.
    02   FILLER                    PIC X(5) VALUE "Hours".
    02   FILLER                    PIC X(8) VALUE SPACES.
    02   FILLER                    PIC X(6) VALUE "Hourly".
    02   FILLER                    PIC X(7) VALUE SPACES.
    02   FILLER                    PIC X(7) VALUE "Regular".
    02   FILLER                    PIC X(8) VALUE SPACES.
    02   FILLER                    PIC X(8) VALUE "Overtime".
    02   FILLER                    PIC X(10) VALUE SPACES.
    02   FILLER                    PIC X(5) VALUE "Gross".
```

*Figure 4.1* This program produces a multipage payroll report such as the one in Figure 4.2. A footing line showing the number of employees processed and the total gross wages is printed at the bottom of the last page of the report.

The FD entry for PAYROLL-REPORT-FILE does not contain a LINAGE clause, even though a multiple-page report is to be printed. Instead, the program keeps track of the number of lines printed on each page and uses a WRITE statement with

```
01   HEADING-LINE-2.                      PIC X VALUE SPACE.
     02   FILLER                          PIC X(6) VALUE "Number".
     02   FILLER                          PIC X(7) VALUE SPACES.
     02   FILLER                          PIC X(6) VALUE "Worked".
     02   FILLER                          PIC X(8) VALUE SPACES.
     02   FILLER                          PIC X(4) VALUE "Rate".
     02   FILLER                          PIC X(9) VALUE SPACES.
     02   FILLER                          PIC X(5) VALUE "Wages".
     02   FILLER                          PIC X(11) VALUE SPACES.
     02   FILLER                          PIC X(5) VALUE "Wages".
     02   FILLER                          PIC X(11) VALUE SPACES.
     02   FILLER                          PIC X(5) VALUE "Wages".

01   DETAIL-LINE.
     02   FILLER                          PIC X VALUE SPACE.
     02   DL-EMPLOYEE-NUMBER              PIC X(6).
     02   FILLER                          PIC X(8) VALUE SPACES.
     02   DL-HOURS-WORKED                 PIC Z9.9.
     02   FILLER                          PIC X(8) VALUE SPACES.
     02   DL-HOURLY-RATE                  PIC $$9.99.
     02   FILLER                          PIC X(6) VALUE SPACES.
     02   DL-REGULAR-WAGES                PIC $$,$$9.99.
     02   FILLER                          PIC X(7) VALUE SPACES.
     02   DL-OVERTIME-WAGES               PIC $$,$$9.99.
     02   FILLER                          PIC X(7) VALUE SPACES.
     02   DL-GROSS-WAGES                  PIC $$,$$9.99.

01   FOOTING-LINE.
     02   FILLER                          PIC X(10) VALUE "Employees ".
     02   FL-EMPLOYEE-COUNT               PIC ZZ9.
     02   FILLER                          PIC X(38) VALUE SPACES.
     02   FILLER                          PIC X(18)
                                          VALUE "Total Gross Wages ".
     02   FL-TOTAL-GROSS-WAGES            PIC $$$$,$$9.99.

01   CONSTANTS.
     02   MAXIMUM-REGULAR-HOURS           PIC 99 VALUE 40.
     02   OVERTIME-MULTIPLIER             PIC 9V9 VALUE 1.5.
     02   LINES-PER-PAGE                  PIC 99 VALUE 11.

01   INPUT-FILE-CONTROL.
     02   EOF-FLAG                        PIC X.
          88   NO-MORE-INPUT              VALUE "Y".
     02   DOS-FILE-NAME                   PIC X(15).

01   PRINTER-CONTROL.
     02   LINE-SPACING                    PIC 9.
     02   LINES-PRINTED                   PIC 99.

01   SYSTEM-DATE.
     02   SD-YEAR                         PIC 99.
     02   SD-MONTH                        PIC 99.
     02   SD-DAY                          PIC 99.

01   WORK-FIELDS.
     02   REGULAR-HOURS                   PIC 99V9.
     02   OVERTIME-HOURS                  PIC 999V99.
     02   REGULAR-WAGES                   PIC 9(4)V99.
     02   OVERTIME-WAGES                  PIC 9(4)V99.
     02   GROSS-WAGES                     PIC 9(4)V99.
```

*Figure 4.1 (continued)*

**100**

```
01   COUNTERS-AND-ACCUMULATOR.
     02   EMPLOYEE-COUNT          PIC 999.
     02   PAGE-NUMBER             PIC 99.
     02   TOTAL-GROSS-WAGES       PIC 9(6)V99.


PROCEDURE DIVISION.
PRINT-PAYROLL-REPORT.
    PERFORM GET-DOS-FILE-NAME.
    OPEN INPUT PAYROLL-FILE
         OUTPUT PAYROLL-REPORT-FILE.
    PERFORM ASSIGN-INITIAL-VALUES.
    READ PAYROLL-FILE
         AT END MOVE "Y" TO EOF-FLAG.
    PERFORM PROCESS-PAYROLL-RECORD
         UNTIL NO-MORE-INPUT.
    PERFORM PRINT-FOOTING-LINE.
    CLOSE PAYROLL-FILE
          PAYROLL-REPORT-FILE.
    STOP RUN.

GET-DOS-FILE-NAME.
    DISPLAY (1, 1) ERASE.
    DISPLAY (5, 1) "Name of payroll file? ".
    ACCEPT (LIN, COL) DOS-FILE-NAME WITH PROMPT.

ASSIGN-INITIAL-VALUES.
    MOVE "N" TO EOF-FLAG.
    MOVE ZERO TO EMPLOYEE-COUNT
                 TOTAL-GROSS-WAGES.
    MOVE 1 TO PAGE-NUMBER.
    MOVE LINES-PER-PAGE TO LINES-PRINTED.

PROCESS-PAYROLL-RECORD.
    PERFORM CALCULATE-WAGES.
    PERFORM UPDATE-COUNT-AND-TOTAL.
    PERFORM PRINT-DETAIL-LINE.
    READ PAYROLL-FILE
         AT END MOVE "Y" TO EOF-FLAG.

PRINT-FOOTING-LINE.
    MOVE EMPLOYEE-COUNT TO FL-EMPLOYEE-COUNT.
    MOVE TOTAL-GROSS-WAGES TO FL-TOTAL-GROSS-WAGES.
    WRITE PAYROLL-REPORT-RECORD
          FROM FOOTING-LINE
          AFTER ADVANCING 2 LINES.

CALCULATE-WAGES.
    IF NO-OVERTIME
        MOVE PR-HOURS-WORKED TO REGULAR-HOURS
        MOVE ZERO TO OVERTIME-HOURS
    ELSE
        MOVE MAXIMUM-REGULAR-HOURS TO REGULAR-HOURS
        SUBTRACT MAXIMUM-REGULAR-HOURS FROM PR-HOURS-WORKED
            GIVING OVERTIME-HOURS
        MULTIPLY OVERTIME-MULTIPLIER BY OVERTIME-HOURS.
    MULTIPLY REGULAR-HOURS BY PR-HOURLY-RATE
        GIVING REGULAR-WAGES ROUNDED.
    MULTIPLY OVERTIME-HOURS BY PR-HOURLY-RATE
        GIVING OVERTIME-WAGES ROUNDED.
    ADD REGULAR-WAGES OVERTIME-WAGES
        GIVING GROSS-WAGES.
```

*Figure 4.1 (continued)*

```
UPDATE-COUNT-AND-TOTAL.
    ADD 1 TO EMPLOYEE-COUNT.
    ADD GROSS-WAGES TO TOTAL-GROSS-WAGES.

PRINT-DETAIL-LINE.
    MOVE PR-EMPLOYEE-NUMBER TO DL-EMPLOYEE-NUMBER.
    MOVE PR-HOURS-WORKED TO DL-HOURS-WORKED.
    MOVE PR-HOURLY-RATE TO DL-HOURLY-RATE.
    MOVE REGULAR-WAGES TO DL-REGULAR-WAGES.
    MOVE OVERTIME-WAGES TO DL-OVERTIME-WAGES.
    MOVE GROSS-WAGES TO DL-GROSS-WAGES.
    IF LINES-PRINTED = LINES-PER-PAGE
        PERFORM PRINT-HEADINGS
    ELSE
        MOVE 1 TO LINE-SPACING.
    WRITE PAYROLL-REPORT-RECORD
        FROM DETAIL-LINE
        AFTER ADVANCING LINE-SPACING LINES.
    ADD LINE-SPACING TO LINES-PRINTED.

PRINT-HEADINGS.
    MOVE PAGE-NUMBER TO TL-PAGE-NUMBER.
    ADD 1 TO PAGE-NUMBER.
    WRITE PAYROLL-REPORT-RECORD
        FROM TITLE-LINE-1
        AFTER ADVANCING PAGE.
    ACCEPT SYSTEM-DATE FROM DATE.
    MOVE SD-YEAR TO TL-YEAR.
    MOVE SD-MONTH TO TL-MONTH.
    MOVE SD-DAY TO TL-DAY.
    WRITE PAYROLL-REPORT-RECORD
        FROM TITLE-LINE-2
        AFTER ADVANCING 1 LINE.
    WRITE PAYROLL-REPORT-RECORD
        FROM HEADING-LINE-1
        AFTER ADVANCING 3 LINES.
    WRITE PAYROLL-REPORT-RECORD
        FROM HEADING-LINE-2
        AFTER ADVANCING 1 LINE.
    MOVE 6 TO LINES-PRINTED.
    MOVE 2 TO LINE-SPACING.
```

*Figure 4.1 (continued)*

ADVANCING PAGE to go to a new page when necessary. An advantage of this approach is that an initial WRITE with ADVANCING PAGE will position the printer at the top of the next physical page, assuring that the report starts at the top of a new page even if the printer was left in the middle of a page by the previous program that ran on the computer. (When the LINAGE clause is present, ADVANCING PAGE skips one logical page but does not position the printer at the top of a physical page. If the program were started with the printer positioned in the middle of a page, ADVANCING PAGE would just move the printer to the middle of the next page.)

```
Payroll Report                                                    Page  1
Ajax Products                                                     02/25/83


Employee      Hours       Hourly       Regular      Overtime      Gross
 Number       Worked       Rate         Wages        Wages        Wages

 235749        35.7       $17.59        $627.96        $0.00      $627.96
 365487        48.4       $24.45        $978.00      $308.07    $1,286.07
 498773        50.2        $9.63        $385.20      $147.34      $532.54
 644569        31.6       $14.75        $466.10        $0.00      $466.10


Payroll Report                                                    Page  2
Ajax Products                                                     02/25/83


Employee      Hours       Hourly       Regular      Overtime      Gross
 Number       Worked       Rate         Wages        Wages        Wages

 772549        49.3       $30.84      $1,233.60      $430.22    $1,663.82
 891546        20.5       $10.62        $217.71        $0.00      $217.71
 944576        40.0       $18.65        $746.00        $0.00      $746.00
 963254        45.7       $26.25      $1,050.00      $224.44    $1,274.44

Employees    8                         Total Gross Wages     $6,814.64
```

*Figure 4.2*    A two-page payroll report printed by the program in Figure 4.1. Note the footing line at the bottom of the second page.

## Title and Footing Lines

This program illustrates another style for titles. The title is not centered, but rather parts of it are positioned at the left and right margins. There are two title lines; the first gives the report title and the page number, and the second gives the company name and the date of the report.

### The date

The date maintained by the system—the one you enter after turning on your computer—can be obtained with an ACCEPT statement of the form:

ACCEPT *data-name* FROM DATE.

The date assigned to *data-name* has the form YYMMDD—a two-digit year followed by a two-digit month followed by a two-digit day. For example, February 25, 1983 would be represented by 830225. The advantage of this form is that we can determine which of two dates is earlier by comparing the corresponding numbers—the number representing the earlier date will always be less than the one representing the later date.

For printing, however, we need to convert the date to the usual MM/DD/YY or MM-DD-YY form. The program accepts the date

ACCEPT SYSTEM-DATE FROM DATE.

and stores it in the record

```
01   SYSTEM-DATE.
     02   SD-YEAR              PIC 99.
     02   SD-MONTH             PIC 99.
     02   SD-DAY               PIC 99.
```

which is defined in the Working-Storage Section. Storing the date in this record breaks it down into a two-digit year, a two-digit month, and a two-digit day. The fields of SYSTEM-DATE are then moved to the corresponding fields of TITLE-LINE-2:

```
MOVE SD-YEAR TO TL-YEAR.
MOVE SD-MONTH TO TL-MONTH.
MOVE SD-DAY TO TL-DAY.
```

The fields of TITLE-LINE-2 are in the desired order and are separated by FILLER items containing the desired slashes.

### The footing line

The payroll report ends with a footing line giving the number of employees processed and the total gross wages earned. The corresponding record FOOTING-LINE contains the fields FL-EMPLOYEE-COUNT and FL-TOTAL-GROSS-WAGES. Since these fields have numeric-edited pictures (and so their contents cannot be used for arithmetic), the actual counting and totaling takes place in the numeric fields EMPLOYEE-COUNT and TOTAL-GROSS-WAGES. The contents of these fields are moved to the contents of the corresponding fields of FOOTING-LINE before the footing line is printed.

### Other Working-Storage Items

Two problems arise when literals such as 40, 1.5, and 11 appear in the Procedure Division. First, the significance of the literals may not be obvious to someone reading the program. Second, if a program modification requires that a particular value be changed, we must find every place in the Procedure Division where the corresponding literal appears. We can alleviate these problems by assigning the needed values to data names and using the data names in the Procedure Division:

```
01   CONSTANTS.
     02   MAXIMUM-REGULAR-HOURS        PIC 99 VALUE 40.
     02   OVERTIME-MULTIPLIER          PIC 9V9 VALUE 1.5.
     02   LINES-PER-PAGE               PIC 99 VALUE 11.
```

The data names indicate the significance of each value. And if a value needs to be changed, we can change the VALUE clause and do not have to locate every occurrence of the value in the Procedure Division.

Some programmers define all constant values in the Working-Storage Section, so that literals never appear in the Procedure Division. The programs in this book don't go quite that far—literals whose significance is obvious from the context in which they appear and that are unlikely to be changed are used in the Procedure Division.

LINES-PER-PAGE, the number of printed lines on each page, is set to 11 so our small test file will give two pages of printout. Values in the range 56 to 60 would be typical for standard-size pages. Note that LINES-PER-PAGE does *not* include the two lines for the footing; so we must leave enough room at the bottom of each page to print the footing, even though the footing will only be printed on the final page of the report.

As usual, `EOF-FLAG` and `DOS-FILE-NAME` are used in connection with the input file:

```
01    INPUT-FILE-CONTROL.
      02    EOF-FLAG                PIC X.
            88    NO-MORE-INPUT     VALUE "Y".
      02    DOS-FILE-NAME           PIC X(15).
```

The condition `NO-MORE-INPUT` is defined to be true when `EOF-FLAG` has the value `"Y"`. Records from the input file will be processed until `NO-MORE-INPUT` is true.

For printer control we use `LINE-SPACING` and `LINES-PRINTED`:

```
01    PRINTER-CONTROL.
      02    LINE-SPACING            PIC 9.
      02    LINES-PRINTED           PIC 99.
```

`LINE-SPACING`, which controls the spacing of detail lines, has the value 2 for the first detail line on a page and 1 for the remaining detail lines on the page. `LINES-PRINTED` is the number of lines printed so far on the current page. When the value of `LINES-PRINTED` equals that of `LINES-PER-PAGE`, it's time to go to a new page.

The work fields defined by

```
01    WORK-FIELDS.
      02    REGULAR-HOURS           PIC 99V9.
      02    OVERTIME-HOURS          PIC 999V99.
      02    REGULAR-WAGES           PIC 9(4)V99.
      02    OVERTIME-WAGES          PIC 9(4)V99.
      02    GROSS-WAGES             PIC 9(4)V99.
```

hold results that will be needed in later calculations. Note that results that are to be both printed and used in later calculations cannot be stored directly in the corresponding fields of `DETAIL-LINE`. The fields of `DETAIL-LINE` are numeric-edited, so their contents cannot be used in later calculations. Results to be used later must be stored in work fields having numeric pictures.

The fields defined by

```
01    COUNTERS-AND-ACCUMULATOR.
      02    EMPLOYEE-COUNT          PIC 999.
      02    PAGE-NUMBER             PIC 99.
      02    TOTAL-GROSS-WAGES       PIC 9(6)V99.
```

are used for counting (`EMPLOYEE-COUNT` and `PAGE-NUMBER`) and accumulating a total (`TOTAL-GROSS-WAGES`).

**The Procedure Division**

Figure 4.3 shows a *structure chart* of the Procedure Division of `PAYROLL-REPORT`. A structure chart, which looks much like the organizational chart of a business, is useful for displaying the structure of a Procedure Division and for outlining a

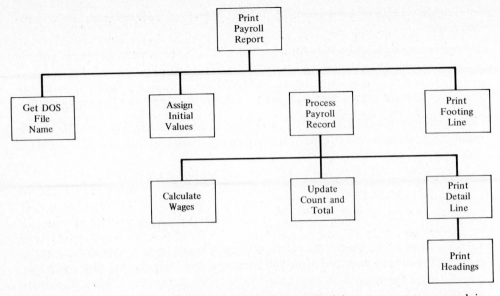

*Figure 4.3* A structure chart for the program in Figure 4.1. Each box represents a paragraph in the Procedure Division of the COBOL program. Each line connecting two boxes indicates that the paragraph represented by the uppermost box performs the paragraph represented by the lower box. If a paragraph is performed by more than one other paragraph, the box representing it may appear more than once in the structure chart, even though the paragraph itself appears only once in the COBOL program.

Procedure Division before it is written. Each block in the structure chart represents a COBOL paragraph. The top-level block represents the first paragraph, the one that oversees the operation of the entire program. The blocks immediately below and connected to a given block represent paragraphs performed by the paragraph corresponding to the given block. The lowest level blocks represent paragraphs that do their work without performing any other paragraphs.

### PRINT-PAYROLL-REPORT

As the top-level paragraph, PRINT-PAYROLL-REPORT accomplishes most of its work by performing other paragraphs. Some of the jobs that previously have been included in the top-level paragraph, such as getting the DOS file name and assigning initial values, have (for greater clarity) been put in subordinate paragraphs.

### GET-DOS-FILE-NAME

This paragraph gets the value of DOS-FILE-NAME from the user.

### ASSIGN-INITIAL-VALUES

As usual, EOF-FLAG is given the initial value "N". EMPLOYEE-COUNT and TOTAL-GROSS-WAGES are given initial values of zero. (Note the use of a MOVE statement with more than one receiving field.) PAGE-NUMBER is given the initial value 1. The reason for the final initialization is a bit tricky. Whenever the value of LINES-PRINTED equals that of LINES-PER-PAGE, the program goes to the top of a new page and prints a set of page headings. By setting the initial value of LINES-PRINTED to the value of LINES-PER-PAGE, we assure that the program will go to the top of a new page and print the page headings for the first page before printing any detail lines.

### PROCESS-PAYROLL-RECORD

PRINT-PAYROLL-RECORD performs PROCESS-PAYROLL-RECORD once for each record read from the input file (that is, until NO-MORE-INPUT is true). When PROCESS-PAYROLL-RECORD is executed, the input record to be processed has already been read. PROCESS-PAYROLL-RECORD performs paragraphs to do the wage calculations, update EMPLOYEE-COUNT and TOTAL-GROSS-WAGES, and print a detail line. Finally, PROCESS-PAYROLL-RECORD reads the next input record to be processed.

### PRINT-FOOTING-LINE

After all input records have been processed and all detail lines printed, PRINT-PAYROLL-REPORT performs PRINT-FOOTING-LINE to move the accumulated employee count and total gross wages to the footing line and then print the footing line.

### CALCULATE-WAGES

Since regular hours (the first 40) are treated differently from overtime hours (hours in excess of 40), the first step is to break up the hours worked into regular hours and overtime hours. If no overtime was worked (NO-OVERTIME is true), all the hours are regular hours. The value of PR-HOURS-WORKED is moved to REGULAR-HOURS, and OVERTIME-HOURS is set to zero:

```
MOVE PR-HOURS-WORKED TO REGULAR-HOURS
MOVE ZERO TO OVERTIME-HOURS
```

If the employee did work overtime, the first 40 hours worked are regular hours and all the rest are overtime hours. The value of MAXIMUM-REGULAR-HOURS (which is 40) is moved to REGULAR-HOURS, and the result of subtracting MAXIMUM-REGULAR-HOURS from PR-HOURS-WORKED is stored in OVERTIME-HOURS. Finally, the value of OVERTIME-HOURS is multiplied by the value of OVERTIME-MULTIPLIER (which is 1.5) so that each overtime hour is counted as an hour and a half:

```
MOVE MAXIMUM-REGULAR-HOURS TO REGULAR-HOURS
SUBTRACT MAXIMUM-REGULAR-HOURS FROM PR-HOURS-WORKED
     GIVING OVERTIME-HOURS
MULTIPLY OVERTIME-MULTIPLIER BY OVERTIME-HOURS.
```

The value of PR-HOURS-WORKED has one decimal place; after MAXIMUM-REGULAR-HOURS has been subtracted the result still has one decimal place. After multiplying by OVERTIME-MULTIPLER, which also has one decimal place, the result can have two decimal places. OVERTIME-HOURS has a picture of 999V99 so that both decimal places can be stored without the need for rounding or truncation.

The remainder of the calculation is the same regardless of whether or not the employee worked overtime. The value of REGULAR-HOURS is multiplied by that of PR-HOURLY-RATE; the result, rounded to two decimal places, becomes the value of REGULAR-WAGES. In the same way the value of OVERTIME-WAGES is computed from the values of OVERTIME-HOURS and PR-HOURLY-RATE. Finally, the values of REGULAR-WAGES and OVERTIME-WAGES are added to get the value of GROSS-WAGES:

```
MULTIPLY REGULAR-HOURS BY PR-HOURLY-RATE
    GIVING REGULAR-WAGES ROUNDED,
MULTIPLY OVERTIME-HOURS BY PR-HOURLY-RATE
    GIVING OVERTIME-WAGES ROUNDED,
ADD REGULAR-WAGES OVERTIME-WAGES
    GIVING GROSS-WAGES,
```

### UPDATE-COUNT-AND-TOTAL

*Counting* and *accumulating totals* are two operations frequently performed by COBOL programs. For the first, the data item that serves as a *counter* is cleared to zero before counting begins. The value of the counter is increased by one for each item to be counted. Likewise, the data item that serves as an *accumulator* is cleared to zero before accumulation begins. Each item to be included in the total is added in turn to the value of the accumulator.

In this program, EMPLOYEE-COUNT serves as a counter and TOTAL-GROSS-WAGES serves as an accumulator. Both are cleared to zero in the paragraph ASSIGN-INITIAL-VALUES:

```
MOVE ZERO TO EMPLOYEE-COUNT
             TOTAL-GROSS-WAGES,
```

UPDATE-COUNT-AND-TOTAL counts one employee by adding 1 to the value of EMPLOYEE-COUNT. The gross wages earned by the employee are added to the value of TOTAL-GROSS-WAGES, which is the running total of the gross wages for all employees processed so far:

```
ADD 1 TO EMPLOYEE-COUNT,
ADD GROSS-WAGES TO TOTAL-GROSS-WAGES,
```

### PRINT-DETAIL-LINE

This paragraph begins by moving the values to be printed from the fields of the input record and from work fields to the corresponding fields of DETAIL-LINE. If the value of LINES-PRINTED equals that of LINES-PER-PAGE, the current page is full, so PRINT-HEADINGS is called to go to the top of a new page and print page headings. PRINT-HEADINGS sets LINE-SPACING to 2 so that a line will be skipped between the last heading line and the first detail line. If the current page is not full, LINE-SPACING is set to 1, so that detail lines after the first will be single spaced:

```
IF LINES-PRINTED = LINES-PER-PAGE
      PERFORM PRINT-HEADINGS
ELSE
      MOVE 1 TO LINE-SPACING.
```

The contents of DETAIL-LINE are then printed using the value of LINE-SPACING set by either PRINT-HEADINGS or the MOVE statement. The value of LINES-PRINTED is increased by the value of LINE-SPACING—the number of lines printed or skipped by the WRITE statement:

```
WRITE PAYROLL-REPORT-RECORD
      FROM DETAIL-LINE
      AFTER ADVANCING LINE-SPACING LINES.
ADD LINE-SPACING TO LINES-PRINTED.
```

### PRINT-HEADINGS

First, the current page number is moved to the appropriate field of TITLE-LINE-1, 1 is added to the value of the current page number, and TITLE-LINE-1 is printed. Next, the date is obtained and stored in SYSTEM-DATE. The fields of system date are moved to the corresponding fields of TITLE-LINE-2, rearranging the components of the date in the process, and TITLE-LINE-2 is printed. After that, the two lines of column headings are printed. Finally, PRINT-HEADINGS sets LINES-PRINTED to 6, since the titles and headings take up six lines, and sets LINE-SPACING to 2, so that a line will be skipped between the headings and the first detail line.

## *EXERCISES*

1. Modify PAYROLL-REPORT so that (a) a relation condition is used to determine whether or not an employee worked overtime and (b) a condition name is used to determine when the end of a page has been reached.

2. Which statement in the paragraph CALCULATE-WAGES could (in the face of very unrealistic data) cause a size error? Modify the program to handle this error as follows. At the beginning of CALCULATE-WAGES the flag SIZE-ERROR-FLAG is set to "N". If the size error occurs, the value of SIZE-ERROR-FLAG is set to "Y". PRINT-DETAIL-LINE checks the value of SIZE-ERROR-FLAG. If no size error occurred, the usual detail line is printed. If a size error did occur, the program prints the data from the input record followed by an error message.

3. Modify `CALCULATE-WAGES` to use `COMPUTE` statements instead of `ADD`, `SUBTRACT`, and `MULTIPLY` statements. Which *two* statements can be replaced by the following?

```
COMPUTE OVERTIME-HOURS = OVERTIME-MULTIPLIER *
     (PR-HOURS-WORKED - MAXIMUM-REGULAR-HOURS)
```

Why are the parentheses needed in this statement?

4. Modify `PAYROLL-REPORT` so that the second title line shows the time as well as the date on which the report was printed. The date and time should be printed at the right-hand side of the page in the following form:

```
Date: 02/25/83   Time: 11:45
```

The time can be obtained with the statement

```
ACCEPT data-name FROM TIME.
```

The value assigned to *data-name* has the form HHMMSSFF where HH is hours, MM is minutes, SS is seconds, and FF is hundredths of a second. Thus `11452085` represents the time that would be written conventionally as 11:45:20.85.

5. Salespeople at a certain company earn a 10% commission on the first $5000 of sales and a 15% commission on sales in excess of $5000. Write a program to compute each salesperson's commission from the amount that person sold. The input to the program is a file containing records defined as follows:

| Field | Size | Type of Data |
|---|---|---|
| Salesperson number | 6 | Alphanumeric |
| Amount of sales | 7 | Numeric—two decimal places |

The program should print a report showing, for each salesperson, the salesperson number, the amount sold, the commission earned at the 10% rate, the commission earned at the 15% rate, the total commission earned by the salesperson, and the sales income received by the company after the salesperson's commission has been deducted. At the end of the report a footing line should be printed showing the total commission paid out to salespeople and the total sales income received by the company.

# 5

## Screen Formatting

IBM COBOL uses the ACCEPT and DISPLAY statements to handle *interactive screens*—forms displayed on the screen and filled in by the user with the data to be accepted. The ACCEPT statement provides extensive data validation by rejecting input that does not conform to the picture of the item being accepted. The Data Division is provided with a *Screen Section* for support of the screen-oriented ACCEPT and DISPLAY statements.

Some properties of ACCEPT and DISPLAY that were introduced in previous chapters are reviewed here for completeness.

### POSITION SPECIFICATIONS

Both the ACCEPT and DISPLAY statements use *position specifications* to designate positions on the display. (*Position specification* is often abbreviated to *position-spec*.) A position specification has the following form:

 ( *line-number* ,  *column-number* )

The line number, the column number, or both, can be omitted, but the comma and the space following it must always be present.

For the monochrome display, line numbers range from 1 through 25 and column numbers range from 1 through 80. Thus, ( 1 , 1 ) represents the upper left corner of the display, ( 1 , 80 ) represents the upper right corner, ( 25 , 1 ) represents the lower left corner, and ( 25 , 80 ) represents the lower right corner. ( 13 , 40 ) represents the approximate center of the display.

If the line or column number is omitted, the current line or column—the line or column in which the cursor is currently positioned—is assumed. Thus ( 10 , ) represents the intersection of line 10 and the column containing the cursor, ( , 30 ) represents the intersection of column 30 and the line containing the cursor, and ( , ) represents the current cursor position. Note that the comma and the space following it are always present.

The predefined data names LIN and COL can be used to represent the current line and column. Thus ( LIN , COL ) represents the current cursor position; ( 10 , COL ) represents the intersection of line 10 with the column containing the cursor; and so on.

According to the reference manual, line and column specifications of the form

        LIN + *integer*     LIN - *integer*
        COL + *integer*     COL - *integer*

can be used to designate positions relative to the current values of LIN and COL. Thus, the position specification

        (LIN + 5, COL - 3)

should designate a line number of 5 greater than the current line number and a column number 3 less than the current column number. This feature does not work properly in version 1.00 of IBM COBOL. When it is used, the items being positioned appear in unpredictable locations.

## THE DISPLAY STATEMENT

A DISPLAY statement consists of the word DISPLAY followed by a list of items to be displayed. The items to be displayed can be specified by identifers* or literals. The list of items can also contain the word ERASE, which erases the screen from the current cursor position to the end of the screen.

---

*An *identifier* is a data name together with any additional information needed to identify a unique memory area. For example, if FIELD-A is a field of both RECORD-A and RECORD-B, then FIELD-A is a data name but not an identifier, since it does not identify a unique memory area. On the other hand, the qualified names

        FIELD-A OF RECORD-A
        FIELD-A OF RECORD-B

identify unique memory areas and hence are identifiers. Most data names do refer to unique memory areas and hence are also identifiers.

Each entry in the list of items to be displayed (including ERASE) can be preceded by a position specification. When a position specification is encountered, the cursor is moved to the designated position. The item following the position specification is displayed beginning at the designated position. ERASE is effective only if a position specification has occurred earlier in the DISPLAY statement.

For example, the statement

```
DISPLAY (5, 10) "ONE" (8, 5) "TWO", (1, 1) "THREE",
```

displays "ONE" in columns 10 through 12 of line 5, "TWO" in columns 5 through 7 of line 8, and "THREE" in columns 1 through 5 of line 1. In our previous programs we have DISPLAY statements similar to the following.

```
DISPLAY (1, 1) ERASE,
DISPLAY (5, 1) "Name of input file? ",
```

These two DISPLAY statements can be combined into one:

```
DISPLAY (1, 1) ERASE (5, 1) "Name of input file? ",
```

or

```
DISPLAY (1, 1) ERASE
        (5, 1) "Name of input file? ",
```

In either case, the cursor is positioned to the upper left corner of the screen, the screen is erased from the cursor position to the end (thus the entire screen is erased), the cursor is positioned to line 5, column 1, and the message "Name of input file? " is displayed.

The position of the cursor after a DISPLAY statement is executed depends on whether any position specifications appear in the DISPLAY statement. If at least one position specification appears, the cursor is positioned immediately following the last displayed item. Thus, after

```
DISPLAY (5, 1) "Name of input file? ",
```

the cursor is positioned as follows:

```
Name of input file? _
```

On the other hand, if no position specification appears in the entire DISPLAY statement, the cursor is moved to the beginning of the line following the last displayed item, the screen scrolling up if necessary to make room for a new line at the bottom. Thus, after

```
DISPLAY "Name of input file? ",
```

the cursor is positioned as follows:

```
Name of input file?
_
```

One exception—if the only position specification that appears is ( , ), the cursor goes to the beginning of a new line just as if there were no position specification. To prevent the cursor from going to a new line, use (LIN, COL) instead of ( , ).

The DISPLAY statement does no editing on displayed values. For this reason, numeric values should be moved to numeric-edited fields before being displayed. Otherwise, they will be displayed in a hard-to-read internal format. This internal format is particularly hard to read for signed items. For example, suppose FIELD-A is defined by

```
01  FIELD-A              PIC S9(6) VALUE -25.
```

The statement

```
DISPLAY FIELD-A.
```

produces the display

```
00002N
```

The N represents the combined sign-digit code for – and 5, which is the same as the code for the letter N. (See the table in the reference manual entry for the SIGN clause.) On the other hand, if we define FIELD-B by

```
01  FIELD-B              PIC ----,--9.
```

the statements

```
MOVE FIELD-A TO FIELD-B.
DISPLAY FIELD-B.
```

produce the more meaningful display:

```
-25
```

(the minus sign is preceded by five blanks).

Output from a DISPLAY statement can be directed to the printer by using the UPON option. To use the UPON option, we must define a *mnemonic name* for the printer. Mnemonic names are defined in the SPECIAL-NAMES paragraph of the Configuration Section of the Environment Division. (The Configuration Section comes just before the already familiar Input-Output Section.) We can define the mnemonic name LINE-PRINTER as follows:

```
ENVIRONMENT DIVISION.
CONFIGURATION SECTION.
SPECIAL-NAMES.
    PRINTER IS LINE-PRINTER.
```

With this definition, the statement

```
DISPLAY "Can you read me?"
    UPON LINE-PRINTER.
```

prints

```
Can you read me?
```

ERASE and position specifications have no effect on the printer. If they are included in a DISPLAY statement directed to the printer, they will be applied to the screen even though the items to be displayed are sent to the printer.

There is one more form of the DISPLAY statement:

> DISPLAY *screen-name*

*Screen-name* is the name of a screen defined in the Screen Section of the Data Division. This form of the DISPLAY statement will be taken up later in the chapter when we discuss the Screen Section.

## THE ACCEPT STATEMENT

The ACCEPT statement has four formats. Format 1 accepts system data items such as the time. Format 2 is a line-oriented ACCEPT statement that does not provide for cursor positioning or prompting. Format 3 and format 4 are screen-oriented ACCEPT statements. A format 3 ACCEPT statement specifies a single data item whose value is to be accepted. A format 4 ACCEPT statement refers to a screen description which, in turn, may specify any number of data items whose values are to be accepted. We will discuss formats 1 through 3 here; format 4 will be taken up later in the chapter when we discuss the Screen Section.

### Format 1

A format 1 ACCEPT statement has one of the following forms:

> ACCEPT *identifier* FROM DATE
> ACCEPT *identifier* FROM DAY
> ACCEPT *identifier* FROM TIME
> ACCEPT *identifier* FROM ESCAPE KEY

The value accepted from DATE is a six-digit number of the form YYMMDD, where YY is the year, MM is the month, and DD is the day. Thus February 1, 1983 is represented by 830201. The value accepted from DAY is a five-digit number of the form YYNNN, where YY is the year and NNN is the day of the year. Thus, February 1, 1983 is represented by 83032. The value accepted from TIME is an eight-digit number of the form HHMMSSFF where HH is the hour (from 00 through 23), MM is the minutes, SS is the seconds, and FF represents hundredths of a second. Thus 21 hours (9 P.M.), 35 minutes, and 15.68 seconds is represented by 21351568. The value accepted from ESCAPE KEY is a two-digit number whose significance is discussed in connection with the format 3 and format 4 ACCEPT statements.

Each accepted value is an unsigned numeric value. This value is moved to the field specified by *identifier* according to the usual rules for the MOVE statement.

### Format 2

The format 2 ACCEPT statement accepts one line of typed data. When the Enter key is pressed to terminate the typed line, the cursor moves to the beginning of the next line, with the screen scrolling up one line if necessary. The format 2 ACCEPT statement has the following form:

ACCEPT *identifier*

The accepted data is moved to the receiving field designated by *identifier* exactly as if it had been moved from a hypothetical sending field by a MOVE statement. The only exception occurs when the receiving field is alphanumeric-edited, in which case no editing is done. Thus a receiving field with a picture of XBXXBXXX is treated as if its picture were X(8).

The picture for the receiving field determines whether the hypothetical sending field is alphanumeric or numeric. If the receiving field is alphanumeric or alphanumeric-edited, the hypothetical sending field is alphanumeric with a length equal to the number of characters typed. If the receiving field is numeric or numeric-edited, the hypothetical sending field is numeric and has the form:

S9...9V9...9

The number of 9s preceding the implied decimal point is the same as the number of digits preceding the decimal point in the value entered. The number of 9s following the implied decimal point is the same as the number of digits following the decimal point in the value entered. The sign is stored as a separate character; it is negative if a minus sign occurred in the value entered and positive otherwise.

If the receiving field is numeric or numeric-edited, some data validation is done on the value entered. The only characters allowed are the digits 0 through 9, the decimal point, and the plus and minus signs. A decimal point is allowed only if the picture of the receiving field contains an implied or actual decimal point. No more than one decimal point is allowed. A plus or minus sign is allowed only as the first or last character of the value entered and only if the picture of the receiving field contains a sign (specified by S, +, -, CR, or DB). If the value entered is invalid, the message

INVALID NUMERIC INPUT -- PLEASE RETYPE

is displayed and another typed line is read.

Note that the value entered may be too large to be stored in the receiving field. When the value is moved to the receiving field, it will be truncated on the left and right as needed, and no warning will be given that truncation has taken place.

## Format 3

The format 3 ACCEPT statement is screen-oriented. The identifier that specifies the receiving field is preceded by a position specification giving the position of the *data input field*—the area of the screen in which the user will type the data to be accepted. Following the identifier, a WITH phrase can be used to specify further details of how the data will be accepted and processed.

### The WITH phrase

The reserved word WITH is followed by one or more *options*. The various options are briefly introduced here. More information on these options, including a few restrictions on their use, can be found in the reference manual.

PROMPT is by far the most useful option, since it allows the user to see the format of the data input field. For an alphanumeric or alphanumeric-edited receiving field, PROMPT causes the data input field to be filled with periods before any characters are accepted. For a numeric or numeric-edited receiving field, digit positions are filled with zeros, a period is placed in the decimal point position, and a space is placed in the sign position. The following illustrates the initial appearance of typical data input fields:

| | |
|---|---|
| . . . . . . . . . . | Picture for receiving field is X(10) |
| 000.00 | Picture for receiving field is S999V99 |

Characters are entered by the user replace those supplied by the PROMPT option. When user-entered characters are deleted, the PROMPT characters reappear.

UPDATE causes the current contents of the receiving field to be placed in the data input field before any input is accepted. UPDATE cannot be used with numeric-edited receiving fields. For alphanumeric and alphanumeric-edited receiving fields, the data supplied by UPDATE can be edited just as if it had been entered by the user. When satisfied with the edited data, the user can press a terminator key to terminate the ACCEPT statement and send the edited contents of the data input field back to the receiving field. For numeric receiving fields, the user cannot edit the data supplied by UPDATE. Any attempt at editing causes the data supplied by UPDATE to be deleted from the data input field. Thus for numeric receiving fields the user has only two choices: (1) Press a terminator key to leave the contents of the receiving field unchanged, or (2) enter a new value from scratch.

For alphanumeric or alphanumeric-edited receiving fields, SPACE-FILL causes unkeyed character positions (positions for which no characters were entered) of the data input field and the receiving field to be filled with spaces when the ACCEPT statement ends; ZERO-FILL causes the unkeyed character positions to be filled with zeros. If neither option is specified, SPACE-FILL is assumed. For numeric or numeric-edited receiving fields, SPACE-FILL and ZERO-FILL affect only the unkeyed digit positions of the data input field (not the receiving field—unkeyed digit positions in the receiving field are always filled with zeros). What's more, SPACE-FILL affects only unkeyed digit positions to the left of the decimal point.

Alphanumeric items are normally left-justified in the data input field. The RIGHT-JUSTIFY option causes an alphanumeric item to be right-justified in the data input field when the ACCEPT statement ends. This option affects the data input field only; the description of the receiving field in the Data Division determines whether the data will be stored left- or right-justified. The LEFT-JUSTIFY option has no effect, since alphanumeric items are left-justified when no justify option is specified.

The sign of a numeric item normally appears in the leftmost position of the data input field. The TRAILING-SIGN option causes the sign to appear in the rightmost position of the data input field. This option affects only the data input field—the description of the receiving field in the Data Division determines whether the data will be stored with a leading or a trailing sign.

NO-ECHO causes asterisks to be displayed in the data input field instead of the characters actually typed. This is useful for accepting passwords, account numbers, access codes, and other items that should not be visible to someone looking over the user's shoulder.

EMPTY-CHECK requires at least one character to be entered for a field. LENGTH-CHECK requires that all positions of the field be filled. (For a numeric or numeric-edited field, only the digit positions need be filled; no entry need be made for the sign position, and the decimal point can be skipped over with AUTO-SKIP.) AUTO-SKIP causes an ACCEPT to end automatically (without a terminator key being pressed) when all positions of an alphanumeric field or all digit positions of a numeric field have been filled. For numeric and numeric-edited fields, AUTO-SKIP automatically moves the cursor to the right of the decimal point when all digit positions to the left of the decimal point have been filled. BEEP causes the speaker to sound when the ACCEPT statement is ready to accept user input.

### Data entry and editing

For a numeric or numeric-edited field, the digits to the left of the decimal point are entered first, then the decimal point, and finally the digits to the right of the decimal point. If AUTO-SKIP is specified, then when all digits to the left of the decimal point have been entered, the cursor will move to the first position to the right of the decimal point without the user actually entering a decimal point. For a signed field, a + or - sign can be entered at any time—it need not be the first or the last character. Data entry for a field can be terminated at any time by pressing a terminator key (if EMPTY-CHECK or LENGTH-CHECK has been specified, the corresponding requirement must be met before a terminator character will be accepted).

The data being entered can be edited with the Backspace, Cursor Left, and Cursor Right keys and with the key combination Ctrl End. Ctrl End restarts the ACCEPT statement; any data entered by the user or provided by the UPDATE option is deleted. Backspace deletes the last character entered. Cursor Left and Cursor Right can be used to move the cursor to any previously entered character. The user can then *overtype* the previously entered character—type a new character to replace the one at which the cursor is positioned.

When the cursor is positioned for entering a new character—when it is in the position it occupied before Cursor Left or Cursor Right was used—typing a character key enters an new character and typing Backspace deletes the last character entered. When the cursor is not positioned for entering a new character—when it has been moved to some other position with Cursor Left and Cursor Right—Backspace is ignored, and typing a character key does not enter an additional character but instead overtypes the character at which the cursor is positioned.

For example, suppose we have typed the first three characters of an alphanumeric item, so that the data input field looks like this:

        COM.....

The cursor is positioned for entering a new character. If we type a character—say P—that character will be entered following the M:

        COMP....

On the other hand, if we type B a c K s p a c e, the last character entered—M—will be deleted:

     CO̲. . . . . .

Suppose we use C u r s o r  L e f t to move the cursor to some previously entered character, say C:

     C̲OM. . . . .

B a c K s p a c e is now ignored, and typing a character key will not enter an additional character but will replace C with the character typed. If we type H, for example, we get

     H O̲M. . . . .

If we now use C u r s o r  R i g h t to move the cursor as far to the right as possible:

     HOM̲. . . . .

we can continue entering new characters.

### Terminator keys

Data entry for a field can be terminated by pressing one of the following *terminator keys:* E n t e r, T a b, E s c, B a c K t a b, and the function keys F 1 through F 1 0. If EMPTY - CHECK is specified, at least one character must be entered before a terminator key will be accepted. If LENGTH - CHECK is specified, every position must be filled before a terminator key will be accepted. When a field is terminated, the system data item ESCAPE KEY is set to indicate which terminator key was used. The following table shows the value assigned to ESCAPE KEY for each terminator key:

| *Terminator Key* | ESCAPE KEY Value |
|---|---|
| E n t e r or T a b key, or field automatically terminated by AUTO - SK I P option | 0 0 |
| E s c | 0 1 |
| F 1 - F 1 0 | 0 2 - 1 1 |
| B a c K t a b | 9 9 |

After a format 3 ACCEPT statement has been executed, a format 1 ACCEPT statement can be used to get the value of ESCAPE KEY. This value can be used in a conditional statement—such as an I F statement or a PERFORM - UNT I L statement— to determine what action the program will take next. Usually, the E n t e r or T a b key is used for normal termination, while the E s c key indicates some abnormal condition, such as if the user wishes to terminate the program instead of entering another data item. The function keys can be used to request the program to take specific actions.

## THE SCREEN SECTION

We often use the word *line* to refer a particular row of characters. For example, we say that the statement:

```
DISPLAY "IBM Personal Computer".
```

displays the *line:*

```
IBM Personal Computer
```

Likewise, we use the word *screen* to refer to a particular arrangement of characters on the entire display. A screen can contain instructions and data for the user as well as data input fields for the user to fill in. Screens are frequently designed to imitate printed forms, providing office workers—who are used to filling out forms—with an understandable way of interacting with computers.

The Screen Section of the Data Division allows each screen to be specified by a *screen description,* which is similar in form to a record description. A screen description specifies both the items that are to be displayed and the data input fields and receiving fields for the items to be accepted. A single DISPLAY statement displays all the items to be displayed, and a single ACCEPT statement accepts all the data entered by the user. Specifying the entire screen in a single screen description is far simpler (and the program is far easier to read) than if the same result were achieved with a mass of DISPLAY and ACCEPT statements in the Procedure Division. I recommend screen descriptions for all but the simplest screen-oriented input and output.

The Screen Section, when present, is always the last section of the Data Division. It is introduced with the section header

```
SCREEN SECTION.
```

Like record descriptions, screen descriptions are organized by means of level numbers into group items and elementary items. An elementary screen item defines a data item to be displayed or a data input field. A group screen item defines an entire screen, that is, a group of elementary items that will be processed with a single DISPLAY or ACCEPT statement. Usually, a group item is processed by both a DISPLAY statement (to display instructions, field labels, and data) and an ACCEPT statement (to accept values filled in by the user).

### An Example Screen Description

To get a feeling for how screens are described and how screen descriptions are used by ACCEPT and DISPLAY statements, let's consider the following example:

```
01   EMPLOYEE-SCREEN.
     02   BLANK SCREEN.
     02   LINE 10 COLUMN 5 VALUE "Employee Number: ".
     02   PIC XBXXBXXX FROM EMPLOYEE-NUMBER.
     02   LINE 12 COLUMN 5 VALUE "Hours Worked: ".
     02   PIC Z9.9 TO HOURS-WORKED.
     02   LINE 14 COLUMN 5 VALUE "Hourly Rate: ".
     02   PIC $$9.99 TO HOURLY-RATE.
```

EMPLOYEE-SCREEN is the *screen name*—the name that will be used to refer to the screen in ACCEPT and DISPLAY statements. For example, the statement

    DISPLAY EMPLOYEE-SCREEN.

displays all the display items specified in EMPLOYEE-SCREEN. The statement

    ACCEPT EMPLOYEE-SCREEN

accepts the data that the user enters in the data input fields described in EMPLOYEE-SCREEN.

EMPLOYEE-SCREEN refers to three fields defined elsewhere in the Data Division: EMPLOYEE-NUMBER, HOURS-WORKED, and HOURLY-RATE. These fields might be defined in the File Section or Working-Storage Section as follows:

    01   EMPLOYEE-RECORD.
         02   EMPLOYEE-NUMBER PIC X(6).
         02   HOURS-WORKED    PIC 99V9.
         02   HOURLY-RATE     PIC 99V99.

EMPLOYEE-NUMBER provides data to be displayed. HOURS-WORKED and HOURLY-RATE serve as receiving fields for data to be accepted.

The elementary items are processed in the order in which they appear in the screen description. When EMPLOYEE-NAME is processed by a DISPLAY statement, the first elementary item processed is

    02   BLANK SCREEN.

which erases the screen and positions the cursor at line 1, column 1. BLANK SCREEN has the same effect as the DISPLAY statement

    DISPLAY (1, 1) ERASE

The next two elementary items label and display the value of EMPLOYEE-NUMBER:

    02   LINE 10 COLUMN 5 VALUE "Employee Number: ".
    02   PIC XBXXBXXX FROM EMPLOYEE-NUMBER.

The LINE and COLUMN specifications position the cursor at a particular line and column. Thus, LINE 10 COLUMN 5 positions the cursor at the intersection of line 10 and column 5. A VALUE clause specifies a nonnumeric literal to be displayed. Thus the effect of

    02   LINE 10 COLUMN 5 VALUE "Employee Number: ".

is to display

    Employee Number:

beginning at line 10, column 5. In the next elementary item

    02   PIC XBXXBXXX FROM EMPLOYEE-NUMBER.

the phrase `FROM EMPLOYEE-NUMBER` specifies that the value to be displayed is obtained from `EMPLOYEE-NUMBER`. Before being displayed, the value of `EMPLOYEE-NUMBER` is edited using the specified picture. Thus, if the value of `EMPLOYEE-NUMBER` is `123456`, the employee number is displayed as

    1 23 456

If an elementary item does not contain a line and column specification, the corresponding field is positioned immediately after the field described by the previous elementary item. Thus, the displayed value of `EMPLOYEE-NUMBER` is positioned immediately after the label `"Employee Number: "`. The effect of the two elementary items just described is to display

    Employee Number: 1 23 456

beginning at line 10, column 5.
    The next elementary item

    02  LINE 12 COLUMN 5 VALUE "Hours Worked: ",

displays `"Hours Worked: "` beginning at line 12, column 5. In the next elementary item

    02  PIC Z9.9 TO HOURS-WORKED,

the phrase `TO HOURS-WORKED` specifies that data accepted from the user is to be stored in the receiving field `HOURS-WORKED`. Thus, this elementary item defines a data input field. When a field having only a `TO` phrase is processed by a `DISPLAY` statement, the data input field is filled with periods. Thus, when `DISPLAY EMPLOYEE-SCREEN` is executed, the following line appears (beginning at line 12, column 5):

    Hours Worked: ....

When the data input field is processed by an `ACCEPT` statement, the periods are replaced by a prompt identical to the one produced by the prompt option of the format 3 `ACCEPT` statement:

    Hours Worked: 00.0

    The remaining two elementary items

    02  LINE 14 COLUMN 5 VALUE "Hourly Rate: ",
    02  PIC $$9.99 TO HOURLY-RATE,

define and label a data input field for `HOURLY-RATE`.
    When the `DISPLAY` statement

    DISPLAY EMPLOYEE-SCREEN.

is executed, the display is cleared and the field labels are displayed, as is the value of `EMPLOYEE-NUMBER`. The two data input fields are filled with periods:

```
Employee Number: 1 23 456

Hours Worked: ....

Hourly Rate: .....
```

When the statement

```
ACCEPT EMPLOYEE-SCREEN.
```

is executed, the first data input field is processed:

```
EMPLOYEE Number: 1 23 456

Hours Worked: 00.0

Hourly Rate: .....
```

If the value 9.5 is entered, the display looks like this

```
Employee Number: 1 23 456

Hours Worked: 09.5_

Hourly Rate: .....
```

If the Enter key is now pressed, the hours-worked field is edited according to the picture given in the screen description (the leading zero is suppressed) and the cursor is moved to the hourly rate field:

```
Employee Number: 1 23 456

Hours Worked:  9.5

Hourly Rate: 00.00
```

Suppose the user types 10.25 and presses the Enter key. The value entered is edited according to the picture given in the screen description, and (since there are no more data input fields) the ACCEPT statement is terminated. The display now looks like this:

```
Employee Number: 1 23 456

Hours Worked:  9.5

Hourly Rate: $10.25
```

## Specifications for Elementary Screen Items

Each elementary screen item can contain a number of specifications (clauses or phrases) describing the corresponding display item or data input field. Four specifications—AUTO, SECURE, REQUIRED, and FULL—can also be given for a group item, in which case the specification applies to all the elementary items subordinate to the group item. In this section we will look briefly at each of the possible specifications. Additional details and restrictions can be found in the entry for the Screen Section in the reference manual.

### Positioning items

As a screen description is compiled, a current cursor position is maintained so that each display item or data input field can be positioned properly on the display. When a level 01 screen item is encountered, the cursor is set to line 1, column 1. After each elementary item is processed, the cursor is set to the position immediately following the corresponding display item or data input field. Consistent cursor positioning is maintained throughout the entire screen description, even though some of the elementary items will be processed by DISPLAY statements and others will be processed by ACCEPT statements. Both DISPLAY and ACCEPT statements process elementary items in the order in which they appear in the screen description. This need not be the same as the order in which the corresponding fields appear on the display.

The cursor can be positioned explicitly with the LINE and COLUMN specifications. LINE *integer* or COLUMN *integer* sets the cursor to the line or column specified by the integer. Thus

        LINE 5 COLUMN 9

sets the cursor to the intersection of line 5 and column 9. LINE PLUS *integer* or COLUMN PLUS *integer* causes the integer to be added to the current line or column value. For example, if the cursor is positioned at line 5, column 9, the specification

        LINE PLUS 2 COLUMN PLUS 5

changes the cursor position to line 7, column 14.

If COLUMN is specified without LINE, the current line is not changed. If LINE is specified without COLUMN, column 1 is assumed. If the integer following LINE or COLUMN is omitted, LINE PLUS 1 or COLUMN PLUS 1 is assumed. If neither LINE nor COLUMN is specified for an elementary item, the current cursor position is not changed—the corresponding field is positioned immediately after the field corresponding to the preceding elementary item in the screen description.

### Erasing

BLANK SCREEN erases the entire screen and positions the cursor at line 1, column 1. BLANK LINE erases the current line from the cursor position to the end of the line. The cursor position is not changed.

### Defining display and data input fields

Display and data input fields are defined using the VALUE clause or the PICTURE clause combined with the FROM, TO, or USING phrases.

A VALUE clauses specifies a nonnumeric literal to be displayed. In contrast to the use of the VALUE clause in record descriptions, the VALUE clause cannot be used with a PICTURE clause, and the literal must be nonnumeric—numeric literals and figurative constants are not allowed. For example,

```
02   LINE 7 COLUMN 3 VALUE "Account Number".
```

causes

```
Account Number
```

to be displayed beginning at line 7, column 3. Items with value clauses are processed only by DISPLAY statements and have no effect on ACCEPT statements.

FROM defines a display field, TO defines a data input field, and USING defines both a display field and a data input field. USING produces the same effect as the UPDATE option of the format 3 ACCEPT statement. An elementary item with FROM, TO, or USING must be provided with a picture to specify how the data is to be edited for display.

For example, consider the following screen description:

```
01   EXAMPLE-SCREEN.
     02   LINE 5 COLUMN 10 PIC $$$9.99 FROM UNIT-PRICE.
     02   LINE 7 COLUMN 10 PIC ZZ9 TO QUANTITY-ORDERED.
     02   LINE 9 COLUMN 10 PIC Z9.9 FROM OLD-DISCOUNT-RATE
                                    TO NEW-DISCOUNT-RATE.
     02   LINE 11 COLUMN 10 PIC Z9.9 USING TAX-RATE.
```

(For simplicity, we omit displaying identifying labels such as "Unit Price: ", although in any real application such labels are essential.) The FROM phrases define UNIT-PRICE and OLD-DISCOUNT-RATE as sending fields—they will supply data to be displayed on the screen. The TO phrases define QUANTITY-ORDERED and NEW-DISCOUNT-RATE as receiving fields—they will receive values accepted from the user. USING defines TAX-RATE as both a sending field and a receiving field. TAX-RATE will supply data to be displayed and receive data entered by the user.

When the statement

```
DISPLAY EXAMPLE-SCREEN.
```

is executed, the values of all sending fields defined by FROM and USING phrases are edited according to the corresponding pictures and displayed at the designated positions. Thus, the value of UNIT-PRICE is edited with the picture $$$9.99 and displayed beginning at line 5, column 10. The value of OLD-DISCOUNT-RATE is edited with the picture Z9.9 and displayed beginning at line 7, column 10. The value of TAX-RATE is edited with the picture Z9.9 and displayed beginning at line 11, column 10. The data input field corresponding to QUANTITY-ORDERED is filled with periods.

When the statement

```
ACCEPT EXAMPLE-SCREEN.
```

is executed, values are accepted from the user and stored in the receiving fields defined by TO and USING phrases. Since elementary items are processed in the order in which they occur in the screen description, the ACCEPT statement begins with the data input field corresponding to QUANTITY-ORDERED. The dots filling the data input field are replaced by a prompt such as supplied by the PROMPT option of the format 3 ACCEPT statement. If the user enters a data value and presses the Enter key, three things happen:

1. The contents of the data input field are moved to the receiving field QUANTITY-ORDERED.
2. The contents of the data input field are edited with the picture ZZ9, so that after data entry for the field is terminated the data entered appears in edited form.
3. The ACCEPT statement moves to the next data input field defined in the screen description, which in this case is the data input field corresponding to NEW-DISCOUNT-RATE.

The values for NEW-DISCOUNT-RATE and TAX-RATE are accepted in like manner. The prompt for a field with a FROM or USING phrase is filled in with any data supplied by FROM are USING. For example, suppose the DISPLAY statement displays the value

4.5

in the field corresponding to TAX-RATE. When that field is processed by the ACCEPT statement, but before any data is entered by the user, the following prompt will appear:

04.5

Values supplied by FROM or USING are treated like those supplied by the UPDATE option of the format 3 ACCEPT statement. An alphanumeric value can be edited; when data entry for the field terminates, the edited value will be stored in the receiving field. A numeric value supplied by FROM or USING cannot be edited; any attempt at editing will cause the value supplied by FROM or USING to be deleted.

If the user terminates data entry for a field without entering any characters or doing any editing, the receiving field is not changed. In particular, when both FROM and TO are present, the value supplied by the sending field will *not* be moved to the receiving field unless some character is entered or some editing change is made by the user.

### Appearance of displayed items

HIGHLIGHT causes a displayed item to appear in high intensity; BLINK causes the item to blink, and REVERSE-VIDEO displays an item with the foreground and background colors reversed. For the IBM Monochrome Display and Printer Adapter, REVERSE-VIDEO causes the item to be displayed with dark letters on a light background. UNDERLINE causes a displayed item to be underlined; UNDERLINE can only be used with the IBM Monochrome Display and Printer Adapter.

When a Color/Graphics Monitor Adapter is used, we can employ FOREGROUND-COLOR to set the color in which characters will be displayed and BACKGROUND-COLOR to set the color of the background. The background color is specified by an integer in the range 0 through 7, and the foreground color is specified by an integer in the range 0 through 15. If the foreground and background colors are not specified, the background color defaults to black and the foreground color defaults to white. The integers used to specify colors are defined as follows:

| | | | |
|---|---|---|---|
| 0 | Black | 8 | Gray |
| 1 | Blue | 9 | Light blue |
| 2 | Green | 10 | Light green |
| 3 | Cyan | 11 | Light cyan |
| 4 | Red | 12 | Light red |
| 5 | Magenta | 13 | Light magenta |
| 6 | Brown | 14 | Yellow |
| 7 | White | 15 | High intensity white |

Thus

       FOREGROUND-COLOR 4 BACKGROUND-COLOR 2

specifies red letters on a green background. FOREGOUND-COLOR and BACKGROUND-COLOR must be on a line with something else; if alone, they won't work. A good place to put them is on the same line with BLANK SCREEN.

### Other specifications

BELL sounds the speaker when an ACCEPT statement is ready to accept data from the item in question. BLANK WHEN ZERO causes a displayed item to be blank (all spaces) if its value is zero. JUSTIFIED (which can be abbreviated JUST) causes a displayed item to be right-justified in its field. AUTO causes an ACCEPT statement to automatically go to the next data input field when the preceding one has been filled by the user; the user does not have to press a terminator key to go to the next field. SECURE causes characters entered by the user to appear on the display as asterisks, thus protecting the data entered from prying eyes. REQUIRED requires that some entry be made in a data input field before a terminator will be accepted. FULL requires that all positions of a data input field be filled before a terminator will be accepted.

### Correspondence with format 3 ACCEPT statement

A number of the specifications in screen descriptions correspond directly to WITH options for the format 3 ACCEPT statement. The following table gives this correspondence:

| WITH *Option* | *Screen-Description Specification* |
|---|---|
| AUTO-SKIP | AUTO |
| BEEP | BELL |
| EMPTY-CHECK | REQUIRED |
| LENGTH-CHECK | FULL |
| NO-ECHO | SECURE |
| PROMPT | Always in effect |
| RIGHT-JUSTIFY | JUSTIFIED |
| UPDATE | Specify receiving |
| | field with USING |

## Terminator Keys and the Format 4 ACCEPT Statement

The format 4 ACCEPT statement has two forms:

> ACCEPT *screen-name*

and

> ACCEPT *screen-name*
>     ON ESCAPE *imperative-statement*

In each case, *screen-name* is the name of the screen from which data is to be accepted. The ON ESCAPE option specifies a statement that will be executed if the user terminates the ACCEPT statement by pressing the Esc key.

The same terminator keys are used for both the format 3 and format 4 ACCEPT statements. Since each format 3 ACCEPT statement accepts only a single item, each terminator key terminates the ACCEPT statement as well as data entry for the item. Since a single format 4 ACCEPT statement can accept many items—one for each data input field in the corresponding screen description—some terminator keys terminate data entry for individual items while others terminate the entire ACCEPT statement.

The Enter and Tab keys terminate data entry for the current item and move the cursor to the next data input field, if any. (*Previous, first, next,* and *last* refer to the order in which elementary items appear in the screen description—not, necessarily, to the order in which the corresponding data input fields appear on the display.) If the current data input field is the last one, Enter and Tab also terminate the entire ACCEPT statement. The Backtab key terminates data entry for the current item and moves the cursor to the previous data input field, if any. If the current data input field is the first one, the Backtab key merely restarts data entry for the current item. The Backtab key can only terminate data entry for a field; it can never terminate the entire ACCEPT statement.

The Esc key and the function keys F1 through F10 terminate the entire ACCEPT statement as well as data entry for the current item. If the ACCEPT statement is terminated by Esc, and the ON ESCAPE option is present, the statement following ON ESCAPE is executed. When an ACCEPT statement is terminated with Esc, any characters entered for the current item are ignored, and the corresponding TO or USING field is not changed. As with the format 3 ACCEPT statement, the system data item ESCAPE KEY is set to reflect the key used to terminate the entire ACCEPT statement. The codes for the terminator keys are the same as for format 3.

**Caution**

Some screen descriptions are not compiled properly by Version 1.00 of the IBM COBOL Compiler. The compiler does not give any errors or warnings for these screen descriptions, but the computer hangs up when one attempts to execute the compiled program. An example of such a "pathological" screen description is given later in the chapter (in Figure 5.3). The problem is more of an annoyance than a serious limitation since most reasonable screen descriptions do compile properly, and only small changes may be needed to transform a pathological screen description into one that will compile correctly. Keep in mind, however, that if a program containing screen descriptions cannot be executed, one or more of the screen descriptions may well be the cause. Experiment with the screen descriptions (in particular, try simplifying them) until you arrive at versions that will compile correctly.

## CREATING AND UPDATING A FILE

The program in Figure 5.1 creates a customer file on disk from information entered by the user. The program in Figure 5.4 allows the user to update an existing customer file by entering new values for some or all of the fields in each record. Both programs are screen oriented. For creating a new record, the program in Figure 5.1 displays a blank form for the user to fill in with the necessary information. For updating a record, the program in Figure 5.4 displays a form filled in with the current contents of the record. The user can then make any changes desired.

### Creating a File

The program in Figure 5.1 creates the file CUSTOMER-FILE. Looking at the Environment Division, we see that CUSTOMER-FILE is assigned to DISK. Since no ORGANIZATION clause is provided in the FILE-CONTROL-paragraph entry for CUSTOMER-FILE, the organization of CUSTOMER-FILE defaults to regular sequential (not line sequential).

Turning to the File Section of the Data Divison, we see that each record of CUSTOMER-FILE has eight alphanumeric fields (ACCOUNT-NUMBER, LAST-NAME, FIRST-NAME, MIDDLE-INITIAL, STREET-ADDRESS, CITY, STATE, and ZIP) and two numeric fields (BALANCE and CREDIT-LIMIT). Our problem is to provide the user with a convenient and easy-to-understand method of entering the values of these 10 fields for each record in the file being created.

In the Working-Storage Section, we find the usual DOS-FILE-NAME for holding the name entered by the user for the file to be created. END-OF-INPUT-FLAG

```
IDENTIFICATION DIVISION.
PROGRAM-ID. CREATE-CUSTOMER-FILE.

*     Create a customer file from data entered
*     by the user.

ENVIRONMENT DIVISION.
INPUT-OUTPUT SECTION.
FILE-CONTROL.
     SELECT CUSTOMER-FILE ASSIGN TO DISK.

DATA DIVISION.
FILE SECTION.
FD   CUSTOMER-FILE
     LABEL RECORDS STANDARD
     VALUE OF FILE-ID IS DOS-FILE-NAME.
01   CUSTOMER-RECORD.
     02   ACCOUNT-NUMBER   PIC X(6).
     02   LAST-NAME        PIC X(30).
     02   FIRST-NAME       PIC X(20).
     02   MIDDLE-INITIAL   PIC X.
     02   STREET-ADDRESS   PIC X(40).
     02   CITY             PIC X(15).
     02   STATE            PIC XX.
     02   ZIP              PIC X(5).
     02   BALANCE          PIC 9(6)V99.
     02   CREDIT-LIMIT     PIC 9(6)V99.

WORKING-STORAGE SECTION.
01   DOS-FILE-NAME        PIC X(15).
01   END-OF-INPUT-FLAG    PIC X.
     88   FINISHED        VALUE "Y".
```

*Figure 5.1*   This program creates a customer file from data entered by the user via an interactive screen.

has the value " Y " if the user has finished entering records and the value " N " otherwise. The user indicates that no more records are to be entered by pressing the E s c key when a blank form appears on the display. When this occurs, END-OF-INPUT-FLAG is set to " Y " by a statement in the ON ESCAPE option of a format 4 ACCEPT statement.

The Screen Section is always the last section in the Data Division. CUSTOMER-SCREEN produces the screen shown in Figure 5.2. The periods in Figure 5.2 represent data input fields (recall that when a screen description is processed by a DISPLAY statement, the data input fields are filled with periods). On the actual display, the field labels such as Account Number appear in reverse video.

The first elementary item of CUSTOMER-SCREEN:

```
     02   BLANK SCREEN.
```

clears the screen in preparation for accepting values for a new record. Next come 10 pairs of elementary items. The first elementary item of each pair displays a field label; the second item of each pair defines a data input field for accepting a value of one of the fields of CUSTOMER-RECORD.

For example,

```
SCREEN SECTION.
01  CUSTOMER-SCREEN.
    02  BLANK SCREEN.
    02  LINE 4 COLUMN 5 REVERSE-VIDEO VALUE "Account Number".
    02  LINE 5 COLUMN 5 PIC XBXXBXXX TO ACCOUNT-NUMBER
            AUTO.
    02  LINE 8 COLUMN 5 REVERSE-VIDEO VALUE "Last Name".
    02  LINE 9 COLUMN 5 PIC X(30) TO LAST-NAME
            AUTO REQUIRED.
    02  LINE 8 COLUMN 40 REVERSE-VIDEO VALUE "First Name".
    02  LINE 9 COLUMN 40 PIC X(20) TO FIRST-NAME
            AUTO REQUIRED.
    02  LINE 8 COLUMN 65 REVERSE-VIDEO VALUE "Initial".
    02  LINE 9 COLUMN 65 PIC X TO MIDDLE-INITIAL
            AUTO REQUIRED.
    02  LINE 12 COLUMN 5 REVERSE-VIDEO VALUE "Street Address".
    02  LINE 13 COLUMN 5 PIC X(40) TO STREET-ADDRESS
            AUTO REQUIRED.
    02  LINE 16 COLUMN 5 REVERSE-VIDEO VALUE "City".
    02  LINE 17 COLUMN 5 PIC X(15) TO CITY
            AUTO REQUIRED.
    02  LINE 16 COLUMN 25 REVERSE-VIDEO VALUE "State".
    02  LINE 17 COLUMN 25 PIC XX TO STATE
            AUTO FULL.
    02  LINE 16 COLUMN 35 REVERSE-VIDEO VALUE "ZIP".
    02  LINE 17 COLUMN 35 PIC X(5) TO ZIP
            AUTO FULL.
    02  LINE 20 COLUMN 5 REVERSE-VIDEO VALUE "Balance".
    02  LINE 21 COLUMN 5 PIC $$$$,$$9.99 TO BALANCE
            AUTO REQUIRED.
    02  LINE 20 COLUMN 21 REVERSE-VIDEO VALUE "Credit Limit".
    02  LINE 21 COLUMN 21 PIC $$$$,$$9.99 TO CREDIT-LIMIT
            AUTO REQUIRED.

PROCEDURE DIVISION.
CREATE-FILE.
    DISPLAY (1, 1) ERASE (5, 1) "Customer file name? ".
    ACCEPT (, ) DOS-FILE-NAME WITH PROMPT.
    OPEN OUTPUT CUSTOMER-FILE.
    MOVE "N" TO END-OF-INPUT-FLAG.
    DISPLAY CUSTOMER-SCREEN.
    ACCEPT CUSTOMER-SCREEN
        ON ESCAPE MOVE "Y" TO END-OF-INPUT-FLAG.
    PERFORM WRITE-ONE-RECORD
        UNTIL FINISHED.
    CLOSE CUSTOMER-FILE.
    STOP RUN.

WRITE-ONE-RECORD.
    WRITE CUSTOMER-RECORD.
    DISPLAY CUSTOMER-SCREEN.
    ACCEPT CUSTOMER-SCREEN
        ON ESCAPE MOVE "Y" TO END-OF-INPUT-FLAG.
```

*Figure 5.1 (continued)*

```
Account Number
. . . . . .


Last Name                        First Name              Initial
. . . . . . . . . . . . . . . . . . . . . .    . . . . . . . . . . . . . . . . . .    .


Street Address
. . . . . . . . . . . . . . . . . . . . . . . . . . . . . . . . . . . . . .


City                   State      ZIP
. . . . . . . . . . . . . . .    . .        . . . . .


Balance            Credit Limit
. . . . . . . . .        . . . . . . . . .
```

*Figure 5.2*   The screen displayed by the program in Figure 5.1 before any data has been entered. In the actual display, labels such as Account Number are in reverse video.

```
02   LINE 4 COLUMN 5 REVERSE-VIDEO VALUE "Account Number",
```

displays the field label Account Number in reverse video beginning at line 4, column 5; and

```
02   LINE 5 COLUMN 5 PIC XBXXBXXX TO ACCOUNT-NUMBER
         AUTO,
```

defines the data input field corresponding to ACCOUNT-NUMBER. From Figure 5.2 we see that each data input field is positioned immediately below the corresponding label. Thus each label and the corresponding data input field begin in the same column, but the line number for the data input field is one greater than the line number for the label.

(In general, screens are usually simple enough that we can lay them out by trial and error. Pads of video display layout forms are available from dealers in computer supplies. The layout forms are divided into 24 or 25 lines and 80 columns. After positioning the field labels and data input fields on a layout form, we can easily read off the line and column numbers needed for the screen description.)

AUTO is specified for each data input field so that if the user completely fills a field, the cursor will automatically move to the next field. If the user fills the last field, the ACCEPT statement is automatically terminated. To prevent the user from accidentally overlooking any fields, REQUIRED is specified for all but three data input fields. FULL is specified for the data input fields corresponding to STATE and ZIP, requiring the user to enter two characters for the state and five characters for the zip code.

Neither REQUIRED nor FULL is specified for the account-number field. The user terminates the program by pressing Esc with a blank form on the screen and the cursor positioned on the account number field. If REQUIRED, for example, were specified for the account number field, the user would have to enter at least one character of a dummy account number before pressing the Esc key to terminate the program, which would be annoying.

In the Procedure Division, the paragraph CREATE-FILE begins by obtaining the DOS file name for CUSTOMER-FILE, after which CUSTOMER-FILE is opened for output. "N" is moved to END-OF-INPUT-FLAG, indicating that input has not yet been terminated by the user. The statements

```
DISPLAY CUSTOMER-SCREEN,
ACCEPT CUSTOMER-SCREEN
    ON ESCAPE MOVE "Y" TO END-OF-INPUT-FLAG,
```

display CUSTOMER-SCREEN and accept values for the fields of CUSTOMER-RECORD. END-OF-INPUT-FLAG is set to "Y" if the user terminates the ACCEPT by pressing the Esc key. If the user terminates the ACCEPT by any other means, END-OF-INPUT-FLAG retains the value "N".

The PERFORM statement executes the paragraph WRITE-ONE-RECORD repeatedly until the condition FINISHED is true—that is, until the value of END-OF-INPUT-FLAG is "Y". WRITE-ONE-RECORD writes the current value of CUSTOMER-RECORD to the file being created, then uses DISPLAY and ACCEPT to obtain a new value for CUSTOMER-RECORD from the user. If an ACCEPT is terminated by some means other than pressing the Esc key, the program assumes that valid data was accepted, and WRITE-ONE-RECORD is performed to write the data to the file. If an ACCEPT is terminated by pressing the Esc key, the program assumes that no valid data was entered, and WRITE-ONE-RECORD is not executed again. The current value of CUSTOMER-RECORD is not written to the file, so any values accepted before the Esc was pressed are ignored.

When the user terminates input by pressing the Esc key, the execution of the PERFORM statement is terminated, and the computer goes on to the last two statements of CREATE-FILE, which close the file that was created and terminate execution of the program.

### A Pathological Screen Description

Figure 5.3 shows a version of CUSTOMER-SCREEN for which the compiler produces incorrect code. This version differs from the one in Figure 5.1 only in that each data input field has the specifications AUTO REQUIRED. A version of the file-creation program containing this screen description appears to compile and link properly (no error messages are produced). But when the compiled program is invoked for execution, the computer hangs up. Most curiously, the hangup seems to take place while the program is being loaded, before execution of the program actually begins. The runtime system, which is required for program execution, is never loaded. If REQUIRED is deleted from the data input field corresponding to ACCOUNT-NUMBER, the screen description will be compiled properly.

### Updating a File

The program in Figure 5.4 updates a customer file created by the program in Figure 5.1. The program assumes that every record in the file is to be updated; if a particular record is

```
SCREEN SECTION.
01   CUSTOMER-SCREEN.
     02   BLANK SCREEN.
     02   LINE 4 COLUMN 5 REVERSE-VIDEO VALUE "Account Number".
     02   LINE 5 COLUMN 5 PIC XBXXBXXX TO ACCOUNT-NUMBER
            AUTO REQUIRED.
     02   LINE 8 COLUMN 5 REVERSE-VIDEO VALUE "Last Name".
     02   LINE 9 COLUMN 5 PIC X(30) TO LAST-NAME
            AUTO REQUIRED.
     02   LINE 8 COLUMN 40 REVERSE-VIDEO VALUE "First Name".
     02   LINE 9 COLUMN 40 PIC X(20) TO FIRST-NAME
            AUTO REQUIRED.
     02   LINE 8 COLUMN 65 REVERSE-VIDEO VALUE "Initial".
     02   LINE 9 COLUMN 65 PIC X TO MIDDLE-INITIAL
            AUTO REQUIRED.
     02   LINE 12 COLUMN 5 REVERSE-VIDEO VALUE "Street Address".
     02   LINE 13 COLUMN 5 PIC X(40) TO STREET-ADDRESS
            AUTO REQUIRED.
     02   LINE 16 COLUMN 5 REVERSE-VIDEO VALUE "City".
     02   LINE 17 COLUMN 5 PIC X(15) TO CITY
            AUTO REQUIRED.
     02   LINE 16 COLUMN 25 REVERSE-VIDEO VALUE "State".
     02   LINE 17 COLUMN 25 PIC XX TO STATE
            AUTO REQUIRED.
     02   LINE 16 COLUMN 35 REVERSE-VIDEO VALUE "ZIP".
     02   LINE 17 COLUMN 35 PIC X(5) TO ZIP
            AUTO REQUIRED.
     02   LINE 20 COLUMN 5 REVERSE-VIDEO VALUE "Balance".
     02   LINE 21 COLUMN 5 PIC $$$$,$$9.99 TO BALANCE
            AUTO REQUIRED.
     02   LINE 20 COLUMN 21 REVERSE-VIDEO VALUE "Credit Limit".
     02   LINE 21 COLUMN 21 PIC $$$$,$$9.99 TO CREDIT-LIMIT
            AUTO REQUIRED.
```

*Figure 5.3* A pathological screen description. A program containing this screen description appears to compile and link properly, but the computer hangs up when the executable program is run. If REQUIRED is deleted from the sixth line, the program will run properly.

not be be changed, the user must pass over it manually by pressing the Esc key. The program will only modify existing records; it will not add new records or delete existing ones. In Chapter 7 we will look at a more elaborate file-update program that updates only selected records, adds new records, and deletes existing records.

This program does not change the file to be updated but instead creates a new file containing the updated information. The unchanged original file can be retained as a permanent record. What's more, if something goes wrong during the update process, the original file is still available so that another attempt at updating it can be made. In Figure 5.4, CUSTOMER-FILE-IN is the file to be updated, and CUSTOMER-FILE-OUT is the new file to which the updated records will be written. The DOS file names for these two files are stored in DOS-FILE-NAME-IN and DOS-FILE-NAME-OUT.

The record currently being updated is stored in CUSTOMER-RECORD in the Working-Storage Section. The records associated with the two files—CUSTOMER-RECORD-IN and CUSTOMER-RECORD-OUT—are used for reading and writing

```
IDENTIFICATION DIVISION.
PROGRAM-ID. UPDATE-CUSTOMER-FILE.

*    Update records in disk file.

ENVIRONMENT DIVISION.
INPUT-OUTPUT SECTION.
FILE-CONTROL.
     SELECT CUSTOMER-FILE-IN ASSIGN TO DISK.
     SELECT CUSTOMER-FILE-OUT ASSIGN TO DISK.

DATA DIVISION.
FILE SECTION.
FD   CUSTOMER-FILE-IN
     LABEL RECORDS STANDARD
     VALUE OF FILE-ID IS DOS-FILE-NAME-IN.
01   CUSTOMER-RECORD-IN  PIC X(135).

FD   CUSTOMER-FILE-OUT
     LABEL RECORDS STANDARD
     VALUE OF FILE-ID IS DOS-FILE-NAME-OUT.
01   CUSTOMER-RECORD-OUT PIC X(135).

WORKING-STORAGE SECTION.
01   CUSTOMER-RECORD.
     02   ACCOUNT-NUMBER   PIC X(6).
     02   LAST-NAME        PIC X(30).
     02   FIRST-NAME       PIC X(20).
     02   MIDDLE-INITIAL   PIC X.
     02   STREET-ADDRESS   PIC X(40).
     02   CITY             PIC X(15).
     02   STATE            PIC XX.
     02   ZIP              PIC X(5).
     02   BALANCE          PIC 9(6)V99.
     02   CREDIT-LIMIT     PIC 9(6)V99.

01   DOS-FILE-NAME-IN     PIC X(15).
01   DOS-FILE-NAME-OUT    PIC X(15).
01   END-OF-INPUT-FLAG    PIC X.
     88   FINISHED         VALUE "Y".
```

*Figure 5.4*  This program updates records in a disk file; an interactive screen displays existing records and allows the user to make corrections.

customer records but not for updating them. Thus these two records are not divided into fields but are defined as elementary items whose length (135 characters) is the same as that of CUSTOMER-RECORD. To read a record, we use a READ statement with the INTO option:

```
READ CUSTOMER-FILE-IN
     INTO CUSTOMER-RECORD
     AT END MOVE "Y" TO END-OF-INPUT-FLAG.
```

which reads a record from CUSTOMER-FILE into CUSTOMER-RECORD-IN, then moves the contents of CUSTOMER-RECORD-IN to CUSTOMER-RECORD. To write a record, we use a WRITE statement with the FROM option:

```
SCREEN SECTION.
01  CUSTOMER-SCREEN.
    02  BLANK SCREEN.
    02  LINE 4 COLUMN 5 REVERSE-VIDEO VALUE "Account Number".
    02  LINE 5 COLUMN 5 PIC XBXXBXXX USING ACCOUNT-NUMBER
            AUTO.
    02  LINE 8 COLUMN 5 REVERSE-VIDEO VALUE "Last Name".
    02  LINE 9 COLUMN 5 PIC X(30) USING LAST-NAME
            AUTO.
    02  LINE 8 COLUMN 40 REVERSE-VIDEO VALUE "First Name".
    02  LINE 9 COLUMN 40 PIC X(20) USING FIRST-NAME
            AUTO.
    02  LINE 8 COLUMN 65 REVERSE-VIDEO VALUE "Initial".
    02  LINE 9 COLUMN 65 PIC X USING MIDDLE-INITIAL
            AUTO.
    02  LINE 12 COLUMN 5 REVERSE-VIDEO VALUE "Street Address".
    02  LINE 13 COLUMN 5 PIC X(40) USING STREET-ADDRESS
            AUTO.
    02  LINE 16 COLUMN 5 REVERSE-VIDEO VALUE "City".
    02  LINE 17 COLUMN 5 PIC X(15) USING CITY
            AUTO.
    02  LINE 16 COLUMN 25 REVERSE-VIDEO VALUE "State".
    02  LINE 17 COLUMN 25 PIC XX USING STATE
            AUTO.
    02  LINE 16 COLUMN 35 REVERSE-VIDEO VALUE "ZIP".
    02  LINE 17 COLUMN 35 PIC X(5) USING ZIP
            AUTO.
    02  LINE 20 COLUMN 5 REVERSE-VIDEO VALUE "Balance".
    02  LINE 21 COLUMN 5 PIC $$$$,$$9.99 USING BALANCE
            AUTO.
    02  LINE 20 COLUMN 21 REVERSE-VIDEO VALUE "Credit Limit".
    02  LINE 21 COLUMN 21 PIC $$$$,$$9.99 USING CREDIT-LIMIT
            AUTO.

PROCEDURE DIVISION.
UPDATE-FILE.
    DISPLAY (1, 1) ERASE (5, 1) "Name of file to be updated? ".
    ACCEPT (, ) DOS-FILE-NAME-IN WITH PROMPT.
    DISPLAY (7, 1) "Name of updated file? ".
    ACCEPT (, ) DOS-FILE-NAME-OUT WITH PROMPT.
    OPEN INPUT CUSTOMER-FILE-IN
        OUTPUT CUSTOMER-FILE-OUT.
    MOVE "N" TO END-OF-INPUT-FLAG.
    READ CUSTOMER-FILE-IN
        INTO CUSTOMER-RECORD
        AT END MOVE "Y" TO END-OF-INPUT-FLAG.
    PERFORM UPDATE-RECORD
        UNTIL FINISHED.
    CLOSE CUSTOMER-FILE-IN
        CUSTOMER-FILE-OUT.
    STOP RUN.

UPDATE-RECORD.
    DISPLAY CUSTOMER-SCREEN.
    ACCEPT CUSTOMER-SCREEN.
    WRITE CUSTOMER-RECORD-OUT
        FROM CUSTOMER-RECORD.
    READ CUSTOMER-FILE-IN
        INTO CUSTOMER-RECORD
        AT END MOVE "Y" TO END-OF-INPUT-FLAG.
```

*Figure 5.4 (continued)*

```
WRITE CUSTOMER-RECORD-OUT
    FROM CUSTOMER-RECORD.
```

which moves the contents of CUSTOMER-RECORD to CUSTOMER-RECORD-OUT, then writes the contents of CUSTOMER-RECORD-OUT to CUSTOMER-FILE-OUT.

The Screen Section defines CUSTOMER-SCREEN, the screen to be used for updating customer records. The screen description for CUSTOMER-SCREEN is similar to the corresponding one in Figure 5.1 with two exceptions. First, each customer-record field is specified with USING so that the current contents of the field will be displayed before a new value is accepted. Second, all REQUIRED and FULL options have been omitted, giving the user complete freedom not to change any field that does not need changing. If a data input field is not changed by the user, the corresponding field of CUSTOMER-RECORD retains its original value, which was read from the file being updated.

The Procedure Division is similar to that of Figure 5.1. The main difference is that processing is terminated not at the user's request but rather when all the records in CUSTOMER-FILE-IN have been read and processed. The Esc key, which in Figure 5.1 was used to terminate processing, is not given any special treatment—the ACCEPT statement does not contain an ON ESCAPE option nor is an ACCEPT FROM ESCAPE KEY statement used. However, we can still use the Esc key to terminate the ACCEPT statement at any time. Thus if none or only some of the fields of a record are to be changed, we can terminate the ACCEPT statement with Esc instead of having to move the cursor to each field with Enter or Tab. Regardless of how an ACCEPT statement is terminated, the contents of CUSTOMER-RECORD after the ACCEPT statement terminates is considered to be the updated record and is written to CUSTOMER-FILE-OUT.

## EXERCISES

1. Rewrite the screen description for the program in Figure 5.1 so that the labels (such as Account Number) appear *below* the corresponding data input fields instead of above them.
2. Rewrite the screen descriptions for the program in Figure 5.1 so that the program displays the following screen:

```
  Account Number:  . . . . . .
      Last Name:  . . . . . . . . . . . . . . . . . . . . . . . . . . .
     First Name:  . . . . . . . . . . . . . . . . . . . .
        Initial:  .
 Street Address:  . . . . . . . . . . . . . . . . . . . . . . . . . . . . . . . . . . . . . . . .
           City:  . . . . . . . . . . . . . . . .
          State:  . .
            ZIP:  . . . . .
        Balance:  . . . . . . . . . .
   Credit Limit:  . . . . . . . . . .
```

**3.** Write a program to create the monthly sales file described in Chapter 3. The program should use a screen description and format 4 ACCEPT and DISPLAY statements.

**4.** Write a program to update the monthly sales file described in Chapter 3. Assume that only the Unit Price and Number Sold fields are to be updated. All fields of the records will be displayed, but new values will be accepted only for Unit Price and Number Sold. Before writing the updated record, the program will compute an updated value for Sales Income based on the values entered for Unit Price and Number Sold.

**5.** Rewrite the program in Figure 5.4 to use multiple DISPLAY statements and format 3 ACCEPT statements instead of a screen description. Which version of the program is the simplest? For which version is it easiest to determine from reading the program how the screen will be formatted?

# 6

## Table Handling

Many programs must have at hand certain facts and figures in order to carry out their calculations. For example, we might give a program the quantity ordered for a certain item of merchandise and wish the program to calculate the total cost of the order. To do this calculation, the program needs to know the unit price—the price per item—which most likely will depend on the particular item in question as well as on the quantity ordered. There are no mathematical principles that would allow the program to calculate the unit price—the required information must be supplied either by the programmer or by the user.

Computer programs use *tables* to store in an orderly way the information needed for their calculations. Given a particular problem to solve, the program—like a person solving the same problem—must look up the needed data in the available tables. In this chapter, we will see how to incorporate tables in COBOL programs and how to program the computer to look up the data it needs. In passing, we will also look at two other aspects of COBOL: *data representation*—how data is stored inside the computer—and *nested* IF *statements*—IF statements that contain other IF statements, which can in turn contain still other IF statements, and so on.

## TABLES AND SUBSCRIPTS

Suppose we have five items of merchandise, numbered 1 through 5, which are priced as follows:

| Item | Price |
|:----:|:-----:|
| 1 | $  7.95 |
| 2 | 27.50 |
| 3 | 21.25 |
| 4 | 149.95 |
| 5 | 3.49 |

We want to store this information in a COBOL program in such a way that, given the number of an item, the program can determine its price and hence solve such problems as calculating the cost of a given number of a particular item.

Our first thought might be to store the price data in a Working-Storage record as follows:

```
01   PRICE-TABLE,
     02   PRICE-1 PIC 999V99 VALUE 7,95,
     02   PRICE-2 PIC 999V99 VALUE 27,50,
     02   PRICE-3 PIC 999V99 VALUE 21,25,
     02   PRICE-4 PIC 999V99 VALUE 149,95,
     02   PRICE-5 PIC 999V99 VALUE 3,49,
```

As a result of this record description, the value of PRICE-1 is the price of item 1, the value of PRICE-2 is the value of item 2, and so on.

Unfortunately, there is a serious problem with this approach. If we write PRICE-1, say, in a certain program statement, that statement will always refer to the price of item 1. But when we write the program, we do not want to commit ourselves to a particular item. We do not want a program that will do calculations only for item 1—we want our program to do calculations for any of the five items that the user might designate. With only data names like PRICE-1, PRICE-2, and so on at our disposal, our only recourse would be to use IF statements to select statements referring to PRICE-1, statements referring to PRICE-2, and so on depending on which item is designated by the user. This would be very cumbersome.

Fortunately, COBOL provides us with a method of defining tables that avoids this problem. We replace the record description for PRICE-TABLE by the following:

```
01   PRICE-TABLE,
     02   PRICE PIC 999V99 OCCURS 5 TIMES,
```

Instead of writing out five level 02 entries, one for each price, we write one level 02 entry and use the OCCURS *clause:*

```
OCCURS 5 TIMES
```

to specify that the entry we wrote is to be repeated five times. The definition of PRICE-TABLE is equivalent to

```
01   PRICE-TABLE.
     02   PRICE PIC 999V99.
     02   PRICE PIC 999V99.
     02   PRICE PIC 999V99.
     02   PRICE PIC 999V99.
     02   PRICE PIC 999V99.
```

The latter, however, is not legal COBOL—we are not allowed to write the entry for PRICE five times. Instead, we must write the entry for PRICE only once and use an OCCURS clause to state how many times the entry is to be repeated.

The data name PRICE refers to each of the five entries in PRICE-TABLE. To retrieve the price of a particular item, we need to designate a particular entry. This is done with a *subscript*. The subscript is written in parentheses following the data name PRICE. Thus, PRICE ( 1 ) refers to the first entry in the table; PRICE ( 2 ) refers to the second entry; PRICE ( 3 ) refers to the third entry; and so on. Note that there is a space between the data name and the left parenthesis preceding the subscript.

PRICE ( 1 ), PRICE ( 2 ), PRICE ( 3 ), and so on are *subscripted data names*. Along with qualifed data names, subscripted data names are examples of *identifiers*. Each consists of a data name—PRICE—together with the additional information—the subscript—needed to designate a unique memory area. If the values of the five entries in this version of PRICE-TABLE are the same as for the earlier version, the value of PRICE ( 1 ) is (in conventional notation) 7.95, the value of PRICE ( 2 ) is 27.50, the value of PRICE ( 3 ) is 21.25, and so on.

If we always used constants such as 1, 2, 3, and so on for subscripts, we would be no better off than we were when using PRICE-1, PRICE-2, PRICE-3, and so on. The table entries designated by PRICE ( 1 ), PRICE ( 2 ), PRICE ( 3 ), and so on are fixed when the program is written and cannot be changed while the program is executing. The enormous advantage of subscripting lies in that we can use a data name for a subscript. The value of the subscript—and hence the table entry referred to by the subscripted data name—can change as the program is executed. A single subscripted data name can refer to many different table entries (but only one at a time) as required by the needs of the program.

Suppose that ITEM is defined in the Working-Storage Section by

```
01   ITEM PIC 9.
```

Then the subscripted data name

```
PRICE (ITEM)
```

refers to the entry in PRICE-TABLE determined by the current value of ITEM. For example, if the statements

```
MOVE 1 TO ITEM.
DISPLAY PRICE (ITEM).
```

are executed, then the first entry in PRICE-TABLE is displayed. (The computer would display 00795). Likewise, the statements

```
MOVE 3 TO ITEM.
DISPLAY PRICE (ITEM).
```

display the third entry in PRICE-TABLE, and

```
MOVE 5 TO ITEM.
DISPLAY PRICE (ITEM).
```

display the fifth entry. The entry referred to by

```
PRICE (ITEM)
```

is determined not when the program is written but by the current value of ITEM when a statement containing PRICE (ITEM) is executed.

To see how this property of subscripts can be put to use, consider a program for calculating the cost of a particular quantity of a given item. The program might contain the following statements:

```
DISPLAY (5, 1) "Item number? ".
ACCEPT (, ) ITEM.
DISPLAY (7, 1) "Quantity ordered? ".
ACCEPT (, ) QUANTITY-ORDERED.
MULTIPLY PRICE (ITEM) BY QUANTITY-ORDERED
    GIVING EXTENDED-PRICE.
DISPLAY (9, 1) "Cost of order: ", EXTENDED-PRICE.
```

We assume that QUANTITY-ORDERED and EXTENDED-PRICE are defined in the Working-Storage Section with appropriate pictures.

The important point is that the value of ITEM accepted from the user determines which entry of PRICE-TABLE is referred to by the MULTIPLY statement. In a practical program, these statements would most likely be repeated (via a PERFORM statement) many times, once for each total-cost calculation that the user wanted to do. On each execution, the table entry referred to by the MULTIPLY statement would depend on the value entered for ITEM by the user.

Not surprisingly, it is an error to attempt to refer to a nonexistent table entry. It would be an error for the user to enter 6 for ITEM, since PRICE-TABLE has only five entries. To prevent an invalid subscript from being used, we could rewrite the statements as follows:

```
DISPLAY (5, 1) "Item number? ".
ACCEPT (, ) ITEM.
IF ITEM < 1 OR > 5
    DISPLAY (7, 1) "Invalid item number"
ELSE
    DISPLAY (7, 1) "Quantity ordered? "
    ACCEPT (, ) QUANTITY-ORDERED
    MULTIPLY PRICE (ITEM) BY QUANTITY-ORDERED
        GIVING EXTENDED-PRICE
    DISPLAY (9, 1) "Cost of order: ", EXTENDED-PRICE.
```

## STORING DATA IN A TABLE

Basically, there are two methods of providing the data values for a table: (1) We can read the table from a disk file, and (2) we can write the required values into the program. For the moment, we will focus on the second method.

In our original version of PRICE-TABLE we specified the values of the entries by using a VALUE clause for PRICE-1, another VALUE clause for PRICE-2, and so on. This method won't work, however, when the entries are defined with an OCCURS clause. Since the entries are not listed separately, we cannot provide a VALUE clause for each entry.

Instead, we use a REDEFINES clause, which causes two records to occupy the same memory area. Consider the following record descriptions:

```
01   PRICE-DATA.
     02   FILLER PIC 999V99 VALUE 7.95.
     02   FILLER PIC 999V99 VALUE 27.50.
     02   FILLER PIC 999V99 VALUE 21.25.
     02   FILLER PIC 999V99 VALUE 149.95.
     02   FILLER PIC 999V99 VALUE 3.49.

01   PRICE-TABLE REDEFINES PRICE-DATA.
     02   PRICE PIC 999V99 OCCURS 5 TIMES.
```

PRICE-DATA is a record with five fields, each with picture 999V99. Each field is defined by a FILLER item and given a value with a VALUE clause. PRICE-TABLE is also a record with five fields, each with picture 999V99, the five fields being defined with an OCCURS clause. The REDEFINES clause states that PRICE-TABLE occupies the same memory area as PRICE-DATA. Consequently, there is a one-to-one correspondence between the entries in PRICE-TABLE and the FILLER items in PRICE-DATA. Specifically, the values of the entries in PRICE-TABLE are given by the FILLER items in PRICE-DATA. Thus, the value of PRICE (1) is 7.95, the value of PRICE (2) is 27.50, and so on.

The general form of the REDEFINES clause is

*data-name-1* REDEFINES *data-name-2*

The record description for *data-name-1* must follow the record description for *data-name-2*. What's more, the record referred to by *data-name-1* cannot contain a VALUE clause, and the record referred to by *data-name-2* cannot contain an OCCURS clause. In terms of assigning values to tables, these restrictions mean that the record giving the data values always precedes the record that defines the table with an OCCURS clause. The second of these two records—the one that defines the table with an OCCURS clause—is the one that contains the REDEFINES clause. The items referred to by *data-name-1* and *data-name-2* must be the same size.

We can write PRICE-DATA more compactly at the expense of making it far less readable. To begin with, we note that the FILLER items in PRICE-DATA need not be numeric. They can be alphanumeric as long as their values correspond, character by character, with the values that we wish to store in PRICE-TABLE. Thus, we could write PRICE-DATA as

```
01   PRICE-DATA.
     02   FILLER PIC X(5) VALUE "00795".
     02   FILLER PIC X(5) VALUE "02750".
     02   FILLER PIC X(5) VALUE "02125".
     02   FILLER PIC X(5) VALUE "14995".
     02   FILLER PIC X(5) VALUE "00349".
```

The five characters 00795 provide the value for PRICE (1), the five characters 02750 provide the value for PRICE (2), and so on. Note that leading zeros must be used, since each FILLER item must consist of exactly five characters so as to correspond to the picture 999V99.

So far we haven't made PRICE-DATA any smaller, but we can do so by combining all the FILLER items into a single 25-character alphanumeric item:

```
01   PRICE-DATA PIC X(25) VALUE "0079502750021251499500349".
```

The first five characters of PRICE-DATA provide the value of PRICE (1), the second five characters provide the value of PRICE (2), and so on. Of course, we have traded compactness for readability—it's almost impossible for a human reader to look at PRICE-DATA and see at a glance the value of each entry in PRICE-TABLE. Using the compact form, we define PRICE-TABLE and assign it values as follows:

```
01   PRICE-DATA PIC X(25) VALUE "0079502750021251499500349".

01   PRICE-TABLE REDEFINES PRICE-DATA.
     02   PRICE PIC 999V99 OCCURS 5 TIMES.
```

## DATA REPRESENTATION

We have reached the point in our study of COBOL where we need to look briefly at how data is represented inside the computer. In the preceding section, for example, we made use of a one-to-one correspondence between the characters of alphanumeric and numeric values—a correspondence that exists for only one of the several possible methods of representing numeric values. Also, one of the representations for numeric values is particularly suitable for subscripts. Finally, later in the chapter we will take up *indexes,* a data representation specifically designed for accessing data in tables.

All data stored in a computer is represented by combinations of the symbols 0 and 1, which are known as *binary digits* or *bits*. The binary digits constitute the computer's *alphabet*—the computer represents information as strings of 0s and 1s just as we represent information in English as strings of letters, digits, and punctuation marks. There are many ways in which a given alphabet can be used to represent a particular type of information. Using the ABCs, for example, we might record our information in English, French, German, or Spanish. In COBOL, the various ways of representing data by combinations of bits are known as *usages*.

### DISPLAY **Usage**

In DISPLAY usage, each data item is stored as a sequence of characters. The characters themselves are represented according to the American Standard Code for Information

Interchange (ASCII) given in appendix G of the COBOL reference manual and Appendix B of this book. The code for each character occupies eight bits. A memory location that holds eight bits is called a *byte,* so each character occupies one byte of memory. (The appendices give the ASCII codes as numerical values rather than bit patterns, since COBOL programmers never actually have to deal with the bit patterns.)

In COBOL, the default usage is DISPLAY. That is, if we do not specify a particular usage, DISPLAY is assumed. Therefore, in all the programs we have written so far, the data has been stored with DISPLAY usage. DISPLAY is the only usage available for alphanumeric data. For numeric data, however, IBM COBOL provides two other usages that allow arithmetic to be carried out with greater efficiency.

The ASCII code is used for communicating with input and output devices such as the keyboard, the display, and the printer. Data sent to or received from these devices has DISPLAY usage. The ACCEPT and DISPLAY statements will convert between DISPLAY and other usages, so a receiving field for an ACCEPT statement or a source field for a DISPLAY statement can have any usage. When input and output devices are treated as files, however, no conversion is performed. Input data has DISPLAY usage and output data must have DISPLAY usage.

Data stored in line-sequential files must have DISPLAY usage. A line-sequential file is assumed to consist of a sequence of ASCII characters, including the control characters that mark the end of a record and the end of the file. If data with some of other usage were stored in a line-sequential file, some of the codes representing the data might be the same as the end-of-record and end-of-file control characters, and the file would not be processed properly. With a regular-sequential file, however, any usage may be employed. No assumption is made about the codes stored in a regular-sequential file.

When an alphanumeric item is used to provide data for a numeric table, as in

```
01   PRICE-DATA PIC X(25) VALUE "0079502750021251499500349".

01   PRICE-TABLE REDEFINES PRICE-DATA.
     02   PRICE PIC 999V99 OCCURS 5 TIMES.
```

the table entries must have DISPLAY usage. We are assuming a one-to-one correspondence between the characters in the alphanumeric item and those making up the table entries. This correspondence will exist only if each table entry is represented by a sequence of ASCII characters—that is, if it has DISPLAY usage.

## COMP-3 Usage

The ASCII code uses eight bits for each character. The eight bits are needed if we want to be able to store all 256 ASCII characters. If we only need to store the digits 0 through 9, however, we need only four bits. COMPUTATIONAL-3 (invariably abbreviated to COMP-3) usage represents each digit of a numeric value by a group of four bits. COMP-3 usage saves memory by storing numeric values two digits to a byte instead of one digit to a byte as with DISPLAY usage. What's more, the four-bit digit codes can be manipulated more rapidly than the corresponding ASCII codes, so calculations are speeded us as well. COMP-3 is the recommended usage when large amounts of numerical data must be stored or extensive calculations must be carried out.

We associate a usage with a data name by means of a USAGE clause. For example,

```
01    HOURLY-RATE PIC 99V99 USAGE COMP-3.
```

specifies that the value of HOURLY-RATE will be stored with COMP-3 usage. Numeric data items moved to HOURLY-RATE will be converted to COMP-3 usage; if the value of HOURLY-RATE is moved to another data item, the usage will be converted as needed. (Conversions from one usage to another are time-consuming and should be avoided whenever possible; for example, it's best if all the values participating in a particular calculation have the same usage.) The word USAGE can be omitted, so we can also describe HOURLY-RATE by

```
01    HOURLY-RATE PIC 99V99 COMP-3.
```

Both DISPLAY and COMP-3 represent numeric values in *decimal notation,* that is, using the digits 0 through 9, although the digits are coded differently in the two usages. DISPLAY usage for numeric values is sometimes referred to as *external decimal,* since it is a form of decimal notation suitable for communicating with external devices such as printers. COMP-3 is sometimes referred to as *internal decimal,* since it is the form of decimal notation best suited for storing numeric values in computer memory.

## COMP and COMP-0

Instead of using decimal notation, in which numbers are represented by the digits 0 through 9, we can use *binary notation,* which uses only the two digits 0 and 1. Since 0 and 1 are the two symbols that can be stored directly in a computer's memory, it's clear that binary notation is better suited for use with computers than decimal notation. Numbers stored in binary notation can, in fact, be stored more compactly and manipulated more rapidly than is possible with either DISPLAY or COMP-3 usage. On the other hand, converting values between DISPLAY usage and binary notation is more time-consuming than converting between DISPLAY and COMP-3 usages.

For most computer systems, COMPUTATIONAL (abbreviated COMP) usage stores numeric values in binary notation. IBM COBOL provides COMP usage so as to be compatible with other versions of COBOL. In IBM COBOL, however, COMP is the same as DISPLAY and so offers no advantages for data storage or numerical computations. IBM COBOL programmers do not normally employ COMP usage.

IBM COBOL does, however, provide a limited form of binary notation with COMPUTATIONAL-0 (abbreviated COMP-0) usage. COMP-0 items are stored as 16-bit (two-byte) binary numbers. Values of COMP-0 items must be integers (whole numbers) in the range −32,767 through 32,767.

The main reason for specifying COMP-0 is speed. Arithmetic on COMP-0 items can be carried out at high speed directly by the computer hardware, rather than by routines in the COBOL program library. Because of the limited range of values of COMP-0 items, and the requirement that the values be integers, COMP-0 is usually not suitable for business data such as amounts of money. COMP-0 *is* suitable for many of the data items, such as counters, that are used to control the execution of a program.

COMP-0 *is particularly suitable for subscripts.* Subscripts must lie in the range 1 through 1023,* well within the range allowed for COMP-0 values. What's more, table processing often requires extensive manipulation of subscripts, manipulations that can be speeded up enormously by specifying COMP-0 for the subscripts.

### INDEX **Usage**

*Indexes,* which are alternatives to subscripts, are described later in this chapter. We can define an *index data item*—a memory area for storing an index value—by specifying usage INDEX:

        01   CURRENT-TABLE-ENTRY USAGE INDEX.

or just

        01   CURRENT-TABLE-ENTRY INDEX.

Note that an index data item has no picture.

## TABLE LOOKUP

In our previous example of a price table, we assumed that the number used to designate each item was the same as the position of the price of that item in the price table. That is, the price of item 1 was the first price in the price table and was referred to with a subscript value of 1; the price of item 2 was the second price in the price table and was referred to with a subscript value of 2; and so on.

In reality, things seldom work out so simply. Items are designated by complex catalog numbers or stock numbers in which each digit or group of digits has a special meaning. For example, item 625135 might be sold by department 6, obtained from supplier 25, and be the 135th item added to department 6's inventory. Such item numbers are beyond the control of the programmer and cannot be made to correspond to table subscripts.

From the programmer's point of view, both item numbers and item prices are arbitrary data. Both, therefore, must be stored in a price table, which we can picture as a two-column table, with one column containing item numbers and the other containing the corresponding prices:

| Item Number | Item Price |
|---|---|
| 125731 | $   7.95 |
| 243694 | 27.50 |
| 432718 | 21.25 |
| 679132 | 149.95 |
| 731235 | 3.49 |

---

*An OCCURS clause can specify at most 1023 repetitions of a table entry.

To find the price of item 432718, for example, a program must look up 432718 in the first column of the table, then find the corresponding price (21.25) in the second column. If the program is asked for the price of item 720961, it must report that no such item number appears in the table.

Figure 6.1 shows a program for looking up prices in the table just given. Our first job in writing the program is to define the table in COBOL. Each line of the table is an ITEM-ENTRY. The table has five lines, so ITEM-ENTRY occurs five times. Each line contains two values, an item number and an item price, so each ITEM-ENTRY has two fields, ITEM-NUMBER and ITEM-PRICE. Thus we define our price table (which we follow customary usage and call a *price list*) as follows:

```
01   PRICE-LIST REDEFINES PRICE-DATA.
     02   ITEM-ENTRY OCCURS 5 TIMES.
          03   ITEM-NUMBER PIC X(6).
          03   ITEM-PRICE PIC 999V99.
```

Since ITEM-ENTRY occurs five times, we must use a subscript to designate a particular occurrence. Thus ITEM-ENTRY (1) refers to the first occurrence of ITEM-ENTRY (the first line of the table); ITEM-ENTRY (2) refers to the second occurrence of ITEM-ENTRY (the second line of the table); and so on.

Each occurrence of ITEM-ENTRY has ITEM-NUMBER and ITEM-PRICE fields; therefore, ITEM-NUMBER and ITEM-PRICE also occur five times, and for each we must use a subscript to designate a particular occurrence. Thus, ITEM-NUMBER (1), whose value is 125731, is the ITEM-NUMBER field of ITEM-ENTRY (1); ITEM-PRICE (3), whose value (in conventional notation) is 21.25, is the ITEM-PRICE field of ITEM-ENTRY (3); and so on.

PRICE-DATA provides the data for PRICE-LIST. Since ITEM-NUMBER and ITEM-PRICE both have DISPLAY usage, their values can be defined by alphanumeric items. PRICE-DATA contains an alphanumeric filler item for each line of the table. Thus

```
02   FILLER PIC X(11) VALUE "12573100795".
```

provides the data for the first line of the table, which contains an item number of 125731 and a price of 7.95. As usual, all leading zeros must be present in the alphanumeric items.

For a subscript we will use the data name ENTRY-NUMBER, which is defined in the Working-Storage Section with picture 9 and usage COMP-0. To check when our search has reached the end of the table, we will compare ENTRY-NUMBER with NUMBER-OF-ENTRIES, which we give the value 5. As with arithmetical operations, comparisons are most efficient when the values being compared have the same picture and usage; hence, NUMBER-OF-ENTRIES is also given a picture of 9 and a usage of COMP-0.

The simplest way to look up an item number in a price list is to place our finger at the beginning of the item-number column, then run our finger down the column until we find the item number we are looking for. When this occurs, we use our finger to keep our place in the table while we write down the corresponding item price. If our finger runs off the end of the table, then the item number we were looking for is not present in the table.

```
IDENTIFICATION DIVISION.
PROGRAM-ID.  PRICES-1.

*    Look up price corresponding to given item number

ENVIRONMENT DIVISION.

DATA DIVISION.
WORKING-STORAGE SECTION.
01   PRICE-DATA.
     02  FILLER          PIC X(11) VALUE "12573100795".
     02  FILLER          PIC X(11) VALUE "24369402750".
     02  FILLER          PIC X(11) VALUE "43271802125".
     02  FILLER          PIC X(11) VALUE "67913214995".
     02  FILLER          PIC X(11) VALUE "73123500349".

01   PRICE-LIST REDEFINES PRICE-DATA.
     02  ITEM-ENTRY OCCURS 5 TIMES.
         03   ITEM-NUMBER PIC X(6).
         03   ITEM-PRICE  PIC 999V99.

01   ENTRY-NUMBER        PIC 9 COMP-0.
01   NUMBER-OF-ENTRIES   PIC 9 COMP-0 VALUE 5.
01   FOUND               PIC X.
01   TERMINATOR-KEY      PIC 99.
01   TARGET-ITEM-NUMBER  PIC X(6).
01   PRICE-OUT           PIC $$$9.99.
01   DUMMY               PIC X.

PROCEDURE DIVISION.
FIND-PRICES.
     MOVE ZERO TO TERMINATOR-KEY.
     PERFORM FIND-ONE-PRICE
         UNTIL TERMINATOR-KEY NOT = 0.
     STOP RUN.

FIND-ONE-PRICE.
     DISPLAY (1, 1) ERASE (5, 1) "Item number? ".
     ACCEPT (, )  TARGET-ITEM-NUMBER WITH PROMPT.
     PERFORM TABLE-LOOKUP.
     IF FOUND = "Y"
         MOVE ITEM-PRICE (ENTRY-NUMBER) TO PRICE-OUT
         DISPLAY (7, 1) "Item price: " PRICE-OUT
     ELSE
         DISPLAY (7, 1) "Item not found".
     DISPLAY (9, 1)
         "Press Enter to continue, Esc to terminate ".
     ACCEPT (, ) DUMMY.
     ACCEPT TERMINATOR-KEY FROM ESCAPE KEY.

TABLE-LOOKUP.
     MOVE "N" TO FOUND.
     PERFORM CHECK-ENTRY
         VARYING ENTRY-NUMBER FROM 1 BY 1
         UNTIL FOUND = "Y" OR ENTRY-NUMBER > NUMBER-OF-ENTRIES.
     SUBTRACT 1 FROM ENTRY-NUMBER.

CHECK-ENTRY.
     IF TARGET-ITEM-NUMBER = ITEM-NUMBER (ENTRY-NUMBER)
         MOVE "Y" TO FOUND.
```

*Figure 6.1*   This program looks up the prices of items in a price list. This version of the program uses subscripts, and a PERFORM VARYING statement is used for table lookup.

In our COBOL program, the subscript ENTRY-NUMBER plays the role of our finger. Starting our finger at the top of the table means giving ENTRY-NUMBER the initial value 1. As we move our finger down the item-number column, ENTRY-NUMBER takes on the values 2, 3, and so on. For each value of ENTRY-NUMBER, we must compare the value ITEM-NUMBER (ENTRY-NUMBER) with the item number we are trying to find. If the two values are the same, we have found the entry we are looking for and can stop the search. The value of ITEM-PRICE (ENTRY-NUMBER) is the price of the item whose item number we looked up. On the other hand, if at any time during the search the value of ENTRY-NUMBER exceeds that of NUMBER-OF-ENTRIES, we have run off the end of the table. If this occurs, we know that the item number we are looking up is not in the table.

Suppose that the value of TARGET-ITEM-NUMBER is the item number we are looking up. For each value of ENTRY-NUMBER, we must check to see if the value of TARGET-ITEM-NUMBER is equal to that of ITEM-NUMBER (ENTRY-NUMBER)—that is, if the condition

```
TARGET-ITEM-NUMBER = ITEM-NUMBER (ENTRY-NUMBER)
```

holds true. We use a flag FOUND to record whether or not the item we are looking for has been found. Before the search begins, the value of FOUND is set to "N". When an item number is found in the table that is equal to the item number we are looking for, the value of FOUND is set to "Y". The paragraph CHECK-ENTRY checks the table entry designated by ENTRY-NUMBER to see if it is the one we are looking for. Specifically, CHECK-ENTRY compares the value of TARGET-ITEM-NUMBER with that of ITEM-NUMBER (ENTRY-NUMBER) and sets FOUND to "Y" if the two are equal:

```
CHECK-ENTRY,
    IF TARGET-ITEM-NUMBER = ITEM-NUMBER (ENTRY-NUMBER)
        MOVE "Y" TO FOUND,
```

The paragraph TABLE-LOOKUP begins by initializing the value of FOUND to "N":

```
MOVE "N" TO FOUND,
```

To step the value of ENTRY-NUMBER through the possible subscript values—to run our finger down the table—we use a special form of the PERFORM statement:

```
PERFORM CHECK-ENTRY
    VARYING ENTRY-NUMBER FROM 1 BY 1
    UNTIL FOUND = "Y" OR ENTRY-NUMBER > NUMBER-OF-ENTRIES,
```

The VARYING option works like this. When the PERFORM statement is executed, the value of ENTRY-NUMBER is set to 1 (because of the phrase FROM 1) and the paragraph CHECK-ENTRY is performed. After performing CHECK-ENTRY the first time, the PERFORM statement adds 1 to the value of ENTRY-NUMBER (because of the phrase BY 1). The next time CHECK-ENTRY is performed the value of ENTRY-NUMBER is 2. In general, CHECK-ENTRY is performed repeatedly with ENTRY-NUMBER having the value 1 the first time CHECK-ENTRY is performed, 2 the second time, 3 the third time, and so on.

The UNTIL part works just as it does with the PERFORM statements we have used previously—before each execution of CHECK-ENTRY the condition following UNTIL is tested. If the condition is false, CHECK-ENTRY is performed. If the condition is true, the repetitions terminate and the computer goes on to the statement following the PERFORM statement. There are two conditions under which we want to terminate the search—if the item number we are looking for has been found:

```
FOUND = "Y"
```

or if the search has run off the end of the table:

```
ENTRY-NUMBER > NUMBER-OF-ENTRIES
```

When the value ITEM-NUMBER (ENTRY-NUMBER) is found to be equal to the item number we are looking up, we want to retain the current value of ENTRY-NUMBER so we can use ITEM-PRICE (ENTRY-NUMBER) to refer to the corresponding price. (Remember ENTRY-NUMBER represents our finger and we want to leave our finger on the table entry that we found.) Annoyingly, the PERFORM statement works against us in this respect—after the desired value of ENTRY-NUMBER has been found, the VARYING option adds 1 to the value of ENTRY-NUMBER before the UNTIL option terminates the execution of the PERFORM statement.

Specifically, the following events take place. CHECK-ENTRY finds that the values of TARGET-ITEM-NUMBER and ITEM-NUMBER (ENTRY-NUMBER) are equal and sets the value of FOUND to "Y". The VARYING option of the PERFORM statement adds 1 to the value of ENTRY-NUMBER. Finally, the UNTIL option determines that the value of FOUND is "Y" and terminates the execution of the PERFORM statement. Because of the extra addition of 1 to ENTRY-NUMBER, we are left with a value of ENTRY-NUMBER that is one greater than the subscript of the table entry found by the search. Fortunately, the extra addition is easily reversed with a SUBTRACT statement:

```
SUBTRACT 1 FROM ENTRY-NUMBER.
```

The paragraph FIND-ONE-PRICE accepts a value for TARGET-ITEM-NUMBER and performs TABLE-LOOKUP to look up this item number in the price list. After TABLE-LOOKUP has been performed, the value of FOUND is "Y" if the value of TARGET-ITEM-NUMBER was found in the table and "N" if it was not. If the value of FOUND is "Y", the value of ENTRY-NUMBER is the subscript of the entry that was found. After performing TABLE-LOOKUP, then, FIND-ONE-PRICE checks the value of FOUND. If the value FOUND is "Y", the requested price—the value of ITEM-PRICE (ENTRY-NUMBER)—is edited and displayed for the user:

```
MOVE ITEM-PRICE (ENTRY-NUMBER) TO PRICE-OUT
DISPLAY (7, 1) "Item price: " PRICE-OUT
```

If the value of FOUND is "N", the user is informed that the sought-after item number was not found:

```
DISPLAY (7, 1) "Item not found".
```

At this point we want the program to pause while the user examines the item price or the item-not-found message. When ready, the user can press the En t e r key to continue looking up items or the E s c key to terminate the program:

```
DISPLAY (9, 1)
    "Press Enter to continue, Esc to terminate ",
ACCEPT (, ) DUMMY,
ACCEPT TERMINATOR-KEY FROM ESCAPE-KEY,
```

The first ACCEPT statement causes the program to wait until the user presses a terminator key. The second ACCEPT statement stores the code corresponding to the terminator key in TERMINATOR-KEY. The value of TERMINATOR-KEY is checked by the PERFORM statement in paragraph FIND-PRICES. If the value of TERMINATOR-KEY is 0 (the user pressed En t e r or T a b), the program continues. If the user pressed any other terminator key, such as E s c, the PERFORM statement and the program are terminated.

## INDEXING

The entries in a table are numbered beginning with 1 for the first entry. These numbers are called *occurrence numbers*. With subscripting, we always designate table entries by their occurrence numbers. The first entry in a table has an occurrence number of 1 and is designated by a subscript value of 1; the second entry has an occurrence number of 2 and is designated by a subscript value of 2; and so on.

Every location in the computer's memory has a unique *address;* the computer uses these addresses to locate specific memory areas, such as the one corresponding to a given table entry. When we use subscripting to refer to a table entry, the computer must convert the subscript value—the occurrence number of the desired entry—into the corresponding memory address. This conversion can be time-consuming enough to significantly slow down the operation of a program that does extensive table manipulation, such as repeatedly searching a large table.

To alleviate this problem, COBOL allows us to use *indexes* as an alternative to subscripts. Indexes are either memory addresses or closely related to memory addresses. When we refer to a table entry with an index, no conversion from occurrence number to memory address need take place.

A problem with using memory addresses is that methods for addressing memory vary greatly from one computer to another. If a COBOL program were allowed to depend on a particular scheme for addressing memory, it could only be used on one type of computer. To avoid this limitation, COBOL hides from the programmer all details of the internal representation of indexes. All we know—and all we need to know—is that an index is a value that somehow designates a particular table entry. COBOL converts between occurrence numbers and index values when required. In fact, it's often convenient to think of indexes as if they were occurrence numbers and forget that they are represented differently inside the computer.

Figure 6.2 shows a version of our table-lookup program that uses indexing. When we define a table, we must specify if indexing will be used:

```
IDENTIFICATION DIVISION.
PROGRAM-ID.  PRICES-2.

*     Price lookup using indexing.

ENVIRONMENT DIVISION.

DATA DIVISION.
WORKING-STORAGE SECTION.
01   PRICE-DATA.
     02   FILLER          PIC X(11) VALUE "12573100795".
     02   FILLER          PIC X(11) VALUE "24369402750".
     02   FILLER          PIC X(11) VALUE "43271802125".
     02   FILLER          PIC X(11) VALUE "67913214995".
     02   FILLER          PIC X(11) VALUE "73123500349".

01   PRICE-LIST REDEFINES PRICE-DATA.
     02   ITEM-ENTRY OCCURS 5 TIMES
                      INDEXED BY ENTRY-NUMBER.
          03   ITEM-NUMBER PIC X(6).
          03   ITEM-PRICE  PIC 999V99.

01   NUMBER-OF-ENTRIES   PIC 9 COMP-0 VALUE 5.
01   FOUND               PIC X.
01   TERMINATOR-KEY      PIC 99.
01   TARGET-ITEM-NUMBER  PIC X(6).
01   PRICE-OUT           PIC $$$9.99.
01   DUMMY               PIC X.

PROCEDURE DIVISION.
FIND-PRICES.
     MOVE ZERO TO TERMINATOR-KEY.
     PERFORM FIND-ONE-PRICE
          UNTIL TERMINATOR-KEY NOT = 0.
     STOP RUN.

FIND-ONE-PRICE.
     DISPLAY (1, 1) ERASE (5, 1) "Item number? ".
     ACCEPT (, )  TARGET-ITEM-NUMBER WITH PROMPT.
     PERFORM TABLE-LOOKUP.
     IF FOUND = "Y"
          MOVE ITEM-PRICE (ENTRY-NUMBER) TO PRICE-OUT
          DISPLAY (7, 1) "Item price: " PRICE-OUT
     ELSE
          DISPLAY (7, 1) "Item not found".
     DISPLAY (9, 1)
          "Press Enter to continue, Esc to terminate ".
     ACCEPT (, ) DUMMY.
     ACCEPT TERMINATOR-KEY FROM ESCAPE KEY.

TABLE-LOOKUP.
     MOVE "N" TO FOUND.
     PERFORM CHECK-ENTRY
          VARYING ENTRY-NUMBER FROM 1 BY 1
          UNTIL FOUND = "Y" OR ENTRY-NUMBER > NUMBER-OF-ENTRIES.
     SET ENTRY-NUMBER DOWN BY 1.

CHECK-ENTRY.
     IF TARGET-ITEM-NUMBER = ITEM-NUMBER (ENTRY-NUMBER)
          MOVE "Y" TO FOUND.
```

*Figure 6.2*   This version of the price-lookup program uses indexes instead of subscripts. Table lookup is still done with a PERFORM VARYING statement.

**153**

```
01   PRICE-LIST REDEFINES PRICE-DATA.
     02   ITEM-ENTRY OCCURS 5 TIMES
                      INDEXED BY ENTRY-NUMBER.
          03   ITEM-NUMBER PIC X(6).
          03   ITEM-PRICE  PIC 999V99.
```

The INDEXED BY phrase specifies that occurrences of ITEM-ENTRY can be designated by index values. (Since ITEM-NUMBER and ITEM-PRICE are fields of ITEM-ENTRY, the same index values can be used to designate particular item numbers and item prices.) ENTRY-NUMBER is defined as an *index name;* it refers to an index value just as a data name refers to a data value. ENTRY-NUMBER is completely defined by the INDEXED BY clause; no additional definition in the Working-Storage Section is required (or allowed).

As mentioned earlier, if we need additional memory areas in which to store indexes—to save index values for later use, for example—we can define index data items in the Working-Storage Section. In most cases, however, the index names defined in INDEXED BY clauses are sufficient and we do not have to define additional index data items.

Index names are used just like subscripts to designate particular table entries. For example,

```
ITEM-ENTRY (ENTRY-NUMBER)
```

refers to the item entry designated by the current value of ENTRY-NUMBER. More usefully,

```
ITEM-NUMBER (ENTRY-NUMBER)
```

and

```
ITEM-PRICE (ENTRY-NUMBER)
```

refer to the ITEM-NUMBER and ITEM-PRICE fields of the item entry designated by the value of ENTRY-NUMBER.

*Relative indexing* allows us to locate a table entry by its position relative to a table entry designated by an index value. For example,

```
ITEM-ENTRY (ENTRY-NUMBER + 1)
```

refers to the entry immediately following the one designated by the value of ENTRY-NUMBER;

```
ITEM-ENTRY (ENTRY-NUMBER + 2)
```

refers to the second entry following the one designated by the value of ENTRY-NUMBER; and so on. Likewise,

```
ITEM-ENTRY (ENTRY-NUMBER - 1)
```

refers to the entry immediately preceding the one designated by the value of ENTRY-NUMBER;

```
ITEM-ENTRY (ENTRY-NUMBER - 2)
```

refers to the second entry preceding the one designated by the value of ENTRY-NUMBER; and so on. Relative indexing can only be used with indexes; there is no corresponding feature for subscripts.

## The SET Statement

The SET statement is used to move index values from one index name or index data item to another, to convert between index values and occurrence numbers, and to change index values in such a way that the corresponding occurrence numbers are increased or decreased by given amounts. The operations performed on index values with SET statements correspond to operations that would be performed on subscript values with MOVE, ADD, and SUBTRACT.

The statement

```
SET ENTRY-NUMBER TO 1.
```

sets the value of ENTRY-NUMBER to correspond to the occurrence number 1. After SET statement is executed,

```
ITEM-ENTRY (ENTRY-NUMBER)
```

refers to the first entry of PRICE-LIST. Likewise, after

```
SET ENTRY-NUMBER TO 3
```

the value of ENTRY-NUMBER designates the third entry of PRICE-LIST, and after

```
SET ENTRY-NUMBER TO 5
```

ENTRY-NUMBER designates the fifth entry of PRICE-LIST.

The statement

```
SET ENTRY-NUMBER UP BY 1.
```

changes the value of ENTRY-NUMBER in such a way that the corresponding occurrence number is increased by 1. If before this statement was executed the value of ENTRY-NUMBER designated the first entry of PRICE-LIST, afterwards it designates the second entry of PRICE-LIST. Likewise, after the statements

```
SET ENTRY-NUMBER TO 3.
SET ENTRY-NUMBER UP BY 2.
```

are executed, the value of ENTRY-NUMBER designates the fifth entry of PRICE-LIST.

If we use DOWN BY in place of UP BY, the occurrence number is decreased rather than increased. If the value of ENTRY-NUMBER designates the third entry of PRICE-LIST, executing the statement

```
SET ENTRY-NUMBER DOWN BY 1.
```

will cause the value of ENTRY-NUMBER to designate the second entry of PRICE-LIST. Likewise, after the statements

```
SET ENTRY-NUMBER TO 5.
SET ENTRY-NUMBER DOWN BY 4.
```

have been executed, the value of ENTRY-NUMBER refers to the first entry in PRICE-LIST.

## The PERFORM VARYING Statement

As was the case for subscripts, we can use a PERFORM statement with the VARYING option to step an index through a series of values, performing a given paragraph for each index value. For example, consider the statement

```
PERFORM CHECK-ENTRY
    VARYING ENTRY-NUMBER FROM 1 BY 1
    UNTIL FOUND = "N" OR ENTRY-NUMBER > NUMBER-OF-ENTRIES.
```

which looks exactly like the corresponding statement for subscripts. Before CHECK-ENTRY is performed for the first time, the value of ENTRY-NUMBER is set to correspond to the occurrence number 1. The effect is the same as if the statement

```
SET ENTRY-NUMBER TO 1.
```

were executed. Before each succeeding execution of CHECK-ENTRY, the value of ENTRY-NUMBER is changed so as to increase the corresponding occurrence number by 1. The effect is the same as if the statement

```
SET ENTRY-NUMBER UP BY 1.
```

were executed. Thus, CHECK-ENTRY is performed repeatedly with ENTRY-NUMBER being stepped through values corresponding to the occurrence numbers 1, 2, 3, and so on.

In the UNTIL part of the PERFORM statement, the value of ENTRY-NUMBER is compared with that of the numeric data item NUMBER-OF-ENTRIES. For purposes of comparison, index values are always converted to the corresponding occurrence numbers. Thus the condition

```
ENTRY-NUMBER > NUMBER-OF-ENTRIES
```

is true if the *occurrence number corresponding to the value of* ENTRY-NUMBER is greater than the value of NUMBER-OF-ENTRIES and false otherwise. This condition thus serves the desired purpose of terminating the repetitions of CHECK-ENTRY when the search runs off the end of the table.

Because the PERFORM VARYING statement works the same for indexes as for subscripts, the table-lookup procedure is almost exactly the same in Figure 6.2 as in Figure 6.1. As in Figure 6.1, when the PERFORM statement terminates, ENTRY-NUMBER designates the entry *immediately following* the one that was found by the search. In Figure 6.1 we used a SUBTRACT statement to decrease the value of ENTRY-NUMBER by 1. In Figure 6.2, we achieve the same effect with a SET statement:

```
SET ENTRY-NUMBER DOWN BY 1.
```

## THE SEARCH STATEMENT

The SEARCH statement carries out all the index manipulations and comparisons necessary to search a table. The programmer need only specify the point in the table at which the search is to start and the conditions under which the search is to terminate. The SEARCH statement can be used only with indexes, not with subscripts. Since the SEARCH statement does all the index manipulations, the COBOL compiler has an even better opportunity to use simple, fast operations on index values and to avoid time-consuming conversions between index values and occurrence numbers.

Figure 6.3 shows a version of our price-lookup program using the SEARCH statement. The search is carried out in the paragraph TABLE-LOOKUP:

```
TABLE-LOOKUP.
    SET ENTRY-NUMBER TO 1.
    SEARCH ITEM-ENTRY
        AT END MOVE "N" TO FOUND
        WHEN TARGET-ITEM-NUMBER = ITEM-NUMBER (ENTRY-NUMBER)
            MOVE "Y" TO FOUND.
```

Note that no CHECK-ENTRY paragraph is needed.

Since, in general, we may not always want to start a search at the beginning of a table, we must set the value of the index name ENTRY-NUMBER to designate the entry at which the search is to begin. In this case we do want to start the search at the beginning of the table, so we set ENTRY-NUMBER to designate the first entry of PRICE-LIST:

```
    SET ENTRY-NUMBER TO 1.
```

The first line of the SEARCH statement:

```
    SEARCH ITEM-ENTRY
```

specifies that item entries are to be searched. The description of ITEM-ENTRY must contain both an OCCURS clause and an INDEXED BY clause.

The search can terminate in either of two ways: with success, when the desired entry is found, or without success, when the end of the table is reached. The AT END phrase, if present, specifies a statement to be executed when the search terminates without success. Each WHEN clause (there may be more than one) gives a condition for termination and specifies a statement to be executed when the condition in question terminates the search.

As in our previous programs, we use the value of FOUND to indicate whether or not the search was successful. If the search terminates without success, we want to set the value of FOUND to "N":

```
    AT END MOVE "N" TO FOUND
```

The WHEN clause:

```
    WHEN TARGET-ITEM-NUMBER = ITEM-NUMBER (ENTRY-NUMBER)
        MOVE "Y" TO FOUND
```

```
IDENTIFICATION DIVISION.
PROGRAM-ID.  PRICES-3.

*    Price lookup using SEARCH statement.

ENVIRONMENT DIVISION.

DATA DIVISION.
WORKING-STORAGE SECTION.
01  PRICE-DATA.
    02  FILLER          PIC X(11) VALUE "12573100795".
    02  FILLER          PIC X(11) VALUE "24369402750".
    02  FILLER          PIC X(11) VALUE "43271802125".
    02  FILLER          PIC X(11) VALUE "67913214995".
    02  FILLER          PIC X(11) VALUE "73123500349".

01  PRICE-LIST REDEFINES PRICE-DATA.
    02  ITEM-ENTRY OCCURS 5 TIMES
                INDEXED BY ENTRY-NUMBER.
        03  ITEM-NUMBER PIC X(6).
        03  ITEM-PRICE  PIC 999V99.

01  FOUND               PIC X.
01  TERMINATOR-KEY      PIC 99.
01  TARGET-ITEM-NUMBER  PIC X(6).
01  PRICE-OUT           PIC $$$9.99.
01  DUMMY               PIC X.

PROCEDURE DIVISION.
FIND-PRICES.
    MOVE ZERO TO TERMINATOR-KEY.
    PERFORM FIND-ONE-PRICE
        UNTIL TERMINATOR-KEY NOT = 0.
    STOP RUN.

FIND-ONE-PRICE.
    DISPLAY (1, 1) ERASE (5, 1) "Item number? ".
    ACCEPT (, )  TARGET-ITEM-NUMBER WITH PROMPT.
    PERFORM TABLE-LOOKUP.
    IF FOUND = "Y"
        MOVE ITEM-PRICE (ENTRY-NUMBER) TO PRICE-OUT
        DISPLAY (7, 1) "Item price: " PRICE-OUT
    ELSE
        DISPLAY (7, 1) "Item not found".
    DISPLAY (9, 1)
        "Press Enter to continue, Esc to terminate ".
    ACCEPT (, ) DUMMY.
    ACCEPT TERMINATOR-KEY FROM ESCAPE KEY.

TABLE-LOOKUP.
    SET ENTRY-NUMBER TO 1.
    SEARCH ITEM-ENTRY
        AT END MOVE "N" TO FOUND
        WHEN TARGET-ITEM-NUMBER = ITEM-NUMBER (ENTRY-NUMBER)
            MOVE "Y" TO FOUND.
```

*Figure 6.3* This version of the price-lookup program uses a SEARCH statement for table lookup.

specifies the condition for termination with success (the desired item has been found):

```
TARGET-ITEM-NUMBER = ITEM-NUMBER (ENTRY-NUMBER)
```

and a statement to be executed after termination. When the search terminates successfully, we want to set the value of FOUND to "Y":

```
MOVE "Y" TO FOUND
```

When the SEARCH statement is executed, the table is searched beginning with the entry designated by the current value of ENTRY-NUMBER. For each entry examined, ENTRY-NUMBER is set to designate that entry and the condition in the WHEN clause is checked. If the condition is false, the search continues. If the condition is true, the search is terminated and the statement specified in the WHEN statement is executed. ENTRY-NUMBER retains the value that it had when the condition in the WHEN clause was found to be true. As mentioned, if the end of the table is encountered, the search is terminated and the statement following AT END is executed.

More specifically, ENTRY-NUMBER is given values corresponding to the occurrence numbers 1, 2, 3, and so on, just as was done when the PERFORM VARYING statement was used. For each value of ENTRY-NUMBER, the WHEN clause checks to see if the value of the ITEM-NUMBER field in the entry designated by the value of ENTRY-NUMBER is equal to the item number we are searching for. If so, the search terminates, the value of FOUND is set to "Y", and ENTRY-NUMBER continues to designate the entry found by the search. If the end of the table is encountered, the search is terminated and the value of FOUND is set to "N".

When the SEARCH statement terminates, then, the value of FOUND will be "Y" if the search was successful and "N" otherwise. If the value of FOUND is "Y", the value of ENTRY-NUMBER designates the entry found by the search.

## THE SEARCH ALL STATEMENT

Like the search we programmed with PERFORM VARYING, the SEARCH statement starts with the designated table entry and works its way through the table, examining each entry in turn, until the desired entry is found or the end of the table is encountered. This procedure, known as *sequential search,* is grossly inefficient for large tables. Imagine looking up a name in the telephone directory by looking at each name on page 1 of the directory, then each name on page 2, then each name on page 3, and so on. We could find "Aarons" quickly enough, but it might take us days to find "Zimmerman," or to find that the name we were looking up isn't listed.

In reality, of course, we know that the names in a telephone directory or the words in a dictionary are in alphabetical order, and we use this fact to quickly locate the item we are looking for or to determine just as quickly that the item is not listed. The SEARCH ALL statement brings the same efficiency to searches conducted by COBOL programs. The table being searched must be in alphabetical or numerical order according to the *key values,* the values—such as item numbers—that will be examined by the search. The SEARCH ALL statement makes use of this order to promote rapid searching.

SEARCH ALL carries out a *binary search,* which can be illustrated with a dictionary as follows. Open the dictionary at its approximate center and note the first word on the right-hand page. If the word we are looking for precedes (in alphabetical order) the first word on the right-hand page, the desired word is in the first half of the dictionary. If the word we are looking for follows the first word on the right-hand page, the desired word is in the second half of the dictionary. We can thus eliminate half the dictionary in a single step. Now repeat this process with the half selected in the first step, dividing *it* in half and determining in which half the desired word lies. We have now narrowed down our search to a "half of a half" or a fourth of the dictionary. For a 1000-page dictionary, 10 repetitions of the halving process will narrow the search down to a single page. If this page doesn't contain the word we are looking for, that word is not in the dictionary.

Figure 6.4 shows a version of the price lookup program using SEARCH ALL. In the description for the table entries we must designate the key field—the field whose values will be examined during the search. We must also state whether the entries will be arranged with their key fields in *ascending order* (smaller values before larger values) or *descending order* (larger values before smaller values):

```
01   PRICE-LIST REDEFINES PRICE-DATA.
     02   ITEM-ENTRY OCCURS 5 TIMES
                    ASCENDING KEY IS ITEM-NUMBER
                    INDEXED BY ENTRY-NUMBER.
        03   ITEM-NUMBER PIC X(6).
        03   ITEM-PRICE   PIC 999V99.
```

It's up to the programmer to make sure that the entries are actually stored with their key fields in the order specified. If any entries are out of order, the SEARCH ALL statement will not work properly, probably by failing to find some entries that are in fact in the table.

With SEARCH ALL, we cannot specify the entry with which the SEARCH is to begin. As its name implies, SEARCH ALL searches the entire table, and we have no control over the order in which entries will be examined. Therefore, in contrast to the case for SEARCH, we do not assign ENTRY-NUMBER an initial value before executing the SEARCH-ALL statement:

```
TABLE-LOOKUP.
    SEARCH ALL ITEM-ENTRY
        AT END MOVE "N" TO FOUND
        WHEN TARGET-ITEM-NUMBER = ITEM-NUMBER (ENTRY-NUMBER)
            MOVE "Y" TO FOUND.
```

As with SEARCH, when a value of ENTRY-NUMBER is found such that the value ITEM-NUMBER (ENTRY-NUMBER) is equal to the desired item number, the search terminates and the value of FOUND is set to "Y". If the entry sought is not present, the search terminates and the value of FOUND is set to "N".

```
IDENTIFICATION DIVISION.
PROGRAM-ID.   PRICES-4.

*    Price lookup using SEARCH ALL statement.

ENVIRONMENT DIVISION.

DATA DIVISION.
WORKING-STORAGE SECTION.
01   PRICE-DATA.
     02   FILLER           PIC X(11) VALUE "12573100795".
     02   FILLER           PIC X(11) VALUE "24369402750".
     02   FILLER           PIC X(11) VALUE "43271802125".
     02   FILLER           PIC X(11) VALUE "67913214995".
     02   FILLER           PIC X(11) VALUE "73123500349".


01   PRICE-LIST REDEFINES PRICE-DATA.
     02   ITEM-ENTRY OCCURS 5 TIMES
                    ASCENDING KEY IS ITEM-NUMBER
                    INDEXED BY ENTRY-NUMBER.
          03   ITEM-NUMBER PIC X(6).
          03   ITEM-PRICE  PIC 999V99.


01   FOUND                 PIC X.
01   TERMINATOR-KEY        PIC 99.
01   TARGET-ITEM-NUMBER    PIC X(6).
01   PRICE-OUT             PIC $$$9.99.
01   DUMMY                 PIC X.

PROCEDURE DIVISION.
FIND-PRICES.
     MOVE ZERO TO TERMINATOR-KEY.
     PERFORM FIND-ONE-PRICE
          UNTIL TERMINATOR-KEY NOT = 0.
     STOP RUN.


FIND-ONE-PRICE.
     DISPLAY (1, 1) ERASE (5, 1) "Item number? ".
     ACCEPT (, )   TARGET-ITEM-NUMBER WITH PROMPT.
     PERFORM TABLE-LOOKUP.
     IF FOUND = "Y"
          MOVE ITEM-PRICE (ENTRY-NUMBER) TO PRICE-OUT
          DISPLAY (7, 1) "Item price: " PRICE-OUT
     ELSE
          DISPLAY (7, 1) "Item not found".
     DISPLAY (9, 1)
          "Press Enter to continue, Esc to terminate ".
     ACCEPT (, ) DUMMY.
     ACCEPT TERMINATOR-KEY FROM ESCAPE KEY.


TABLE-LOOKUP.
     SEARCH ALL ITEM-ENTRY
          AT END MOVE "N" TO FOUND
          WHEN TARGET-ITEM-NUMBER = ITEM-NUMBER (ENTRY-NUMBER)
               MOVE "Y" TO FOUND.
```

*Figure 6.4*   This version of the price-lookup program uses a SEARCH  ALL statement for table lookup.

## NESTED IF STATEMENTS

Our final program for this chapter uses *nested* IF statements—IF statements containing other IF statements. In this section we will look at a few points that must be kept in mind when using nested IF statements. To illustrate various forms of IF statements in a compact way, it will help to use abbreviations for conditions and statements. We will let c1, c2, c3, and so on stand for conditions, and let s1, s2, s3, and so on stand for statements.

**1.** *No matter how complicated an* IF *statement, there is only one period at the end of the entire* IF *statement.* This has been said before, but it's one of those things that cannot be said too many times. A period embedded within an IF statement will end the statement prematurely. The error may or may not be detected by the compiler. For example, in

```
IF  c1
        s1
        s2.
ELSE
        s3
        s4.
```

the period following s2 terminates the IF statement prematurely. The compiler will detect this error, since the period cuts the IF statement off from its ELSE part. On the other hand, in

```
IF  c1
        s1
        s2
ELSE
        s3.
        s4.
```

the compiler, which pays no attention to the indentation, has no way of knowing that the period following s3 is erroneous. Therefore, the IF statement ends with s3 and has no effect on the execution of s4. The effect is the same as if we had written

```
IF  c1
        s1
        s2
ELSE
        s3.
s4.
```

Although the compiler did not detect the error, the compiled program will not work properly since s4 will always be executed instead of only being executed when c1 is false, as intended.

**2.** *Every statement in a nested* IF *statement is governed by the most recent* IF *or* ELSE. For example, the following statement is not indented correctly:

```
IF c1
    IF c2
        s1
    s2
ELSE
    s3.
```

The indentation suggests that the execution of s2 is controlled only by condition c1, and this is no doubt what the person who wrote the statement intended. But by rule 2, each statement is governed by the nearest preceding IF or ELSE. Thus the correct indentation is

```
IF c1
    IF c2
        s1
        s2
ELSE
    s3.
```

that is, s2 will be executed only when *both* c1 and c2 are true. *There is nothing more misleading in a COBOL program than an* IF *statement whose indentation does not reflect the way in which the statement will be processed by the compiler.*

The only way to get the effect implied by the original, erroneously indented statement is to move the inner IF statement into a performed paragraph:

```
IF c1
    PERFORM CHECK-C2
    s2
ELSE
    s3.
```

Paragraph CHECK-C2 is defined by

```
CHECK-C2.
    IF c2
        s1.
```

Now, c2 has no effect on s2, which is executed whenever c1 is true.

Likewise,

```
IF c1
    IF c2
        s1
    ELSE
        s2
    s3.
```

is incorrectly indented, since s3 is governed by the preceding ELSE. What is the correct indentation? How can we use a PERFORM statement to obtain the behavior implied by the incorrectly indented IF statement?

**3.** *An* ELSE *part goes with the nearest preceding* IF *statement that does not already have an* ELSE *part.* Here is another incorrectly indented IF statement:

```
IF  c1
      IF  c2
            s1
ELSE
      s2,
```

The indentation implies that the ELSE part goes with the first IF statement, so s2 will be executed whenever c1 is false. But by rule 3, the ELSE part goes with the second IF statement, the nearest preceding IF statement that does not already have an ELSE part. The correct indentation is

```
IF  c1
      IF  c2
            s1
      ELSE
            s2,
```

Statement s2 is executed only if c1 is true and c2 is false. Once again, we can get the effect of the erroneously indented IF statement by moving the inner IF statement into a performed paragraph:

```
IF  c1
      PERFORM  CHECK-C2
ELSE
      s2,
```

Paragraph CHECK-C2 is again defined by

```
CHECK-C2,
      IF  c2
            s1,
```

**4.** *When possible, use a multiway-selection construction in preference to more complicated nested* IF *statements.* Having seen some of the pitfalls that can arise in writing nested IF statements, let's look at one nesting scheme which is particularly straightforward:

```
IF  c1
      s1
ELSE
      IF  c2
            s2
      ELSE
            IF  c3
                  s3
            ELSE
                  s4,
```

If c1 is true, s1 is executed. If c1 is false but c2 is true, c2 is executed. If c1 and c2 are false, but c3 is true, s3 is executed. Finally, if all the conditions are false, s4 is executed. One and only one statement is executed, regardless of which conditions are true or false.

The best way to understand this construction is to make a list of the conditions and the corresponding statements:

```
c1          s1
c2          s2
c3          s3
            s4
```

The computer goes down the list of conditions until it finds the first true condition, then executes the corresponding statement. If none of the conditions are true, the final statement, s4, is executed.

This nesting scheme is sometimes referred to as *multiway selection,* since it selects one of a number of statements for execution. To emphasize the correspondence between conditions and statements, a multiway selection is often written like this:

```
IF  c1
      s1
ELSE IF  c2
      s2
ELSE IF  c3
      s3
ELSE
      s4.
```

We can include as many ELSE IF parts as needed. Also, the final ELSE part can be omitted. If the ELSE part is omitted, no statement is executed when none of the conditions are true. Finally, each of the statements s1 through s4 can actually be a series of statements.

## IN-MEMORY INFORMATION RETRIEVAL

Information retrieval obtains information requested by the user from a *database* such as a price list or a telephone directory. For in-memory information retrieval, the database is stored as a table in the computer's main memory while in use. When we have finished using the database, we can store it on disk for later use. We must load it back into main memory, however, before it can be used again. Figure 6.5 shows a program for in-memory information retrieval from a price list.

The table that stores the price list has the same structure as the price-list tables in previous programs, but has 100 entries instead of 5:

```
01   PRICE-LIST.
     02   ITEM-ENTRY OCCURS 100 TIMES.
          03   ITEM-NUMBER   PIC X(6).
          03   ITEM-PRICE    PIC 999V99.
```

Note that this version of PRICE-LIST does not redefine a data table. The data for PRICE-LIST is not written into the program; it will be obtained from the user or read from a disk file when the program is executed. In the Working-Storage Section the data

```
IDENTIFICATION DIVISION.
PROGRAM-ID.  INFORMATION-RETRIEVAL.

*    In-memory information retrieval from price list.

ENVIRONMENT DIVISION.
INPUT-OUTPUT SECTION.
FILE-CONTROL.
     SELECT PRICE-FILE ASSIGN TO DISK.

DATA DIVISION.
FILE SECTION.
FD   PRICE-FILE
     LABEL RECORDS STANDARD
     VALUE OF FILE-ID IS DOS-FILE-NAME.
01   PRICE-RECORD        PIC X(11).

WORKING-STORAGE SECTION.
01   PRICE-LIST.
     02   ITEM-ENTRY OCCURS 100 TIMES.
          03   ITEM-NUMBER PIC X(6).
          03   ITEM-PRICE  PIC 999V99.

01   FOUND               PIC X.
01   END-OF-FILE         PIC X.
01   TERMINATOR-KEY      PIC 99.
01   TARGET-ITEM-NUMBER  PIC X(6).
01   PRICE-OUT           PIC $$$9.99.
01   DUMMY               PIC X.
01   DOS-FILE-NAME       PIC X(15).
01   ENTRY-NUMBER        PIC 999 COMP-0.
01   PREV-ENTRY-NUMBER   PIC 999 COMP-0.
01   FREE                PIC 999 COMP-0.
01   TABLE-SIZE          PIC 999 COMP-0 VALUE 100.

SCREEN SECTION.
01   MENU-SCREEN.
     02   BLANK SCREEN.
     02   LINE 5 COLUMN 30 VALUE "F1   Create entry".
     02   LINE 7 COLUMN 30 VALUE "F2   Delete entry".
     02   LINE 9 COLUMN 30 VALUE "F3   Find price".
     02   LINE 11 COLUMN 30 VALUE "F4   Load file".
     02   LINE 13 COLUMN 30 VALUE "F5   Save file".
     02   LINE 15 COLUMN 30 VALUE "F6   Exit program".
     02   LINE 19 COLUMN 24
             VALUE "Press key for desired function".

PROCEDURE DIVISION.
MAIN-ROUTINE.
     MOVE 1 TO FREE.
     MOVE ZERO TO TERMINATOR-KEY.
     PERFORM GET-AND-CARRY-OUT-FUNCTION
         UNTIL TERMINATOR-KEY = 7.
     STOP RUN.
```

*Figure 6.5* This program for in-memory information retrieval creates entries, deletes entries, and finds prices in a price-list stored in main memory. The price list can be saved in a disk file and loaded from disk when needed.

```
GET-AND-CARRY-OUT-FUNCTION.
    MOVE ZERO TO TERMINATOR-KEY.
    PERFORM DISPLAY-MENU-AND-GET-FUNCTION
        UNTIL TERMINATOR-KEY > 1 AND < 8.
    IF TERMINATOR-KEY = 2
        PERFORM CREATE-ENTRY
    ELSE IF TERMINATOR-KEY = 3
        PERFORM DELETE-ENTRY
    ELSE IF TERMINATOR-KEY = 4
        PERFORM FIND-PRICE
    ELSE IF TERMINATOR-KEY = 5
        PERFORM LOAD-FILE
    ELSE IF TERMINATOR-KEY = 6
        PERFORM SAVE-FILE.

DISPLAY-MENU-AND-GET-FUNCTION.
    DISPLAY MENU-SCREEN.
    ACCEPT (19, 55) DUMMY.
    ACCEPT TERMINATOR-KEY FROM ESCAPE KEY.

CREATE-ENTRY.
    IF FREE > TABLE-SIZE
        DISPLAY (1, 1) ERASE (5, 1) "No room for new item"
                (7, 1) "Press Enter to continue "
        ACCEPT (, ) DUMMY
    ELSE
        DISPLAY (1, 1) ERASE (5, 1) "Item number? "
        ACCEPT (, ) TARGET-ITEM-NUMBER WITH PROMPT
        PERFORM TABLE-LOOKUP
        IF FOUND = "Y"
            DISPLAY (7, 1) "Item already in price list"
                    (9, 1) "Press Enter to continue "
            ACCEPT (, ) DUMMY
        ELSE
            MOVE TARGET-ITEM-NUMBER TO ITEM-NUMBER (FREE)
            DISPLAY (7, 1) "Item price? "
            ACCEPT (, ) ITEM-PRICE (FREE) WITH PROMPT
            ADD 1 TO FREE.

DELETE-ENTRY.
    DISPLAY (1, 1) ERASE (5, 1) "Item number? ".
    ACCEPT (, ) TARGET-ITEM-NUMBER WITH PROMPT.
    PERFORM TABLE-LOOKUP.
    IF FOUND = "N"
        DISPLAY (7, 1) "Item not found"
                (9, 1) "Press Enter to continue "
        ACCEPT (, ) DUMMY
    ELSE
        MOVE ENTRY-NUMBER TO PREV-ENTRY-NUMBER
        ADD 1 TO ENTRY-NUMBER
        PERFORM MOVE-BACK-ONE-POSITION
            VARYING ENTRY-NUMBER FROM ENTRY-NUMBER BY 1
            UNTIL ENTRY-NUMBER = FREE
        SUBTRACT 1 FROM FREE.

MOVE-BACK-ONE-POSITION.
    MOVE ITEM-ENTRY (ENTRY-NUMBER) TO
        ITEM-ENTRY (PREV-ENTRY-NUMBER).
    MOVE ENTRY-NUMBER TO PREV-ENTRY-NUMBER.
```

*Figure 6.5 (continued)*

```
FIND-PRICE.
    DISPLAY (1, 1) ERASE (5, 1) "Item number? ".
    ACCEPT (, ) TARGET-ITEM-NUMBER WITH PROMPT.
    PERFORM TABLE-LOOKUP.
    IF FOUND = "Y"
        MOVE ITEM-PRICE (ENTRY-NUMBER) TO PRICE-OUT
        DISPLAY (7, 1) "Item price: " PRICE-OUT
    ELSE
        DISPLAY (7, 1) "Item not found".
    DISPLAY (9, 1) "Press Enter to continue ".
    ACCEPT (, ) DUMMY.

LOAD-FILE.
    DISPLAY (1, 1) ERASE (5, 1) "File name? ".
    ACCEPT (, ) DOS-FILE-NAME WITH PROMPT.
    OPEN INPUT PRICE-FILE.
    MOVE 1 TO FREE.
    MOVE "N" TO END-OF-FILE.
    READ PRICE-FILE
        AT END MOVE "Y" TO END-OF-FILE.
    PERFORM READ-ONE-RECORD
        UNTIL END-OF-FILE = "Y" OR FREE > TABLE-SIZE.
    CLOSE PRICE-FILE.

READ-ONE-RECORD.
    MOVE PRICE-RECORD TO ITEM-ENTRY (FREE).
    ADD 1 TO FREE.
    READ PRICE-FILE
        AT END MOVE "Y" TO END-OF-FILE.

SAVE-FILE.
    DISPLAY (1, 1) ERASE (5, 1) "File name? ".
    ACCEPT (, ) DOS-FILE-NAME WITH PROMPT.
    OPEN OUTPUT PRICE-FILE.
    PERFORM WRITE-ONE-RECORD
        VARYING ENTRY-NUMBER FROM 1 BY 1
        UNTIL ENTRY-NUMBER = FREE.
    CLOSE PRICE-FILE.

WRITE-ONE-RECORD.
    MOVE ITEM-ENTRY (ENTRY-NUMBER) TO PRICE-RECORD.
    WRITE PRICE-RECORD.

TABLE-LOOKUP.
    MOVE "N" TO FOUND.
    PERFORM CHECK-ENTRY
        VARYING ENTRY-NUMBER FROM 1 BY 1
        UNTIL FOUND = "Y" OR ENTRY-NUMBER = FREE.
    SUBTRACT 1 FROM ENTRY-NUMBER.

CHECK-ENTRY.
    IF TARGET-ITEM-NUMBER = ITEM-NUMBER (ENTRY-NUMBER)
        MOVE "Y" TO FOUND.
```

*Figure 6.5 (continued)*

name TABLE-SIZE is given the value 100. If the program is modified to change the number of entries in PRICE-LIST, the value of TABLE-SIZE must be changed correspondingly.

The program uses subscripts; modifying it to use indexes instead is left as an exercise. Three data names—ENTRY-NUMBER, PREV-ENTRY-NUMBER, and FREE—are used as subscripts. Each is given a picture of 999 and usage COMP-0. ENTRY-NUMBER normally designates the table entry with which the program is currently working. PREV-ENTRY-NUMBER is sometimes used to designate the entry immediately preceding the one designated by ENTRY-NUMBER.

One hundred is the *maximum* number of entries the table can hold; usually it will hold fewer, that is, only part of the table will be in use. We need to keep track of the used and usused parts of the table both to know where new entries can be stored and to prevent searches from running past the part of the table that is actually in use. For this purpose, we use FREE to designate the first unused entry in the table. At any time, all entries preceding ITEM-ENTRY (FREE) are in use; ITEM-ENTRY (FREE) and all entries following are unused and available for storing new data. If all the table entries are in use—there are no unused entries—the value of FREE is 101, one greater than the value of TABLE-SIZE. When the program begins execution, the value of FREE is set to 1, indicating that all the table entries are unused.

The user requests the program to perform various functions by pressing function keys. In the Screen Section we define MENU-SCREEN, which displays the correspondence between function keys and functions to be performed. The code representing the function key pressed is stored as the value of TERMINATOR-KEY. The following table shows the correspondence between function keys, values of TERMINATOR-KEY, and functions to be performed:

| Function Key | Value of TERMINATOR-KEY | Function |
|:---:|:---:|:---|
| F1 | 2 | Create entry |
| F2 | 3 | Delete entry |
| F3 | 4 | Find price |
| F4 | 5 | Load file |
| F5 | 6 | Save file |
| F6 | 7 | Exit program |

In the Procedure Division, MAIN-ROUTINE initializes FREE to 1 (all table entries unused), and sets TERMINATOR-KEY to 0 (to make sure the PERFORM statement will execute at least once—any initial value other than 7 could have been used). The PERFORM statement executes GET-AND-CARRY-OUT-FUNCTION repeatedly. The latter displays the menu, invites the user to press a function key, and stores the code corresponding to the function key in TERMINATOR-KEY. If the user presses F1 through F5, GET-AND-CARRY-OUT-FUNCTION carries out the corresponding function. If F6 is pressed, no function is carried out, but the value of 7 for TERMINATOR-KEY terminates the PERFORM statement. The computer goes on to the following STOP RUN statement, which terminates the program.

GET-AND-CARRY-OUT-FUNCTION sets TERMINATOR-KEY to 0 to assure that the PERFORM statement will be executed at least once. The PERFORM statement calls on DISPLAY-MENU-AND-GET-FUNCTION to display the menu, invite the user to press a function key, and store the corresponding code as the value of TERMINATOR-KEY. DISPLAY-MENU-AND-GET-FUNCTION is repeated until the user presses a valid function key—until the terminator code is in the range 2 through 7.

A multiway selection performs the paragraph that carries out the function requested by the user. If the value of TERMINATOR-KEY is 2, CREATE-ENTRY is performed; if the value of TERMINATOR-KEY is 3, DELETE-ENTRY is performed; and so on. If the value of TERMINATOR-KEY is 7, no paragraph is performed; the value 7 will cause the PERFORM statement in MAIN-ROUTINE to terminate, thereby ending the program.

DISPLAY-MENU-AND-GET-FUNCTION displays MENU-SCREEN. A value is accepted for DUMMY just to get the program to wait until the user presses a function key. A format 3 rather than a format 4 ACCEPT statement is used for DUMMY to prevent a prompt for DUMMY from being displayed. The data that we are actually interested in is obtained by the format 1 ACCEPT statement, which sets TERMINA-TOR-KEY to the code for the key used to terminate the format 3 ACCEPT statement.

CREATE-ENTRY creates a new entry in the price list. Note that it does not create a new entry in the COBOL table, which always has exactly 100 entries. The data for the new price-list is placed in the first unused entry of the COBOL table.

CREATE-ENTRY first checks if the value of FREE is greater than that of TABLE-SIZE; if it is, the table is full, and no new price-list entries can be inserted. A DISPLAY statement informs the user of this unfortunate state of affairs.

If there is room in the table, the program accepts the item number for the new entry. TABLE-LOOKUP is performed to see if an entry with this item number is already present. If it is (the value of FOUND was set to "Y" by TABLE-LOOKUP), a new entry with the same item number cannot be inserted. (If two entries were allowed to have the same item number, TABLE-LOOKUP would only find the one that came first in the table; the data in the second could never be retrieved.) Again, the user is informed of the problem.

If no problems were found, the data for the new price-list entry is stored in the first unused table entry—the one designated by FREE. The item-number already accepted is stored in ITEM-NUMBER (FREE), and a value for ITEM-PRICE (FREE) is accepted from the user. The value of FREE is increased by one so that FREE once again designates the first unused entry.

Note that each new entry is added onto the end of the price list currently stored in memory. No attempt is made to keep the entries in order according to their item-number fields. This means that we can only use sequential search for finding entries; binary search would require the entries to be in order.

DELETE-ENTRY, which deletes the entry having a given item number, is the trickiest routine in the program. The tricky part is that when a price-list entry is deleted, all the following entries have to be moved up one place in the table to fill in the gap left by the deleted entry. DELETE-ENTRY begins by getting the item number of the entry to be deleted and looking it up in the table. The user is informed if no entry with that item number is present.

If an entry with the desired item number is present, TABLE-LOOKUP sets ENTRY-NUMBER to designate the entry to be deleted. The statements

```
MOVE ENTRY-NUMBER TO PREV-ENTRY-NUMBER.
ADD 1 TO ENTRY-NUMBER.
```

set PREV-ENTRY-NUMBER to designate the entry to be deleted and ENTRY-NUMBER to designate the entry following the one to be deleted. The entry following the one to be deleted has to be moved up one position in the table. That is, the price-list entry designated by ENTRY-NUMBER has to be moved to the position designated by PREV-ENTRY-NUMBER. And this process has to be repeated all the way to the end of the price list, so that each entry following the one to be deleted is moved up one position.

The PERFORM statement repeatedly executes MOVE-BACK-ONE-POSITION, which moves the price-list entry designated by ENTRY-NUMBER up (or back) one position in the table. The VARYING phrase

```
VARYING ENTRY-NUMBER FROM ENTRY-NUMBER BY 1
```

starts ENTRY-NUMBER with its current value (FROM ENTRY-NUMBER) and adds 1 to its value (BY 1) after each execution of MOVE-BACK-ONE-POSITION. For example, if before executing the PERFORM statement the value of ENTRY-NUMBER is 28, the PERFORM statement will step ENTRY-NUMBER through the values 28, 29, 30, 31, and so on. The PERFORM statement terminates when the value of ENTRY-NUMBER is equal to that of FREE—when ENTRY-NUMBER designates the first unused record following the price list.

After each price-list entry following the one to be deleted has been moved up one position, the table entry that formerly held the last price-list entry is now unused. The value of FREE is decreased by 1 so that FREE designates the new unused entry:

```
SUBTRACT 1 FROM FREE.
```

MOVE-BACK-ONE-POSITION moves the price-list entry designated by ENTRY-NUMBER to the unused table entry designated by PREV-ENTRY-NUMBER:

```
MOVE ITEM-ENTRY (ENTRY-NUMBER) TO
     ITEM-ENTRY (PREV-ENTRY-NUMBER).
```

The table entry designated by ENTRY-NUMBER is now unused, since its contents have been moved up one position. We move the value of ENTRY-NUMBER to that of PREV-ENTRY-NUMBER:

```
MOVE ENTRY-NUMBER TO PREV-ENTRY-NUMBER.
```

so that PREV-ENTRY-NUMBER once again designates an unused table entry—one into which the contents of the following table entry can be moved. The PERFORM statement will increase the value of ENTRY-NUMBER by 1, so that ENTRY-

NUMBER will once again designate a price-list entry to be moved to the table entry designated by PREV-ENTRY-NUMBER.

FIND-PRICE should be familiar from our previous programs. The item number to be found is obtained from the user and TABLE-LOOKUP is performed to find the desired item. If the search was successful, FOUND is set to "Y" and ENTRY-NUMBER is set to designate the entry found. If the value of FOUND is "Y", the price sought—the value of ITEM-PRICE (ENTRY-NUMBER) is displayed for the user. Otherwise, the user is informed that the entry number entered could not be found.

LOAD-FILE loads a previously saved price list from disk. The price list is read from PRICE-FILE, each record of which corresponds to one price-list entry. LOAD-FILE begins by accepting the DOS file name for the file to be loaded and opening PRICE-FILE for input. FREE is set to 1, indicating that the entire price-list table is unused. (Any data currently in the table is thus discarded.) The flag END-OF-FILE is initialized to "N". The READ statement reads the first record from PRICE-FILE. The PERFORM statement performs READ-ONE-RECORD until the value of END-OF-FILE becomes "Y" (the end of the input file was encountered) or until the value of FREE exceeds that of TABLE-SIZE (there is no more room in the table). After all records have been read, PRICE-FILE is closed.

READ-ONE-RECORD moves the previously read price record to the table entry designated by FREE, the first unused entry in the table. The value of FREE is increased by 1 so that it designates the next table entry, which now becomes the first unused entry. Finally, READ-ONE-RECORD reads a new record from the file, a record that will be stored in the table the next time READ-ONE-RECORD is performed.

SAVE-FILE, which saves the price list in memory as a disk file, begins by accepting the DOS file name for the disk file from the user, then opens PRICE-FILE for output. Note that the same file, PRICE-FILE, is used for input by LOAD-FILE and for output by SAVE-FILE. The paragraph WRITE-ONE-RECORD is performed with ENTRY-NUMBER equal to 1, 2, 3, and so on. The repetition terminates when the value of ENTRY-NUMBER equals that of FREE—the values of all the table entries that are in use have been written to PRICE-FILE. SAVE-FILE finishes by closing PRICE-FILE.

WRITE-ONE-RECORD moves the entry designated by ENTRY-NUMBER to PRICE-RECORD and writes PRICE-RECORD to PRICE-FILE.

TABLE-LOOKUP and CHECK-ENTRY are similar to the corresponding routines in previous programs and do not need additional discussion. The only point to note is that we do not search the entire table but only the part that is currently in use. Therefore, the search terminates when the value of FOUND is "Y" (the desired entry has been found) or the value of ENTRY-NUMBER equals that of FREE (the search has encountered the end of the price list—the end of the part of the table that is in use).

## MULTIPLE-LEVEL TABLES

The tables we have looked at so far were all one-level tables, so called because an OCCURS clause is present on only one level of the record description for the table.

COBOL also allows two-level tables, in which OCCURS clauses are present on two levels, and three-level tables, in which OCCURS clauses are present on three levels.

We know that for a one-level table one subscript or index is required to designate a table entry. Likewise, for a two-level table we need two subscripts or indexes to designate a table entry, and for three-level tables we need three subscripts or indexes to designate a table entry.

## A Two-Level Table

Let's look at a concrete example of a two-level table. Suppose that your company sells four products (numbered 1 through 4) in three sales territories (numbered 1 through 3). You are interested in the sales income from each product in each territory. It's natural to arrange the sales data as a table with three rows (one for each territory) and four columns (one for each product):

| | | *Products* | | |
|---|---|---|---|---|
| | 1 | 2 | 3 | 4 |
| *Territories* 1 | 325.78 | 295.63 | 781.25 | 498.50 |
| 2 | 754.62 | 875.28 | 123.45 | 249.37 |
| 3 | 334.77 | 692.35 | 137.42 | 666.21 |

From the table we can easily see that, for example, in territory 2 the sales for product 3 were 123.45, and in territory 1 the sales for product 4 were 498.50.

Let's translate this table into COBOL in three steps. We represent the entire table by the level 01 item SALES-TABLE:

```
01   SALES-TABLE,
```

SALES-TABLE is composed of three rows, one for each territory. We use an OCCURS clause to define the three rows at level 02:

```
01   SALES-TABLE,
    02   SALES-BY-TERRITORY OCCURS 3 TIMES,
```

Each row of the table—each occurrence of SALES-BY-TERRITORY—contains four numeric values, one for each product. We use another OCCURS clause to define the four product entries at level 03:

```
01   SALES-TABLE,
    02   SALES-BY-TERRITORY OCCURS 3 TIMES,
        03   SALES-BY-TERRITORY-AND-PRODUCT PIC 999V99
                                    OCCURS 4 TIMES,
```

To designate a particular occurrence of SALES-BY-TERRITORY—a particular row of the table—we need a single subscript. Thus

```
SALES-BY-TERRITORY (1)
SALES-BY-TERRITORY (2)
SALES-BY-TERRITORY (3)
```

refer respectively to the first, second, and third rows of the sales table.

Each occurrence of SALES-BY-TERRITORY has subordinate to it four occurrences of SALES-BY-TERRITORY-AND-PRODUCT. To designate a particular table entry, then, we need two subscripts. The first subscript designates a particular row of the table—a particular occurrence of SALES-BY-TERRITORY. The second designates a particular entry in the designated row—one of the four occurrences of SALES-BY-TERRITORY-AND-PRODUCT subordinate to the designated occurrence of SALES-BY-TERRITORY. For example, the value of

```
SALES-BY-TERRITORY-AND-PRODUCT (2, 3)
```

is 123.45—the sales in territory 2 of product 3. Likewise, the value of

```
SALES-BY-TERRITORY-AND-PRODUCT (1, 4)
```

is 498.50—the sales in territory 1 of product 4.

It's instructive to see how the data for this table would be written in the program (even though, in practice, sales data would probably not be written in a program but would be entered by the user or read from disk). SALES-TABLE is defined as a table of three rows, each of which contains four data entries. In the data, then, the four entries for row 1 come first, then the four entries for row 2, and finally the four entries for row 3:

```
01   SALES-DATA.
     02   FILLER PIC X(20) VALUE "32578295637812549850".
     02   FILLER PIC X(20) VALUE "75462875281234524937".
     02   FILLER PIC X(20) VALUE "33477692351374266621".

01   SALES-TABLE REDEFINES SALES-DATA.
     02   SALES-BY-TERRITORY OCCURS 3 TIMES.
          03   SALES-BY-TERRITORY-AND-PRODUCT PIC 999V99
                                              OCCURS 4 TIMES.
```

## A Three-Level Table

If we become interested in the effect of some other factor on product sales, we will have to make our sales table into a three-level table to take the additional factor into account. Suppose we are interested in how sales vary with the month of the year as well as how they vary with territory and product. We might imagine that we have 12 sales reports, one for each month of the year, and each containing a table showing the sales of each product in each territory. We begin by defining the 12 monthly sales reports:

```
01   SALES-TABLE.
     02   SALES-BY-MO OCCURS 12 TIMES.
```

Each monthly sales report contains a table of three rows, one row for each territory:

```
01   SALES-TABLE.
     02   SALES-BY-MO OCCURS 12 TIMES.
          03   SALES-BY-MO-AND-TERR OCCURS 3 TIMES.
```

Each row contains four data entries:

```
01  SALES-TABLE.
    02  SALES-BY-MO OCCURS 12 TIMES.
        03  SALES-BY-MO-AND-TERR OCCURS 3 TIMES.
            04  SALES-BY-MO-TERR-AND-PROD PIC 999V99
                                          OCCURS 4 TIMES.
```

We need one subscript to designate a level 02 item; two subscripts to designate a level 03 item; and three subscripts to designate a level 04 item. Thus, the value of

```
SALES-BY-MO (1)
```

is the January sales report; the value of

```
SALES-BY-MO (2)
```

is the February sales report; and so on. The value of

```
SALES-BY-MO-AND-TERR (2, 3)
```

gives the February sales for territory 3; the value of

```
SALES-BY-MO-AND-TERR (9, 2)
```

gives the September sales for territory 2; and so on. Finally, the value of

```
SALES-BY-MO-TERR-AND-PROD (3, 2, 4)
```

gives the March sales in territory 2 for product 4; the value of

```
SALES-BY-MO-TERR-AND-PROD (1, 3, 2)
```

gives the January sales in territory 3 for product 2.

We won't write a data record for the three-level sales table—the data record would be very long. Note, however, that in such a record, the January data would come first, then the February data, then the March data, and so on. In the data for each month the first row of the table would come first, then the second row, and finally the third row.

## More about PERFORM VARYING

We have seen how the PERFORM VARYING statement will step a subscript or index through a series of values. In processing a two-level table, we may need to step two subscripts or indexes through two series of values, and for a three-level table we may need to step three subscripts or indexes through three series of values. With the aid of AFTER *clauses,* we can extend PERFORM VARYING to manipulate two or three subscripts or indexes.

For example, suppose we want to add up all the entries in the two-level version of SALES-TABLE to get the total sales for all products in all territories. Let's use the subscript T to designate a particular territory and the subscript P to designate a particular product:

```
MOVE ZERO TO TOTAL.
PERFORM ADD-ONE-ENTRY
    VARYING T FROM 1 BY 1 UNTIL T > 3
    AFTER P FROM 1 BY 1 UNTIL P > 4.
```

Paragraph ADD-ONE-ENTRY is defined as follows:

```
ADD-ONE-ENTRY.
    ADD SALES-BY-TERRITORY-AND-PRODUCT (T, P) TO TOTAL.
```

When the PERFORM statement is executed, both T and P are set to 1. With the value of T remaining 1, ADD-ONE-ENTRY is performed with the value of P equal to 1, 2, 3, and 4. Since ADD-ONE-ENTRY adds the entry designated by the values of T and P to TOTAL, all the entries in the first row are added to TOTAL.

Next, T is set to 2 and ADD-ONE-ENTRY is again performed with the value of P equal to 1, 2, 3, and 4, adding the entries in the second row to TOTAL. Finally, the value of T is set to 3, and ADD-ONE-ENTRY is again performed with the value of P equal to 1, 2, 3, and 4, adding the entries in the third row to TOTAL. When the PERFORM statement terminates, ADD-ONE-ENTRY has been executed for each combination of valid values of T and P, thus adding all the table entries to TOTAL. Note that the value of T changes only after P been stepped through its complete range of values, which is why we say that T is varied *after* P.

To add up all the entries in the three-level version of SALES-TABLE, we must manipulate three subscripts: M (month), T (territory), and P (product):

```
MOVE ZERO TO TOTAL.
PERFORM ADD-ONE-ENTRY
    VARYING M FROM 1 BY 1 UNTIL M > 12
    AFTER T FROM 1 BY 1 UNTIL T > 3
    AFTER P FROM 1 BY 1 UNTIL P > 4.
```

ADD-ONE-ENTRY is now defined by

```
ADD-ONE-ENTRY.
    ADD SALES-BY-MO-TERR-AND-PROD (M, P, T) TO TOTAL.
```

When the PERFORM statement is executed, M, T, and P are set to 1. With the values of M and T equal to 1, ADD-ONE-ENTRY is performed with the value of P equal to 1, 2, 3, and 4. The value of T is set to 2, and ADD-ONE-ENTRY is again performed for the value of P equal to 1, 2, 3, and 4. This process is repeated still again with the value of T equal to 3. At this point, all the entries in the January table have been added to TOTAL.

Next the value of M is set to 2, and the entire process of varying P and T is repeated, thus adding the entries in the February table to TOTAL. The value of M is set to 3, and ADD-ONE-ENTRY is again performed for all combinations of valid values of T and P, adding the entries in the March table to TOTAL; and so on. When the PERFORM statement terminates, ADD-ONE-ENTRY will have been executed for every combination of valid values of M, T, and P.

## EXERCISES

**1.** The unit price of an item depends on the quantity ordered as follows:

| Quantity Ordered | Unit Price |
| --- | --- |
| 1–99 | $29.95 |
| 100–199 | 28.45 |
| 200–299 | 26.87 |
| 300 and over | 23.99 |

Write a program to compute the total cost of an order given the number of items ordered.

The kind of table search required here is sometimes called *inexact* search, since we need only find which range of values contains the value being sought. This is in contrast to *exact search,* for which we must find a value equal to the one being sought. Since the quantity ranges are contiguous—each begins where the preceding one leaves off—we need only store the upper limit for each range in the COBOL table:

```
QTY-UPPER-LIMIT        UNIT-PRICE
      99                 29.95
     199                 28.45
     299                 26.87
     999                 23.99
```

We search the table for the first value of `QTY-UPPER-LIMIT` that equals or exceeds the quantity actually ordered. That is, we want to find the first value of `ENTRY-NUMBER` for which

```
QUANTITY-ORDERED NOT > QTY-UPPER-LIMIT (ENTRY-NUMBER)
```

If the quantity ordered is greater than 999, the last price in the table (23.99) should be used. Therefore, if the search is unsuccessful, the value of `ENTRY-NUMBER` should be set to 4.

An inexact search can be programmed with `PERFORM VARYING` or with `SEARCH`, but not with `SEARCH ALL`. For inexact search, entries must be examined in the order in which they appear in the table; with `SEARCH ALL`, we have no control over the order in which table entries are examined.

**2.** Write each of the following `IF` statements in indented form with the indentation reflecting the way the statement will be processed by the COBOL compiler:

(a) `IF c1 s1 IF c2 s2 s3.`

(b) `IF c1 s1 IF c2 s2 ELSE s3.`

(c) `IF c1 IF c2 s2 ELSE s3 s4.`

(d) `IF c1 s1 IF c2 s2 ELSE s3 s4 ELSE s5.`

(e) `IF c1 s1 IF c2 s2 ELSE s3 IF c3 s4 ELSE s5 ELSE s6 s7.`

3. (a) Rewrite the information-retrieval program (Figure 6.5) to use indexes rather than subscripts. Note that more than one index can be associated with a table in an INDEXED BY clause. For example,

```
INDEXED BY ENTRY-NUMBER
          PREV-ENTRY-NUMBER
          FREE
```

associates the three indexes ENTRY-NUMBER, PREV-ENTRY-NUMBER, and FREE with the table in question. All MOVE, ADD, and SUBTRACT statements used to manipulate subscripts must be replaced by SET statements for manipulating indexes. Note that a SET statement often seems backwards with respect to the corresponding MOVE, ADD, or SUBTRACT statement. For example

```
MOVE ENTRY-NUMBER TO PREV-ENTRY-NUMBER.
```

is replaced by

```
SET PREV-ENTRY-NUMBER TO ENTRY-NUMBER.
```

(b) With the aid of relative indexing, modify the program to eliminate the need for the index PREV-ENTRY-NUMBER.

4. Modify the indexing version of the information-retrieval program (see Exercise 3) to search the table with SEARCH instead of PERFORM VARYING. When more than one index is defined for a table entry, SEARCH uses the index that appears first in the INDEXED BY clause, which would be ENTRY-NUMBER for the INDEXED BY clause given in Exercise 3. Since the entire COBOL table is not to be searched, we cannot rely on the AT END phrase to terminate the search when the end of the price list is reached. Instead, we must provide a WHEN clause for this purpose:

```
WHEN ENTRY-NUMBER = FREE
     MOVE "N" TO FOUND
```

Incidentally, SEARCH ALL cannot be used for two reasons: (1) The entries are not necessarily in order according to their key fields; and (2) we are not searching the entire COBOL table.

5. A price list consists of five items with four quantity ranges for each item. Write a program to compute the cost of an order for a single item, given the item number and the quantity ordered.

We store the price list as a two-level table as follows:

```
01   PRICE-LIST.
     02   ITEM-ENTRY OCCURS 5 TIMES.
          03   ITEM-NUMBER PIC X(6).
          03   QUANTITY-ENTRY OCCURS 4 TIMES.
               04   QTY-UPPER-LIMIT PIC 999.
               04   UNIT-PRICE PIC 999V99.
```

Let the value of subscript I designate a particular occurrence of ITEM-ENTRY; for each value of I let the value of subscript Q designate a particular occurrence of QUANTITY-ENTRY. Note that only a single subscript is needed to designate a value of ITEM-NUMBER:

```
ITEM-NUMBER (I)
```

whereas two subscripts are required to designate a value of `QTY-UPPER-LIMIT` or `UNIT-PRICE`:

```
QTY-UPPER-LIMIT (I, Q)
UNIT-PRICE (I, Q)
```

Two searches are required to use this table. First, we perform an exact search to find the value of I such that

```
TARGET-ITEM-NUMBER = ITEM-NUMBER (I)
```

Without changing the value of I, we perform an inexact search to determine the first value of Q such that

```
QUANTITY-ORDERED NOT > QTY-UPPER-LIMIT (I, Q)
```

The values found for I and Q designate the unit price

```
UNIT-PRICE (I, Q)
```

to be used in calculating the cost of the order.

# 7

---

# More About Sequential File Processing

*Sequential access* and *random access* are two general methods for storing records in files and retrieving records from files. With sequential access, input records are processed in the order in which they are stored in the file, and output records are processed in the order in which they are to be stored in the file. With random access, records can be processed in any desired order, regardless of the order in which they are stored or will be stored in a file.

A file for which only sequential access is possible is often called a *sequential file*. Used in this general way, "sequential file" applies not only to IBM COBOL regular-sequential files but also to line-sequential files and files assigned to the printer. Thus, all our work so far has been done with sequential files. In this chapter, we will look at some additional properties of sequential files and at some programming techniques that are particularly applicable to them.

## REASSIGNING DISK FILES TO OTHER DEVICES

A file assigned to DISK in the SELECT entry of the FILE-CONTROL paragraph can be reassigned to other devices by using the appropriate DOS file name:

| DOS File Name | Device |
|---|---|
| LPT1<br>PRN | Printer |
| AUX<br>COM1 | RS-232 port |
| CON<br>USER (see below) | Display |

The reference manual recommends the file name USER for the display. Characters written to USER (it is said) are sent immediately to the display, whereas output written to CON is stored in a buffer area and sent to the display in blocks of 512 characters. With CON, nothing appears on the display until 512 characters of output have accumulated. The only problem is that version 1.00 of IBM COBOL does not recognize USER as a name for the display; when USER is given as a DOS file name, the program creates a disk file named USER. CON is recognized but, as described, causes output to be processed in blocks of 512 characters.

Files to be reassigned should have line-sequential organization; regular-sequential files do not have the format expected by external devices such as the printer and the display. Data sent to output devices must have DISPLAY usage. As far as the COBOL program is concerned, the files are processed as if they were disk files. In particular, COBOL features intended for use with the printer, such as the ADVANCING option and the LINAGE clause, cannot be used with files assigned to DISK, even if they are to be reassigned to the printer.

The DOS file names AUX and COM1 refer to the Asynchronous Communications Adapter, also known as the RS-232 port. There are two types of printers used with the IBM Personal Computer: *parallel* printers and *serial* printers. Parallel printers connect to the Parallel Printer Adapter or the Monochrome Display and Parallel Printer Adapter; serial printers connect to the RS-232 port. The RS-232 port can also be connected to a *modem,* which allows data to be sent and received over telephone lines, or it can be connected directly to another computer.

Before a COBOL program can use the RS-232 port, the Asynchronous Communications Adapter must be initialized with the DOS command MODE:

MODE COM1 :*baud ,parity ,databits ,stopbits ,*P

COM1 refers to Asynchronous Communications Adapter number 1. The remaining parameters define the *communications protocol*. It is up to you to determine the protocol required by the device with which you wish to communicate. The following is a brief description of the parameters and their possible values:

*Baud* is the number of bits per second at which data will be transmitted and received. Possible values are 110, 150, 300, 600, 1200, 2400, 4800, and 9600. Only the first two digits (11, 15, 30, . . . ) need be given.

*Parity* refers to a bit used for error checking. Possible values are N (none), O (odd), and E (even). If the *parity* parameter is omitted, the default is E (even parity).

*Databits* is the number of bits used to transmit each character. Possible values are 7 and 8. If this parameter is omitted, the default is seven bits.

*Stopbits* is the number of bits used to signal the end of a character; possible values are 1 and 2. The default is 2 if *baud* is 110 and 1 otherwise.

The P option causes the system to repeatedly try the RS-232 port rather than give a time-out error if the device connected to the port is not ready. This option is usually used if the RS-232 port is connected to a printer.

For example, the MODE command

        MODE COM1:12,E,7,1

specifies transmission at 1200 bits per second with even parity, 7 data bits, and one stop bit. The P option is not used. The MODE command

        MODE COM1:30,,,,P

specifies transmission at 300 bits per second. The P option is used, and the default values are used for *parity, databits,* and *stopbits*.

Another form of the MODE command can be used to redirect output from the parallel printer to the RS-232 port. For example, after the DOS command

        MODE LPT1:=COM1

files assigned to PRINTER in COBOL programs will be sent to the RS-232 port.

Any required MODE commands must be given to the DOS before executing a COBOL program that sends output to the RS-232 port. It may be convenient to create a batch file containing the MODE commands followed by the command line that invokes the COBOL program.

## THE REWRITE STATEMENT

In Chapter 5 we looked at a program (Figure 5.4) for updating a disk file. The program did not change the file to be updated, however, but created a new, updated file. Advantages of this approach are that the original file is not damaged if some human or mechanical error occurs during updating, and the unchanged original file can be retained as a permanent record. On the other hand, if we make a backup copy of the file to be updated—which should be done anyway, in case the disk is damaged—there is no reason for not changing the original file. The backup copy will serve as a permanent copy and as a means for recovering from errors.

REWRITE allows us to update a file without creating a new copy of it. REWRITE is always used after a READ statement; the record written by REWRITE is stored in the file in the same position as the record that was read by READ. Thus, we can read a record, change it as needed, and store the updated record back in the original file in the position occupied by the record that was read. For a file with which REWRITE is to be used, we must specify I-O (instead of INPUT, OUTPUT, or EXTEND) in the OPEN statement.

Figure 7.1 shows the use of REWRITE in a version of the file-update program from Chapter 5. Figure 7.1 is simpler than Figure 5.4, since the program has one file instead of two to deal with. Since there is only one customer file to be concerned with, CUSTOMER-RECORD can be defined as the record for that file instead of being defined in the Working-Storage section as was done in Figure 5.4.

In the Procedure Division, paragraph UPDATE-FILE accepts the DOS file name for CUSTOMER-FILE and opens CUSTOMER-FILE for input and output:

```
OPEN I-O CUSTOMER-FILE.
```

END-OF-FILE-FLAG is initialized to "N", and the first record is read from CUSTOMER-FILE. UPDATE-RECORD is performed repeatedly until all records in CUSTOMER-FILE have been processed, at which time CUSTOMER-FILE is closed and the program terminates.

```
IDENTIFICATION DIVISION.
PROGRAM-ID. UPDATE-CUSTOMER-FILE.

*      Update file using REWRITE

ENVIRONMENT DIVISION.
INPUT-OUTPUT SECTION.
FILE-CONTROL.
     SELECT CUSTOMER-FILE ASSIGN TO DISK.

DATA DIVISION.
FILE SECTION.
FD   CUSTOMER-FILE
     LABEL RECORDS STANDARD
     VALUE OF FILE-ID IS DOS-FILE-NAME.
01   CUSTOMER-RECORD.
     02   ACCOUNT-NUMBER   PIC X(6).
     02   LAST-NAME        PIC X(30).
     02   FIRST-NAME       PIC X(20).
     02   MIDDLE-INITIAL   PIC X.
     02   STREET-ADDRESS   PIC X(40).
     02   CITY             PIC X(15).
     02   STATE            PIC XX.
     02   ZIP              PIC X(5).
     02   BALANCE          PIC 9(6)V99.
     02   CREDIT-LIMIT     PIC 9(6)V99.

WORKING-STORAGE SECTION.
01   DOS-FILE-NAME        PIC X(15).
01   END-OF-FILE-FLAG     PIC X.
     88   FINISHED        VALUE "Y".
```

*Figure 7.1*  This program uses the REWRITE statement to update a customer file. The program modifies the existing file rather than creating a new, updated file. You should always make a backup copy of the unmodified file before running this type of program.

```
SCREEN SECTION.
01  CUSTOMER-SCREEN.
    02  BLANK SCREEN.
    02  LINE 4 COLUMN 5 REVERSE-VIDEO VALUE "Account Number".
    02  LINE 5 COLUMN 5 PIC XBXXBXXX USING ACCOUNT-NUMBER
            AUTO.
    02  LINE 8 COLUMN 5 REVERSE-VIDEO VALUE "Last Name".
    02  LINE 9 COLUMN 5 PIC X(30) USING LAST-NAME
            AUTO.
    02  LINE 8 COLUMN 40 REVERSE-VIDEO VALUE "First Name".
    02  LINE 9 COLUMN 40 PIC X(20) USING FIRST-NAME
            AUTO.
    02  LINE 8 COLUMN 65 REVERSE-VIDEO VALUE "Initial".
    02  LINE 9 COLUMN 65 PIC X USING MIDDLE-INITIAL
            AUTO.
    02  LINE 12 COLUMN 5 REVERSE-VIDEO VALUE "Street Address".
    02  LINE 13 COLUMN 5 PIC X(40) USING STREET-ADDRESS
            AUTO.
    02  LINE 16 COLUMN 5 REVERSE-VIDEO VALUE "City".
    02  LINE 17 COLUMN 5 PIC X(15) USING CITY
            AUTO.
    02  LINE 16 COLUMN 25 REVERSE-VIDEO VALUE "State".
    02  LINE 17 COLUMN 25 PIC XX USING STATE
            AUTO.
    02  LINE 16 COLUMN 35 REVERSE-VIDEO VALUE "ZIP".
    02  LINE 17 COLUMN 35 PIC X(5) USING ZIP
            AUTO.
    02  LINE 20 COLUMN 5 REVERSE-VIDEO VALUE "Balance".
    02  LINE 21 COLUMN 5 PIC $$$$,$$9.99 USING BALANCE
            AUTO.
    02  LINE 20 COLUMN 21 REVERSE-VIDEO VALUE "Credit Limit".
    02  LINE 21 COLUMN 21 PIC $$$$,$$9.99 USING CREDIT-LIMIT
            AUTO.

PROCEDURE DIVISION.
UPDATE-FILE.
    DISPLAY (1, 1) ERASE (5, 1) "Name of file to be updated? ".
    ACCEPT (, ) DOS-FILE-NAME WITH PROMPT.
    OPEN I-O CUSTOMER-FILE.
    MOVE "N" TO END-OF-FILE-FLAG.
    READ CUSTOMER-FILE
        AT END MOVE "Y" TO END-OF-FILE-FLAG.
    PERFORM UPDATE-RECORD
        UNTIL FINISHED.
    CLOSE CUSTOMER-FILE.
    STOP RUN.

UPDATE-RECORD.
    DISPLAY CUSTOMER-SCREEN.
    ACCEPT CUSTOMER-SCREEN.
    REWRITE CUSTOMER-RECORD.
    READ CUSTOMER-FILE
        AT END MOVE "Y" TO END-OF-FILE-FLAG.
```

*Figure 7.1 (continued)*

As usual in sequential file processing, the record-processing paragraph UPDATE-RECORD begins by processing the record read by the initial READ statement in UPDATE-FILE or by a previous execution of UPDATE-RECORD. The previously read record is displayed for the user and the user's changes are accepted:

```
DISPLAY CUSTOMER-SCREEN.
ACCEPT CUSTOMER-SCREEN.
```

The source and receiving fields defined in CUSTOMER-SCREEN are the fields of CUSTOMER-RECORD. Thus after the DISPLAY and ACCEPT statement have been executed, CUSTOMER-RECORD contains the updated record. We write the updated record back to the file with

```
REWRITE CUSTOMER-RECORD.
```

UPDATE-RECORD finishes by reading the next record from CUSTOMER-FILE, the record that will be updated the next time UPDATE-RECORD is performed.

## EXTEND MODE

A regular- or line-sequential disk file can be opened in EXTEND mode:

```
OPEN EXTEND FILE-A.
```

EXTEND mode is the same as OUTPUT mode except that records written by the program are stored at the end of an existing file instead of in a newly created file. A file opened in EXTEND mode must already exist on the disk; EXTEND mode cannot be used to create a new file.

## CONTROL TOTALS

We often want to provide a report with *control totals*—totals and subtotals summarizing various levels of business activity. For example, suppose a company's marketing area is divided into *territories;* a number of *salespeople* work in each territory; and each salesperson handles a variety of *products*. We are interested in three kinds of total: the total sales for each territory, the total sales by each salesperson in each territory, and the total sales of each product by each salesperson in each territory.

Each business activity that we want to summarize is referred to as a *level*. Thus, we want to consider sales at the *territory level,* the *salesperson level,* and the *product level*. The most inclusive level, the territory level, is said to be the *major level*. The least inclusive level, the product level, is said to be the *minor level*. In between is the salesperson level, which is therefore known as the *intermediate level*. A program that provides totals for the territory, salesperson, and product levels is said to provide *three levels of control totals*. The printing of one or more totals is called a *control break*.

Figure 7.2 shows a program for printing control totals. Figure 7.3 shows a sample data file and the report produced when the sample file is processed by the program. The program's input data is read from SALES-DATA-FILE, which is assigned to DISK. SALES-DATA-FILE is given line-sequential organization so that small test files can be prepared with a text editor. The report is written to SALES-REPORT-FILE, which is assigned to the printer.

Each input record gives the amount of one sale of a particular product. In order for the amount of the sale to be included in the proper totals, the input record must identify

```
IDENTIFICATION DIVISION.
PROGRAM-ID.  CONTROL-TOTALS.

*    Print product, salesperson, and territory totals.

ENVIRONMENT DIVISION.
INPUT-OUTPUT SECTION.
FILE-CONTROL.
    SELECT SALES-DATA-FILE ASSIGN TO DISK
        ORGANIZATION IS LINE SEQUENTIAL.
    SELECT SALES-REPORT-FILE ASSIGN TO PRINTER.

DATA DIVISION.
FILE SECTION.
FD  SALES-DATA-FILE
    LABEL RECORDS STANDARD
    VALUE OF FILE-ID IS DOS-FILE-NAME.
01  SALES-DATA-RECORD.
    02   TERRITORY-NUMBER          PIC X(3).
    02   SALESPERSON-NUMBER        PIC X(3).
    02   PRODUCT-NUMBER            PIC X(3).
    02   SALES-AMOUNT              PIC 9999V99.

FD  SALES-REPORT-FILE
    LABEL RECORDS OMITTED.
01  SALES-REPORT-RECORD           PIC X(80).

WORKING-STORAGE SECTION.
01  HEADING-LINE.
    02   FILLER                    PIC X(3)  VALUE SPACES.
    02   FILLER                    PIC X(7)  VALUE "Product".
    02   FILLER                    PIC X(6)  VALUE SPACES.
    02   FILLER                    PIC X(5)  VALUE "Total".
    02   FILLER                    PIC X(6)  VALUE SPACES.
    02   FILLER                    PIC X(11) VALUE "Salesperson".
    02   FILLER                    PIC X(5)  VALUE SPACES.
    02   FILLER                    PIC X(5)  VALUE "Total".
    02   FILLER                    PIC X(6)  VALUE SPACES.
    02   FILLER                    PIC X(9)  VALUE "Territory".
    02   FILLER                    PIC X(6)  VALUE SPACES.
    02   FILLER                    PIC X(5)  VALUE "Total".

01  DETAIL-LINE.
    02   FILLER                    PIC X(5).
    02   DL-PRODUCT-NUMBER         PIC X(3).
    02   FILLER                    PIC X(6).
    02   DL-PRODUCT-TOTAL          PIC $$,$$9.99.
    02   FILLER                    PIC X(8).
    02   DL-SALESPERSON-NUMBER     PIC X(3).
    02   FILLER                    PIC X(7).
    02   DL-SALESPERSON-TOTAL      PIC $$,$$9.99.
    02   FILLER                    PIC X(7).
    02   DL-TERRITORY-NUMBER       PIC X(3).
    02   FILLER                    PIC X(7).
    02   DL-TERRITORY-TOTAL        PIC $$,$$9.99.
```

*Figure 7.2*   This program prints a report containing three levels of control totals.

```
01   ACCUMULATORS.
     02   TERRITORY-TOTAL         PIC 9999V99.
     02   SALESPERSON-TOTAL       PIC 9999V99.
     02   PRODUCT-TOTAL           PIC 9999V99.


01   CURRENT-NUMBERS.
     02   CURRENT-TERRITORY-NUMBER      PIC X(3).
     02   CURRENT-SALESPERSON-NUMBER    PIC X(3).
     02   CURRENT-PRODUCT-NUMBER        PIC X(3).


01   INPUT-FILE-CONTROL.
     02   END-OF-INPUT-FLAG       PIC X.
     02   DOS-FILE-NAME           PIC X(15).

PROCEDURE DIVISION.
MAIN-ROUTINE.
     PERFORM OPEN-FILES-AND-PRINT-HEADINGS.
     MOVE "N" TO END-OF-INPUT-FLAG.
     MOVE ZERO TO TERRITORY-TOTAL
                    SALESPERSON-TOTAL
                    PRODUCT-TOTAL.
     READ SALES-DATA-FILE
         AT END MOVE "Y" TO END-OF-INPUT-FLAG.
     IF END-OF-INPUT-FLAG  = "N"
         MOVE TERRITORY-NUMBER TO CURRENT-TERRITORY-NUMBER
         MOVE SALESPERSON-NUMBER TO CURRENT-SALESPERSON-NUMBER
         MOVE PRODUCT-NUMBER TO CURRENT-PRODUCT-NUMBER.
     PERFORM PROCESS-ONE-RECORD
         UNTIL END-OF-INPUT-FLAG = "Y".
     PERFORM PRINT-TERRITORY-TOTAL.
     CLOSE SALES-DATA-FILE
           SALES-REPORT-FILE.
     STOP RUN.


OPEN-FILES-AND-PRINT-HEADINGS.
     DISPLAY (1, 1) ERASE (5, 1) "Name of input file? ".
     ACCEPT (, ) DOS-FILE-NAME WITH PROMPT.
     OPEN INPUT SALES-DATA-FILE
          OUTPUT SALES-REPORT-FILE.
     WRITE SALES-REPORT-RECORD
         FROM HEADING-LINE.
     MOVE SPACES TO SALES-REPORT-RECORD.
     WRITE SALES-REPORT-RECORD.


PROCESS-ONE-RECORD.
     IF TERRITORY-NUMBER NOT = CURRENT-TERRITORY-NUMBER
         PERFORM PRINT-TERRITORY-TOTAL
     ELSE IF SALESPERSON-NUMBER NOT = CURRENT-SALESPERSON-NUMBER
         PERFORM PRINT-SALESPERSON-TOTAL
     ELSE IF PRODUCT-NUMBER NOT = CURRENT-PRODUCT-NUMBER
         PERFORM PRINT-PRODUCT-TOTAL.
     ADD SALES-AMOUNT TO TERRITORY-TOTAL.
     ADD SALES-AMOUNT TO SALESPERSON-TOTAL.
     ADD SALES-AMOUNT TO PRODUCT-TOTAL.
     READ SALES-DATA-FILE
         AT END MOVE "Y" TO END-OF-INPUT-FLAG.
```

*Figure 7.2 (continued)*

```
PRINT-TERRITORY-TOTAL.
    PERFORM PRINT-SALESPERSON-TOTAL.
    MOVE SPACES TO DETAIL-LINE.
    MOVE CURRENT-TERRITORY-NUMBER TO DL-TERRITORY-NUMBER.
    MOVE TERRITORY-TOTAL TO DL-TERRITORY-TOTAL.
    WRITE SALES-REPORT-RECORD
        FROM DETAIL-LINE.
    MOVE TERRITORY-NUMBER TO CURRENT-TERRITORY-NUMBER.
    MOVE ZERO TO TERRITORY-TOTAL.

PRINT-SALESPERSON-TOTAL.
    PERFORM PRINT-PRODUCT-TOTAL.
    MOVE SPACES TO DETAIL-LINE.
    MOVE CURRENT-SALESPERSON-NUMBER TO DL-SALESPERSON-NUMBER.
    MOVE SALESPERSON-TOTAL TO DL-SALESPERSON-TOTAL.
    WRITE SALES-REPORT-RECORD
        FROM DETAIL-LINE.
    MOVE SALESPERSON-NUMBER TO CURRENT-SALESPERSON-NUMBER.
    MOVE ZERO TO SALESPERSON-TOTAL.

PRINT-PRODUCT-TOTAL.
    MOVE SPACES TO DETAIL-LINE.
    MOVE CURRENT-PRODUCT-NUMBER TO DL-PRODUCT-NUMBER.
    MOVE PRODUCT-TOTAL TO DL-PRODUCT-TOTAL.
    WRITE SALES-REPORT-RECORD
        FROM DETAIL-LINE.
    MOVE PRODUCT-NUMBER TO CURRENT-PRODUCT-NUMBER.
    MOVE ZERO TO PRODUCT-TOTAL.
```

*Figure 7.2 (continued)*

the territory in which the sale was made, the salesperson who made the sale, and the product that was sold. We assume that each territory, salesperson, and product is identified by a three-digit number. Thus the record for SALES-DATA-FILE is defined as follows:

```
01    SALES-DATA-RECORD.
      02    TERRITORY-NUMBER      PIC X(3).
      02    SALESPERSON-NUMBER    PIC X(3).
      02    PRODUCT-NUMBER        PIC X(3).
      02    SALES-AMOUNT          PIC 9999V99.
```

For example, input data record

```
bb7bb3bb5003995
```

(where the b's stand for blanks, as usual) represents a sale in territory 7 by salesperson 3 of product 5. The amount of the sale (in conventional notation) is $39.95.

We recall that the records in a sequential file must be processed in the order in which they are stored in the file. Before the file can be processed, therefore, it must be sorted so that the records are in the required order. In the case at hand, the records need to be sorted first by territory, then by salesperson, and finally by product. That is, the records for territory 1 must come before those for territory 2, and so on. Within the records for each territory, the records for salesperson 1 must come before the records for salesperson 2, and so on. Finally, within the records for each salesperson, the records for product 1 must come before the records for product 2, and so on.

(a)
```
1   1   1030000
1   1   1010000
1   2   1050000
1   2   2070000
2   3   1040000
2   3   2010000
2   3   2090000
2   4   3060000
2   4   3050000
3   4   3040000
3   5   1020000
3   5   2010000
```

(b)

| Product | Total | Salesperson | Total | Territory | Total |
|---------|-------|-------------|-------|-----------|-------|
| 1 | $400.00 | | | | |
| | | 1 | $400.00 | | |
| 1 | $500.00 | | | | |
| 2 | $700.00 | | | | |
| | | 2 | $1,200.00 | | |
| | | | | 1 | $1,600.00 |
| 1 | $400.00 | | | | |
| 2 | $1,000.00 | | | | |
| | | 3 | $1,400.00 | | |
| 3 | $1,100.00 | | | | |
| | | 4 | $1,100.00 | | |
| | | | | 2 | $2,500.00 |
| 3 | $400.00 | | | | |
| | | 4 | $400.00 | | |
| 1 | $200.00 | | | | |
| 2 | $100.00 | | | | |
| | | 5 | $300.00 | | |
| | | | | 3 | $700.00 |

*Figure 7.3*   (a) A data file for the control-totals program in Figure 7.2. (b) The report produced when the data file is processed.

We can achieve the required order by arranging the records in ascending order according to the first nine characters of each record. Since alphanumeric values are compared from left to right, a record with a smaller territory number will precede a record with a larger territory number. If two records have the same territory number, the one with the smallest salesperson number will come first. And if two records have the same territory number and salesperson number, the one with the smallest product number will come first. (Note the order of the records in the sample data file in Figure 7.3.) It was with sorting in mind that TERRITORY-NUMBER was chosen as the first field of the record, SALESPERSON-NUMBER as the second field, and SALES-AMOUNT as the third field.

Standard COBOL provides a SORT statement for placing the records of a file in order according to one or more fields. Unfortunately, the SORT statement is one of the advanced features omitted from IBM COBOL. Much the same effect, however, can be had with the *indexed files* described in Chapter 9, which allow records to be stored in such a way that they can later be read in ascending order according to a particular field. Also, DOS 2.00 provides a SORT command that can be used to sort line-sequential files.

The format of the report in Figure 7.3 has been made as simple as possible so that we can concentrate on the logic of the program rather than on the details of producing fancy reports. There is no title, page number, or provisions for handling multiple-page reports. The output is arranged in six columns, two for each level, with the columns for the minor level on the left and those for the major level on the right. Of the two columns for a given level, the left gives the territory, salesperson, or product number and the right gives the corresponding total.

Totals need to be printed after processing all the records for a particular product, salesperson, or territory. That is, each *change* in the product, salesperson, or territory number causes the corresponding total to be produced. Whenever a salesperson total is produced, a product total is also produced, even if the product number remains the same—we want separate product totals for sales of the same product by different salespeople. Likewise, whenever a territory total is produced, salesperson and product totals are also produced even if the salesperson and product numbers remain the same—we want separate product and salesperson totals for sales made in different territories.

In the Working-Storage Section, `HEADING-LINE` provides the line of column headings. `DETAIL-LINE` defines six data fields, one for each column in the report. Examining Figure 7.3, however, we see that only two data fields are used in each line, the fields corresponding to the remaining columns being blank. Before printing a detail line, we move `SPACES` to `DETAIL-LINE`, filling all the fields with blanks. We then move values to the two data fields that are to be used; the remaining data fields remain blank. Incidentally, we do not have to specify `VALUE SPACES` for the `FILLER` items; moving `SPACES` to the entire record also blanks out the `FILLER` items.

The accumulators `TERRITORY-TOTAL`, `SALESPERSON-TOTAL`, and `PRODUCT-TOTAL` are used to maintain the three totals computed by the program. `CURRENT-TERRITORY-NUMBER`, `CURRENT-SALESPERSON-NUMBER`, and `CURRENT-PRODUCT-NUMBER` are used to keep track of the territory, salesperson, and product for which records are currently being processed. When a new record is read, its territory, salesperson, and product numbers are compared with the current ones. If all the numbers match, the sales amount for the new record is added to all the totals and the program reads the next input record. If any of the numbers do not match, the territory, product, or salesperson has changed, and a control break must be produced before processing the new record.

In the Procedure Division, paragraph `MAIN-ROUTINE` starts by performing `OPEN-FILES-AND-PRINT-HEADINGS` to get the DOS file name for the input file, to open the input and print files, and to print the heading line at the top of the report. Next, `MAIN-ROUTINE` initializes `END-OF-INPUT-FLAG` to `"N"`, clears the three accumulators to zero, and reads the first record from the input file. If a valid record was read—the value of `END-OF-INPUT-FLAG` is still `"N"`—`CURRENT-TERRITORY-NUMBER`, `CURRENT-SALESPERSON-NUMBER`, and `CURRENT-PRODUCT-NUMBER` are initialized to the corresponding numbers for the first record. Paragraph `PROCESS-ONE-RECORD` is performed repeatedly until all input records have been processed. `PRINT-TERRITORY-TOTAL` is performed to print totals for the last territory processed, after which the files are closed and the program terminated.

When PROCESS-ONE-RECORD is performed, a record has been read but not yet processed. The first job of PROCESS-ONE-RECORD is to determine if a control-break must be produced before processing the new record. A control break is produced when there is a change in the territory, salesperson, or product number—when one or more of these numbers in the record just read differ from the corresponding numbers currently being processed by the program. For example, if the program is currently processing records for territory 3, and the record just read is for territory 4, the program must print summarizing totals for territory 3 before processing the first record for territory 4.

A multiway selection determines whether to print a territory total, salesperson total, or product total, or whether to produce no control break at all. We want to produce totals at as high a level as is necessary—we would not want to just print a product total when the salesperson or the territory has also changed. Therefore, the program begins by checking for a change at the highest level—it checks if the territory number has changed; if it has, PRINT-TERRITORY-TOTAL is performed. Otherwise, the program checks if the salesperson number has changed; if it has, PRINT-SALESPERSON-TOTAL is performed. Finally, the program checks if the product number has changed; if it has, PRINT-PRODUCT-TOTAL is performed. If none of the identifying numbers have changed, none of the print-total paragraphs are performed, and so no control break is produced.

Regardless of whether or not a control break was produced, PROCESS-ONE-RECORD now processes the record just read by adding the value of SALES-AMOUNT to each of the three accumulators, after which a new record is read from the input file.

Paragraphs PRINT-TERRITORY-TOTAL, PRINT-SALESPERSON-TOTAL, and PRINT-PRODUCT-TOTAL each handles one level of totals; the three paragraphs have much the same structure. As mentioned, when a salesperson total is printed, the current product total is also printed, since we want a separate product total for each salesperson who sells a product. Therefore, PRINT-SALESPERSON-TOTAL first performs PRINT-PRODUCT-TOTAL to print the product total, then goes on to print the salesperson total. Likewise, PRINT-TERRITORY-TOTAL performs PRINT-SALESPERSON-TOTAL to print the salesperson and product totals, then goes on to print the territory total.

Selecting PRINT-PRODUCT-TOTAL for detailed study, we see that the first step is to blank out the detail line:

```
MOVE SPACES TO DETAIL-LINE.
```

Next, the current product number and the corresponding product total are moved to the corresponding fields of DETAIL-LINE, after which DETAIL-LINE is written to the output file:

```
MOVE CURRENT-PRODUCT-NUMBER TO DL-PRODUCT-NUMBER.
MOVE PRODUCT-TOTAL TO DL-PRODUCT-TOTAL.
WRITE SALES-REPORT-RECORD
    FROM DETAIL-LINE.
```

The final step is to prepare for processing a new product. CURRENT-PRODUCT-NUMBER is set to the new product number—the product number in the record that triggered the control break—and PRODUCT-TOTAL is reset to zero:

```
MOVE PRODUCT-NUMBER TO CURRENT-PRODUCT-NUMBER.
MOVE ZERO TO PRODUCT-TOTAL.
```

## MERGING

Suppose we have two sequential files with the records in each file in ascending order according to values of a key field—an identifying field such as an employee number or an account number. We wish to *merge* the two files—to combine them in such a way that the records in the combined file are also in ascending order according to values of the key field. Only the methods of sequential file processing can be used—records must be read from each file to be merged in the order in which they are stored in that file, and records must be written to the merged file in the order in which they are to be stored.

Merging has many applications. We might use it, for example, to merge mailing lists obtained from different sources. If two companies merge, corresponding files for the two companies, such as their employee and customer account files, will need to be merged. Since merging builds a larger sorted file out of two smaller sorted files, it is the basis for many sorting programs. Variations on merging allow us to compare the contents of two files in various ways. For example, we could use a variation of merging to compare an automobile registration file with a property tax file, producing a list of automobile owners who have not paid property taxes on their cars.

The principle of merging is very simple. To being with, only two records are accessible to the merging program—the first record in each of the files being merged. Since the records in the merged file are to be in ascending order according to values of the key field, the record with the smallest key is written to the merged file, and a new record is read from the file whose first record had the smallest key.

This process is repeated for the remaining records in the files being merged. At any time, the merging program will have in memory two records, one from each of the files being merged. The program compares the keys of these two records, writes the record with the smallest key to the merged file, and reads a new record from the file whose record had the smallest key. When one of the files being merged is exhausted, the remaining records in the other file are copied to the merged file.

To see that this procedure works, let's consider two very small files, A and B. The records in each file will be represented by their key values, which are two digit numbers. We can illustrate the two files as follows:

```
A:  11   59
B:  21   70   85   94
```

Note that the records in each file are in ascending order according to their key values. To begin, the keys of the first record in each file (the leftmost record in the illustrations) are compared. The record with the smallest key is transferred to the merged file, which we call file C:

```
A: 59
                                    C:  11
B: 21   70   85   94
```

Continuing, the keys of the next record to be read from each file (again, the leftmost record in the illustration) are compared. The record with the smallest key is transferred to the merged file:

```
A: 59
                                    C:  11   21
B: 70   85   94
```

The next step exhausts file A:

```
A:
                                    C:  11   21   59
B: 70   85   94
```

When one file is exhausted, all the records in the remaining file are transferred to the merged file:

```
                    C:  11   21   59   70   85   94
```

Figure 7.4 shows a merging program and Figure 7.5 shows two files to be merged and the resulting merged file. Following the notation in the example, the files to be merged are named A-FILE and B-FILE, and the merged file is called C-FILE. All three files are assigned to DISK; all are given line-sequential organization so that test files can be created with a text editor and printed out as in Figure 7.5.

In the File Section, each record associated with each file is defined to be 13 characters long. In the Working-Storage Section, we define memory areas A-REC and B-REC to hold the current records read from A-FILE and B-FILE. Each record has a six-character key field. The merging program works only with the key fields—the remainder of the record can have whatever structure is required by a particular application. For simplicity, we give each record only one additional field, a *balance* field with picture 9(5)V99. In Figure 7.5, each record in A-FILE is given a balance of 9999999 and each record in B-FILE is given a balance of 1111111, thus making it easy to see which records in the merged file originated in A-FILE and which originated in B-FILE.

In the Procedure Division, MERGE-FILES begins by obtaining the DOS file names for the three files. A-FILE and B-FILE are opened for input, and C-FILE is opened for output. Paragraphs READ-A-FILE and READ-B-FILE are performed to read the first record from each of the two input files.

READ-A-FILE reads the next record from A-FILE into A-REC. If there are no more records in A-FILE, HIGH-VALUE is moved to A-KEY. READ-B-FILE carries out the corresponding operations for B-FILE and B-REC. HIGH-VALUE is a value that is larger than all other values having the same picture. We assume that no valid record has a key equal to HIGH-VALUE so HIGH-VALUE is larger than the key of any valid record. A value of HIGH-VALUE for either A-KEY or B-KEY signals the end of the corresponding file. The reason for using HIGH-VALUE for this

```
IDENTIFICATION DIVISION.
PROGRAM-ID.  MERGE.

*    Merge A-FILE and B-FILE to form C-FILE.

ENVIRONMENT DIVISION.
INPUT-OUTPUT SECTION.
FILE-CONTROL.
    SELECT A-FILE ASSIGN TO DISK
        ORGANIZATION IS LINE SEQUENTIAL.
    SELECT B-FILE ASSIGN TO DISK
        ORGANIZATION IS LINE SEQUENTIAL.
    SELECT C-FILE ASSIGN TO DISK
        ORGANIZATION IS LINE SEQUENTIAL.

DATA DIVISION.
FILE SECTION.
FD  A-FILE
    LABEL RECORDS STANDARD
    VALUE OF FILE-ID IS DOS-FILE-NAME-A.
01  A-RECORD            PIC X(13).

FD  B-FILE
    LABEL RECORDS STANDARD
    VALUE OF FILE-ID IS DOS-FILE-NAME-B.
01  B-RECORD            PIC X(13).

FD  C-FILE
    LABEL RECORDS STANDARD
    VALUE OF FILE-ID IS DOS-FILE-NAME-C.
01  C-RECORD            PIC X(13).

WORKING-STORAGE SECTION.
01  A-REC.
    02  A-KEY           PIC X(6).
    02  A-BALANCE       PIC 9(5)V99.

01  B-REC.
    02  B-KEY           PIC X(6).
    02  B-BALANCE       PIC 9(5)V99.

01  DOS-FILE-NAME-A     PIC X(15).
01  DOS-FILE-NAME-B     PIC X(15).
01  DOS-FILE-NAME-C     PIC X(15).
```

*Figure 7.4*  This program merges two files. The two input files are F I L E - A and F I L E - B. The merged records are written to F I L E - C.

purpose is that when one file is exhausted, we want all the records in the other file to be copied to the merged file. The program always moves the record with the smaller key to the merged file, so if the value of one of the keys is H I G H - V A L U E, the remaining records in the other file, having keys smaller than H I G H - V A L U E, will be transferred to the merged file as desired.

Returning to M E R G E - F I L E S, after reading the first record from each file to be merged, the program performs P R O C E S S - O N E - R E C O R D until both A - K E Y and

```
PROCEDURE DIVISION.
MERGE-FILES.
     DISPLAY (1, 1) ERASE (5, 1) "First input file? ".
     ACCEPT (, ) DOS-FILE-NAME-A WITH PROMPT.
     DISPLAY (7, 1) "Second input file? ".
     ACCEPT (, ) DOS-FILE-NAME-B WITH PROMPT.
     DISPLAY (9, 1) "Output file? ".
     ACCEPT (, ) DOS-FILE-NAME-C WITH PROMPT.
     OPEN INPUT A-FILE
          INPUT B-FILE
          OUTPUT C-FILE.
     PERFORM READ-A-FILE.
     PERFORM READ-B-FILE.
     PERFORM PROCESS-ONE-RECORD
          UNTIL A-KEY = HIGH-VALUE AND B-KEY = HIGH-VALUE.
     CLOSE A-FILE
           B-FILE
           C-FILE.
     STOP RUN.

PROCESS-ONE-RECORD.
     IF A-KEY < B-KEY
          WRITE C-RECORD
               FROM A-REC
          PERFORM READ-A-FILE
     ELSE
          WRITE C-RECORD
               FROM B-REC
          PERFORM READ-B-FILE.

READ-A-FILE.
     READ A-FILE
          INTO A-REC
          AT END MOVE HIGH-VALUE TO A-KEY.

READ-B-FILE.
     READ B-FILE
          INTO B-REC
          AT END MOVE HIGH-VALUE TO B-KEY.
```

*Figure 7.4 (continued)*

B-KEY are equal to HIGH-VALUE—that is, until both input files have been exhausted. At that point, the files are closed and the program terminated.

When PROCESS-ONE-RECORD is performed, A-REC and B-REC each contain a record read from the corresponding file (the key of one record may equal HIGH-VALUE, indicating that the corresponding file has been exhausted). The keys of the two records are compared. If A-REC has the smaller key, the contents of A-REC are written to C-FILE, and new record is read from A-FILE. Otherwise, the contents of B-REC are written to C-FILE, and a new record is read from B-FILE.

## MORE ABOUT UPDATING SEQUENTIAL FILES

We have previously looked at file-update programs in which the data in each record can be changed, but the number of records remain the same after the update as before. We

| (a) | (b) | (c) |
|-----|-----|-----|
| 1000009999999 | 0500001111111 | 0500001111111 |
| 2000009999999 | 2500001111111 | 1000009999999 |
| 3000009999999 | 3500001111111 | 2000009999999 |
| 4000009999999 | 3700001111111 | 2500001111111 |
| 5000009999999 | 5500001111111 | 3000009999999 |
| 6000009999999 | 8000001111111 | 3500001111111 |
| 7000009999999 | 9500001111111 | 3700001111111 |
| 8000009999999 | 9700001111111 | 4000009999999 |
| 9000009999999 | 9900001111111 | 5000009999999 |
|  |  | 5500001111111 |
|  |  | 6000009999999 |
|  |  | 7000009999999 |
|  |  | 8000001111111 |
|  |  | 8000009999999 |
|  |  | 9000009999999 |
|  |  | 9500001111111 |
|  |  | 9700001111111 |
|  |  | 9900001111111 |

*Figure 7.5*   Parts (a) and (b) are input files for the merging program in Figure 7.3. Part (c) is the merged file produced by the program.

now want to consider a more general file-update program that can add new records to the file and delete no longer needed ones, as well as modify records that are to be retained.

We are concerned with two files, a *master file* and a *transaction file*. The master file contains permanent records such as customer accounts. The transaction file contains records specifying modifications to the master file, such as records of purchases and payments as well as records opening new accounts and closing old ones. Specifically, a transaction record can request any of three operations; *add* a new record to the master file, *update* an existing record, or *delete* a record from the master file.

Because records are to be added and deleted, the update program must create a new, updated copy of the master file. (REWRITE allows us to modify records in a sequential file, but not to find room for new records or close up gaps left by deleted records.) The master file to be updated is called the *old master file,* and the updated file is called the *new master file*. File updates are usually performed periodically—say, once a month. The new master file produced by last month's update becomes this month's old master file. The new master file produced by this month's update will become next month's old master file, and so on.

Sequential file update is one of the variations of merging mentioned earlier. The records in the old master file and the transaction file are in ascending order according to values of a key field. The file-update program reads the old master file and the transaction file, producing a new master file whose records are also in ascending order. But instead of merely combining the old master file and the transaction file—as a straight merging program would do—the file-update program carries out the operations on each master record that are specified by all transaction records having the same key as the master record.

Figure 7.6 shows the file-update program. OLD-MASTER-FILE, NEW-MASTER-FILE, and TRANSACTION-FILE are all assigned to DISK. All three

```
      IDENTIFICATION DIVISION.
      PROGRAM-ID.  SEQUENTIAL-FILE-UPDATE.

*        Update master file from transaction file.

      ENVIRONMENT DIVISION.
      INPUT-OUTPUT SECTION.
      FILE-CONTROL.
          SELECT OLD-MASTER-FILE ASSIGN TO DISK
              ORGANIZATION IS LINE SEQUENTIAL.
          SELECT NEW-MASTER-FILE ASSIGN TO DISK
              ORGANIZATION IS LINE SEQUENTIAL.
          SELECT TRANSACTION-FILE ASSIGN TO DISK
              ORGANIZATION IS LINE SEQUENTIAL.

      DATA DIVISION.
      FILE SECTION.
      FD  OLD-MASTER-FILE
          LABEL RECORDS STANDARD
          VALUE OF FILE-ID IS DOS-FILE-NAME-OM.
      01  OLD-MASTER-RECORD         PIC X(13).

      FD  NEW-MASTER-FILE
          LABEL RECORDS STANDARD
          VALUE OF FILE-ID IS DOS-FILE-NAME-NM.
      01  NEW-MASTER-RECORD         PIC X(13).

      FD  TRANSACTION-FILE
          LABEL RECORDS STANDARD
          VALUE OF FILE-ID IS DOS-FILE-NAME-TR.
      01  TRANSACTION-RECORD        PIC X(15).

      WORKING-STORAGE SECTION.
      01  OLD-MASTER-REC.
          02  OM-KEY                PIC X(6).
          02  OM-BALANCE            PIC 9(5)V99.

      01  NEW-MASTER-REC.
          02  NM-KEY                PIC X(6).
          02  NM-BALANCE            PIC 9(5)V99.

      01  TRANSACTION-REC.
          02  TR-KEY                PIC X(6).
          02  TR-FUNCTION           PIC X.
          02  TR-AMOUNT             PIC S9(5)V99
                                    SIGN IS TRAILING SEPARATE.

      01  ERROR-RECORD.
          02  FILLER                PIC X(14) VALUE "Error for key ".
          02  ER-KEY                PIC X(6).
          02  FILLER                PIC X(2) VALUE ": ".
          02  ER-MESSAGE            PIC X(40).

      01  CURRENT-KEY               PIC X(6).
      01  OCCUPIED                  PIC X.
      01  DOS-FILE-NAME-OM          PIC X(15).
      01  DOS-FILE-NAME-NM          PIC X(15).
      01  DOS-FILE-NAME-TR          PIC X(15).
```

*Figure 7.6*  This program updates a master file from a transaction file. The records in both the master file and the transaction file must be in ascending order according to their key values.

```
PROCEDURE DIVISION.
MAIN-ROUTINE.
     DISPLAY (1, 1) ERASE (5, 1) "Old master file? ".
     ACCEPT (, ) DOS-FILE-NAME-OM WITH PROMPT.
     DISPLAY (7, 1) "Transaction file? ".
     ACCEPT (, ) DOS-FILE-NAME-TR WITH PROMPT.
     DISPLAY (9, 1) "New master file? ".
     ACCEPT (, ) DOS-FILE-NAME-NM WITH PROMPT.
     DISPLAY (1, 1) ERASE.
     OPEN INPUT OLD-MASTER-FILE
          INPUT TRANSACTION-FILE
          OUTPUT NEW-MASTER-FILE.
     PERFORM READ-OLD-MASTER-FILE.
     PERFORM READ-TRANSACTION-FILE.
     PERFORM PROCESS-ONE-KEY
          UNTIL OM-KEY = HIGH-VALUE AND
               TR-KEY = HIGH-VALUE.
     CLOSE OLD-MASTER-FILE
           TRANSACTION-FILE
           NEW-MASTER-FILE.
     STOP RUN.

READ-OLD-MASTER-FILE.
     READ OLD-MASTER-FILE
          INTO OLD-MASTER-REC
          AT END MOVE HIGH-VALUE TO OM-KEY.

READ-TRANSACTION-FILE.
     READ TRANSACTION-FILE
          INTO TRANSACTION-REC
          AT END MOVE HIGH-VALUE TO TR-KEY.

PROCESS-ONE-KEY.
     PERFORM SELECT-KEY.
     PERFORM PROCESS-TRANSACTION-RECORD
          UNTIL TR-KEY NOT = CURRENT-KEY.
     IF OCCUPIED = "Y"
          WRITE NEW-MASTER-RECORD
               FROM NEW-MASTER-REC.

SELECT-KEY.
     IF OM-KEY < TR-KEY OR = TR-KEY
          MOVE OM-KEY TO CURRENT-KEY
          MOVE OLD-MASTER-REC TO NEW-MASTER-REC
          PERFORM READ-OLD-MASTER-FILE
          MOVE "Y" TO OCCUPIED
     ELSE
          MOVE TR-KEY TO CURRENT-KEY
          MOVE "N" TO OCCUPIED.
```

*Figure 7.6 (continued)*

files are given line-sequential organization for the usual reason that we want to create old master and transaction test files and print or display the new master file produced when the test files are processed.

In the Working-Storage section we define the memory areas that will hold the current old master, new master, and transaction records. The records in the old master

```
PROCESS-TRANSACTION-RECORD.
    IF TR-FUNCTION = "A"
        PERFORM ADD-RECORD
    ELSE IF TR-FUNCTION = "U"
        PERFORM UPDATE-RECORD
    ELSE IF TR-FUNCTION = "D"
        PERFORM DELETE-RECORD
    ELSE
        MOVE TR-KEY TO ER-KEY
        MOVE "Invalid transaction code" TO ER-MESSAGE
        DISPLAY ERROR-RECORD.
    PERFORM READ-TRANSACTION-FILE.

ADD-RECORD.
    IF OCCUPIED = "N"
        MOVE TR-KEY TO NM-KEY
        MOVE TR-AMOUNT TO NM-BALANCE
        MOVE "Y" TO OCCUPIED
    ELSE
        MOVE TR-KEY TO ER-KEY
        MOVE "Record already present--cannot add" TO
            ER-MESSAGE
        DISPLAY ERROR-RECORD.

UPDATE-RECORD.
    IF OCCUPIED = "Y"
        ADD TR-AMOUNT TO NM-BALANCE
    ELSE
        MOVE TR-KEY TO ER-KEY
        MOVE "Record not present--cannot update" TO
            ER-MESSAGE
        DISPLAY ERROR-RECORD.

DELETE-RECORD.
    IF OCCUPIED = "Y"
        MOVE "N" TO OCCUPIED
    ELSE
        MOVE TR-KEY TO ER-KEY
        MOVE "Record not present--cannot delete" TO
            ER-MESSAGE
        DISPLAY ERROR-RECORD.
```

*Figure 7.6 (continued)*

file have the same structure as those processed by the merging program—a six-digit key followed by balance field with picture 9(5)V99. The structure of the transaction records is slightly different. Following the six-character key, TR-KEY, is a one-character field, TR-FUNCTION, which gives the operation specified by this transaction record. If the value of TR-FUNCTION is "A", the transaction *adds* a new record to the master file; if the value is "U", the transaction record *updates* the master record whose key is equal to TR-KEY. If the value is "D", the transaction record *deletes* the master record whose key is equal to TR-KEY.

The field TR-AMOUNT serves different purposes depending on the function of the transaction. If a new record is being added, TR-AMOUNT gives the initial balance for the new record. If a master record is being updated, the value of TR-AMOUNT is added to the balance field of the master record. If a master record is being deleted, TR-AMOUNT is not used and can be omitted. (An unneeded field at the end of a record can always be omitted; COBOL fills the memory area corresponding to the omitted field with blanks.)

When a record is being updated, we may need to increase the value of the balance field (as when a new purchase is made) or to decrease it (as when a payment is made). Therefore, we make TR-AMOUNT a signed field, with positive values representing additions to the balance field and negative values representing subtractions from the balance field. To make it easy to enter signed numbers with a text editor, we specify SIGN IS TRAILING SEPARATE. Thus, an increase of $375.98 in the balance is represented by 0037598+, whereas a decrease of $5426.35 is represented by 0542635-.

ERROR-RECORD is used to report erroneous transactions, such as an invalid value for TR-FUNCTION or an attempt to update a record that is not in the old master file.

The data items CURRENT-KEY and OCCUPIED play central roles in the operation of the program. A number of transactions can be applied to a single master record—a customer might make a number of purchases and payments during the course of a month, for example. The value of CURRENT-KEY is the key of the master record currently being updated; all transactions whose keys equal the value of CURRENT-KEY must be processed before the program goes on to the next master record.

The master record currently being processed is stored in NEW-MASTER-REC. Whether or not NEW-MASTER-REC contains a valid record can vary as transactions are processed. For example, a transaction can create a record in NEW-MASTER-REC even if no record with that key was present in the old master file. Likewise, a transaction can delete the record in NEW-MASTER-REC regardless of whether that record came from the old master file or was created by a preceding transaction. We use the value of OCCUPIED to keep track of whether NEW-MASTER-REC represents a valid master record. The value of OCCUPIED is set to "Y" if NEW-MASTER-REC contains a valid record and to "N" otherwise.

In the Procedure Division, MAIN-ROUTINE is very similar to the corresponding routine for the merging program. The DOS file names for the three files are obtained and the files are opened. Paragraphs READ-OLD-MASTER-FILE and READ-TRANSACTION-FILE are performed to read the first record from each file. As in the merging program, when an input file is exhausted the read-file paragraph sets the corresponding record key to HIGH-VALUE. Paragraph PROCESS-ONE-KEY is performed until the values of both OM-KEY and TR-KEY equal HIGH-VALUE—that is, until both the old master and the transaction file are exhausted. When both input files are exhausted, all files are closed and the program is terminated.

In the merging program, the main routine performed a paragraph PROCESS-ONE-RECORD which processed one record from one of the two input files. In the file-update program, we cannot guarantee that the corresponding paragraph will always process exactly one record. Master records can be created and destroyed with Add and Delete transactions, and many transaction records may need to be applied to the same master record. The file update program, then, focuses not on records but on key values.

Whereas the merging program merged records, the file-update program merges key values. The paragraph corresponding to PROCESS-ONE-RECORD, then, is PROCESS-ONE-KEY.

PROCESS-ONE-KEY performs paragraph SELECT-KEY to set the value of CURRENT-KEY to the next key to be processed. Next PROCESS-TRANSACTION-RECORD is performed for each transaction record whose key is equal to the value of CURRENT-KEY. After all the transactions—which can include additions and deletions—have been processed, NEW-MASTER-REC may or may not contain a valid record. If the value of OCCUPIED is "Y", NEW-MASTER-REC does contain a valid record, which is written to NEW-MASTER-FILE.

If we remember that our program merges keys, the logic of SELECT-KEY becomes clear. The two keys currently available are those of the current old master and transaction records. If the value of OM-KEY is less than or equal to that of TR-KEY, CURRENT-KEY is set to the value of OM-KEY; otherwise, CURRENT-KEY is set to the value of TR-KEY. If the value of OM-KEY is selected, there is a record in the old master file whose key is equal to the current key. This record is moved to NEW-MASTER-REC for possible updating, a new record is read from the old master file, and OCCUPIED is set to "Y", indicating that NEW-MASTER-REC contains a valid master record with key equal to the current key. If the value of TR-KEY is selected, there is no record in the old master file whose key is equal to the current key. (How can we be sure of this?) OCCUPIED is set to "N" indicating that NEW-MASTER-REC does not contain a master record with key equal to the current key.

PROCESS-TRANSACTION-RECORD uses a multiway selection on the value of TR-FUNCTION to perform the proper paragraph for processing the current transaction record. If the value of TR-FUNCTION is "A", ADD-RECORD is performed; if the value is "U", UPDATE-RECORD is performed; if the value is "D", DELETE-RECORD is performed. If some other value is present, the program complains of an invalid transaction code and ignores the transaction record. After the current transaction has been processed, the next record from the transaction file is read.

ADD-RECORD creates a new master record from the data in the transaction record. If the value of OCCUPIED is "N", ADD-RECORD moves TR-KEY to NM-KEY, TR-AMOUNT to NM-BALANCE, and sets OCCUPIED to "Y", indicating that NEW-MASTER-REC now contains valid data. If the value of OCCUPIED was originally "Y", however, NEW-MASTER-REC already contains a record whose key equals that of the transaction record, and the program complains that a new record with that key cannot be added.

UPDATE-RECORD increases or decreases the balance of the record being updated. If the value of OCCUPIED is "Y", NEW-MASTER-REC contains a master record to be updated, and the (positive or negative) value of TR-AMOUNT is added to the value of NM-BALANCE. If the value of OCCUPIED is "N", however, NEW-MASTER-REC does not contain a record to be updated (there is no record in the old master file whose key equals the key of the transaction record), and the program complains that it cannot update a nonexistent record.

DELETE-RECORD deletes the contents of NEW-MASTER-REC simply by setting the value of occupied to "N", so the program will no longer consider NEW-MASTER-REC to contain valid data. If the value of OCCUPIED is already "N", the program complains that it cannot delete a nonexistent record.

Figure 7.7 shows sample old master and transaction files along with the resulting new master file. Note the trailing signs in the transaction records. The first three transaction records represent valid transactions and produce the changes shown in the master file. The last four transactions are invalid and cause the error messages in Figure 7.7d to be displayed.

## EXERCISES

**1.** Modify the control-total program (Figure 7.2) so that it prints at the end of the report a total line giving the grand total of all sales regardless of territory, salesperson, or product. After the program has processed all the input records, instead of executing

```
PERFORM PRINT-TERRITORY-TOTAL
```

as it does now, it should instead execute

```
PERFORM PRINT-FINAL-TOTAL
```

In analogy with the other print-total paragraphs, PRINT-FINAL-TOTAL should begin by performing PRINT-TERRITORY-TOTAL, so subtotals will be printed for the last product, salesperson, and territory before the final-total line is printed.

**2.** Often it is not possible to arrange control totals in columns as in Figure 7.3. For each record read we may have to print a detail line that takes up the entire width of the page, leaving no room for totals columns. Instead, at each control break we interrupt the printing of detail lines to print one or more total lines, such as

(a)
```
1111110010099
2222220020099
3333330030099
4444440040099
5555550050099
6666660060099
7777770070099
8888880080099
9999990090099
```

(b)
```
200000A0004995+
444444U0006000-
666666D
777777Z
888888A0009995+
900000U0007995+
950000D
```

(c)
```
1111110010099
2000000004995
2222220020099
3333330030099
4444440034099
5555550050099
7777770070099
8888880080099
9999990090099
```

(d)
```
Error for key 777777: Invalid transaction code
Error for key 888888: Record already present--cannot add
Error for key 900000: Record not present--cannot update
Error for key 950000: Record not present--cannot delete
```

*Figure 7.7* Part (a) is a master file, and part (b) is a transaction file, to be processed by the file-update program in Figure 7.6. Part (c) is the updated file produced by the program, and part (d) is the display produced by the erroneous records in the transaction file.

```
Product Total          $700,00
Salesperson Total    $1,200,00
Territory Total      $1,600,00
```

Modify the payroll program of Figure 4.1 to print totals in this way. Assume that the first digit of an employee number designates the division, the second the plant, and the third the department in which the employee works. After processing all employees in a given department, the program should print a department total; after processing all employees in a given plant, the program should print a department total for the last department processed and then a plant total. After processing all the employees in a given division, the program should print department and plant totals for the last department and plant processed and then print a division total.

Page control can be troublesome when detail and total lines are printed by different parts of a program. One solution is to have a single paragraph—say PRINT-REPORT-LINE—for printing all detail and total lines. This paragraph keeps track of the number of lines printed on each page and goes to a new page when necessary. To print a line, the program moves the line to the record associated with the output file, moves the desired line spacing to LINE-SPACING, and performs PRINT-REPORT-LINE. Note that this method involves giving up the convenience of the FROM option of the WRITE statement—we must use a MOVE statement to move each line to the record associated with the output file.

3. One variation of merging writes a record to the output file only when records with matching keys are found in both input files. For example, one input file might contain the names of people receiving welfare payments, and the other file might contain the names of people known to have larger incomes than are allowed for welfare recipients. We want the program to produce a file of all those who are receiving payments illegally. Modify the merging program (Figure 7.4) for this variation. *Hint:* On each cycle of operation the program compares the keys of the current records from each input file. If the keys differ, the record with the smaller key is discarded. (We discard a record by just reading in another record from the corresponding file.) If the two records have the same key, one of them—say the one from A-FILE—is written to the output file, after which both records are discarded.

4. Another variation of merging finds records that are present in one file but not in another. As mentioned in the text, this variation could be used to find persons who had registered cars but were not paying property taxes on them. Modify the merging program (Figure 7.4) for this variation. *Hint:* If the value of A-KEY is less than that of B-KEY, no record with key equal to value of A-KEY occurs in B-FILE. Why?

5. Modify the file-update program (Figure 7.6) so that transactions are entered by the user rather than read from a file. When the program is ready for the next transaction, it will prompt the user to enter a key and the operation to be performed. If the operation is Add, a screen will be displayed on which the user can fill in the details of the record to be added. If the operation is Update, a screen will be displayed showing the current contents of the master record and on which the user can make changes. If

the operation is Delete, the corresponding record is deleted without further ado. The user must enter transaction keys in ascending order; an error message should be given if the user enters a transaction key smaller than the current key. Be sure and retain the overall structure of the file-update program in spite of the substantial changes in the way transaction records are processed. When the user indicates (say by pressing a certain function key) that all transactions have been processed, the current transaction key—corresponding to TR-KEY—should be set to HIGH-VALUE.

# 8

## Relative Files
## and
## Hashing

Random access allows us to process the records of a file in whatever order we wish. With this freedom, however, comes the responsibility of designating which record we wish to process—it's no longer sufficient, for example, just to tell the computer to read a record; we must also tell it which record to read.

COBOL provides two file organizations, *relative* and *indexed,* that allow random access. The two organizations differ in the way in which records are designated. With relative organization, the records are numbered very much like the entries in a table—the first record in the file is record 1, the next is record 2, and so on. We use record numbers to designate particular records in a relative file just as we use subscript values to designate particular entries in a table. With indexed organization, on the other hand, records are designated by key values such as account numbers.

We will look at relative files in this chapter and indexed files in Chapter 9. *Hashing,* a frequently used technique for accessing records in relative files, is also described in this chapter and illustrated with an information-retrieval program.

## STATEMENTS FOR PROCESSING RELATIVE FILES

Relative files allow three kinds of access—sequential, random, and dynamic. As usual, sequential access means that the records are processed in the order in which they are stored in the file. Sequential access with relative files provides some features not available with regular- or line-sequential files—processing can start with any designated record, and records can be deleted. With random access, records are designated by record numbers. Dynamic access allows us to switch between sequential access and random access at will.

### The Environment Division

As with other files, each relative file must be described in a SELECT entry in the FILE-CONTROL paragraph of the Input-Output Section of the Environment Division. Relative files must be assigned to DISK:

SELECT *file-name* ASSIGN TO DISK

The corresponding DOS file name must assign the file to a disk file—not to an input or output device such as a printer or the display.

The access mode for the file must be specified with one of the following three ACCESS clauses:

ACCESS IS SEQUENTIAL
ACCESS IS RANDOM
ACCESS IS DYNAMIC

The organization of a relative file is specified as RELATIVE:

ORGANIZATION IS RELATIVE

Finally, we must designate the data item in which we will store the record number of the record we wish to process:

RELATIVE KEY IS *data-name*

The RELATIVE KEY clause can be omitted for sequential-access mode unless a START statement is to be used to specify that processing will begin at some point other than the beginning of the file.

The following is a typical SELECT entry for a relative file with random access:

SELECT R-FILE ASSIGN TO DISK
    ACCESS IS RANDOM
    ORGANIZATION IS RELATIVE
    RELATIVE KEY IS RECORD-NUMBER.

### The Data Division

In the File Section we must provide an FD entry for each relative file. The FD entry has the same form as for any disk file:

```
FD   R-FILE
     LABEL RECORDS STANDARD
     VALUE OF FILE-ID IS DOS-FILE-NAME.
```

The data name referred to in the RELATIVE KEY clause must be defined in the Working-Storage Section. This item must have an integer picture—no decimal places may be specified. Record numbers for relative files can range from 1 through 32767, so the item need have no more than five digits. Usage COMP-0 will relieve the program from having to perform time-consuming conversions:

```
01   RECORD-NUMBER PIC 9(5) COMP-0.
```

Note that the relative key data item is *not* a field of the records stored in the file.

## The Procedure Division

### Sequential access

A relative file with sequential-access mode can be opened for input, output, or input-output. When the file is opened in INPUT mode, its records can be read with READ statements identical to those used for regular- and line-sequential files. For example,

```
READ R-FILE
     INTO DATA-RECORD
     AT END MOVE "Y" TO EOF-FLAG.
```

obtains the next record from the file and stores it both in the record associated with R-FILE and in DATA-RECORD. If all the records in the file have been processed, the statement following AT END is executed. If a RELATIVE KEY data item was defined for the file, the value of that data item is set to the record number of the record that was read.

If we do not specify otherwise, the first READ statement reads record 1, the next READ statement reads record 2, and so on. In contrast to the case for regular- and line-sequential files, however, we can use a START statement to specify the number of the record with which sequential processing is to begin. A RELATIVE KEY data item must be defined when START is used; before executing the START statement, the value of the RELATIVE KEY data item must be set to the number of the record with which processing is to begin. Assuming that RECORD-NUMBER is the RELATIVE KEY data item for the file, the following statements cause sequential processing of R-FILE to begin with record 25:

```
MOVE 25 TO RECORD-NUMBER.
START R-FILE
     INVALID KEY MOVE "N" TO NO-SUCH-RECORD.
```

After this statement is executed, the next READ statement will read record 25, the READ statement after that will read record 26, and so on.

An *invalid-key error* arises if the designated record is not in the file—if, in our example, record 25 has been deleted or was never stored. The optional

INVALID KEY clause allows us to specify a statement to be executed if an invalid-key error occurs. In Chapter 10 we will see other ways of handling invalid-key and other file-processing errors.

By including a KEY clause, we can specify that the START statement is to skip over nonexistent records. For example, the START statement:

```
MOVE 25 TO RECORD-NUMBER.
START R-FILE
    KEY IS GREATER THAN RECORD-NUMBER
    INVALID KEY MOVE "N" TO NO-SUCH-RECORD.
```

causes sequential processing to begin with the first record in the file with a record number greater than 25. If there is no such record, the statement in the INVALID KEY clause is executed. Likewise,

```
MOVE 25 TO RECORD-NUMBER.
START R-FILE
    KEY IS NOT LESS THAN RECORD-NUMBER
    INVALID KEY MOVE "Y" TO NO-SUCH-RECORD.
```

causes sequential processing to begin with the first available record whose record number is 25 or greater. Note that the data item RECORD-NUMBER referred to by the KEY clause must be the RELATIVE KEY data item.

When a file is opened in OUTPUT mode, a new file is always created. Any existing file with the same DOS file name is deleted. For a relative file with sequential access, only the WRITE statement is allowed in OUTPUT mode. The first WRITE statement writes record 1, the second WRITE statement writes record 2, and so on. If a RELATIVE KEY data item was defined, it is set to the record number of the record just written. An invalid-key error occurs if there is insufficient disk space for the record. Except for the optional INVALID KEY clause, the WRITE statement is the same as used for regular- and line-sequential files:

```
WRITE R-RECORD
    FROM DATA-RECORD
    INVALID KEY MOVE "Y" TO NO-ROOM.
```

Only an existing file can be opened in I-O mode; new files can be created only in OUTPUT mode. For a relative file with sequential access opened in I-O mode, we can read records with READ and use START to specify the record with which reading will begin. After reading a record, we can use REWRITE to replace the record just read with a new record, or we can use DELETE to delete the record just read. Note that with sequential access, WRITE is not allowed in I-O mode.

The REWRITE statement is the same as for regular- and line-sequential files: The most recently read record is replaced in the file by the record written with REWRITE. For example,

```
REWRITE R-RECORD
    FROM DATA-RECORD.
```

replaces the most recently read record with the value of DATA-RECORD. No invalid key clause is needed (or allowed), since the successful execution of the preceding READ statement assures that the record to be replaced exists in the file.

Like REWRITE, DELETE is executed after a READ statement; the record read by the preceding READ statement is deleted from the file. For example,

```
DELETE R-FILE RECORD.
```

deletes the record most recently read from R-FILE. Note that DELETE refers to a file name, not a record name. As with REWRITE, no INVALID KEY clause is needed or allowed, since the successful execution of the preceding READ statement assures that the record to be deleted is present in the file.

The deleted record is not actually removed from the file—the size of the disk file does not change. Rather, the area occupied by the deleted record is filled with a special character—the character with ASCII code 0—that designates a deleted record. Deleted records are skipped during sequential access; during random access, attempting to read a deleted record causes an invalid-key error.

### Random access

With random access, the number of the record affected by a given operation must be moved to the RELATIVE KEY data item before the operation is carried out. An invalid-key error results if the specified record number is not valid for the operation in question. The INVALID KEY clause is allowed for all file processing statements (except OPEN and CLOSE) and should be used unless an invalid-key error is logically impossible or unless errors are being handled by one of the alternative methods described in Chapter 10.

INPUT mode is used to read records from an existing file. The only statement allowed is READ. For example, the statement

```
MOVE 135 TO RECORD-NUMBER.
READ R-FILE
    INTO DATA-RECORD
    INVALID KEY MOVE "Y" TO NO-SUCH-RECORD.
```

reads record 135 of R-FILE into DATA-RECORD. Records can be read in any order, but the number of each record to be read must be moved to the RELATIVE KEY data item (RECORD-NUMBER in our examples) before executing the READ statement. An invalid-key error occurs if there is no record in the file corresponding to the designated record number—either because no record was ever stored with that record number or because the record with that number was deleted.

As usual, OUTPUT mode is used to create a new file. A relative file can be created either *sequentially* or *randomly*. When the file is created sequentially, then, as described previously, the first record written to the file is stored as record 1, the second as record 2, and so on. When the file is created randomly, records are stored with specified record numbers. For example,

```
MOVE 200 TO RECORD-NUMBER.
WRITE R-RECORD
     FROM DATA-RECORD
     INVALID KEY MOVE "N" TO OCCUPIED.
```

The records can be written in any order, and we need not write a record for every record number within the file—we can leave gaps in the file if we wish. An invalid-key error occurs if a record has already been written for the designated record number (this is called a "duplicate-key error") or if there isn't room on the disk for another record.

In I-O mode, all statements are allowed except START, which is meaningful only for sequential access. READ and WRITE are as described for INPUT and OUTPUT modes. WRITE can be used only to write new records; REWRITE must be used to replace existing records. Attempting to WRITE a record with a record number for which a record is already present in the file causes an invalid-key error.

REWRITE and DELETE do not have to follow a READ statement for the record to be replaced or deleted. Instead, we move the number of the record to be affected to the RELATIVE KEY data item before executing REWRITE or DELETE. Thus

```
MOVE 29 TO RECORD-NUMBER.
REWRITE R-RECORD
     FROM DATA-RECORD
     INVALID KEY MOVE "Y" TO NOT-FOUND.
```

replaces the current contents of record 29 with the value of DATA-RECORD, and

```
MOVE 199 TO RECORD-NUMBER.
DELETE R-FILE RECORD
     INVALID KEY MOVE "Y" TO NOT-FOUND.
```

deletes record 199. An invalid-key error occurs if the record to be replaced or deleted is not present in the file.

### Dynamic access

Dynamic access allows both sequential and random access. A sequential form of the READ statement is available, and the START statement can be used to specify where sequential reading will begin. The remaining statements are the same as for random access.

In INPUT mode, only START and READ are allowed. As usual, if we do not wish to start sequential processing with record 1, we can use START to specify the first record to be processed sequentially:

```
MOVE 100 TO RECORD-NUMBER.
START R-FILE
     KEY IS NOT LESS THAN RECORD-NUMBER
     INVALID KEY MOVE "Y" TO BAD-START.
```

Records can be read either randomly or sequentially. For random access, the READ statement is the same as in random-access mode. For sequential access, a special form of the READ statement is used:

```
READ R-FILE NEXT RECORD
    INTO DATA-RECORD
    AT END MOVE "Y" TO EOF-FLAG.
```

The phrase NEXT RECORD designates the sequential form of the READ statement. The next available record is read—any nonexistent records are skipped. Attempting to read beyond the end of the file causes an AT END condition rather than an invalid-key error. If the read is successful, the RELATIVE KEY data item is set to the number of the record read.

In OUTPUT mode, only the WRITE statement is allowed. There is no special sequential-access form of the WRITE statement. The random-access form is used, with the value of the RELATIVE KEY data item being manipulated as needed to store the records sequentially. Thus

```
MOVE 1 TO RECORD-NUMBER.
```

can be used to begin writing with the first record of the file. And the statements

```
WRITE R-RECORD
    FROM DATA-RECORD
    INVALID KEY MOVE "Y" TO OUT-OF-SPACE.
ADD 1 TO RECORD-NUMBER.
```

write the contents of DATA-RECORD in the position given by the current contents of RECORD-NUMBER, then increase the value of RECORD-NUMBER by 1 so that the next record will be written in the immediately following file position.

All statements are allowed in I-O mode, including both the random and sequential forms of the READ statement. The REWRITE and DELETE statements work as with random access—the RELATIVE KEY data item must be set to the desired record number before executing the statement. Recall, however, that the sequential form of the READ statement sets the RELATIVE KEY data item to the number of the record that was read. Executing a REWRITE or DELETE statement after a sequential READ statement will replace or delete the record read, just as in sequential-access mode.

## HASHING

With sequential access, we usually process an entire file at one time. Random access, however, allows us to select for processing only those records needed for the purpose at hand. To use random access, we need some way of identifying the records we wish to process, and our programs need ways of locating in a file the records we designate.

As we saw in Chapter 7, records are usually identified by *key values* such as account numbers, catalog numbers, and so on. For relative files, each record is designated by a unique record number. What we need are ways of translating the key value that identifies a record into the record number that specifies where the record is stored in the file. This is usually done in one of three ways:

1. *Use the record numbers as key values*. The record for account 1 will be stored as record 1; the record for account 2 will be stored as record 2; and so on. This is by far the best method if it can be used. But, as pointed out in Chapter 5 in

connection with table-handling, key values are usually chosen for purposes other than information retrieval. Various digits or groups of digits may encode information about the items identified by the keys, for example. Such lengthy, complex keys are not practical for use as record numbers.

2. *Provide the file with an index*—a table giving the record number corresponding to each key value.* To locate a particular record in the file, the program looks up its key value in the index to obtain the corresponding record number. The main disadvantage of indexes is the additional disk space required to store the index. (In some complex information retrieval systems, the space required to store the indexes exceeds that required for the data file.) In some situations, the time required to look up records in the index may be significant. As we will see in Chapter 9, COBOL provides easy-to-use indexed files for which the COBOL runtime system automatically creates and maintains indexes and looks up key values in them as needed. If we wish to use indexes, we will usually use the indexed files provided by COBOL instead of trying to construct our own indexes for relative files.

3. *Hashing.* Instead of doing a possibly time-consuming lookup in a space-consuming index, it would be nice if we could do some calculation on the key value to yield the corresponding record number. In most cases we cannot do this perfectly, but we can come close—we can devise a calculation that will yield the approximate location of the record we are seeking. A (usually) short search through the file will then yield the desired record. This method is called *hashing* because the key-to-record-number calculation scrambles, or "makes a hash of," the key value. The advantage of hashing is that no space for the index or time for looking up keys in an index is required. A disadvantage is that records are stored in the file in random order, so they cannot be processed sequentially in order of ascending key values. Another problem is that there are many different methods of hashing, so some knowledge of hashing techniques and perhaps some experimentation may be needed to choose the hashing method best suited for a particular application.

For users of IBM COBOL, indexes no doubt have the advantage over hashing, since a powerful indexing system is built into COBOL whereas we must program hashing for ourselves. Nevertheless, as an important information retrieval technique and a good illustration of the use of relative files, hashing is well worth looking at in detail.

We begin our discussion with the hashing calculation (often called the *hashing function*) which converts key values into record numbers. For randomly chosen key values, we would like the corresponding record numbers to be evenly distributed throughout the file, with record numbers that are in use intermingled with those that are available for storing new records. That way, when we store a new record, there is a good chance the hashing calculation will yield a record number that is available for use. If a *collision* occurs—the record number yielded by the hashing calculation is already in

---

*Don't confuse the use of the word *index* in this chapter and the next with the quite different use found in Chapter 5. We use the word here with the familiar meaning exemplified by the index to a book or encyclopedia.

use—we should still be able to find an available record location very close to the one designated by the hashing calculation. When time comes to retrieve the record, it will be found at or very close to the location designated by the hashing calculation.

Fortunately, there is a very simple calculation with the desired property. We assume that the key value is a number (alphanumeric keys must be converted to numbers—we will not go into the often tricky methods of doing this). We divide the key value by the file size—the largest record number allowed for the file—and take the remainder (not the quotient) of the division. The remainder can range from 0 through one less than the file size. Adding 1 to the remainder gives us the record number, which—as required—lies in the range of 1 through the file size.

In standard COBOL the DIVIDE statement has a REMAINDER option for computing remainders. Since this option has few uses aside from hashing calculations, it is one of the little-used features omitted from IBM COBOL. To compute a remainder in IBM COBOL, we proceed as in elementary arithmetic. For example, to divide 60 by 23 and get the remainder, we arrange our work as follows:

$$
\begin{array}{r}
2 \quad \text{Quotient} \\
23\overline{)60} \\
46 \quad \text{Product} \\
14 \quad \text{Remainder}
\end{array}
$$

We divide 23 into 60 getting the integer quotient, 2. (The part of the quotient to the right of the decimal point is discarded.) We then multiply the quotient (2) by the divisor (23) and subtract the product (46) from the dividend (60) to get the remainder (14).

The same method works in COBOL. Suppose the value of TARGET-ACCOUNT-NO is the key value for the desired record, and the calculated record number is to be stored in REC-NO. The value of FILE-SIZE is the largest record number allowed for the file. We use QUOTIENT and PRODUCT for temporary storage. QUOTIENT must have an integer picture so that any quotient digits to the right of the decimal point will be discarded. The following statements do the hashing calculation:

```
DIVIDE TARGET-ACCOUNT-NO BY FILE-SIZE
    GIVING QUOTIENT.
MULTIPY QUOTIENT BY FILE-SIZE
    GIVING PRODUCT.
SUBTRACT PRODUCT FROM TARGET-ACCOUNT-NO
    GIVING REC-NO.
ADD 1 TO REC-NO.
```

The value of TARGET-ACCOUNT-NO is divided by that of FILE-SIZE, and the remainder is stored in REC-NO. The value of REC-NO is then increased by 1 to get a value in the range of 1 through the value of FILE-SIZE.

In order for this hashing calculation to distribute records evenly throughout the file, the file size must be a *prime number*—a number that is not evenly divisible by any number other than 1 and itself. Here are the first nine prime numbers:

2, 3, 5, 7, 11, 13, 17, 19, 23

Additional prime numbers can be looked up in mathematical handbooks or worked out by computer programs. For the information-retrieval program described later in this chapter, we will use a small test file with 19 records.

When we store a new record in the file, we hope the hashing calculation will yield the number of an unused record location; when we retrieve a record, we hope the hashing calculation will yield the record number of the desired record. Our hopes are sometimes not fulfilled, however, and we have to search through the file for an unused record location or for the record we are trying to retrieve.

The question then arises as to the order in which the record locations should be examined when searching the file. The most obvious answer is to search the record locations sequentially—if the record location designated by the hashing calculation is not the one we want, we add one to the record number and look at the next record location. If that location doesn't fulfill our needs, we add one to the record number again, and so on.

This method does have a disadvantage—it leads to the formation of clusters of adjacent records. If we are looking for an unused record location and our hashing calculation lands us in a cluster, we will have to search all the way to the end of the cluster to find an unused location. The record we are trying to store will be placed at the end of the cluster, making the cluster even bigger.

This disadvantage, however, is often outweighed by an enormous advantage for diskette files. The system usually reads several adjacent records at a time from diskette into main memory. A sequential search can examine these adjacent records at high speed before requiring another time-consuming diskette access. More sophisticated search methods that jump around in the file are best used with the faster fixed disks.

When searching, we may run off the end of the file—the record number may exceed the value of FILE-SIZE. But since the search started somewhere within the file, we are not finished when we reach the end of the file—we must go back to the beginning of the file and continue. Thus if the value of REC-NO designates the record just examined, the following statements set it to designate the next record to be examined:

```
ADD 1 TO REC-NO.
IF REC-NO > FILE-SIZE
    MOVE 1 TO REC-NO.
```

The file is treated as if it were in the shape of a ring, with the last record location adjacent to the first one. When we step off the last record location of the file, we step onto the first one.

Another question arises—when do we call off the search for a record and conclude that the record is not in the file? Certainly, if our search carries us back to the record we began with, the one designated by the hashing calculation, we will have examined every record in the file and know that the record we are seeking is not there. But examining every record in a large file can be very time-consuming—can we find some way to call off the search sooner?

When we store a record in the file, we start with the record designated by the hashing calculation, search for an empty record location, and place the new record in the first empty record location found. The important point is that there are no empty record locations between the record designated by hashing calculation and the location in which the record is actually stored. When searching for a record, we can call off the search the first time we encounter an empty record location, for we know that if the record sought were present, it would lie between the record designated by the hashing calculation and the first empty record location.

This method of stopping searches does require us to be careful when we delete records. For suppose we delete one of the records separating the record designated by a hashing calculation from the location holding the record for which the calculation was done. When we search for the latter record, the empty record produced by the deletion will cause the search to be called off prematurely.

One solution—which we will use here—is to distinguish between empty records, which have never been used, and deleted records, which have been used but whose contents have been deleted. Locations containing both empty and deleted records are available for storing new records. However, only an empty record can terminate a search.

To implement this scheme, we include a one-character REC-STATUS field in each record. REC-STATUS can have three values—"E" for empty, "D" for deleted, or "F" for full (contains useful data). Any location holding a record with "D" or "E" status can be used to store a new record. Only a record with "E" status, however, can terminate a search.

When the hash file is created, a record with status "E" is written for each record number from 1 through the value of FILE-SIZE. When a new record is stored in the file, the new record, with status "F", replaces an existing record with "D" or "E" status. To delete a record, we simply change its status to "D". (Note that we do not delete a record by removing it with the COBOL DELETE statement, but merely by changing the value of its REC-STATUS field.)

A hash file needs a good supply of unused record locations if we are to have a good chance of finding an unused location near the one designated by a hashing calculation. No more than about 70% of the locations in a hash file should contain data records, the remaining records being deleted or empty. If this *loading factor* of 70% is exceeded, collisions will become frequent and searches will become lengthy.

## INFORMATION RETRIEVAL USING HASHING

Figure 8.1 shows a program for creating a new, empty hash file, and Figure 8.2 shows a program for information storage and retrieval using the file created by the program in Figure 8.1. The information storage and retrieval program is similar in structure to the in-memory information retrieval program of Figure 6.5 except that the information is stored on disk instead of in main memory. Also, the information stored consists not of price-list entries but of customer records such as those in file-update programs of Figures 5.1, 5.4, and 7.1.

The program in Figure 8.1 initializes a hash file by writing an empty record for every record number of the file. Note that the records are "empty" only because the REC-STATUS field of each record has the value "E". COBOL treats our "empty" records just like any other data records.

```
IDENTIFICATION DIVISION.
PROGRAM-ID.  INITIALIZE-HASH-FILE.

*     Create an empty hash file.

ENVIRONMENT DIVISION.
INPUT-OUTPUT SECTION.
FILE-CONTROL.
     SELECT CUSTOMER-FILE ASSIGN TO DISK
          ACCESS IS SEQUENTIAL
          ORGANIZATION IS RELATIVE.

DATA DIVISION.
FILE SECTION.
FD   CUSTOMER-FILE
     LABEL RECORDS STANDARD
     VALUE OF FILE-ID IS DOS-FILE-NAME.
01   CUSTOMER-RECORD      PIC X(136).

WORKING-STORAGE SECTION.
01   EMPTY-RECORD.
     02   REC-STATUS      PIC X VALUE "E".
     02   FILLER          PIC X(135) VALUE SPACES.

01   FILE-SIZE           PIC 99 COMP-0 VALUE 19.
01   DOS-FILE-NAME       PIC X(15).

PROCEDURE DIVISION.
MAIN-ROUTINE.
     DISPLAY (1, 1) ERASE (5, 1) "File name? ".
     ACCEPT (, ) DOS-FILE-NAME WITH PROMPT.
     OPEN OUTPUT CUSTOMER-FILE.
     PERFORM WRITE-EMPTY-RECORD
          FILE-SIZE TIMES.
     CLOSE CUSTOMER-FILE.
     STOP RUN.


WRITE-EMPTY-RECORD.
     WRITE CUSTOMER-RECORD
          FROM EMPTY-RECORD
          INVALID KEY DISPLAY (7, 1) "Disk full"
                    STOP RUN.
```

*Figure 8.1*    This program creates an empty hash file. The file is filled with empty records, that is, records whose REC-STATUS fields have the value "E".


In the Environment Division, CUSTOMER-FILE—the file to be initialized—is assigned to DISK and given relative organization. Since the task at hand is most easily accomplished with sequential processing, sequential access is specified for CUSTOMER-FILE. In the File Section of the Data Division, the FD entry for CUSTOMER-FILE is the usual one for files assigned to DISK. CUSTOMER-RECORD is defined to be 136 characters long; this size is determined by the more detailed description of CUSTOMER-RECORD given in Figure 8.2.

In the Working-Storage Section we begin by defining EMPTY-RECORD whose value will be written in each record location of the file. The first field of an empty record is REC-STATUS, which has the value "E". The contents of the remainder of an

```
IDENTIFICATION DIVISION.
PROGRAM-ID.  HASHING.

*     Information storage and retrieval using hashing.

ENVIRONMENT DIVISION.
INPUT-OUTPUT SECTION.
FILE-CONTROL.
     SELECT CUSTOMER-FILE ASSIGN TO DISK
          ACCESS IS RANDOM
          ORGANIZATION IS RELATIVE
          RELATIVE KEY IS RECORD-NUMBER.

DATA DIVISION.
FILE SECTION.
FD   CUSTOMER-FILE
     LABEL RECORDS STANDARD
     VALUE OF FILE-ID IS DOS-FILE-NAME.
01   CUSTOMER-RECORD.
     02   REC-STATUS          PIC X.
     02   ACCOUNT-NUMBER      PIC 9(6).
     02   LAST-NAME           PIC X(30).
     02   FIRST-NAME          PIC X(20).
     02   MIDDLE-INITIAL      PIC X.
     02   STREET-ADDRESS      PIC X(40).
     02   CITY                PIC X(15).
     02   STATE               PIC XX.
     02   ZIP                 PIC X(5).
     02   BALANCE             PIC 9(6)V99.
     02   CREDIT-LIMIT        PIC 9(6)V99.

WORKING-STORAGE SECTION.
01   FOUND               PIC X.
01   NO-SPACE            PIC X.
01   DOS-FILE-NAME       PIC X(15).
01   TERMINATOR-KEY      PIC 99.
01   RECORD-NUMBER       PIC 99 COMP-0.
01   REC-NO              PIC 99 COMP-0.
01   FIRST-REC-NO        PIC 99 COMP-0.
01   FREE-REC-NO         PIC 99 COMP-0.
01   FILE-SIZE           PIC 99 COMP-0 VALUE 19.
01   TARGET-ACCOUNT-NO   PIC 9(6) COMP-3.
01   QUOTIENT            PIC 9(6) COMP-3.
01   PRODUCT             PIC 9(6) COMP-3.
01   DUMMY               PIC X.

SCREEN SECTION.
01   MENU-SCREEN.
     02   BLANK SCREEN.
     02   LINE 5 COLUMN 30 VALUE "F1  Enter new record".
     02   LINE 7 COLUMN 30 VALUE "F2  Update record".
     02   LINE 9 COLUMN 30 VALUE "F3  Delete record".
     02   LINE 11 COLUMN 30 VALUE "F4  Exit program".
     02   LINE 15 COLUMN 25
              VALUE "Press key for desired function".
```

*Figure 8.2*   This information-storage-and-retrieval program uses hashing for storing and retrieving records in a relative file.

```
01   ENTER-SCREEN.
     02  BLANK SCREEN.
     02  LINE 4 COLUMN 5 REVERSE-VIDEO VALUE "Account Number".
     02  LINE 5 COLUMN 5 PIC 9B99B999 FROM ACCOUNT-NUMBER.
     02  LINE 8 COLUMN 5 REVERSE-VIDEO VALUE "Last Name".
     02  LINE 9 COLUMN 5 PIC X(30) TO LAST-NAME
             AUTO REQUIRED.
     02  LINE 8 COLUMN 40 REVERSE-VIDEO VALUE "First Name".
     02  LINE 9 COLUMN 40 PIC X(20) TO FIRST-NAME
             AUTO REQUIRED.
     02  LINE 8 COLUMN 65 REVERSE-VIDEO VALUE "Initial".
     02  LINE 9 COLUMN 65 PIC X TO MIDDLE-INITIAL
             AUTO REQUIRED.
     02  LINE 12 COLUMN 5 REVERSE-VIDEO VALUE "Street Address".
     02  LINE 13 COLUMN 5 PIC X(40) TO STREET-ADDRESS
             AUTO REQUIRED.
     02  LINE 16 COLUMN 5 REVERSE-VIDEO VALUE "City".
     02  LINE 17 COLUMN 5 PIC X(15) TO CITY
             AUTO REQUIRED.
     02  LINE 16 COLUMN 25 REVERSE-VIDEO VALUE "State".
     02  LINE 17 COLUMN 25 PIC XX TO STATE
             AUTO FULL.
     02  LINE 16 COLUMN 35 REVERSE-VIDEO VALUE "ZIP".
     02  LINE 17 COLUMN 35 PIC X(5) TO ZIP
             AUTO FULL.
     02  LINE 20 COLUMN 5 REVERSE-VIDEO VALUE "Balance".
     02  LINE 21 COLUMN 5 PIC $$$$,$$9.99 TO BALANCE
             AUTO REQUIRED.
     02  LINE 20 COLUMN 21 REVERSE-VIDEO VALUE "Credit Limit".
     02  LINE 21 COLUMN 21 PIC $$$$,$$9.99 TO CREDIT-LIMIT
             AUTO REQUIRED.

01   UPDATE-SCREEN.
     02  BLANK SCREEN.
     02  LINE 4 COLUMN 5 REVERSE-VIDEO VALUE "Account Number".
     02  LINE 5 COLUMN 5 PIC 9B99B999 FROM ACCOUNT-NUMBER.
     02  LINE 8 COLUMN 5 REVERSE-VIDEO VALUE "Last Name".
     02  LINE 9 COLUMN 5 PIC X(30) USING LAST-NAME
             AUTO.
     02  LINE 8 COLUMN 40 REVERSE-VIDEO VALUE "First Name".
     02  LINE 9 COLUMN 40 PIC X(20) USING FIRST-NAME
             AUTO.
     02  LINE 8 COLUMN 65 REVERSE-VIDEO VALUE "Initial".
     02  LINE 9 COLUMN 65 PIC X USING MIDDLE-INITIAL
             AUTO.
     02  LINE 12 COLUMN 5 REVERSE-VIDEO VALUE "Street Address".
     02  LINE 13 COLUMN 5 PIC X(40) USING STREET-ADDRESS
             AUTO.
     02  LINE 16 COLUMN 5 REVERSE-VIDEO VALUE "City".
     02  LINE 17 COLUMN 5 PIC X(15) USING CITY
             AUTO.
     02  LINE 16 COLUMN 25 REVERSE-VIDEO VALUE "State".
     02  LINE 17 COLUMN 25 PIC XX USING STATE
             AUTO.
     02  LINE 16 COLUMN 35 REVERSE-VIDEO VALUE "ZIP".
     02  LINE 17 COLUMN 35 PIC X(5) USING ZIP
             AUTO.
     02  LINE 20 COLUMN 5 REVERSE-VIDEO VALUE "Balance".
     02  LINE 21 COLUMN 5 PIC $$$$,$$9.99 USING BALANCE
             AUTO.
     02  LINE 20 COLUMN 21 REVERSE-VIDEO VALUE "Credit Limit".
     02  LINE 21 COLUMN 21 PIC $$$$,$$9.99 USING CREDIT-LIMIT
             AUTO.
```

*Figure 8.2 (continued)*

```
PROCEDURE DIVISION.
MAIN-ROUTINE.
    DISPLAY (1, 1) ERASE (5, 1) "File name? ".
    ACCEPT (, ) DOS-FILE-NAME WITH PROMPT.
    OPEN I-O CUSTOMER-FILE.
    MOVE ZERO TO TERMINATOR-KEY.
    PERFORM GET-AND-DO-FUNCTION
        UNTIL TERMINATOR-KEY = 5.
    CLOSE CUSTOMER-FILE.
    STOP RUN.

GET-AND-DO-FUNCTION.
    MOVE ZERO TO TERMINATOR-KEY.
    PERFORM DISPLAY-MENU
        UNTIL TERMINATOR-KEY > 1 AND < 6.
    IF TERMINATOR-KEY = 2
        PERFORM ENTER-RECORD
    ELSE IF TERMINATOR-KEY = 3
        PERFORM UPDATE-RECORD
    ELSE IF TERMINATOR-KEY = 4
        PERFORM DELETE-RECORD.

DISPLAY-MENU.
    DISPLAY MENU-SCREEN.
    ACCEPT (15, 56) DUMMY.
    ACCEPT TERMINATOR-KEY FROM ESCAPE KEY.

ENTER-RECORD.
    DISPLAY (1, 1) ERASE (5, 1) "Account number? ".
    ACCEPT (, ) TARGET-ACCOUNT-NO WITH PROMPT.
    PERFORM GET-RECORD.
    IF FOUND = "Y"
        DISPLAY (7, 1) "Record already in file"
        PERFORM WAIT-FOR-USER
    ELSE IF NO-SPACE = "Y"
        DISPLAY (7, 1) "No room in file"
        PERFORM WAIT-FOR-USER
    ELSE
        MOVE "F" TO REC-STATUS
        MOVE TARGET-ACCOUNT-NO TO ACCOUNT-NUMBER
        DISPLAY ENTER-SCREEN
        ACCEPT ENTER-SCREEN
        REWRITE CUSTOMER-RECORD.

UPDATE-RECORD.
    DISPLAY (1, 1) ERASE (5, 1) "Account Number? ".
    ACCEPT (, ) TARGET-ACCOUNT-NO WITH PROMPT.
    PERFORM GET-RECORD.
    IF FOUND = "N"
        DISPLAY (7, 1) "Record not found"
        PERFORM WAIT-FOR-USER
    ELSE
        DISPLAY UPDATE-SCREEN
        ACCEPT UPDATE-SCREEN
        REWRITE CUSTOMER-RECORD.
```

*Figure 8.2 (continued)*

```
DELETE-RECORD.
     DISPLAY (1, 1) ERASE (5, 1) "Account number? ".
     ACCEPT (, ) TARGET-ACCOUNT-NO WITH PROMPT.
     PERFORM GET-RECORD.
     IF FOUND = "N"
         DISPLAY (7, 1) "Record not found"
         PERFORM WAIT-FOR-USER
     ELSE
         MOVE "D" TO REC-STATUS
         REWRITE CUSTOMER-RECORD.

WAIT-FOR-USER.
     DISPLAY (9, 1) "Press Enter to continue ".
     ACCEPT (, ) DUMMY.

GET-RECORD.
     MOVE "N" TO FOUND
                 NO-SPACE.
     MOVE ZERO TO FREE-REC-NO.
     PERFORM GET-FIRST-REC-NO.
     PERFORM EXAMINE-RECORD.
     PERFORM EXAMINE-RECORD
         UNTIL REC-NO = FIRST-REC-NO OR
               REC-STATUS = "E" OR
               FOUND = "Y".
     IF FREE-REC-NO > 0 AND FOUND = "N"
         MOVE FREE-REC-NO TO RECORD-NUMBER.
     IF REC-NO = FIRST-REC-NO AND
         FREE-REC-NO = 0 AND
         REC-STATUS NOT = "E"
         MOVE "Y" TO NO-SPACE.

EXAMINE-RECORD.
     MOVE REC-NO TO RECORD-NUMBER.
     READ CUSTOMER-FILE.
     IF REC-STATUS = "F" AND
         ACCOUNT-NUMBER = TARGET-ACCOUNT-NO
         MOVE "Y" TO FOUND.
     IF FREE-REC-NO = 0 AND REC-STATUS = "D"
         MOVE REC-NO TO FREE-REC-NO.
     PERFORM GET-NEXT-REC-NO.

GET-FIRST-REC-NO.
     DIVIDE TARGET-ACCOUNT-NO BY FILE-SIZE
         GIVING QUOTIENT.
     MULTIPLY QUOTIENT BY FILE-SIZE
         GIVING PRODUCT.
     SUBTRACT PRODUCT FROM TARGET-ACCOUNT-NO
         GIVING REC-NO.
     ADD 1 TO REC-NO.
     MOVE REC-NO TO FIRST-REC-NO.

GET-NEXT-REC-NO.
     ADD 1 TO REC-NO.
     IF REC-NO > FILE-SIZE
         MOVE 1 TO REC-NO.
```

*Figure 8.2 (continued)*

empty record are unimportant; we represent the remainder of the record by a 135-character FILLER item with VALUE SPACES.

Since we want to create a small test file with 19 record locations, we give FILE-SIZE the value 19. For a different-sized file, the value of FILE-SIZE must be changed in both Figure 8.1 and Figure 8.2. Remember that the new file size must also be a prime number.

In the Procedure Division, paragraph MAIN-ROUTINE gets the DOS-FILE-NAME for CUSTOMER-FILE and opens the file in OUTPUT mode. Remember that opening a file for OUTPUT always creates a new file; any existing file with the same DOS file name is deleted.

Paragraph WRITE-EMPTY-RECORD is performed for each empty record to be written to the file. Since we know in advance how many records are to be written (not usually the case in COBOL programs), we can use the form of the PERFORM statement that lets us specify how many times the performed paragraph will be executed:

```
PERFORM WRITE-EMPTY-RECORD
    FILE-SIZE TIMES.
```

Since the value of FILE-SIZE is 19, WRITE-EMPTY-RECORD will be performed 19 times. When the PERFORM statement terminates, CUSTOMER-FILE is closed and the program is terminated.

Each time it is performed, WRITE-EMPTY-RECORD writes the contents of EMPTY-RECORD to CUSTOMER-FILE. Should an invalid-key error occur, the message Disk full is displayed and execution of the program is terminated.

The program in Figure 8.2 uses the hashing techniques discussed earlier for information storage and retrieval. As in Figure 8.1, CUSTOMER-FILE has relative organization and is assigned to DISK, but this time random access is specified. RECORD-NUMBER is designated as the RELATIVE KEY data item—the one used to hold the record number of the record to be accessed.

CUSTOMER-RECORD is defined in detail in the File Section. The first field is REC-STATUS. The remaining fields are as in Figure 5.1 with one exception. ACCOUNT-NUMBER is now defined as a numeric rather than an alphanumeric field, since we require a number for our hashing calculation.

In the Working-Storage Section, FOUND and NO-SPACE are flags for indicating whether a search found the desired record and whether any space for new records—any empty or deleted records—remain in the file. DOS-FILE-NAME and TERMINATOR-KEY have their usual functions. As mentioned, RECORD-NUMBER is the RELATIVE KEY data item in which we must store the number of the record to be accessed by a record-processing operation. The values of REC-NO, FIRST-REC-NO, and FREE-REC-NO are also used to designate records, but their values must be moved to RECORD-NUMBER if we wish to access the designated records. The value of FILE-SIZE specifies that the file contains 19 records.

TARGET-ACCOUNT-NO contains the account number of the record to be stored or retrieved. QUOTIENT and PRODUCT are used for temporary storage by the hashing calculation. To make the calculation as efficient as possible, all three fields are given COMP-3 usage (the values involved are too large for COMP-0, which would be even more efficient). DUMMY is a dummy alphanumeric item that serves as a receiving field for ACCEPT statements that merely wait until the user presses a terminator key.

This program defines three screens. MENU-SCREEN is used to display a menu of the options available to the user. By pressing the proper function key as given in the menu, the user can elect to enter a new record, update an existing record, delete a record, or exit the program. The update function is also used for retrieving information from the file.

ENTER-SCREEN, which is used when a new record is entered, is with one exception the same as the screen description in the program CREATE-CUSTOMER-FILE, Figure 5.1. UPDATE-SCREEN, which is used for updating a record, is with one exception identical to the screen description in the program UPDATE-CUSTOMER-FILE, Figure 5.4. In both cases the exception is the third level-02 item. In this program, the data input field corresponding to ACCOUNT-NUMBER is given a numeric-edited picture, since ACCOUNT-NUMBER is itself numeric. What's more, ACCOUNT-NUMBER is designated (with FROM) as a source field only—its value cannot be changed by the user. When ENTRY-SCREEN or UPDATE-SCREEN is displayed, the account number has already been entered. The value of ACCOUNT-NUMBER is displayed for the user's convenience, but the user is not allowed to change it.

In the Procedure Division, paragraph MAIN-ROUTINE obtains the DOS file name for the hash file and opens the file in I-O mode. Recall that a file opened in I-O mode must already exist, which is why a separate program was used to create the file. Paragraph GET-AND-DO-FUNCTION is performed until the value of TERMINATOR-KEY becomes 5, which corresponds to the exit-program function. When the PERFORM statement terminates, the file is closed and the program is terminated.

GET-AND-DO-FUNCTION is called to display MENU-SCREEN and get a value of TERMINATOR-KEY corresponding to the function the user wishes performed. DISPLAY-MENU is repeated until a TERMINATOR-KEY value in the range 2 through 5 (corresponding to function keys F1 through F4) is returned.

A multiway selection executes the paragraph corresponding to the function key pressed. If the value of TERMINATOR-KEY is 2 (F1 pressed), ENTER-RECORD is performed. If the value is 3 (F2 pressed), UPDATE-RECORD is performed. If the value is 4 (F3 pressed), DELETE-RECORD is performed. No paragraph is performed for a value of 5 (F4 pressed); this value terminates the PERFORM statement in MAIN-ROUTINE and thus terminates the program.

Paragraph DISPLAY-MENU displays MENU-SCREEN. The format 3 ACCEPT statement then waits until the user presses a terminator key. The format 1 ACCEPT statement stores the code for the key pressed in TERMINATOR-KEY.

Paragraph ENTER-RECORD allows the user to store a new record in the file. The account number of the new record is obtained from the user and stored in TARGET-ACCOUNT-NO, after which GET-RECORD is performed to see if a record with that account number is in the file. GET-RECORD sets the flags FOUND and NO-SPACE. FOUND is set to "Y" if a record with account number equal to the value of TARGET-

ACCOUNT-NO was found, and to "N" otherwise. NO-SPACE is set to "Y" if there is no room in the file for a new record, and to "N" otherwise.

If the value of FOUND is "Y", the user is informed that a record with the given account number is already in the file, so a new record with that account number cannot be inserted. If the value of NO-SPACE is "Y", the user is informed that there is no room in the file for a new record.

If the values of both FOUND and NO-SPACE are "N", GET-RECORD sets RECORD-NUMBER to the record number of the empty or deleted record to be replaced by the new record. The record status for the new record is set to "F", and the account number is set to the value of TARGET-ACCOUNT-NO. To obtain values for the remaining fields of CUSTOMER-RECORD, ENTER-SCREEN is displayed and then accepted. Finally, the REWRITE statement stores the new customer record in the location designated by RECORD-NUMBER. The INVALID KEY clause is omitted from all record processing statements, since GET-RECORD always sets RECORD-NUMBER to a valid record number—a value in the range of 1 through the value of FILE-SIZE.

Paragraph UPDATE-RECORD displays the contents of a designated record and allows the user to modify the contents if desired. Like ENTER-RECORD, GET-RECORD begins by getting the desired account number and calling GET-RECORD to find the record with that account number in the file. IF GET-RECORD set FOUND to "N", the user is informed that the requested record was not found. If the value of FOUND is "Y", GET-RECORD has set RECORD-NUMBER to the number of the desired record and has read the record into CUSTOMER-RECORD. The contents of CUSTOMER-RECORD are displayed to the user (via UPDATE-SCREEN), and any modifications the user wishes to make are accepted. The updated record is then rewritten to the file.

Paragraph DELETE-RECORD is similar to UPDATE-RECORD except that, instead of updating the fields of the record, DELETE-RECORD deletes the record by setting its REC-STATUS field to "D" and rewriting it to the file.

Paragraph WAIT-FOR-USER uses a dummy ACCEPT statement to wait until the user, having read the information currently on the screen, presses the En t e r key (or any other terminator key) to continue.

Paragraph GET-RECORD searches the file for a record whose account number is equal to the value of TARGET-ACCOUNT-NO. GET-RECORD is a bit tricky mainly because it has several jobs to do. If the sought-after record is present, GET-RECORD must set RECORD-NUMBER to the number of the desired record, read the record into CUSTOMER-RECORD, and set FOUND to "Y". If the desired record is not found, FOUND must be set to "N". In that case, if space remains for a new record, NO-SPACE must be set to "N" and RECORD-NUMBER must be set to the number of the first empty or deleted record found during the search. If no empty or deleted record was found, NO-SPACE must be set to "Y".

GET-RECORD begins by initializing FOUND and NO-SPACE to "N". FREE-REC-NO will be set to the number of the first deleted record encountered during the search. Its value is set initially to zero—an invalid record number—indicating that no deleted record has been encountered so far. Paragraph GET-FIRST-REC-NO is performed to carry out the hashing calculation and set REC-NO to the number of the first record to be examined. This record number is also stored in FIRST-REC-NO, where it is used to determine when the search has examined all the records in the file and returned to its starting point.

Paragraph EXAMINE-RECORD is performed to examine the record designated by the value of REC-NO. If necessary, the same paragraph is performed repeatedly to examine succeeding records in the file. The search continues until terminated by any of three conditions:

1. REC-NO = FIRST-REC-NO. The search has examined all the records in the file and returned to its starting point.
2. REC-STATUS = "E". An empty record has been encountered.
3. FOUND = "Y". The desired record has been found.

When the search terminates, the program must see that RECORD-NUMBER and NO-SPACE are set properly. If the desired record was not found, RECORD-NUMBER should be set to the first empty or deleted record (if any) encountered during the search. If the value of FREE-REC-NO is greater than 0, this value is the number of the first deleted record encountered during the search. Hence if the value of FREE-REC-NO is greater than 0 and that of FREE is "N", the value of FREE-REC-NO is moved to RECORD-NUMBER.

There is no space for new records in the file if the following three conditions hold:

1. REC-NO = FIRST-REC-NO. The search has returned to its starting point after examining all records in the file.
2. FREE-REC-NO = 0. No deleted records were found.
3. REC-STATUS NOT = "E". The last record examined was not empty.

If all three conditions hold, the value of NO-SPACE is set to "Y".

Paragraph EXAMINE-RECORD reads the record designated by REC-NO and determines if this is the desired record. Also, if this is the first deleted record encountered during the search, its record number is moved to FREE-REC-NO.

EXAMINE-RECORD begins by moving the value of REC-NO to RECORD-NUMBER and reading the designated record from CUSTOMER-FILE. If the record contains valid data (REC-STATUS = "F") and its account number equals the value of TARGET-ACCOUNT-NO, the desired record has been found and the value of FOUND is set to "Y". If no deleted record has been found so far (FREE-REC-NO = 0) and the record just read is deleted (REC-STATUS = "D"), FREE-REC-NO is set to the record number of the deleted record. Finally, GET-NEXT-REC-NO is performed to set the value of REC-NO to designate the next record to be examined.

Paragraph GET-FIRST-REC-NO does the hashing calculation as described previously. Both REC-NO and FIRST-REC-NO are set to the result of the hashing calculation. GET-NEXT-REC-NO changes the value of REC-NO so that it designates the next record to be examined. Note that by changing GET-FIRST-REC-NO and GET-NEXT-REC-NO, we could change the hashing calculation and the search strategy without affecting the rest of the program.

## EXERCISES

1. Suppose that in a certain application it *is* possible to use record numbers as key values—the record for account 1 will be stored as record 1; the record for account 2 will be stored as record 2, and so on. Write an information storage and retrieval program based on this approach. Records will be retrieved with READ statements, stored with WRITE statements, updated with READ and REWRITE statements, and deleted with DELETE statements. Use INVALID KEY clauses to detect user errors such as attempting to read a nonexistent record or attempting to store a new record with a record number that is already in use. Usually, the best approach is to have an INVALID KEY clause set the value of a flag. The value of the flag is tested later with an IF statement. The file should be created by a separate program. Note that you can create an empty relative file by opening the file for OUTPUT and then closing it, without writing any records to it.

2. Modify the program of Figure 8.2 so that it can create a new file. After the DOS file name has been entered, but before the file has been opened in I‐O mode, the user is asked if a new file should be created. The dialog should go like this:

   ```
   File name? B:CUSTOMER.DAT
   Create new file (Y/N)? Y
   Are you sure (Y/N)? Y
   ```

   Since creating a new file destroys an existing one with the same DOS file name, the user is asked to confirm the request to create a new file. If the request is made and confirmed, the program should perform a paragraph that opens the file for OUTPUT, fills it with empty records, and then closes it. Note that since the file has random-access mode, the program must step the value of record number from 1 through the value of FILE‐SIZE as the empty records are written.

3. Modify the program of Figure 8.2 to add a "retrieve record" function that displays a requested record but does not allow the user to update it. This function would help prevent records from being changed accidentally, as might happen if they were retrieved using the update function.

4. Modify the in-memory information retrieval program (Figure 6.5) so that the price list is stored in a hash file on disk rather than in main memory.

5. After many deletions have been made in a hash file, most of the unused records will be deleted rather than empty. Searches for nonexistent records will become time-consuming, since only an empty record can terminate such a search before every record in the file has been examined. One solution is "rehashing"—read the records from the old hash file and store all the valid data records (records with status "F") in a new hash file. In the new hash file all unused records will be empty rather than deleted. Write a program to create a new customer file and store the valid data records from the old customer file into the new one. Records are read sequentially from the old customer file; records with status "D" or "E" are ignored. Each data record is stored in the new customer file using hashing. The hashing procedure employed in Figure 8.2 can be used. However, this procedure can be simplified, since (1) there are no deleted records in the new customer file, and (2) the old customer file contains no more than one record for each account number so we can store a new record without having to check whether a record with the same account number is already present.

# 9

---

# Indexed
# Files

It's easy to provide a simple index for a relative file. We can use a one-level table with each entry containing a key value and the record number of the corresponding record. A SEARCH statement could be used to look up key values in the index.

On the other hand, when we must be able to insert and delete records in both the index and the data file, when both sequential and random access are required and both must be carried out with reasonable speed, and when the index is too large to all fit in main memory at once, then a much more complicated index is needed along with more complex procedures for looking up key values.

Fortunately, COBOL programmers don't have to worry about these complexities. When we specify indexed organization for a file, COBOL automatically creates and maintains both a data file and an index file. The index file is used to provide sequential, random, and dynamic access to the records in the data file.

The combination of random and sequential access is particularly useful. We can store records in the file in any order, then process them in ascending order of their key values, as we might need to do to produce a report whose detail lines are ordered according to key values.

For each indexed file we define a *record key,* which is a field of the record description associated with the file. Be careful not to confuse relative keys (for relative files) and record keys (for indexed files). Relative keys are not fields of the records stored in the file, and their values are record numbers. Record keys *are* fields of the records stored in the file, and their values are defined by the user to identify records and to control the order in which the records will be processed sequentially. A record-key value must uniquely identify the corresponding record—no two records in an indexed file can have the same value for their record keys.

The record key can be up to 60 characters long, and can be either a group item or an alphanumeric elementary item. The main reason for using a group item is to control the order in which records are processed sequentially. For example, if the record key is defined as

```
02   REC-KEY.
     03   ZIP-CODE        PIC  X(5).
     03   ACCOUNT-NUMBER  PIC  X(6).
```

records will be processed sequentially in ascending order of their ZIP codes. Records with the same ZIP code will be processed in order of their account numbers. Likewise, if we want to process a file of transactions to produce control totals for each territory, salesperson, and product, we could defined the record key like this:

```
02   REC-KEY.
     03   TERRITORY-NUMBER     PIC  X(3).
     03   SALESPERSON-NUMBER   PIC  X(3).
     03   PRODUCT-NUMBER       PIC  X(3).
     03   TRANSACTION-NUMBER   PIC  X(5).
```

Records will be processed sequentially in order of their territory numbers. Records with the same territory number will be processed in order of their salesperson numbers. Records with the same territory and salesperson numbers will be processed in order of their product numbers. Finally, records with the same territory, salesperson, and product number will be processed in order of their transaction numbers.

Note that even if transaction numbers are not used in the processing, they are necessary to assure that each record has a unique record-key value. Transaction numbers need to be unique only for a particular combination of territory number, salesperson number, and product number. In practice, transactions would probably be numbered separately for each salesperson, so each record for a particular salesperson would have a different transaction number, but records for different salespeople could have the same transaction number.

The SELECT entry for indexed files is similar to that for relative files. The file organization is INDEXED. Access can be specified as either SEQUENTIAL, RANDOM, or DYNAMIC. A record-field key field must always be designated; in contrast to the corresponding case for relative keys, under no circumstances can the RECORD KEY clause can be omitted. Here is a typical SELECT entry for an indexed file:

```
SELECT ACCTS-FILE ASSIGN TO DISK
    ACCESS IS RANDOM
    ORGANIZATION IS INDEXED
    RECORD KEY IS ACCOUNT-NUMBER.
```

The corresponding FD entry in the File Section of the Data Division might look like this:

```
FD   ACCTS-FILE
     LABEL RECORDS STANDARD
     VALUE OF FILE-ID IS DOS-FILE-NAME.
01   ACCTS-RECORD.
     02   ACCOUNT-NUMBER.
          03   REGION          PIC X.
          03   STORE           PIC X(3).
          03   CUSTOMER        PIC X(4).
     02   BALANCE              PIC 9(5)V99.
```

Indexed files must be assigned to DISK, and the DOS file name must designate a disk file—not an input or output device such as the printer. For each indexed file COBOL actually creates two files—the *data file,* which contains the data records, and the *key file,* which contains the index. The data file has the DOS file name provided by the user; the key file has the same name but with the extension KEY in place of whatever extension (if any) that was provided by the user. The extension provided by the user must *not* be KEY, because if it were the system would have no way of creating a distinct name for the key file.

For example, if the user provides the DOS file name CUSTOMER.DAT, the data file will be named CUSTOMER.DAT and the key file will be named CUSTOMER.KEY. If the user provides the DOS file name CUSTOMER, the data file will be named CUSTOMER and the key file will be named CUSTOMER.KEY.


## STATEMENTS FOR PROCESSING INDEXED FILES

### Sequential Access

When the file is opened in INPUT mode, only the READ and START statements are allowed. The READ statement is the same one used for processing sequential files:

```
READ ACCTS-FILE
     INTO DATA-RECORD
     AT END MOVE "Y" TO EOF-FLAG.
```

Records are read in ascending order according to their record-key values. Unless specified otherwise, sequential processing begins with the record having the smallest record-key value.

We can specify some other starting point for sequential processing by using a START statement. The key of the first record to be processed is moved to the record-key field, after which the START statement is executed:

```
MOVE "78132564" TO ACCOUNT-NUMBER.
START ACCTS-FILE
    INVALID KEY MOVE "Y" TO BAD-START.
```

The START statement arranges for sequential file processing to begin with the record having the record-key value "78132564". If no record with this key value is present, an invalid-key error occurs.

Alternatively, we can specify that sequential processing will begin with the first record whose record key is greater than a given value:

```
MOVE "37210000" TO ACCOUNT-NUMBER.
START ACCTS-FILE
    KEY IS GREATER THAN ACCOUNT-NUMBER
    INVALID KEY MOVE "Y" TO BAD-START.
```

Note that a record with a key of "37210000" will not be processed. If we want a record with the given key value to be processed also, we specify NOT LESS THAN instead of GREATER THAN:

```
MOVE "50010001" TO ACCOUNT-NUMBER.
START ACCTS-FILE
    KEY IS NOT LESS THAN ACCOUNT-NUMBER
    INVALID KEY MOVE "Y" TO BAD-START.
```

In either case, if no record satisfying the stated condition is found, an invalid-key error occurs.

As usual, OUTPUT mode is used only to create new files; an existing file with the same DOS file name is deleted. Opening a file for OUTPUT and then closing it without writing to it creates an empty file—one containing no records. In OUTPUT mode, only the WRITE statement is allowed:

```
WRITE ACCTS-RECORD
    FROM DATA-RECORD
    INVALID KEY MOVE "Y" TO WRITE-ERROR.
```

Records must be written in ascending order according to their key values. An invalid-key error occurs if the key of the record being written is the same as or less than the key of a record already in the file. An invalid-key error also occurs if there is no room on the disk for another record.

In I-O mode, READ, START, REWRITE, and DELETE are allowed, but WRITE is not. READ and START work the same as in INPUT mode.

As usual for sequential processing, REWRITE must follow a successful execution of READ. The record written by REWRITE replaces in the file the record read by the most recent execution of READ. The new record must have the same record key as the record it replaces; otherwise, an invalid-key error occurs. The following statement replaces the most recently read record with the contents of DATA-RECORD:

```
REWRITE ACCTS-RECORD
    FROM DATA-RECORD
    INVALID KEY MOVE "Y" TO KEY-CHANGED.
```

If the logic of the program guarantees that the record being written has the same record key as the record most recently read, no invalid-key error can occur and the INVALID KEY clause can be omitted.

Like REWRITE, DELETE can be executed only after the successful execution of a READ statement; the record that was read by the READ statement is removed from the file. No invalid-key error can occur with DELETE, since the preceding READ statement assures that the record to be deleted is present in the file. The statement

```
DELETE ACCTS-FILE RECORD.
```

deletes the record most recently read from ACCTS-FILE.

### Random Access

With random access, the contents of the record-key field determines which record will be read from the file or the key under which a record written to the file will be stored. When writing a record to the file or replacing an existing record, the new record to be sent to the file has the proper record key, so the record-key field does not have to be set as a separate operation. Before reading or deleting a record, however, the record-key field must be set to the key of the record to be read or deleted.

In INPUT mode, only READ is allowed. The value of the record-key field determines which record will be read. Thus, the statements

```
MOVE "52315432" TO ACCOUNT-NUMBER.
READ ACCTS-FILE
     INTO DATA-RECORD
     INVALID KEY MOVE "Y" TO NOT-THERE.
```

read the record with account number "52315432" into DATA-RECORD. If no record with that account number is present in the file, an invalid-key error occurs.

In OUTPUT mode, only WRITE is allowed. The record-key field of the record to be written determines the key under which that record will be stored in the file. For example,

```
WRITE ACCTS-RECORD
      FROM DATA-RECORD
      INVALID KEY MOVE "Y" TO BAD-WRITE.
```

stores the value of DATA-RECORD in the file. Before the WRITE takes place, the value of DATA-RECORD is moved to ACCTS-RECORD, thus setting the record-key field of ACCTS-RECORD to the key of the record to be written. An invalid-key error occurs if the key of the record being written is the same as that of a record already in the file, or if there is no room for additional records on the disk.

In I-O mode, READ, WRITE, REWRITE, and DELETE are allowed. READ functions the same as in INPUT mode, and WRITE functions the same as in OUTPUT mode. WRITE can only be used to write new records to the file, not to replace existing records. As in OUTPUT mode, attempting to write a record whose key is the same as that of a record already in the file causes an invalid-key error.

In random-access mode, we do not have to read a record before replacing it with REWRITE or deleting it with DELETE. The value of the record-key field determines which record will be replaced or deleted. For REWRITE, the key of the replacement record determines which record will be replaced. For example, the statement

```
REWRITE ACCTS-RECORD
     FROM DATA-RECORD
     INVALID KEY MOVE "Y" TO NOT-THERE.
```

replaces an existing record with the value of DATA-RECORD. The record chosen for replacement is the one having the same key as the value of DATA-RECORD. (When the FROM option moves the value of DATA-RECORD to ACCTS-RECORD, the key of the value of DATA-RECORD is moved to the record-key field.) If the record to be replaced is not present in the file, an invalid-key error occurs.

Before deleting a record with DELETE, we must set the record-key field to the key of the record to be deleted. Thus,

```
MOVE "29134578" TO ACCOUNT-NUMBER.
DELETE ACCTS-FILE RECORD
     INVALID KEY MOVE "Y" TO NOT-THERE.
```

removes from the file the record with account number "29134578". If no record with that account number is present in the file, an invalid-key error occurs.

**Dynamic Access**

Dynamic access allows a program to switch between sequential and random processing.

In INPUT mode, START and READ are allowed. START can be used to set a starting record for sequential processing. There are two versions of READ, one for random access and one for sequential access. The random-access version of READ is the same as for random-access mode. Thus, the statements

```
MOVE "98342187" TO ACCOUNT-NUMBER.
READ ACCTS-FILE
     INTO DATA-RECORD
     INVALID KEY MOVE "Y" TO NOT-THERE.
```

reads the record with key "98342187" into DATA-RECORD, with an invalid-key error if no such record is in the file.

The words NEXT RECORD (only NEXT is required) distinguish the sequential-access READ statement from the random-access one. Thus

```
READ ACCTS-FILE NEXT RECORD
     INTO DATA-RECORD
     AT END MOVE "Y" TO EOF-FLAG.
```

reads the record following (in ascending order of key values) the previous record read from the file. Attempting to read beyond the last record in the file causes the statement in the AT END phrase to be executed.

In OUTPUT mode, ony the WRITE statement is allowed. The same WRITE statement serves for both random and sequential access. The records being written can be stored in any order, which, of course, includes sequential order. An invalid-key error occurs if we attempt to write a record with the same key as a record already in the file, or if there is no room on the disk for another record.

In I-O mode, READ, WRITE, REWRITE, START, and DELETE are all valid. As in INPUT mode, there are two versions of READ, one for random access and one for sequential access. WRITE, REWRITE, and DELETE are the same for both random and sequential processing. As usual, when a record value is sent to the file with WRITE or REWRITE, the key of the record value determines the key under which the value will be stored in the file. Before DELETE is executed, the record-key field must be set to the key of the record to be deleted. This can be done by reading the record before executing the DELETE statement (as in sequential access) or by moving the desired key to the record-key field (as in random access).

## THE REBUILD UTILITY

One problem with relying on an index is that if something happens to the index, we can no longer access the records in the file. For example, all or part of an index is usually kept in main memory during processing. If processing is terminated prematurely by a power failure or a hardware or software malfunction, the index on the disk may not be properly updated from the one in main memory. The index in the key file on the disk is then useless, since it no longer corresponds to the data file.

To cope with this problem, IBM COBOL provides a utility program called REBUILD, which reads a data file and produces a new data file and key file. In addition to recovering damaged files, REBUILD will also recover the disk space taken up by records that have been deleted.

The REBUILD program is described in appendix K of the reference manual. Detailed instructions are also displayed when the program is run. To use the program with a diskette file, proceed as follows. With the DOS displaying the prompt

        A>

insert the diskette containing the file to be recovered in drive A, insert your COBOL diskette in drive B, and enter the command B:REBUILD.

REBUILD will create a new version of the file to be recovered—it does not erase the existing file. If the diskette in drive A doesn't have room for both the old and the new files, the new file must be stored on drive B. In this case, after REBUILD has been loaded and its initial message has appeared on the screen, remove the COBOL diskette from drive B and insert the diskette that is to receive the rebuilt file.

The first two things REBUILD asks for are the key length (in bytes) and the byte position of the key. In the usual case (and the only one we will consider), the key field and all fields preceding it have DISPLAY usage, so that each character occupies one byte. We need, then, to determine the length of the key in characters and the position in the record of the first character of the key.

For example, suppose the records in the file have the following structure:

```
01   TRANSACTION-RECORD,
     02   CUST-NAME              PIC X(30),
     02   CUST-ADDRESS           PIC X(30),
     02   REC-KEY,
          03   TERRITORY-NO      PIC X(3),
          03   SALESPERSON-NO    PIC X(3),
          03   PRODUCT-NO        PIC X(3),
          03   TRANSACTION-NO    PIC X(5),
     02   QUANTITY-ORDERED       PIC 9(4) COMP-0,
     02   UNIT-PRICE             PIC 9(3)V99 COMP-3,
     02   EXTENDED-PRICE         PIC 9(6)V99 COMP-3,
```

The first three fields of REC-KEY contain three characters each, and the last field contains five characters. The entire key, then, contains 14 characters, and 14 should be entered when the key length is requested. REC-KEY is preceded by two fields of 30 characters each, for a total of 60 characters. REC-KEY, then, begins with the 61st character of the record, so 61 should be entered when the key position is requested. The fields following REC-KEY have no effect on the key length or position.

Next, REBUILD asks for the "source filename," the DOS file name for the file to be rebuilt. Enter the name of the data file, not the key file. For example, if the data and key files being rebuilt are TRANSACT.DAT and TRANSACT.KEY, enter TRANSACT.DAT for the source filename.

Finally, REBUILD asks for the "target filename," the name to be given to the rebuilt file. Again, enter the desired name for the data file. If the target file is to be stored on the same diskette as the source file, the target filename must be different from the source filename. If you want to send the rebuilt file to the diskette in drive B, be sure to include the drive specifier B: in the target filename. For example, a target filename of B:TRANSACT.DAT stores the rebuilt data and key files on the diskette in drive B with the names TRANSACT.DAT and TRANSACT.KEY. The target filename TRANS-.DAT stores the rebuilt data and key files on the diskette in drive A with the names TRANS.DAT and TRANS.KEY.

After the target filename is entered, REBUILD does its work without further user intervention. After the rebuilt data and key files have been created, REBUILD asks for the key length for the next file to be rebuilt. If no more files are to be rebuilt, press Enter to terminate the program.

## AN INFORMATION-RETRIEVAL PROGRAM

Figure 9.1 shows a program for information storage and retrieval using an indexed file. This version of the information-retrieval program is considerably simpler than the version using hashing (Figure 8.2). With hashing, we had to program our own record-lookup procedures, whereas with indexed files the record-lookup procedures are built into the COBOL system and invoked automatically by statements such as READ and REWRITE.

```
IDENTIFICATION DIVISION.
PROGRAM-ID.  INDEXED-FILE.

*    Information storage and retrieval using an indexed file.

ENVIRONMENT DIVISION.
INPUT-OUTPUT SECTION.
FILE-CONTROL.
     SELECT CUSTOMER-FILE ASSIGN TO DISK
          ACCESS IS RANDOM
          ORGANIZATION IS INDEXED
          RECORD KEY IS ACCOUNT-NUMBER.

DATA DIVISION.
FILE SECTION.
FD   CUSTOMER-FILE
     LABEL RECORDS STANDARD
     VALUE OF FILE-ID IS DOS-FILE-NAME.
01   CUSTOMER-RECORD.
     02   ACCOUNT-NUMBER    PIC X(6).
     02   LAST-NAME         PIC X(30).
     02   FIRST-NAME        PIC X(20).
     02   MIDDLE-INITIAL    PIC X.
     02   STREET-ADDRESS    PIC X(40).
     02   CITY              PIC X(15).
     02   STATE             PIC XX.
     02   ZIP               PIC X(5).
     02   BALANCE           PIC 9(6)V99.
     02   CREDIT-LIMIT      PIC 9(6)V99.

WORKING-STORAGE SECTION.
01   RESPONSE              PIC X.
01   OK                    PIC X.
01   DOS-FILE-NAME         PIC X(15).
01   TERMINATOR-KEY        PIC 99.
01   DUMMY                 PIC X.

SCREEN SECTION.
01   MENU-SCREEN.
     02   BLANK SCREEN.
     02.  LINE 5 COLUMN 30 VALUE "F1  Enter new record".
     02   LINE 7 COLUMN 30 VALUE "F2  Update record".
     02   LINE 9 COLUMN 30 VALUE "F3  Delete record".
     02   LINE 11 COLUMN 30 VALUE "F4  Exit program".
     02   LINE 15 COLUMN 25
               VALUE "Press key for desired function".
```

*Figure 9.1*  This information-storage-and-retrieval program is similar to Figure 8.2 but uses an indexed file instead of a relative file and hashing. This program is simpler than Figure 9.1, since procedures for storing new records in an indexed file and for finding a record with a particular key value are built into the COBOL system and do not have to be written by the COBOL programmer.

In the SELECT entry, CUSTOMER-FILE is assigned to DISK and given RANDOM access mode and INDEXED organization. ACCOUNT-NUMBER, the first field of the record associated with the file, is designated as the record-key field.

In the File Section, CUSTOMER-FILE is defined as usual for files assigned to DISK. CUSTOMER-RECORD is the same as for the program in Figure 8.2,

```
01  ENTER-SCREEN.
    02  BLANK SCREEN.
    02  LINE 4 COLUMN 5 REVERSE-VIDEO VALUE "Account Number".
    02  LINE 5 COLUMN 5 PIC XBXXBXXX TO ACCOUNT-NUMBER
            AUTO.
    02  LINE 8 COLUMN 5 REVERSE-VIDEO VALUE "Last Name".
    02  LINE 9 COLUMN 5 PIC X(30) TO LAST-NAME
            AUTO REQUIRED.
    02  LINE 8 COLUMN 40 REVERSE-VIDEO VALUE "First Name".
    02  LINE 9 COLUMN 40 PIC X(20) TO FIRST-NAME
            AUTO REQUIRED.
    02  LINE 8 COLUMN 65 REVERSE-VIDEO VALUE "Initial".
    02  LINE 9 COLUMN 65 PIC X TO MIDDLE-INITIAL
            AUTO REQUIRED.
    02  LINE 12 COLUMN 5 REVERSE-VIDEO VALUE "Street Address".
    02  LINE 13 COLUMN 5 PIC X(40) TO STREET-ADDRESS
            AUTO REQUIRED.
    02  LINE 16 COLUMN 5 REVERSE-VIDEO VALUE "City".
    02  LINE 17 COLUMN 5 PIC X(15) TO CITY
            AUTO REQUIRED.
    02  LINE 16 COLUMN 25 REVERSE-VIDEO VALUE "State".
    02  LINE 17 COLUMN 25 PIC XX TO STATE
            AUTO FULL.
    02  LINE 16 COLUMN 35 REVERSE-VIDEO VALUE "ZIP".
    02  LINE 17 COLUMN 35 PIC X(5) TO ZIP
            AUTO FULL.
    02  LINE 20 COLUMN 5 REVERSE-VIDEO VALUE "Balance".
    02  LINE 21 COLUMN 5 PIC $$$$,$$9.99 TO BALANCE
            AUTO REQUIRED.
    02  LINE 20 COLUMN 21 REVERSE-VIDEO VALUE "Credit Limit".
    02  LINE 21 COLUMN 21 PIC $$$$,$$9.99 TO CREDIT-LIMIT
            AUTO REQUIRED.

01  UPDATE-SCREEN.
    02  BLANK SCREEN.
    02  LINE 4 COLUMN 5 REVERSE-VIDEO VALUE "Account Number".
    02  LINE 5 COLUMN 5 PIC XBXXBXXX FROM ACCOUNT-NUMBER.
    02  LINE 8 COLUMN 5 REVERSE-VIDEO VALUE "Last Name".
    02  LINE 9 COLUMN 5 PIC X(30) USING LAST-NAME
            AUTO.
    02  LINE 8 COLUMN 40 REVERSE-VIDEO VALUE "First Name".
    02  LINE 9 COLUMN 40 PIC X(20) USING FIRST-NAME
            AUTO.
    02  LINE 8 COLUMN 65 REVERSE-VIDEO VALUE "Initial".
    02  LINE 9 COLUMN 65 PIC X USING MIDDLE-INITIAL
            AUTO.
    02  LINE 12 COLUMN 5 REVERSE-VIDEO VALUE "Street Address".
    02  LINE 13 COLUMN 5 PIC X(40) USING STREET-ADDRESS
            AUTO.
    02  LINE 16 COLUMN 5 REVERSE-VIDEO VALUE "City".
    02  LINE 17 COLUMN 5 PIC X(15) USING CITY
            AUTO.
    02  LINE 16 COLUMN 25 REVERSE-VIDEO VALUE "State".
    02  LINE 17 COLUMN 25 PIC XX USING STATE
            AUTO.
    02  LINE 16 COLUMN 35 REVERSE-VIDEO VALUE "ZIP".
    02  LINE 17 COLUMN 35 PIC X(5) USING ZIP
            AUTO.
    02  LINE 20 COLUMN 5 REVERSE-VIDEO VALUE "Balance".
    02  LINE 21 COLUMN 5 PIC $$$$,$$9.99 USING BALANCE
            AUTO.
    02  LINE 20 COLUMN 21 REVERSE-VIDEO VALUE "Credit Limit".
    02  LINE 21 COLUMN 21 PIC $$$$,$$9.99 USING CREDIT-LIMIT
            AUTO.
```

*Figure 9.1 (continued)*

```
PROCEDURE DIVISION.
MAIN-ROUTINE.
    DISPLAY (1, 1) ERASE (5, 1) "File name? ".
    ACCEPT (, ) DOS-FILE-NAME WITH PROMPT.
    DISPLAY (7, 1) "Create new file (Y/N)? ".
    ACCEPT (, ) RESPONSE.
    IF RESPONSE = "Y" OR "y"
        DISPLAY (9, 1) "Are you sure (Y/N)? "
        ACCEPT (, ) RESPONSE
        IF RESPONSE = "Y" OR "y"
            OPEN OUTPUT CUSTOMER-FILE
            CLOSE CUSTOMER-FILE.
    OPEN I-O CUSTOMER-FILE.
    MOVE ZERO TO TERMINATOR-KEY.
    PERFORM GET-AND-DO-FUNCTION
        UNTIL TERMINATOR-KEY = 5.
    CLOSE CUSTOMER-FILE.
    STOP RUN.

GET-AND-DO-FUNCTION.
    MOVE ZERO TO TERMINATOR-KEY.
    PERFORM DISPLAY-MENU
        UNTIL TERMINATOR-KEY > 1 AND < 6.
    IF TERMINATOR-KEY = 2
        PERFORM ENTER-RECORD
    ELSE IF TERMINATOR-KEY = 3
        PERFORM UPDATE-RECORD
    ELSE IF TERMINATOR-KEY = 4
        PERFORM DELETE-RECORD.

DISPLAY-MENU.
    DISPLAY MENU-SCREEN.
    ACCEPT (15, 56) DUMMY.
    ACCEPT TERMINATOR-KEY FROM ESCAPE KEY.

ENTER-RECORD.
    DISPLAY ENTER-SCREEN.
    ACCEPT ENTER-SCREEN.
    MOVE "Y" TO OK.
    WRITE CUSTOMER-RECORD
        INVALID KEY MOVE "N" TO OK.
    IF OK = "N"
        DISPLAY (1, 1) ERASE
                (5, 1) "Account number already"
                (6, 1) "in file or disk full"
        PERFORM WAIT-FOR-USER.

UPDATE-RECORD.
    DISPLAY (1, 1) ERASE (5, 1) "Account Number? ".
    ACCEPT (, ) ACCOUNT-NUMBER WITH PROMPT.
    MOVE "Y" TO OK.
    READ CUSTOMER-FILE
        INVALID KEY MOVE "N" TO OK.
    IF OK = "Y"
        DISPLAY UPDATE-SCREEN
        ACCEPT UPDATE-SCREEN
        REWRITE CUSTOMER-RECORD
    ELSE
        DISPLAY (7, 1) "Record not found"
        PERFORM WAIT-FOR-USER.
```

*Figure 9.1 (continued)*

```
DELETE-RECORD.
    DISPLAY (1, 1) ERASE (5, 1) "Account number? ".
    ACCEPT (, ) ACCOUNT-NUMBER WITH PROMPT.
    MOVE "Y" TO OK.
    DELETE CUSTOMER-FILE RECORD
        INVALID KEY MOVE "N" TO OK.
    IF OK = "N"
        DISPLAY (7, 1) "Record not found"
        PERFORM WAIT-FOR-USER.

WAIT-FOR-USER.
    DISPLAY (9, 1) "Press Enter to continue ".
    ACCEPT (, ) DUMMY.
```

*Figure 9.1 (continued)*

except that ACCOUNT-NUMBER is an alphanumeric field, as required for indexed files, rather than a numeric field, as needed for hashing. Also, the REC-STATUS field is not present, since we no longer have to distinguish full, empty, and deleted records.

The Working-Storage Section is considerably simpler than in Figure 8.2, since we do not need the work fields used in the hashing calculation and the file search. RESPONSE receives a "Y" or "N" response from the user. OK has the value "N" if an invalid-key error occurred and the value "Y" otherwise. DOS-FILE-NAME, TERMINATOR-KEY, and DUMMY play their usual roles.

MENU-SCREEN is the same as in Figure 8.2. ENTER-SCREEN and UPDATE-SCREEN are the same as in Figure 8.2, except that the screen field corresponding to ACCOUNT-NUMBER has an alphanumeric picture. Also, in ENTER-SCREEN the value for ACCOUNT-NUMBER is accepted along with the other fields of CUSTOMER-RECORD, instead of being accepted separately as in Figure 8.2. In UPDATE-SCREEN, however, the entry corresponding to ACCOUNT-NUMBER still defines a display field only—the user is not allowed to change the account number when updating a record.

In the Procedure Division, paragraph MAIN-ROUTINE begins by getting the DOS file name from the user. The user is then asked if a new file is to be created. Because creating a new file destroys an existing file with the same DOS file name, the user is asked to confirm a request to create a new file. (Alas, requests for confirmation may be of limited benefit, since people have been known to repeatedly confirm the most absurd commands, even when the commands are challenged by a human recipient.) If the user confirms that a new file should be created, CUSTOMER-FILE is opened in OUTPUT mode and then closed, creating an empty file.

Whether or not a new file was created, CUSTOMER-FILE is opened in I-O mode. The rest of MAIN-ROUTINE, as well as GET-AND-DO-FUNCTION and DISPLAY-MENU, work as in Figure 8.2. Each time the menu is displayed, the function key pressed by the user determines whether ENTER-RECORD, UPDATE-RECORD, or DELETE-RECORD should be performed, or whether the program should be terminated.

ENTER-RECORD displays and accepts ENTER-SCREEN to get the value of CUSTOMER-RECORD to be written to the file. Note that the value of the record key, ACCOUNT-NUMBER, is entered along with the other fields of CUSTOMER-RECORD. OK is initialized to "Y", and the value of CUSTOMER-RECORD is written to the file. If an invalid-key error occurs, OK is set to "N". In that case the user is informed that a record with the given account number is already in the file, or there is no room for another record on the disk.

UPDATE-RECORD asks the user for the account number of the record to be updated, then attempts to read this record from the file. If no invalid-key error occurs, UPDATE-SCREEN is displayed and accepted to allow the user to update ACCOUNT-RECORD, and the updated record is rewritten to the file. Since UPDATE-SCREEN does not allow the user to change the ACCOUNT-NUMBER field, the account number in the updated record is the same as that of the record read from the file, so no invalid-key error can occur when REWRITE is executed. If the READ statement caused an invalid-key error, the user is informed that the requested record is not in the file.

DELETE-RECORD obtains the account number of the record to be deleted and removes that record with a DELETE statement. If the DELETE statement causes an invalid-key error, the user is informed that the record to be deleted was not present in the file.

## EXERCISES

1. Add a "print contents" command to the information-retrieval program. When this command is given, the program will print the account number, balance, and credit limit for each record in the customer file. The account numbers should be in ascending order.

2. Write a program to print mailing labels from the contents of the customer file created by the information-retrieval program. The first line of each label gives the customer's account number; the remaining three lines give the name and address in the usual order. The labels should be printed in order of ZIP code, with labels having the same ZIP code being ordered according to their account numbers. *Hint:* The program should begin by creating a new indexed file containing the information for the mailing labels. A judicious choice of record key for this new file will make it easy to print the mailing labels in the desired order.

3. Modify the program of Exercise 2 so that the user can specify the range of ZIP codes for which labels are to be printed. The user will enter the smallest and largest ZIP codes for which labels are to be printed; the ZIP codes entered may or may not occur in the file. *Hint:* Use START to start processing with the first ZIP code not less than the lower limit. Terminate processing when the ZIP code of the most recently read record exceeds the upper limit.

4. Modify the control-totals program (Figure 7.2) to use an indexed file. First, write a simple program to accept sales-data records in any order and store them in an indexed file. To make sure that each record has a unique record key, add a transaction-number field such that all records for a given salesperson have different transaction numbers. The records should be stored in such a way that, when the file is processed sequential-

ly, the records will be processed in the order required by the control-totals program. Now modify the program of Figure 7.2 so that it processes the indexed file sequentially and prints the desired control totals.

5. Write a telephone-directory program to store names, addresses, and telephone numbers in an indexed file. Entries are to be retrieved by name. The program should allow new entries to be made in the file, no-longer-needed entries to be deleted, and existing entries to be examined and updated.

# 10

## Debugging and Error Handling

Programming often seems like a continual battle against errors. The first time we attempt to compile a program, the compiler is likely to detect numerous small errors in spelling, punctuation, or statement format. Even when the errors detected by the compiler have been corrected, we are not home free, for the program probably still contains *bugs*—errors in logic that will prevent it from working as we wish. And after the program is *debugged* and ready for use, the user will enter inappropriate commands, attempt to access nonexistent files or send output to nonexistent devices, and enter data that is incorrect in form, content, or both. In this chapter we will look at those features of COBOL that help us find the bugs in our programs and let us write programs able to handle errors committed by the user.

### DEBUGGING AIDS

Debugging a program is like solving a murder mystery. The incorrect output produced by the program, together with any runtime error messages, constitute "the scene of the crime." There is where we find out something is wrong and there is where we will find the clues that we hope will lead us to the culprit—the incorrect program statements. Unfortunately, the clues at the scene of the crime are not always sufficient to solve the mystery. Particularly frustrating are programs that terminate without producing any output or error messages, or which hang up and have to be terminated manually. In such cases we need some way of digging up more clues, and the COBOL debugging aids are just the tools to dig with.

### The Configuration Section and the DEBUGGING MODE Phrase

The Environment Division has a Configuration Section that—in IBM COBOL, at least—is rarely used. When the Configuration Section is used, it is the first section in the Environment Division. The Configuration Section can contain up to three paragraphs:

```
ENVIRONMENT DIVISION.
CONFIGURATION SECTION.
SOURCE-COMPUTER. IBM-PC.
OBJECT-COMPUTER. IBM-PC.
SPECIAL-NAMES.
     PRINTER IS LINE-PRINTER.
     CURRENCY SIGN IS "L".
     DECIMAL POINT IS COMMA.
     SWITCH-1 IS REPORT-FORMAT
          ON IS YEAR-END-REPORT
          OFF IS MONTHLY-REPORT.
```

The SOURCE-COMPUTER paragraph specifies the computer on which a program was compiled, and the OBJECT-COMPUTER paragraph specifies the computer on which the compiled program is to be executed. The IBM COBOL compiler does not use this information, so the SOURCE-COMPUTER and OBJECT-COMPUTER paragraphs are usually omitted.

The SOURCE-COMPUTER paragraph, however, does have an application in debugging. Following the computer name, we can specify WITH DEBUGGING MODE:

```
SOURCE-COMPUTER. IBM-PC WITH DEBUGGING MODE.
```

The DEBUGGING MODE phrase controls the processing of lines having a D in column 7, the indicator area. If WITH DEBUGGING MODE is specified, lines marked with a D in column 7 are compiled the same as any other lines; if WITH DEBUGGING MODE is not specified, such lines are not compiled.

Thus we can insert statements that will help us debug the program but that we do not want to be included in the final debugged program. While we are debugging, we specify WITH DEBUGGING MODE and the statements marked with D are compiled. When we compile the final version of the program, we remove the WITH DEBUGGING MODE phrase so that the statements put in for debugging are not compiled. However, the debugging statements remain in the source program and can be reinstated once again if future problems prove that our final version was not as final as we had hoped. Later in this chapter we will look at two statements, EXHIBIT and TRACE, that are often marked for use with debugging mode.

The SPECIAL-NAMES paragraph is home for an assortment of miscellaneous definitions. As mentioned in Chapter 5 in connection with the DISPLAY statement, we can define a mnemonic name, such as LINE-PRINTER, with which to refer to the printer:

```
PRINTER IS LINE-PRINTER.
```

The mnemonic name for the printer can also be used in the EXHIBIT statement, discussed later in this chapter.

The SPECIAL-NAMES paragraph allows us to specify another symbol to replace the dollar sign, such as L, which approximates the pound sign used in England and elsewhere. We can also specify that numbers will be written according to the European convention, where the roles of the comma and decimal point are reversed:

```
CURRENCY SIGN IS "L".
DECIMAL POINT IS COMMA.
```

Finally, we can define switches whose settings control the operation of the program. Switch definitions hark back to the days when every computer had a set of "sense switches" on its control panel, the settings of which could be detected by programs and used to control program operation. When switches are defined in IBM COBOL, the user is prompted to enter the switch settings before execution of the program begins.

There are eight possible switches, denoted SWITCH-1 through SWITCH-8. The following SPECIAL-NAMES-paragraph entry allows us to use the setting of SWITCH-1 to determine whether a program produces a monthly report or a year-end report:

```
SWITCH-1 IS REPORT-FORMAT
    ON IS YEAR-END-REPORT
    OFF IS MONTHLY-REPORT.
```

The switch name REPORT-FORMAT is for documentation only and is not used by the COBOL program. YEAR-END-REPORT and MONTHLY-REPORT, however, are defined as condition names; the condition YEAR-END-REPORT is true if SWITCH-1 is on and false if SWITCH-1 is off. The condition MONTHLY-REPORT, on the other hand, is true if SWITCH-1 is off and false if SWITCH-1 is on. In the Procedure Division, we can use statements such as

```
IF MONTHLY-REPORT
    PERFORM PRINT-MONTHLY-REPORT
ELSE
    PERFORM PRINT-YEARLY-REPORT.
```

to determine whether a monthly or a yearly report should be printed.

When a program containing switch definitions begins execution, the user is prompted to enter switch settings as follows:

```
Enter switch settings (blank=OFF, non-blank=ON):
12345678
X    X X
```

The Xs entered by the user turn on switches 1,6, and 8. The remaining switches are off.

Switches can occasionally be useful in debugging. Suppose a program maintains complex tables whose contents are not normally printed out. If the program appears to be malfunctioning, however, we would like to see if the internal tables have the proper contents. We could use a switch to cause the tables to be printed out at the end of a program run, or to enable a command to cause the tables to be printed at the user's request. If a user calls to complain of a program malfunction, we can instruct the user to turn on the switch that dumps the tables and send us the results.

### The TRACE and EXHIBIT Statements

If the output produced by a malfunctioning program is insufficient to pinpoint the trouble, we usually need two kinds of additional information. First, because of IF and PERFORM UNTIL statements, which statements a program executes usually depends on the data the program is processing. We want to determine if the proper statements are being executed for the data at hand. Second, we want to determine if data names are being given the proper values. Even though the value of a data name does not appear directly in the output, an erroneous value for that data name will probably produce errors in the values that *are* displayed or printed. To find the cause of errors in the output, then, we may have to look at values that are not normally displayed or printed.

#### The TRACE statement

The TRACE statement displays procedure (paragraph and section) names as the corresponding procedures are executed. Thus, you can see which paragraphs are executed and the order in which the program executes them. For example, if different kinds of input data are to be processed by different paragraphs, you can determine that the proper paragraph is being performed for each kind of data. Or if the TRACE statement reveals that execution of a paragraph referred to by a PERFORM UNTIL statement is being repeated indefinitely, we know that an error is preventing the PERFORM UNTIL statement from terminating. (The error could be in the PERFORM UNTIL statement or in the statements that calculate the data tested by the PERFORM UNTIL statement.)

The statement

```
READY TRACE
```

turns tracing on—that is, causes the program to begin displaying procedure names as they are encountered. The statement

```
RESET TRACE
```

turns tracing off—that is, causes the program to cease displaying procedure names. If you want to trace the execution of the entire program, you can make READY TRACE the first statement of the program and not use RESET TRACE at all. If, however, you have already narrowed the trouble down to a particular part of the program—a particular paragraph, say—then you can make READY TRACE the first statement of the suspect paragraph and RESET TRACE the last statement. Since lengthy traces can be difficult to interpret, it's usually best to trace as small a portion of the program as will provide the needed information.

Since the TRACE statement only displays procedure names, the more paragraphs a program performs and the fewer the statements in each paragraph, the more detailed the information that a trace can give us about the functioning of the program. A trace will tell us nothing about the internal functioning of a paragraph that does not perform any other paragraphs. This property of traces encourages us to write programs with many relatively small paragraphs rather than only a few large ones.

### The EXHIBIT statement

Even if the correct program statements are being executed, those statements may not be calculating data values properly. To see that the calculations are being done correctly, we need to know not only the values that are printed or displayed as output but the intermediate results that are not normally displayed or printed. The EXHIBIT statement allows us to display or print the value of any data name at any time during the execution of the program. The EXHIBIT statement is identical to the DISPLAY statement except that when we exhibit the value of a data name, the data name itself is displayed along with its value. Thus if GROSS-WAGES has a picture of 9(4)V99 and the value (in conventional notation) of 132.57, the statement

        EXHIBIT GROSS-WAGES

causes the program to display

        GROSS-WAGES = 013257

Note that values are displayed in their internal form, so you will have to provide decimal points mentally and ignore leading zeros. You will also have to use the table given in the SIGN-clause entry in the reference manual to interpret the combined sign-digit characters displayed for signed values.

As with the DISPLAY statement, you can use a position specification—such as (25, 1)—to specify where on the screen the exhibited data will appear. You can also use the UPON option along with a mnemonic name defined in the SPECIAL-NAMES paragraph to send the exhibited data to the printer instead of to the display. (Unfortunately, no similar option is available for the TRACE statement, which always sends its data to the display.)

For both TRACE and EXHIBIT, we may sometimes find it convenient to place a D in column 7, so that the statements will only be effective when WITH DEBUGGING MODE is specified. Note that if such a statement takes up more than one program line, each line must have a D in column 7.

## HANDLING FILE ERRORS

So far we have handled file-processing errors with the AT END and INVALID KEY clauses, which allow us to specify statements to be executed when end-of-file conditions and invalid-key errors arise. COBOL provides two additional methods—file-status codes and declaratives—which can be used separately and in combination to provide better handling for file-processing errors.

### File-Status Codes

The SELECT entry in the FILE-CONTROL paragraph has a FILE STATUS option with the following form:

    FILE STATUS *data-name*

*Data-name* corresponds to a two-character data item. After each operation on the file, the value of *data-name* is set to reflect the outcome of the operation—if it was completed successfully or, if not, what error occurred. The following is a typical SELECT entry with the FILE STATUS option:

    SELECT INVENTORY-FILE ASSIGN TO DISK
        FILE STATUS IS ERROR-CODE
        ACCESS IS RANDOM
        ORGANIZATION IS INDEXED
        RECORD KEY IS REC-KEY.

After each operation on INVENTORY-FILE, a two-character value representing the outcome of the operation will be assigned to ERROR-CODE.

A file-status code of 00 always indicates successful completion of a file operation. Some of the remaining codes differ for sequential, relative, and indexed files. The following are the file-status codes for regular-sequential and line-sequential files:

    00    Successful completion
    10    End of file
    30    Permanent error
    34    Disk space full
    91    File damaged

The codes for relative files are

    00    Successful completion
    10    End of file
    22    Attempt to write a duplicate key
    23    Record not found
    24    Disk space full
    30    Permanent error
    91    File structure destroyed

The codes for indexed files are

| 00 | Successful completion |
| 10 | End of file |
| 21 | Key not in sequence |
| 22 | Attempt to write a duplicate key |
| 23 | Record not found |
| 24 | Disk space full |
| 30 | Permanent error |
| 91 | File structure destroyed |

Following an OPEN INPUT or OPEN I-O statement, a file status of 30 means "file not found." For relative and indexed files, a file status beginning with 2 indicates an invalid-key error. For indexed files, a file status of 21 can occur in sequential-access mode for two situations: (1) An attempt was made to write a record whose key is out of sequence—less than the key of a previously written record. (2) When a READ statement is followed by a REWRITE statement, the record-key of the record read is changed before executing the REWRITE statement.

## Declaratives

We can provide the Procedure Division with a *declarative part* for handling file errors. Statements in the declarative part, like those in an AT END phrase or an INVALID KEY clause, are executed only when an error occurs. The declarative part must come immediately after the division header, before the first paragraph of the "nondeclarative part"—the remainder of the Procedure Division. The declarative part is introduced by the word DECLARATIVES and terminated by the words END DECLARATIVES:

```
PROCEDURE DIVISION.
DECLARATIVES.
declarative-part
END DECLARATIVES.
nondeclarative-part
```

The declarative part is divided into *sections*. In fact, sections can be used in both the declarative and nondeclarative parts of the Procedure Division. Each section is introduced by a section header

```
section-name  SECTION
```

with *section-name* beginning at the A margin (column 8). A section can contain any number of paragraphs. Each section except the last is terminated by the occurence of another section header. The last section in the declarative part is terminated by END DECLARATIVES; the last section in the nondeclarative part is terminated by the end of the program. Modern COBOL programmers organize their programs into paragraphs and avoid sections where possible. In a few places, however, COBOL forces us to use sections, and the declarative part is one of those places.

The declarative part has a section for each file or group of files for which error handing is to be provided. A single section can provide error handling for more than one file. Each section header is followed by a USE sentence that defines the files whose errors are to be handled by the section in question.

The USE sentence has the following form:

```
USE AFTER ERROR PROCEDURE ON files
```

ON can be followed by a list of the file names of all the files for which the declarative section is to be used. Alternatively, ON can be followed by one of the words INPUT, OUTPUT, I-O, and EXTEND. INPUT indicates that the declarative section is to be used for all files opened in INPUT mode; OUTPUT indicates that the declarative section is to be used for all files opened in OUTPUT mode; and so on.

Following the USE sentence are one or more paragraphs (usually only one) to be executed when an error occurs for the designated files. The following is a simple declarative part:

```
DECLARATIVES.
EMPLOYEE-FILE-ERRORS SECTION.
    USE AFTER ERROR PROCEDURE ON EMPLOYEE-FILE.
EF-ERRORS.
    MOVE "Y" TO EMPLOYEE-FILE-ERROR-FLAG.
TIME-CARD-FILE-ERRORS SECTION.
    USE AFTER ERROR PROCEDURE ON TIME-CARD-FILE.
TCF-ERRORS.
    MOVE "Y" TO TIME-CARD-FILE-ERROR-FLAG.
END DECLARATIVES.
```

In the following declarative section, INPUT and OUTPUT are used in place of specific file names:

```
DECLARATIVES.
INPUT-ERRORS SECTION.
    USE AFTER ERROR PROCEDURE ON INPUT.
I-ERRORS.
    MOVE "Y" TO INPUT-ERROR-FLAG.
OUTPUT-ERRORS SECTION.
    USE AFTER ERROR PROCEDURE ON OUTPUT.
O-ERRORS.
    MOVE "Y" TO OUTPUT-ERROR-FLAG.
END DECLARATIVES.
```

## Combining Error-Handling Methods

The various methods of handling file errors—AT END and INVALID KEY options, file-status codes, and declaratives—can be combined according to the following rules.

If a file-status item is defined, its value is set after each operation on the file, regardless of what other error-handling mechanisms may be provided. Thus file-status items can be used in combination with both AT END and INVALID KEY options and with declaratives.

If a file-processing statement includes an AT END or INVALID KEY option, and the corresponding error occurs, the statement in the AT END or INVALID KEY option is executed, after which execution continues with program statement following the one that caused the error. The declarative section for the file (if any) is not executed.

If a file-processing statement does not have an AT END or INVALID KEY option, but a declarative section is defined for the file, all errors, including end-of-file and invalid-key errors, cause the declarative section to be executed. After the declarative section has been executed, program execution continues with the statement following the one that caused the error.

If an error occurs that is not handled by an AT END or INVALID KEY option or by a declarative section, the action taken by the system depends on whether a file-status item has been defined for the file. If a file-status item has been defined, execution continues with the statement following the one that caused the error. It is assumed that the program will check the value of the file-status item, discover the error, and take the appropriate action. If no file-status item has been defined for the file, however, an error that is not handled by an AT END or INVALID KEY option or by a declarative section causes the program to terminate with an error message.

### Handling File Errors for an Information-Retrieval Program

Figure 10.1 shows a version of the information-retrieval program discussed in Chapter 9. This version uses a file-status item and a declarative section for error checking, as opposed to the INVALID KEY clauses used in the original version.

ERROR-CODE is designated in the SELECT entry as the file-status item:

```
SELECT CUSTOMER-FILE ASSIGN TO DISK
    FILE STATUS IS ERROR-CODE
    ACCESS IS RANDOM
    ORGANIZATION IS INDEXED
    RECORD KEY IS ACCOUNT-NUMBER.
```

In the Working-Storage Section, ERROR-CODE is defined as a two-character data item:

```
01  ERROR-CODE          PIC XX.
```

The declarative part of the Procedure Division contains a single declarative section:

```
PROCEDURE DIVISION.
DECLARATIVES.
ERROR-MESSAGE SECTION.
    USE AFTER ERROR PROCEDURE ON CUSTOMER-FILE.
DISPLAY-MESSAGE.

        ...

END DECLARATIVES.
```

Paragraph DISPLAY-MESSAGE erases the screen, displays the error message corresponding to the value of ERROR-CODE, and waits for the user to press the Enter key to continue. After the Enter key is pressed, control returns to the statement following the one that caused the error. (When the statement that caused the error is the last statement in a paragraph, control returns from that paragraph to the one

```
IDENTIFICATION DIVISION.
PROGRAM-ID.  INDEXED-FILE.

*    Information storage and retrieval using an indexed file.

ENVIRONMENT DIVISION.
INPUT-OUTPUT SECTION.
FILE-CONTROL.
     SELECT CUSTOMER-FILE ASSIGN TO DISK
          FILE STATUS IS ERROR-CODE
          ACCESS IS RANDOM
          ORGANIZATION IS INDEXED
          RECORD KEY IS ACCOUNT-NUMBER.

DATA DIVISION.
FILE SECTION.
FD   CUSTOMER-FILE
     LABEL RECORDS STANDARD
     VALUE OF FILE-ID IS DOS-FILE-NAME.
01   CUSTOMER-RECORD.
     02   ACCOUNT-NUMBER  PIC X(6).
     02   LAST-NAME       PIC X(30).
     02   FIRST-NAME      PIC X(20).
     02   MIDDLE-INITIAL  PIC X.
     02   STREET-ADDRESS  PIC X(40).
     02   CITY            PIC X(15).
     02   STATE           PIC XX.
     02   ZIP             PIC X(5).
     02   BALANCE         PIC 9(6)V99.
     02   CREDIT-LIMIT    PIC 9(6)V99.

WORKING-STORAGE SECTION.
01   RESPONSE            PIC X.
01   OK                  PIC X.
01   DOS-FILE-NAME       PIC X(15).
01   TERMINATOR-KEY      PIC 99.
01   ERROR-CODE          PIC XX.
01   DUMMY               PIC X.

SCREEN SECTION.
01   MENU-SCREEN.
     02   BLANK SCREEN.
     02   LINE 5 COLUMN 30 VALUE "F1  Enter new record".
     02   LINE 7 COLUMN 30 VALUE "F2  Update record".
     02   LINE 9 COLUMN 30 VALUE "F3  Delete record".
     02   LINE 11 COLUMN 30 VALUE "F4  Exit program".
     02   LINE 15 COLUMN 25
               VALUE "Press key for desired function".
```

*Figure 10.1*  This version of Figure 9.1 uses a file-status data item and a declaratives section to handle errors for CUSTOMER-FILE.

that performed it, just as it would have if the erroneous statement had been successfully executed.)

The file-status code 00 cannot occur, since the declarative section is not invoked when an operation is completed successfully. Codes 10 and 21, which apply only to sequential access, also cannot occur. For each remaining code a message is printed:

```
01   ENTER-SCREEN.
     02  BLANK SCREEN.
     02  LINE 4 COLUMN 5 REVERSE-VIDEO VALUE "Account Number".
     02  LINE 5 COLUMN 5 PIC XBXXBXXX TO ACCOUNT-NUMBER
             AUTO.
     02  LINE 8 COLUMN 5 REVERSE-VIDEO VALUE "Last Name".
     02  LINE 9 COLUMN 5 PIC X(30) TO LAST-NAME
             AUTO REQUIRED.
     02  LINE 8 COLUMN 40 REVERSE-VIDEO VALUE "First Name".
     02  LINE 9 COLUMN 40 PIC X(20) TO FIRST-NAME
             AUTO REQUIRED.
     02  LINE 8 COLUMN 65 REVERSE-VIDEO VALUE "Initial".
     02  LINE 9 COLUMN 65 PIC X TO MIDDLE-INITIAL
             AUTO REQUIRED.
     02  LINE 12 COLUMN 5 REVERSE-VIDEO VALUE "Street Address".
     02  LINE 13 COLUMN 5 PIC X(40) TO STREET-ADDRESS
             AUTO REQUIRED.
     02  LINE 16 COLUMN 5 REVERSE-VIDEO VALUE "City".
     02  LINE 17 COLUMN 5 PIC X(15) TO CITY
             AUTO REQUIRED.
     02  LINE 16 COLUMN 25 REVERSE-VIDEO VALUE "State".
     02  LINE 17 COLUMN 25 PIC XX TO STATE
             AUTO FULL.
     02  LINE 16 COLUMN 35 REVERSE-VIDEO VALUE "ZIP".
     02  LINE 17 COLUMN 35 PIC X(5) TO ZIP
             AUTO FULL.
     02  LINE 20 COLUMN 5 REVERSE-VIDEO VALUE "Balance".
     02  LINE 21 COLUMN 5 PIC $$$$,$$9.99 TO BALANCE
             AUTO REQUIRED.
     02  LINE 20 COLUMN 21 REVERSE-VIDEO VALUE "Credit Limit".
     02  LINE 21 COLUMN 21 PIC $$$$,$$9.99 TO CREDIT-LIMIT
             AUTO REQUIRED.

01   UPDATE-SCREEN.
     02  BLANK SCREEN.
     02  LINE 4 COLUMN 5 REVERSE-VIDEO VALUE "Account Number".
     02  LINE 5 COLUMN 5 PIC XBXXBXXX FROM ACCOUNT-NUMBER.
     02  LINE 8 COLUMN 5 REVERSE-VIDEO VALUE "Last Name".
     02  LINE 9 COLUMN 5 PIC X(30) USING LAST-NAME
             AUTO.
     02  LINE 8 COLUMN 40 REVERSE-VIDEO VALUE "First Name".
     02  LINE 9 COLUMN 40 PIC X(20) USING FIRST-NAME
             AUTO.
     02  LINE 8 COLUMN 65 REVERSE-VIDEO VALUE "Initial".
     02  LINE 9 COLUMN 65 PIC X USING MIDDLE-INITIAL
             AUTO.
     02  LINE 12 COLUMN 5 REVERSE-VIDEO VALUE "Street Address".
     02  LINE 13 COLUMN 5 PIC X(40) USING STREET-ADDRESS
             AUTO.
     02  LINE 16 COLUMN 5 REVERSE-VIDEO VALUE "City".
     02  LINE 17 COLUMN 5 PIC X(15) USING CITY
             AUTO.
     02  LINE 16 COLUMN 25 REVERSE-VIDEO VALUE "State".
     02  LINE 17 COLUMN 25 PIC XX USING STATE
             AUTO.
     02  LINE 16 COLUMN 35 REVERSE-VIDEO VALUE "ZIP".
     02  LINE 17 COLUMN 35 PIC X(5) USING ZIP
             AUTO.
     02  LINE 20 COLUMN 5 REVERSE-VIDEO VALUE "Balance".
     02  LINE 21 COLUMN 5 PIC $$$$,$$9.99 USING BALANCE
             AUTO.
     02  LINE 20 COLUMN 21 REVERSE-VIDEO VALUE "Credit Limit".
     02  LINE 21 COLUMN 21 PIC $$$$,$$9.99 USING CREDIT-LIMIT
             AUTO.
```

*Figure 10.1 (continued)*

```
PROCEDURE DIVISION.
DECLARATIVES.
ERROR-MESSAGE SECTION.
    USE AFTER ERROR PROCEDURE ON CUSTOMER-FILE.
DISPLAY-MESSAGE.
    DISPLAY (1, 1) ERASE.
    IF ERROR-CODE = "22"
        DISPLAY (5, 1) "Account number already in file"
    ELSE IF ERROR-CODE = "23"
        DISPLAY (5, 1) "Record not found"
    ELSE IF ERROR-CODE = "24"
        DISPLAY (5, 1) "Disk space full"
    ELSE IF ERROR-CODE = "30"
        DISPLAY (5, 1) "File not found"
    ELSE IF ERROR-CODE = "91"
        DISPLAY (5, 1) "File structure destroyed"
    ELSE
        DISPLAY (5, 1) "File error".
    DISPLAY (7, 1) "Press Enter to continue ".
    ACCEPT (, ) DUMMY.
END DECLARATIVES.

MAIN-ROUTINE.
    DISPLAY (1, 1) ERASE (5, 1) "File name? ".
    ACCEPT (, ) DOS-FILE-NAME WITH PROMPT.
    DISPLAY (7, 1) "Create new file (Y/N)? ".
    ACCEPT (, ) RESPONSE.
    IF RESPONSE = "Y" OR "y"
        DISPLAY (9, 1) "Are you sure (Y/N)? "
        ACCEPT (, ) RESPONSE
        IF RESPONSE = "Y" OR "y"
            OPEN OUTPUT CUSTOMER-FILE
            CLOSE CUSTOMER-FILE.
    OPEN I-O CUSTOMER-FILE.
    IF ERROR-CODE = "00"
        MOVE ZERO TO TERMINATOR-KEY
        PERFORM GET-AND-DO-FUNCTION
            UNTIL TERMINATOR-KEY = 5
        CLOSE CUSTOMER-FILE.
    STOP RUN.

GET-AND-DO-FUNCTION.
    MOVE ZERO TO TERMINATOR-KEY.
    PERFORM DISPLAY-MENU
        UNTIL TERMINATOR-KEY > 1 AND < 6.
    IF TERMINATOR-KEY = 2
        PERFORM ENTER-RECORD
    ELSE IF TERMINATOR-KEY = 3
        PERFORM UPDATE-RECORD
    ELSE IF TERMINATOR-KEY = 4
        PERFORM DELETE-RECORD.

DISPLAY-MENU.
    DISPLAY MENU-SCREEN.
    ACCEPT (15, 56) DUMMY.
    ACCEPT TERMINATOR-KEY FROM ESCAPE KEY.
```

*Figure 10.1 (continued)*

```
ENTER-RECORD.
    DISPLAY ENTER-SCREEN.
    ACCEPT ENTER-SCREEN.
    WRITE CUSTOMER-RECORD.

UPDATE-RECORD.
    DISPLAY (1, 1) ERASE (5, 1) "Account Number? ".
    ACCEPT (, ) ACCOUNT-NUMBER WITH PROMPT.
    READ CUSTOMER-FILE.
    IF ERROR-CODE = "00"
        DISPLAY UPDATE-SCREEN
        ACCEPT UPDATE-SCREEN
        REWRITE CUSTOMER-RECORD.

DELETE-RECORD.
    DISPLAY (1, 1) ERASE (5, 1) "Account number? ".
    ACCEPT (, ) ACCOUNT-NUMBER WITH PROMPT.
    DELETE CUSTOMER-FILE RECORD.
```

*Figure 10.1 (continued)*

```
22  Account number already in file
23  Record not found
24  Disk space full
30  File not found
91  File structure destroyed
```

Just in case there are any other, undocumented, file-status codes, the noncommittal message File error is printed if some code other than the ones just given occurs. If the list of file-status codes in the reference manual is correct, this last error message will never be printed.

The paragraphs ENTER-RECORD, UPDATE-RECORD, and DELETE-RECORD are similar to those discussed in Chapter 9, but somewhat simpler since no INVALID KEY clauses are needed, nor need any flags be set or tested. Note, however, that after attempting to read a record from CUSTOMER-FILE, UPDATE-RECORD proceeds with the update only if the value of ERROR-CODE is 00, indicating that a record was successfully read.

## DATA VALIDATION

Almost all so-called computer errors result from incorrect data being entered into the computer. Of the remaining errors, most are caused by incorrect programs. Very few are caused by malfunctioning hardware, although malfunctioning hardware can, of course, have other serious effects, such as delaying processing until the computer is fixed.

Because of the likelihood and seriousness of data-entry errors, we would like our programs to catch as many of them as possible. Checks for correct data format can prevent programs from terminating abnormally when they attempt to do arithmetic on nonnumeric data. Use of check digits in key fields can prevent merchandise from being shipped or bills being sent to the wrong person. Reasonableness checks will catch the $500,000 paycheck for the janitor and the $100,000 tax bill for a 10-year old automobile. This kind of checking is known as *data validation*.

Most programs in textbooks—including those in this one—don't do nearly enough data validation, if they do any at all. The reason isn't hard to see. Example programs are written to illustrate particular language features and principles of computer programming. Including statements for data validation, which might take up as much or more space than all the other statements in the Procedure Division, would intimidate beginners and obscure the principles that the program was intended to illustrate. If we wish to use a program from a textbook in a real-world situation, we must usually be prepared to provide many additional statements for data validation and other error checking.

Format errors normally occur with numeric items which, we know, can contain only digits and (depending on the picture for the item) a leading or trailing sign or a leading or trailing combined sign-digit code. Any other characters, such as spaces, decimal points, commas, and dollar signs, will cause a runtime error when the program attempts an arithmetical operation on the data item. So will invalid uses of allowed characters, such as more than one sign character, a trailing sign when a leading sign is specified for the item (or vice versa), or a sign character embedded within the data item.

(Note that just because an item has a numeric picture does not guarantee that it contains valid numeric data. Suppose, for example, that the item in question is a field of the record description associated with an input file. When a record is read from the file, whatever characters occupy the corresponding field of the record will become the value of the numeric data item, without any check being made to see if they actually represent valid numeric data.)

By far the best way to avoid format errors in numeric data is to create data files with IBM COBOL programs using format 3 and format 4 ACCEPT statements. (The format 3 ACCEPT statements should use the PROMPT option.) These statements display the correct format for the user, then check the data as it is entered and refuse to accept erroneous characters. Leading zeros are automatically filled in, a decimal point appears on the screen even though it is not stored in the numeric field, and a sign can be entered at any time, without the operator having to worry about whether the sign is leading or trailing or whether it is to be stored as a separate character or as a combined sign-digit code.

Even though data is in the correct form, its content may still be incorrect. There are, of course, limits to how well a computer program can check content, because usually the program has no way of knowing what the content should be. Still, the program can check for unreasonable values. The $500,000 check to the janitor and the $100,000 tax bill should be caught, since each is unreasonably large. Also, if a company has divisions numbered 1 through 5, then records purporting to come from divisions 6, 7, 8, and 9 should not be accepted. Like format checking, content checking is best done by the programs that create and update a file rather than those that process it.

Limit and range checks are easily made with IF statements. For example, we can check that a value is not less than the value of LOWER-LIMIT with:

```
IF DATA-FIELD < LOWER-LIMIT
    MOVE "Y" TO BAD-DATA-FLAG.
```

We can check that a value is not greater than the value of UPPER-LIMIT with

```
IF DATA-FIELD > UPPER-LIMIT
    MOVE "Y" TO BAD-DATA-FLAG.
```

and we can check that a value lies in the range defined by the values of LOWER-LIMIT and UPPER-LIMIT with

```
IF DATA-FIELD < LOWER-LIMIT OR > UPPER-LIMIT
    MOVE "Y" TO BAD-DATA-FLAG.
```

Except for short test files, it is recommended that all files be created by COBOL programs and that validity checks be made when the file is created. But since IBM Personal Computers are sometimes used to process files prepared on other computers and either transferred to IBM-PC diskettes or transmitted over communications lines, the COBOL programmer may have no control over how the data is prepared. In that case, the worst must be expected, and programs that process a data file must check the data for correct form and content. In the rest of this chapter we will look at how a file-processing program can do this kind of data validation.

## The INSPECT Statement

The INSPECT statement allows us to do two things. First, we can count the number of times a specified character occurs in a data item. Sometimes we may be interested in the exact number of occurrences; other times we may only be interested in whether the character occurs at all—whether the number of occurrences is zero or nonzero. Second, we can cause a specified character to be replaced with another character. This capability can sometimes be used to change an invalid data item into a valid one—for example, by changing leading spaces to leading zeros to produce a valid numeric data item.

The INSPECT statement has the following general form:

```
INSPECT data-name
    TALLYING clause
    REPLACING clause
```

*Data-name* designates the data item whose value is to be examined and (possibly) modified. This item must have display usage, since it will be processed character by character. The TALLYING clause specifies which appearances of a character are to be counted; the REPLACING clause specifies the replacement of certain appearances of a character with another character. An INSPECT statement can have a TALLYING clause, a REPLACING clause, or both. In the latter case, the TALLYING clause comes first.

We use one of the following phrases to specify which characters are to be tallied or replaced:

```
ALL operand
LEADING operand
FIRST operand          (REPLACING clause only)
CHARACTERS
```

*Operand,* which must specify a single character, can be a data name, literal, or figurative constant. ALL *operand* specifies all occurrences of the operand character. Thus,

        ALL "A"

specifies that all uppercase As are to be counted or replaced,

        ALL SPACES

specifies that all spaces are to be counted or replaced, and so on. LEADING *operand* specifies those occurrences of the operand character that precede any other character. Thus, in

        0009050

the first three zeros are leading zeros but the remaining two are not. FIRST *operand* refers to the first (leftmost) occurrence of the operand character. This option is only allowed in the REPLACING clause. Finally, CHARACTERS designates all characters in the data item being processed.

One of the phrases

        BEFORE INITIAL *operand*
        AFTER INITIAL *operand*

can be used to specify where in the data item processing will begin or end. The operand character in the BEFORE and AFTER phrases need not be the same as the one in the ALL, LEADING, and FIRST phrases. For example,

        BEFORE INITIAL "D"

specifies that only those characters preceding the first "D" will be processed, and

        AFTER INITIAL SPACE

specifies that only those characters following the first space will be processed.

The following complete INSPECT statement illustrates the TALLYING clause:

        INSPECT FIELD-A
            TALLYING COUNTER FOR
            ALL "P"
            AFTER INITIAL "C".

FIELD-A is the field to be inspected. COUNTER is a numeric data item used to record the count. The count is added to the current contents of COUNTER, so if we want the count stored in COUNTER, then we must move zero to COUNTER before executing the INSPECT statement. If the value of FIELD-A is

        "PECK OF PICKLED PEPPERS"

the value of COUNT is increased by 4, since there are four Ps following the first C. With the same value for FIELD-A, the statement

```
INSPECT FIELD-A
    TALLYING COUNTER FOR
    ALL "P"
    BEFORE INITIAL "C".
```

would increase the value of COUNTER by 1, and

```
INSPECT FIELD-A
    TALLYING COUNTER FOR
    ALL "P".
```

would increase the value of COUNTER by 5.

The following complete INSPECT statement illustrates the REPLACING clause:

```
INSPECT FIELD-B
    REPLACING ALL "P"
    BY "T"
    AFTER INITIAL "E".
```

If the value of FIELD-B is

```
"PEPPER"
```

its value after the INSPECT statement is executed will be

```
"PETTER"
```

If the statement

```
INSPECT FIELD-B
    REPLACING ALL "P"
    BY "L".
```

is now executed, the value of FIELD-B becomes

```
"LETTER"
```

## A Program with Data Validation

Figure 10.2 shows a version of the payroll-report program (Figure 4.1) that incorporates data validation. The program checks the format of the input data as well as for size errors in those arithmetic operations for which size errors are possible. Additional checks, such as range and limit checks on the values of input data items, can easily be included.

Since the payroll-report program was discussed in Chapter 4, only the parts of Figure 10.2 having to do with data validation will be discussed here. In the Working-Storage section, ERROR-RECORD is used for setting up error messages to be displayed. The erroneous record is moved to ER-PAYROLL-RECORD, so each error message begins by displaying the record that caused the problem. The FILLER item defines a dash to separate the bad record from the error message. A message describing the nature of the problem is stored in ER-MESSAGE.

It is usually best to set a flag when an error occurs rather than attempt to handle the error at the point where it is detected. All the flags are fields of the record ERROR-

```
IDENTIFICATION DIVISION.
PROGRAM-ID. PAYROLL-REPORT.

*    Payroll-report program with data validation.

ENVIRONMENT DIVISION.
INPUT-OUTPUT SECTION.
FILE-CONTROL.
     SELECT PAYROLL-FILE ASSIGN TO DISK
          ORGANIZATION IS LINE SEQUENTIAL.
     SELECT PAYROLL-REPORT-FILE ASSIGN TO PRINTER.

DATA DIVISION.
FILE SECTION.
FD   PAYROLL-FILE
     LABEL RECORDS STANDARD
     VALUE OF FILE-ID IS DOS-FILE-NAME.
01   PAYROLL-RECORD.
     02  PR-EMPLOYEE-NUMBER       PIC X(6).
     02  PR-HOURS-WORKED          PIC 99V9.
         88  NO-OVERTIME          VALUES 0 THRU 40.
     02  PR-HOURLY-RATE           PIC 99V99.

FD   PAYROLL-REPORT-FILE
     LABEL RECORDS OMITTED.
01   PAYROLL-REPORT-RECORD        PIC X(80).

WORKING-STORAGE SECTION.
01   TITLE-LINE-1.
     02  FILLER                   PIC X(14) VALUE "Payroll Report".
     02  FILLER                   PIC X(59) VALUE SPACES.
     02  FILLER                   PIC X(5) VALUE "Page ".
     02  TL-PAGE-NUMBER           PIC Z9.

01   TITLE-LINE-2.
     02  FILLER                   PIC X(13) VALUE "Ajax Products".
     02  FILLER                   PIC X(59) VALUE SPACES.
     02  TL-MONTH                 PIC 99.
     02  FILLER                   PIC X VALUE "/".
     02  TL-DAY                   PIC 99.
     02  FILLER                   PIC X VALUE "/".
     02  TL-YEAR                  PIC 99.

01   HEADING-LINE-1.
     02  FILLER                   PIC X(8) VALUE "Employee".
     02  FILLER                   PIC X(6) VALUE SPACES.
     02  FILLER                   PIC X(5) VALUE "Hours".
     02  FILLER                   PIC X(8) VALUE SPACES.
     02  FILLER                   PIC X(6) VALUE "Hourly".
     02  FILLER                   PIC X(7) VALUE SPACES.
     02  FILLER                   PIC X(7) VALUE "Regular".
     02  FILLER                   PIC X(8) VALUE SPACES.
     02  FILLER                   PIC X(8) VALUE "Overtime".
     02  FILLER                   PIC X(10) VALUE SPACES.
     02  FILLER                   PIC X(5) VALUE "Gross".
```

*Figure 10.2* This version of the payroll-report program (Figure 4.1) detects format errors in its input data and size errors in arithmetical calculations.

```
01   HEADING-LINE-2.
     02  FILLER                     PIC X VALUE SPACE.
     02  FILLER                     PIC X(6) VALUE "Number".
     02  FILLER                     PIC X(7) VALUE SPACES.
     02  FILLER                     PIC X(6) VALUE "Worked".
     02  FILLER                     PIC X(8) VALUE SPACES.
     02  FILLER                     PIC X(4) VALUE "Rate".
     02  FILLER                     PIC X(9) VALUE SPACES.
     02  FILLER                     PIC X(5) VALUE "Wages".
     02  FILLER                     PIC X(11) VALUE SPACES.
     02  FILLER                     PIC X(5) VALUE "Wages".
     02  FILLER                     PIC X(11) VALUE SPACES.
     02  FILLER                     PIC X(5) VALUE "Wages".

01   DETAIL-LINE.
     02  FILLER                     PIC X VALUE SPACE.
     02  DL-EMPLOYEE-NUMBER         PIC X(6).
     02  FILLER                     PIC X(8) VALUE SPACES.
     02  DL-HOURS-WORKED            PIC Z9.9.
     02  FILLER                     PIC X(8) VALUE SPACES.
     02  DL-HOURLY-RATE             PIC $$9.99.
     02  FILLER                     PIC X(6) VALUE SPACES.
     02  DL-REGULAR-WAGES           PIC $$,$$9.99.
     02  FILLER                     PIC X(7) VALUE SPACES.
     02  DL-OVERTIME-WAGES          PIC $$,$$9.99.
     02  FILLER                     PIC X(7) VALUE SPACES.
     02  DL-GROSS-WAGES             PIC $$,$$9.99.

01   FOOTING-LINE.
     02  FILLER                     PIC X(10) VALUE "Employees ".
     02  FL-EMPLOYEE-COUNT          PIC ZZ9.
     02  FILLER                     PIC X(38) VALUE SPACES.
     02  FILLER                     PIC X(18)
                                        VALUE "Total Gross Wages ".
     02  FL-TOTAL-GROSS-WAGES       PIC $$$$,$$9.99.

01   ERROR-RECORD.
     02  ER-PAYROLL-RECORD          PIC X(13).
     02  FILLER                     PIC X(4) VALUE " -- ".
     02  ER-MESSAGE                 PIC X(60).

01   CONSTANTS.
     02  MAXIMUM-REGULAR-HOURS      PIC 99 VALUE 40.
     02  OVERTIME-MULTIPLIER        PIC 9V9 VALUE 1.5.
     02  LINES-PER-PAGE             PIC 99 VALUE 11.

01   INPUT-FILE-CONTROL.
     02  EOF-FLAG                   PIC X.
         88  NO-MORE-INPUT          VALUE "Y".
     02  DOS-FILE-NAME              PIC X(15).

01   PRINTER-CONTROL.
     02  LINE-SPACING               PIC 9.
     02  LINES-PRINTED              PIC 99.

01   SYSTEM-DATE.
     02  SD-YEAR                    PIC 99.
     02  SD-MONTH                   PIC 99.
     02  SD-DAY                     PIC 99.
```

*Figure 10.2 (continued)*

```
01   WORK-FIELDS.
     02   REGULAR-HOURS          PIC 99V9.
     02   OVERTIME-HOURS         PIC 999V99.
     02   REGULAR-WAGES          PIC 9(4)V99.
     02   OVERTIME-WAGES         PIC 9(4)V99.
     02   GROSS-WAGES            PIC 9(4)V99.

01   COUNTERS-AND-ACCUMULATOR.
     02   SPACE-COUNT            PIC 9.
     02   EMPLOYEE-COUNT         PIC 999.
     02   PAGE-NUMBER            PIC 99.
     02   TOTAL-GROSS-WAGES      PIC 9(6)V99.

01   ERROR-FLAGS.
     02   BAD-EMPLOYEE-NUMBER    PIC X.
     02   BAD-HOURS-WORKED       PIC X.
     02   BAD-HOURLY-RATE        PIC X.
     02   BAD-GROSS-WAGES        PIC X.
     02   BAD-RECORD             PIC X.
     02   FATAL-ERROR            PIC X.

PROCEDURE DIVISION.
PRINT-PAYROLL-REPORT.
     PERFORM GET-DOS-FILE-NAME.
     OPEN INPUT PAYROLL-FILE
          OUTPUT PAYROLL-REPORT-FILE.
     PERFORM ASSIGN-INITIAL-VALUES.
     READ PAYROLL-FILE
          AT END MOVE "Y" TO EOF-FLAG.
     PERFORM PROCESS-PAYROLL-RECORD
          UNTIL NO-MORE-INPUT OR FATAL-ERROR = "Y".
     IF FATAL-ERROR NOT = "Y"
          PERFORM PRINT-FOOTING-LINE
          DISPLAY "Program terminated normally"
     ELSE
          DISPLAY "Fatal error--program terminated abnormally".
     CLOSE PAYROLL-FILE
           PAYROLL-REPORT-FILE.
     STOP RUN.

GET-DOS-FILE-NAME.
     DISPLAY (1, 1) ERASE.
     DISPLAY (5, 1) "Name of payroll file? ".
     ACCEPT (LIN, COL) DOS-FILE-NAME WITH PROMPT.
     DISPLAY (1, 1) ERASE.

ASSIGN-INITIAL-VALUES.
     MOVE "N" TO EOF-FLAG.
     MOVE SPACE TO FATAL-ERROR.
     MOVE ZERO TO EMPLOYEE-COUNT
                  TOTAL-GROSS-WAGES.
     MOVE 1 TO PAGE-NUMBER.
     MOVE LINES-PER-PAGE TO LINES-PRINTED.
```

*Figure 10.2 (continued)*

```
PROCESS-PAYROLL-RECORD.
     MOVE SPACES TO ERROR-FLAGS.
     PERFORM CHECK-PAYROLL-RECORD.
     IF BAD-RECORD NOT = "Y"
          PERFORM CALCULATE-WAGES.
     IF BAD-RECORD NOT = "Y"
          PERFORM UPDATE-COUNT-AND-TOTAL
          PERFORM PRINT-DETAIL-LINE
     ELSE
          PERFORM DISPLAY-ERROR-MESSAGE.
     READ PAYROLL-FILE
          AT END MOVE "Y" TO EOF-FLAG.

PRINT-FOOTING-LINE.
     MOVE EMPLOYEE-COUNT TO FL-EMPLOYEE-COUNT.
     MOVE TOTAL-GROSS-WAGES TO FL-TOTAL-GROSS-WAGES.
     WRITE PAYROLL-REPORT-RECORD
          FROM FOOTING-LINE
          AFTER ADVANCING 2 LINES.

CHECK-PAYROLL-RECORD.
     MOVE ZERO TO SPACE-COUNT.
     INSPECT PR-EMPLOYEE-NUMBER
          TALLYING SPACE-COUNT FOR ALL SPACES.
     IF SPACE-COUNT > 0
          MOVE "Y" TO BAD-EMPLOYEE-NUMBER
                      BAD-RECORD.
     INSPECT PR-HOURS-WORKED
          REPLACING LEADING SPACES BY ZEROS.
     IF PR-HOURS-WORKED IS NOT NUMERIC
          MOVE "Y" TO BAD-HOURS-WORKED
                      BAD-RECORD.
     INSPECT PR-HOURLY-RATE
          REPLACING LEADING SPACES BY ZEROS.
     IF PR-HOURLY-RATE IS NOT NUMERIC
          MOVE "Y" TO BAD-HOURLY-RATE
                      BAD-RECORD.

CALCULATE-WAGES.
     IF NO-OVERTIME
          MOVE PR-HOURS-WORKED TO REGULAR-HOURS
          MOVE ZERO TO OVERTIME-HOURS
     ELSE
          MOVE MAXIMUM-REGULAR-HOURS TO REGULAR-HOURS
          SUBTRACT MAXIMUM-REGULAR-HOURS FROM PR-HOURS-WORKED
               GIVING OVERTIME-HOURS
          MULTIPLY OVERTIME-MULTIPLIER BY OVERTIME-HOURS.
     MULTIPLY REGULAR-HOURS BY PR-HOURLY-RATE
          GIVING REGULAR-WAGES ROUNDED.
     MULTIPLY OVERTIME-HOURS BY PR-HOURLY-RATE
          GIVING OVERTIME-WAGES ROUNDED.
     ADD REGULAR-WAGES OVERTIME-WAGES
          GIVING GROSS-WAGES
          ON SIZE ERROR MOVE "Y" TO BAD-GROSS-WAGES
                                    BAD-RECORD.
```

*Figure 10.2 (continued)*

```
UPDATE-COUNT-AND-TOTAL.
    ADD 1 TO EMPLOYEE-COUNT
        ON SIZE ERROR
            DISPLAY "Employee Count too large"
            MOVE "Y" TO FATAL-ERROR.
    ADD GROSS-WAGES TO TOTAL-GROSS-WAGES
        ON SIZE ERROR
            DISPLAY "Total Gross Wages too large"
            MOVE "Y" TO FATAL-ERROR.

PRINT-DETAIL-LINE.
    MOVE PR-EMPLOYEE-NUMBER TO DL-EMPLOYEE-NUMBER.
    MOVE PR-HOURS-WORKED TO DL-HOURS-WORKED.
    MOVE PR-HOURLY-RATE TO DL-HOURLY-RATE.
    MOVE REGULAR-WAGES TO DL-REGULAR-WAGES.
    MOVE OVERTIME-WAGES TO DL-OVERTIME-WAGES.
    MOVE GROSS-WAGES TO DL-GROSS-WAGES.
    IF LINES-PRINTED = LINES-PER-PAGE
        PERFORM PRINT-HEADINGS
    ELSE
        MOVE 1 TO LINE-SPACING.
    WRITE PAYROLL-REPORT-RECORD
        FROM DETAIL-LINE
        AFTER ADVANCING LINE-SPACING LINES.
    ADD LINE-SPACING TO LINES-PRINTED.

PRINT-HEADINGS.
    MOVE PAGE-NUMBER TO TL-PAGE-NUMBER.
    ADD 1 TO PAGE-NUMBER.
    WRITE PAYROLL-REPORT-RECORD
        FROM TITLE-LINE-1
        AFTER ADVANCING PAGE.
    ACCEPT SYSTEM-DATE FROM DATE.
    MOVE SD-YEAR TO TL-YEAR.
    MOVE SD-MONTH TO TL-MONTH.
    MOVE SD-DAY TO TL-DAY.
    WRITE PAYROLL-REPORT-RECORD
        FROM TITLE-LINE-2
        AFTER ADVANCING 1 LINE.
    WRITE PAYROLL-REPORT-RECORD
        FROM HEADING-LINE-1
        AFTER ADVANCING 3 LINES.
    WRITE PAYROLL-REPORT-RECORD
        FROM HEADING-LINE-2
        AFTER ADVANCING 1 LINE.
    MOVE 6 TO LINES-PRINTED.
    MOVE 2 TO LINE-SPACING.

DISPLAY-ERROR-MESSAGE.
    MOVE PAYROLL-RECORD TO ER-PAYROLL-RECORD.
    IF BAD-EMPLOYEE-NUMBER = "Y"
        MOVE "Invalid Employee Number" TO ER-MESSAGE
        DISPLAY ERROR-RECORD.
    IF BAD-HOURS-WORKED = "Y"
        MOVE "Invalid Hours Worked" TO ER-MESSAGE
        DISPLAY ERROR-RECORD.
    IF BAD-HOURLY-RATE = "Y"
        MOVE "Invalid Hourly Rate" TO ER-MESSAGE
        DISPLAY ERROR-RECORD.
    IF BAD-GROSS-WAGES = "Y"
        MOVE "Gross Wages too large" to ER-MESSAGE
        DISPLAY ERROR-RECORD.
```

*Figure 10.2 (continued)*

FLAGS. Each flag whose name begins with the word BAD indicates a problem with the corresponding data item—that is, the value of BAD-HOURS-WORKED indicates whether or not the value of HOURS-WORKED has the correct format. For an error in the input record (including data that causes a size error when the gross wages are computed), BAD-RECORD is set in addition to the flag corresponding to the erroneous field. FATAL-ERROR is set for an error that prevents program execution from continuing—specifically, a size error in the computation of the value of EMPLOYEE-COUNT or GROSS-WAGES. Each flag is initialized to a space and set to "Y" if the corresponding error occurs. The reason for initializing the flags to spaces instead of Ns is that the former is easily done with the statement

```
MOVE SPACES TO ERROR-FLAGS.
```

In the Procedure Division, the PERFORM statement in paragraph PRINT-PAYROLL-REPORT performs PROCESS-PAYROLL-RECORD until there is no more input or until the value of FATAL-ERROR is equal to "Y", the latter indicating that a fatal error occurred, making it impossible for the program to continue. FATAL-ERROR is initialized to a space in the paragraph ASSIGN-INITIAL-VALUES to assure that the PERFORM statement will be executed the first time. After the PERFORM statement terminates, the value of FATAL-ERROR is checked. If no fatal error occurred, the message Program terminated normally is displayed. Otherwise, the program displays the message Fatal error--program terminated abnormally.

PROCESS-PAYROLL-RECORD begins by moving spaces to all the error flags. Paragraph CHECK-PAYROLL-RECORD is then performed to check the current input record. If no problem was found in the record—the value of BAD-RECORD is not "Y"—CALCULATE-WAGES is performed. If there was no problem with the calculation—the value of BAD-RECORD is still not "Y"—then UPDATE-COUNT-AND-TOTAL and PRINT-DETAIL-LINE are performed. If the value of BAD-RECORD is "Y", then the count and total are not updated nor is a detail line printed for the current record. Instead, DISPLAY-ERROR-MESSAGE is called to display an error message for the current record.

CHECK-PAYROLL-RECORD checks the input record for format errors. We will make only one check on the employee number—we assume that no spaces are allowed in the employee number, so that the presence of a space indicates an error. An INSPECT statement is used to count the number of spaces in EMPLOYEE-NUMBER:

```
MOVE ZERO TO SPACE-COUNT.
INSPECT PR-EMPLOYEE-NUMBER
     TALLYING SPACE-COUNT FOR ALL SPACES.
```

If one or more spaces are present, the employee number is flagged as erroneous:

```
IF SPACE-COUNT > 0
     MOVE "Y" TO BAD-EMPLOYEE-NUMBER
                 BAD-RECORD.
```

We will allow numeric values to be entered with leading spaces instead of leading zeros. An INSPECT statement replaces the leading spaces by zeros:

```
INSPECT PR-HOURS-WORKED
      REPLACING LEADING SPACES BY ZEROS.
```

If after this replacement, the value of PR-HOURS-WORKED is not numeric, the value is flagged as erroneous:

```
IF PR-HOURS-WORKED IS NOT NUMERIC
   MOVE "Y" TO BAD-HOURS-WORKED
             BAD-RECORD.
```

PR-HOURLY-RATE is checked in the same way as PR-HOURS-WORKED.

A size error, we recall, occurs when a computed value is too large to fit the field in which it is to be stored. The only computation in CALCULATE-WAGES that can give a size error is the addition of regular and overtime wages to get gross wages. The size error only occurs for unreasonable input data, such as 90 hours worked at $90 per hour, so reasonableness checks on the values of PR-HOURS-WORKED and PR-HOURLY-RATE would eliminate the possibility of this size error. To illustrate size-error checking, however, we will check for the size error rather than checking the reasonableness of the input data:

```
ADD REGULAR-WAGES OVERTIME-WAGES
    GIVING GROSS-WAGES
    ON SIZE ERROR MOVE "Y" TO BAD-GROSS-WAGES
                            BAD-RECORD.
```

Paragraph UPDATE-COUNT-AND-TOTAL checks for size errors in the calculation of the employee count and the total gross wages. These are considered to be fatal errors—the program cannot continue if an accurate count and total cannot be maintained. The SIZE ERROR option on each ADD statement displays the cause of the error and sets the value of FATAL-ERROR to "Y".

Paragraph DISPLAY-ERROR-MESSAGE displays error messages for a bad input record. The bad record is moved to ER-PAYROLL-RECORD for display. The flags are then checked one by one. For each flag whose value is "Y", the appropriate message is moved to ER-MESSAGE and the value of ERROR-RECORD is displayed. Note that a multiway selection construction is *not* used here, since more than one error message can be displayed for the same record, as when both the hours-worked and hourly rate fields are bad.

Figure 10.3 shows the display produced for an input file containing four bad records. The payroll report produced is not shown; however, it contains detail lines for the valid records only, and only the valid records were included in the employee count and the total gross wages.

```
521 762523477 -- Invalid Employee Number
6347223 14577 -- Invalid Hours Worked
75822335924 3 -- Invalid Hourly Rate
8246549179329 -- Gross Wages too large
Program terminated normally
```

*Figure 10.3* The display produced by the program in Figure 10.2 when processing a file containing four erroneous records.

## EXERCISES

**1.** Modify the sequential-file-update program (Figure 7.6) to display an appropriate message if an error occurs for any of the three files manipulated by the program. The error message should identify both the file and the nature of the error.

**2.** Modify the information-retrieval program in Figure 6.5 so that it will display an appropriate message if an error occurs while the program is attempting to load or save a file.

**3.** Suppose that employees at a certain plant are not allowed to work more than 60 hours a week, and their wages are never less than $5 per hour nor more than $25 per hour. Modify the payroll program (Figure 10.2) to reject with an error message any payroll record not meeting these restrictions.

**4.** Modify the information-retrieval program in Figure 10.1 to reject any new or updated customer record with a credit limit in excess of $250,000 or a balance in excess of the credit limit. When an invalid record is entered, the program should display an appropriate error message and leave the database unchanged.

**5.** Identifying numbers are often provided with a check digit calculated from the other digits of the number. To check for an error in the number, we calculate the check digit and compare the calculated check digit with the one actually present in the number—if the two do not match, the number is in error. A match, however, does not guarantee that the number is correct, since no method of calculating check digits can detect all possible errors. A simple* method of calculating check digits is to add up all the digits of the number to be checked and use the rightmost digit of the sum as the check digit. For example, if the number to be checked is

    79231

we compute the check digit by adding the digits of the number

    7 + 9 + 2 + 3 + 1 = 22

and using the rightmost digit of the sum (2) as the check digit. The check digit is usually adjoined to the right end of the identifying number:

    792312

Modify the program in Figure 10.2 to check employee numbers according to this method. Test the program with a data file containing both valid and invalid employee numbers. Hint: Make PR-EMPLOYEE-NUMBER a numeric item with picture 9(6). Check that the value of PR-EMPLOYEE-NUMBER is numeric before attempting the check-digit calculation. To get access to the individual digits of the employee number, move PR-EMPLOYEE-NUMBER to a group item having six fields, each with a picture of 9.

---

*Too simple for practical use, in fact, since this method will not detect transposed digits, one of the most common human errors.

# 11

## Additional COBOL Features

This chapter introduces some miscellaneous features of IBM COBOL that were "left over" after the preceding chapters were written. Some of these, such as subprograms, chaining, and segmentation, are mainly used for very large programs. Others, such as the `GO TO` and `ALTER` statements, are introduced only for the purpose of warning you not to use them.

### SUBPROGRAMS

A *subprogram* (also called a *subroutine*) is a program invoked by another program rather than directly by the user. The subprogram is given access to certain data names in the calling program for the purpose of passing data between the calling program and the subprogram. The subprogram can use the values of these data names and can assign new values to them. The main program and its subprograms are each compiled separately, producing separate object files that are then combined with the linker.

Subprograms are useful for breaking a large program down into manageable parts.

Once the conventions for calling the subprograms have been decided on, different people can work independently on the main program and on each subprogram. A program that is too large for the compiler to handle can be broken down into a main program and subprograms, each of which is small enough to be compiled. Subprograms can be written in languages other than COBOL. Assembly-language subprograms are often used to communicate with nonstandard hardware devices, such as point-of-sale terminals or remote data-entry stations. Database management systems (DBMS) can provide subprograms for COBOL programs to call to gain access to the database.

A COBOL program calls a subprogram with a `CALL` statement:

```
CALL "MYSUB",
```

`"MYSUB"` is the name of the subprogram; specifically, it is the name specified in the `PROGRAM-ID` entry for the subprogram.* Note that the subprogram name must be enclosed in quotation marks. The `CALL` statement works very much like a `PERFORM` statement. Control is transferred to the subprogram when the `CALL` statement is executed. When the execution of the subprogram terminates, execution of the calling program continues with the statement following the `CALL` statement.

Usually we need to give the subprogram access to certain data names in the calling program. The data names to be passed to the subprogram are included in the `CALL` statement in a `USING` *list*:

```
CALL "SUBPROG" USING FIELD-A, FIELD-B, FIELD-C,
```

This statement calls the subprogram `SUBPROG` and gives it access to `FIELD-A`, `FIELD-B`, and `FIELD-C`, which are data names defined in Data Division of the calling program. Data names passed to subprograms are referred to as *parameters*.

A COBOL subprogram has the same general structure as a main program but with a few additional features for communicating with the calling program. The division header for the Procedure Division contains a `USING` list naming the parameters passed from the calling program:

```
PROCEDURE DIVISION USING ITEM-1, ITEM-2, ITEM-3,
```

The parameters listed in the Procedure-Division header of the subprogram correspond to those listed in the `CALL` statement in the calling program. The correspondence is based on position in the `USING` list, not on name. Thus, if the subprogram called with

```
CALL "SUBPROG" USING FIELD-A, FIELD-B, FIELD-C,
```

contains the Procedure-Division header

```
PROCEDURE DIVISION USING ITEM-1, ITEM-2, ITEM-3,
```

then `ITEM-1` in the subprogram corresponds to `FIELD-A` in the calling program, `ITEM-2` in the subprogram corresponds to `FIELD-B` in the calling program, and so on. Put another way, any reference to `ITEM-1` in the Procedure Division of the

---

*The compiler uses only the first six characters of a `PROGRAM-ID` entry, so the names of subprograms called by the same main program should differ in their first six characters.

subprogram actually refers to FIELD-A in the calling program, any reference to ITEM-2 actually refers to FIELD-B, and so on.

If no parameters are passed to a subprogram—if the CALL statement does not have a USING list—then the Procedure Division header of the subprogram does not have a USING list either. Thus, a subprogram called by

```
CALL "MYPROG".
```

has the Procedure Division header:

```
PROCEDURE DIVISION.
```

In the subprogram, parameters are defined in a special section of the Data Division called the Linkage Section. The Linkage Section does not define any memory areas in the subprogram, but rather sets up the links needed for the subprogram parameters to refer to memory areas defined in the calling program. The Linkage Section follows the Working-Storage section and precedes the Screen Section. ITEM-1, ITEM-2, and ITEM-3 might be defined in the Linkage Section as follows:

```
LINKAGE SECTION.
01   ITEM-1     PIC X(10).
01   ITEM-2     PIC 9(6)V99 COMP-3.
01   ITEM-3     PIC S9(5) COMP-0.
```

The number of parameters in the Procedure-Division header must be the same as the number in the CALL statement. Each parameter listed in the Procedure-Division header must be defined (in the Linkage Section) to have the same length and usage as the corresponding parameter in the CALL statement. Failure to observe these rules cannot be detected by the compiler but will cause unpredictable behavior when the subprogram is called.

As with a main program, execution of a subprogram begins with the first paragraph in the nondeclarative part of the Procedure Division. A subprogram, however, is terminated not with a STOP RUN statement but with an EXIT PROGRAM statement, which returns control to the calling program. Unlike the STOP RUN statement, the EXIT PROGRAM statement has to be in a paragraph by itself. The following arrangement seems to be the most reasonable one:

```
PROCEDURE DIVISION.
MAIN-ROUTINE.

        . . .


EXIT-ROUTINE.
     EXIT PROGRAM.
```

When the subprogram is called, execution begins with paragraph MAIN-ROUTINE. When all the statements in this paragraph have been executed, the computer goes on to the next paragraph, EXIT-ROUTINE. When the EXIT PROGRAM statement is executed, the subprogram is terminated and execution of the calling program resumes with the statement following the CALL statement. Any paragraphs performed by MAIN-ROUTINE are written following the EXIT-ROUTINE paragraph.

Figure 11.1 illustrates a simple main program and subprogram. In the main program, MAIN, data names BOB, JANE, SUM, and SUM-E are defined in the Working-Storage Section. In the Procedure Division, values are assigned to BOB and JANE, and the subprogram "SUB" is called with BOB, JANE, and SUM as parameters. The subprogram is to display the values of BOB and JANE, add these two values, and store the result in SUM. After the subprogram returns, the main program moves the value of SUM to SUM-E (for editing) and displays the value of SUM-E.

SUB, the name of the subprogram, is given in the subprogram's PROGRAM-ID paragraph. The parameters JACK, SUE, and TOTAL in the subprogram correspond to BOB, JANE, and SUM in the main program. JACK, SUE, and TOTAL are defined in the Linkage Section, each with the same picture as the corresponding parameter in the main program. The Procedure Division of the subprogram displays the values of JACK and SUE, adds the two values, stores the sum in TOTAL, and returns to the calling program.

Note that each reference to JACK, SUE, or TOTAL in the subprogram is actually a reference to BOB, JANE, or SUM in the main program. For example, the statement

```
ADD JACK SUE GIVING TOTAL.
```

actually adds the values of BOB and JANE, and stores the result in SUM.

To compile and link the main program and subprogram, we begin by creating two source files, one (say, MAIN.COB) for the main program and the other (say, SUB.COB) for the subprogram. The COBOL compiler is invoked twice, once to compile MAIN.COB into the object file MAIN.OBJ, and once to compile SUB.COB into the object file SUB.OBJ. To link MAIN.OBJ and SUB.OBJ, the linker is invoked with the command:

```
A:LINK MAIN SUB;
```

All object files to be linked are listed in the linker command line, with the file for the main program first and those for subprograms following in any order. The linker produces the executable file MAIN.EXE, which we execute in the usual way by entering the file name in response to the DOS prompt:

```
B>MAIN
```

When executed, the program displays the following three lines:

```
First person has    $999.99
Second person has $3,499.49
Both together have $4,499.48
```

The first two lines are displayed by the subprogram; the last line is displayed by the main program.

Information on writing assembly language subprograms can be found in chapter 10 of the reference manual and in Appendix D of this book.

```
IDENTIFICATION DIVISION.
PROGRAM-ID.  MAIN.

ENVIRONMENT DIVISION.

DATA DIVISION.
WORKING-STORAGE SECTION.
01  BOB          PIC 9(4)V99.
01  JANE         PIC 9(4)V99.
01  SUM          PIC 9(4)V99.
01  SUM-E        PIC $$,$$9.99.

PROCEDURE DIVISION.
MAIN-ROUTINE.
     MOVE 999.99 TO BOB.
     MOVE 3499.49 TO JANE.
     CALL "SUB" USING BOB, JANE, SUM.
     MOVE SUM TO SUM-E.
     DISPLAY "Both together have " SUM-E.
     STOP RUN.
```

```
IDENTIFICATION DIVISION.
PROGRAM-ID.  SUB.

ENVIRONMENT DIVISION.

DATA DIVISION.
WORKING-STORAGE SECTION.
01  JACK-E       PIC $$,$$9.99.
01  SUE-E        PIC $$,$$9.99.

LINKAGE SECTION.
01  JACK         PIC 9(4)V99.
01  SUE          PIC 9(4)V99.
01  TOTAL        PIC 9(4)V99.

PROCEDURE DIVISION USING JACK, SUE, TOTAL.
MAIN-ROUTINE.
     MOVE JACK TO JACK-E.
     DISPLAY "First person has " JACK-E.
     MOVE SUE TO SUE-E.
     DISPLAY "Second person has " SUE-E.
     ADD JACK SUE GIVING TOTAL.

EXIT-ROUTINE.
     EXIT PROGRAM.
```

*Figure 11.1*  A demonstration main program and subprogram. The main program and subprogram are compiled separately, producing two object files which are joined by the linker.

## CHAINING

Chaining allows one program to transfer control to another. The program that receives control is loaded into memory, replacing the program that transferred control. Data can be passed from the program that transfers control (the *chaining* program) to the one that receives control (the *chained* program) by using parameters in much the same way as for subprograms. Only the data passed via parameters survives the chaining process. Any other data being manipulated by the chaining program is irretrievably lost.

One application of chaining occurs when a large data processing job can be broken down into a series of smaller steps that can be carried out one after the other. We can write a separate program for each step. When the program for the first step has finished its work, it can chain to the program for the second step; the program for the second step can chain to the program for the third step; and so on. The programs can pass to one another such needed information as the DOS file names of the files being processed. Since only one program is in main memory at a time, the entire series of programs, taken together, can occupy much more space than is available in the computer's main memory.

Here is another application. Suppose we have a set of programs, each of which does a different job. Rather than make the user remember the DOS file name of each program, we can have the user begin by executing a menu program. The menu program will display a menu of the job each program can do and ask the user to make a selection—say, by pressing a function key. The menu program can then chain to the program that carries out the selected task. Other information entered by the user, such as DOS file names, can be passed to the chained program by means of parameters.

When the chained program has finished its work, it can chain back to the menu program. When this is done, however, the menu program is executed anew from the beginning with no memory of its previous incarnation. There is no way to return to a chaining program and continue its execution from the point where it left off when it chained to another program.

A program transfers control to another program by means of a CHAIN statement, such as

```
CHAIN "NEXTPROG.EXE"
```

NEXTPROG.EXE is the DOS file name of the program that is to receive control. Note that a CHAIN statement refers to the chained program by means of its DOS file name, whereas a CALL statement refers to a subprogram by means of its PROGRAM-ID.

The name of the chained program can also be given by the value of an identifier:

```
CHAIN NEXT-PROG-DOS-FILE-NAME.
```

The value of NEXT-PROG-DOS-FILE-NAME must be the DOS file name of the chained program. The DOS file name must be terminated by at least one space.

Parameters are specified in a USING list, just as for the CALL statement:

```
CHAIN "PHASE2.EXE" USING FIELD-A, FIELD-B, FIELD-C.
```

The identifiers in the USING list can be defined in the Working-Storage section, the

Linkage Section,* or in the record area of a file open at the time the CHAIN statement is processed.

If the CHAIN statement has a USING list, there must be a corresponding CHAINING list in the Procedure-Division header of the chained program:

PROCEDURE DIVISION CHAINING ITEM-1, ITEM-2, ITEM-3,

The identifiers in the CHAINING list must be defined in the Working-Storage Section of the chained program. When the chained program receives control, each identifier in the CHAINING list will have the same value that the corresponding identifier in the USING list had when the CHAIN statement was executed.

## SEGMENTATION

*Segmentation* is an alternative to chaining. Both incorporate the same idea—a program too large to fit into main memory can be broken down into smaller parts, not all of which have to be in memory at the same time. With segmentation, the Procedure Division is divided into segments that take turns residing in main memory. The memory areas defined in the Data Division are not affected by segmentation. This is in contrast to chaining, where, we have seen, all data in the chaining program is lost except that explicitly passed to the chained program via parameters.

For segmentation, the Procedure Division must be divided into sections, each of which is assigned a *segment number* in the range 0 through 99. All sections with the same segment number make up a *program segment* and must be grouped together in the Procedure Division. Sections in the declarative part of the Procedure Division must have segment numbers in the range 0 through 49. The segment number of each section is given following the word SECTION in the section header. For example, the section header

MENU SECTION 25,

assigns a segment number of 25 to Menu Section. (That is, Menu Section is part of segment 25.)

Segments with numbers in the range 0 through 49 are called *fixed segments* and remain in main memory. Segments with numbers in the range 50 through 99 are called *independent segments*. Independent segments are loaded into main memory as needed; only one independent segment is in main memory at a time.

Control is transferred from one paragraph to another by means of PERFORM statements, just as with unsegmented programs. A PERFORM statement in a fixed segment can perform any other paragraph in the program. A PERFORM statement in an independent segment can perform a paragraph in a fixed segment or a paragraph in the same independent segment, but it cannot perform a paragraph in another independent segment.

Once control is transferred to an independent segment, a substantial amount of processing should be done before control leaves that segment. Put another way, when a PERFORM statement in a fixed segment performs a paragraph in an independent segment, the computer should do substantial processing before it reaches the end of the performed paragraph and returns to the fixed segment. Usually, the performed para-

---

*A CHAIN statement can occur in a subprogram even though it must chain to a main program.

graph will do much of this processing by performing other paragraphs in the independent segment.

What we are trying to avoid is control passing into and out of a number of independent segments in rapid succession, with each independent segment making only a small contribution to the overall job to be done. When that happens, a phenomenon called *thrashing* takes place, in which the computer spends more time loading segments into main memory than doing useful work.

## THE COPY STATEMENT

The COPY statement causes text from a disk file to be inserted into a source program. The program is compiled as if the COPY statement were replaced by the text from the designated file. The COPY statement can be used in any division but is particularly useful in the Data Division. Once the record formats for a data file have been decided upon, the necessary COBOL record descriptions can be stored on disk and copied into each program that will manipulate the data file. Screen descriptions and records defining report formats are likewise sometimes used in more than one program, in which case they can be stored once and copied into each program that needs them.

For example, consider the following program fragment:

```
DATA DIVISION.
FILE SECTION.
FD   PAYROLL-FILE
     LABEL RECORDS STANDARD
     VALUE OF FILE-ID IS "PAYDAT".
COPY RECDSCR.COB.
```

The word COPY is followed by the DOS file name of the file to be copied. The file name is *not* enclosed in quotation marks. Suppose that the file RECDSCR.COB contains the text

```
01   PAYROLL-RECORD.
     02   PR-EMPLOYEE-NUMBER   PIC X(6).
     02   PR-HOURS-WORKED      PIC 99V9.
     02   PR-HOURLY-RATE       PIC 99V99.
```

The source program will be compiled as if the following had been written:

```
FILE SECTION.
FD   PAYROLL-FILE
     LABEL RECORDS STANDARD
     VALUE OF FILE-ID IS "PAYDAT".
01   PAYROLL-RECORD.
     02   PR-EMPLOYEE-NUMBER   PIC X(6).
     02   PR-HOURS-WORKED      PIC 99V9.
     02   PR-HOURLY-RATE       PIC 99V99.
```

As an alternative to the COPY statement, many text editors allow text in disk files to be inserted in the source file as the source program is edited. The source program will probably be easier to read if the required text is actually inserted with a text editor instead of being merely referred to by a COPY statement.

## THE SAME RECORD AREA CLAUSE

Two memory areas are associated with a file assigned to DISK: a *physical buffer area* that holds sectors read from or destined for the disk and a *logical record area* that holds records read from or destined for the file. The logical record area corresponds to the record descriptions associated with the file. The SAME RECORD AREA clause allows us to specify that two or more files share the same physical buffer area, thus conserving memory space. The SAME RECORD AREA clause is particularly useful when a program contains several files, only one of which will be open at a time. Since only one file at a time will be using its physical buffer area, there is no reason why one physical buffer area can't serve for all the files.

The SAME RECORD AREA clause occurs in the I-O-CONTROL paragraph, which follows the FILE-CONTROL paragraph in the Input-Output Section of the Environment Division. For example, the I-O-CONTROL paragraph

```
    I-O-CONTROL.
        SAME RECORD AREA FOR STATE-TAX-TABLE
                             FEDERAL-TAX-TABLE
                             EMPLOYEE-FILE.
```

states that the files STATE-TAX-TABLE, FEDERAL-TAX-TABLE, and EMPLOYEE-FILE will share the same physical buffer area. Any number of SAME RECORD AREA clauses can appear in the I-O-CONTROL paragraph. However, no file name can appear in more than one SAME RECORD AREA clause.

## LEVEL-77 ITEMS

COBOL allows stand-alone data items—elementary items that are not fields of records—to be given the special level number 77 in the Working-Storage and Linkage Sections:

```
    77  REGULAR-WAGES       PIC 9(4)V99.
    77  OVERTIME-WAGES      PIC 9(4)V99.
    77  GROSS-WAGES         PIC 9(4)V99.
```

Current COBOL programming practice is not to use level-77 items. Stand-alone items are either given level numbers of 01:

```
    01  REGULAR-WAGES       PIC 9(4)V99.
    01  OVERTIME-WAGES      PIC 9(4)V99.
    01  GROSS-WAGES         PIC 9(4)V99.
```

or they are grouped into records for documentation purposes:

```
    01  WORK-AREAS.
        02  REGULAR-WAGES   PIC 9(4)V99.
        02  OVERTIME-WAGES  PIC 9(4)V99.
        02  GROSS-WAGES     PIC 9(4)V99.
```

## THE GO TO STATEMENT

The GO TO statement has the form

> GO TO *procedure-name*

where *procedure-name* is a paragraph or section name. When the GO TO statement is executed, the computer jumps to the beginning of the paragraph or section named and continues execution from that point. Unlike the case for the PERFORM statement, there is no automatic return to the paragraph containing the GO TO statement. When the computer reaches the end of the paragraph or section, it goes on to the next paragraph or section in the program, and continues in this way until another GO TO statement transfers control to some other paragraph or section.

GO TO statements appeared frequently in early COBOL programs, with the result that the computer was sent jumping from paragraph to paragraph in a completely undisciplined manner. Diagramming these jumps with flowcharts confirmed the maze-like structure of the program but did nothing to make it easier to follow. Paragraph names were used only as targets for GO TO statements, and the idea of each paragraph performing a well-defined function was almost completely absent.

In the late 1960s, programmers began to realize how detrimental GO TO statements were to our ability to write, read, and understand complex programs. There arose a movement known as *structured programming,* one of whose precepts is to eliminate the use of GO TO statements in all languages for which this is practical.

COBOL is such a language—the various forms of the IF and PERFORM statements are the only control statements needed to program any data-processing task. The setting and testing of flags, which we have used extensively in this book, is characteristic of structured programming and allows many GO TO statements to be eliminated. Nowadays, a COBOL program filled with GO TO statements has an out-of-date feeling to it, like a novel whose characters use the slang and speech patterns of a bygone era.*

There is one form of the GO TO statement that, while not normally recommended, may occasionally be justifiable. The GO TO DEPENDING ON statement provides a form of multiway selection; it can serve as an alternative to the nested IF statement form of multiway selection with which we are already familiar.

The GO TO DEPENDING ON statement has the form:

> GO TO *procedure-name-1*
> *procedure-name-2*
>
> . . .
>
> *procedure-name-n*
> DEPENDING ON *data-name*

*Data-name* must be an elementary numeric item with no decimal places. The value of *data-name* determines the action taken by the GO TO DEPENDING ON statement.

---

*Alas, not everybody has gotten the message about GO TO statements, as witness the number of GO TO statements in the examples in the COBOL reference manual.

If the value of *data-name* is 1, the computer jumps to *procedure-name-1*; if the value of *data-name* is 2; the computer jumps to *procedure-name-2*; and so on. If the value of *data-name* is less than 1 or greater than the number of procedure names listed, the computer goes on to the next statement in the program, the one following the GO TO DEPENDING ON statement.

To illustrate the GO TO DEPENDING ON statement, we will modify the information-retrieval program in Figure 10.1 so that the multiway selection in the GET-AND-DO-FUNCTION paragraph is implemented with GO TO statements instead of nested IF statements. Figure 11.2 shows the nondeclarative part of the Procedure Division of the modified program.

To begin with, note that the PERFORM statement in MAIN-ROUTINE no longer performs a single paragraph but rather a *range* of paragraphs:

```
PERFORM GET-AND-DO-FUNCTION THRU FUNCTION-EXIT
    UNTIL TERMINATOR-KEY = 4.
```

On each repetition, the PERFORM statement transfers control to GET-AND-DO-FUNCTION, the first paragraph of the range. Control is returned to the PERFORM statement only when the computer reaches the end of FUNCTION-EXIT, the last paragraph in the range.

The last paragraph in a range is often a dummy paragraph whose only purpose is to provide a terminal point for the range. For writing such dummy paragraphs, COBOL provides the EXIT statement (not to be confused with the EXIT PROGRAM statement):

```
FUNCTION-EXIT.
    EXIT.
```

Whenever the computer reaches the FUNCTION-EXIT paragraph, control is immediately returned to the PERFORM statement in MAIN-ROUTINE. Depending on the value of TERMINATOR-KEY, the PERFORM statement may terminate or it may perform GET-AND-DO-FUNCTION through FUNCTION-EXIT again.

As in Figure 10.1, GET-AND-DO-FUNCTION initializes TERMINATOR-KEY to zero and performs DISPLAY-MENU until a value of TERMINATOR-KEY in the range 2 through 5 is returned. The value of TERMINATOR-KEY is then decreased by 1, giving a value in the range 1 through 4, as required by the GO TO DEPENDING ON statement:

```
GO TO ENTER-RECORD
      UPDATE-RECORD
      DELETE-RECORD
      FUNCTION-EXIT
   DEPENDING ON TERMINATOR-KEY.
```

When the GO TO DEPENDING ON statement is executed, a value of 1 for TERMINATOR-KEY causes the computer to jump to ENTER-RECORD; a value of 2 causes the computer to jump to UPDATE-RECORD; a value of 3 causes the computer to jump to DELETE-RECORD; and a value of 4 causes the computer to jump to

```
MAIN-ROUTINE.
    DISPLAY (1, 1) ERASE (5, 1) "File name? ".
    ACCEPT (, ) DOS-FILE-NAME WITH PROMPT.
    DISPLAY (7, 1) "Create new file (Y/N)? ".
    ACCEPT (, ) RESPONSE.
    IF RESPONSE = "Y" OR "y"
        DISPLAY (9, 1) "Are you sure (Y/N)? "
        ACCEPT (, ) RESPONSE
        IF RESPONSE = "Y" OR "y"
            OPEN OUTPUT CUSTOMER-FILE
            CLOSE CUSTOMER-FILE.
    OPEN I-O CUSTOMER-FILE.
    IF ERROR-CODE = "00"
        MOVE ZERO TO TERMINATOR-KEY
        PERFORM GET-AND-DO-FUNCTION THRU FUNCTION-EXIT
            UNTIL TERMINATOR-KEY = 4.
        CLOSE CUSTOMER-FILE.
    STOP RUN.

GET-AND-DO-FUNCTION.
    MOVE ZERO TO TERMINATOR-KEY.
    PERFORM DISPLAY-MENU
        UNTIL TERMINATOR-KEY > 1 AND < 6.
    SUBTRACT 1 FROM TERMINATOR-KEY.
    GO TO ENTER-RECORD
            UPDATE-RECORD
            DELETE-RECORD
            FUNCTION-EXIT
        DEPENDING ON TERMINATOR-KEY.

ENTER-RECORD.
    DISPLAY ENTER-SCREEN.
    ACCEPT ENTER-SCREEN.
    WRITE CUSTOMER-RECORD.
    GO TO FUNCTION-EXIT.

UPDATE-RECORD.
    DISPLAY (1, 1) ERASE (5, 1) "Account Number? ".
    ACCEPT (, ) ACCOUNT-NUMBER WITH PROMPT.
    READ CUSTOMER-FILE.
    IF ERROR-CODE = "00"
        DISPLAY UPDATE-SCREEN
        ACCEPT UPDATE-SCREEN
        REWRITE CUSTOMER-RECORD.
    GO TO FUNCTION-EXIT.

DELETE-RECORD.
    DISPLAY (1, 1) ERASE (5, 1) "Account number? ".
    ACCEPT (, ) ACCOUNT-NUMBER WITH PROMPT.
    DELETE CUSTOMER-FILE RECORD.
    GO TO FUNCTION-EXIT.

FUNCTION-EXIT.
    EXIT.

DISPLAY-MENU.
    DISPLAY MENU-SCREEN.
    ACCEPT (15, 56) DUMMY.
    ACCEPT TERMINATOR-KEY FROM ESCAPE KEY.
```

*Figure 11.2* This version of the Procedure Division of Figure 10.1 uses a GO TO DEPENDING ON statement to implement multiway selection. This is a demonstration only, not a recommended application. The GO TO DEPENDING ON statement is justified only when the selection is to be made from a very large number of paragraphs or when the selection must be made as fast as possible, neither of which applies here.

276

FUNCTION-EXIT. Thus when the value of TERMINATOR-KEY is 4 (corresponding to the Exit Program function), control is returned to the MAIN-ROUTINE PERFORM statement via FUNCTION-EXIT without any processing being done. On detecting that the value of TERMINATOR-KEY is 4, the PERFORM statement terminates the repetitions of GET-AND-DO-FUNCTION through FUNCTION-EXIT.

Paragraphs ENTER-RECORD, UPDATE-RECORD, and DELETE-RECORD each carries out its appointed function as in Figure 10.1. However, since each paragraph was entered with a GO TO statement, there is no automatic return at the end of the paragraph. Each paragraph must end with a GO TO statement transferring control to FUNCTION-EXIT and hence back to the MAIN-ROUTINE PERFORM statement.

(We could omit the GO TO FUNCTION-EXIT statement at the end of DELETE-RECORD; when the end of the paragraph is reached, the computer will "fall into" the next paragraph, FUNCTION-EXIT. The GO TO statement is probably a good idea, however, since it assures the program will continue to work if an additional paragraph is inserted between DELETE-RECORD and FUNCTION-EXIT, as might be done if a new function is added to the program.)

Under what conditions can the GO TO statement form of multiway selection be justified? First, we note that the GO TO DEPENDING ON statement, considered by itself, is somewhat easier to read than the nested IF statements, since the names of the paragraphs that perform the various functions are listed one after the other, without any intervening IFs, ELSE IFs, conditions, or PERFORMs. This simplicity of the GO TO DEPENDING ON statement, however, is paid for by greater complexity in the rest of the Procedure Division. Nevertheless, if a selection must be made from among a large number of paragraphs, the nested IF statements can become long and cumbersome, and the simplicity of the GO TO DEPENDING ON statement may outweigh increased complexity elsewhere.

The other justification for the GO TO DEPENDING ON statement is that it is faster than nested IF statements. The latter must evaluate one condition after another until the first true condition is found. If the number of paragraphs from which the selection is to be made is large, many conditions may have to be evaluated to determine which paragraph is to be performed. For the GO TO DEPENDING ON statement, on the other hand, the compiler creates a table of the memory addresses of all the paragraphs whose names appear in the statement. The data name following DEPENDING ON is used as a subscript to select an entry from this table. This table access is generally faster than the repeated testing of conditions.

Only rarely, however, will this difference in speed be of any significance. Most COBOL programs are *input-output bound,* meaning their speeds are limited not by how fast the computations are carried out but by the speeds of input and output devices, such as the printers, disk drives, and users typing on keyboards.

Neither of these possible justifications apply to the information-retrieval program. The number of paragraph names is small enough so that the selection with nested IF statements is easily read. And the nested IF statements provide seemingly instantaneous response when a function key is pressed. Therefore, the Procedure Division in Figure 10.1 is the superior one, and Figure 11.2 is an abomination in the sight of all structured programmers.

## THE ALTER STATEMENT

GO TO statements, we have seen, allow the computer to jump from paragraph to paragraph in an undisciplined way, making it extremely difficult for someone reading the program to determine what path the computer will follow. Is there any way to make matters worse? Yes, we can alter a GO TO statement so that the computer does not necessarily jump to the paragraph named in the GO TO statement, but can jump to any paragraph in the program. Under these conditions, determining the path the computer will take through the program becomes not merely difficult, but next to impossible. Yet the infamous ALTER statement allows just this kind of tampering with GO TO statements.

An ALTER statement changes the destination paragraph of a designated GO TO statement. A GO TO statement to be tampered with by an ALTER statement must appear in a paragraph by itself:

```
SWITCH.
    GO TO PARA-1.
```

This GO TO statement will send the computer to paragraph PARA-1 *unless* its destination is changed by an ALTER statement, in which case it will send the computer to some other paragraph. We can even omit the paragraph name from the GO TO statement:

```
SWITCH.
    GO TO.
```

This GO TO statement must be altered to give it a destination before control reaches it.

Persons who maintain (correct and update) COBOL programs recoil with horror when they find a GO TO statement in a paragraph by itself, for this most likely indicates that the GO TO statement is tampered with by one or more ALTER statements located who-knows-where in the program.

An ALTER statement specifies a new destination for a GO TO statement. Thus, after

```
ALTER SWITCH TO PROCEED TO PARA-2.
```

the GO TO statement in paragraph SWITCH will send the computer to PARA-2. After

```
ALTER SWITCH TO PROCEED TO PARA-3.
```

is executed, the GO TO statement in SWITCH will send the computer to PARA-3, and so on.

The ALTER statement has no redeeming merit; it is just an invitation to make a program unreadable and incomprehensible; its use can be condemned without reservation.

# Appendix A

## Reserved Words

The following is a list of the reserved words in IBM Personal Computer COBOL. Optional parts of words are enclosed in parentheses. Thus, the entry `PIC(TURE)` indicates that both `PIC` and `PICTURE` are reserved words.

| | |
|---|---|
| ACCEPT | AT |
| ACCESS | AUTHOR |
| ADD | AUTO |
| ADVANCING | AUTO-SKIP |
| AFTER | |
| ALL | BACKGROUND-COLOR |
| ALPHABETIC | BEEP |
| ALTER | BEFORE |
| AND | BELL |
| ARE | BLANK |
| AREA(S) | BLINK |
| ASCENDING | BLOCK |
| ASCII | BOTTOM |
| ASSIGN | BY |

CALL
CHAIN
CHAINING
CHARACTER(S)
CLOSE
CODE-SET
COL
COLLATING
COLUMN
COMMA
COMP
COMPUTATIONAL
COMPUTATIONAL-0
COMPUTATIONAL-3
COMPUTE
COMP-0
COMP-3
CONFIGURATION
CONTAINS
COPY
COUNT
CURRENCY

DATA
DATE
DATE-COMPILED
DATE-WRITTEN
DAY
DEBUGGING
DECIMAL-POINT
DECLARATIVES
DELETE
DELIMITED
DELIMITER
DEPENDING
DESCENDING
DISK
DISPLAY
DIVIDE
DIVISION
DOWN
DYNAMIC

ELSE
EMPTY-CHECK
END
END-OF-PAGE
ENVIRONMENT
EOP

EQUAL
ERASE
ERROR
ESCAPE
EXCEPTION
EXHIBIT
EXIT
EXTEND

FD
FILE
FILE-CONTROL
FILE-ID
FILLER
FIRST
FOOTING
FOR
FOREGROUND-COLOR
FROM
FULL

GIVING
GO
GREATER

HIGHLIGHT
HIGH-VALUE(S)

IDENTIFICATION
IF
IN
INDEX
INDEXED
INITIAL
INPUT
INPUT-OUTPUT
INSPECT
INSTALLATION
INTO
INVALID
IS
I-O
I-O-CONTROL

JUST(IFIED)

KEY

LABEL
LEADING

LEFT
LEFT-JUSTIFY
LENGTH-CHECK
LESS
LIN
LINAGE
LINAGE-COUNTER
LINE(S)
LINKAGE
LOCK
LOW-VALUE(S)

MEMORY
MERGE
MODE
MODULES
MOVE
MULTIPLY

NAMES
NATIVE
NEGATIVE
NEXT
NO-ECHO
NOT
NUMBER
NUMERIC

OBJECT-COMPUTER
OCCURS
OMITTED
OPEN
ORGANIZATION
OVERFLOW

PAGE
PERFORM
PIC(TURE)
PLUS
POINTER
POSITIVE
PRINTER
PROCEDURE(S)
PROCEED
PROGRAM
PROGRAM-ID
PROMPT

QUOTE

RANDOM
READ
READY
RECORD(S)
REDEFINES
RELATIVE
RELEASE
REMOVAL
REPLACING
REQUIRED
RERUN
RESERVE
RESET
RETURN
REVERSE-VIDEO
REWRITE
RIGHT
RIGHT-JUSTIFY
ROUNDED
RUN

SAME
SCREEN
SEARCH
SECTION
SECURE
SECURITY
SELECT
SENTENCE
SEPARATE
SEQUENCE
SEQUENTIAL
SET
SIGN
SIZE
SORT
SORT-MERGE
SOURCE-COMPUTER
SPACE(S)
SPACE-FILL
SPECIAL-NAMES
STANDARD
STANDARD-1
START
STATUS
STRING

| | |
|---|---|
| SUBTRACT | UPDATE |
| SWITCH-1 | UPON |
| SWITCH-2 | USAGE |
| SWITCH-3 | USE |
| SWITCH-4 | USER |
| SWITCH-5 | USING |
| SWITCH-6 | |
| SWITCH-7 | VALUE(S) |
| SWITCH-8 | VARYING |
| SYNC(HRONIZED) | |
| | WHEN |
| TALLYING | WITH |
| THAN | WORDS |
| THROUGH | WORKING-STORAGE |
| THRU | WRITE |
| TIME | |
| TIMES | ZERO((E)S) |
| TO | ZERO-FILL |
| TOP | |
| TRACE | |
| TRAILING | - |
| TRAILING-SIGN | * |
| | |
| UNDERLINE | ** |
| UNSTRING | |
| UNTIL | \ |
| UP | |

# Appendix B

## ASCII
## Codes

The table on the following page gives the ASCII codes for the characters commonly used by COBOL programmers. Excluded are the control characters (codes 0 through 31) and the graphics characters (codes 127 through 255). A complete table of all ASCII codes is given in appendix G of the COBOL reference manual. For comparing alphanumeric items, "alphabetical order" is defined as the order in which the characters appear in this table.

| ASCII Code | Character | ASCII Code | Character | ASCII Code | Character |
|---|---|---|---|---|---|
| 32 | space | 64 | @ | 96 | ` |
| 33 | ! | 65 | A | 97 | a |
| 34 | " | 66 | B | 98 | b |
| 35 | # | 67 | C | 99 | c |
| 36 | $ | 68 | D | 100 | d |
| 37 | % | 69 | E | 101 | e |
| 38 | & | 70 | F | 102 | f |
| 39 | ' | 71 | G | 103 | g |
| 40 | ( | 72 | H | 104 | h |
| 41 | ) | 73 | I | 105 | i |
| 42 | * | 74 | J | 106 | j |
| 43 | + | 75 | K | 107 | k |
| 44 | , | 76 | L | 108 | l |
| 45 | - | 77 | M | 109 | m |
| 46 | . | 78 | N | 110 | n |
| 47 | / | 79 | O | 111 | o |
| 48 | 0 | 80 | P | 112 | p |
| 49 | 1 | 81 | Q | 113 | q |
| 50 | 2 | 82 | R | 114 | r |
| 51 | 3 | 83 | S | 115 | s |
| 52 | 4 | 84 | T | 116 | t |
| 53 | 5 | 85 | U | 117 | u |
| 54 | 6 | 86 | V | 118 | v |
| 55 | 7 | 87 | W | 119 | w |
| 56 | 8 | 88 | X | 120 | x |
| 57 | 9 | 89 | Y | 121 | y |
| 58 | : | 90 | Z | 122 | z |
| 59 | ; | 91 | [ | 123 | { |
| 60 | < | 92 | \ | 124 | \| |
| 61 | = | 93 | ] | 125 | } |
| 62 | > | 94 | ^ | 126 | ~ |
| 63 | ? | 95 | _ | | |

# Appendix C

# The Forms-Layout Program

This appendix presents a BASIC program (Figure C.1) for determining the proper spacing between printed items on a report. The program relieves the need for much tedious calculation or trial and error. As written, the program can be run with any version of IBM-PC BASIC. With some modification, the program can run on pocket computers and notebook-size computers, which may be handier for forms layout than a larger machine. Detailed instructions for using the program are given below; an example of the program's use is given in Chapter 3.

Before running the program, write down on a piece of scratch paper the titles, column headings, and detail items that are to appear in the printed report. (See the example in Chapter 3.) Each detail item can be represented by its COBOL picture. Note the width of each item—the number of characters in it—since you will need to provide the program with this information.

Figure 3.6 illustrates a run of the forms-layout program. The program begins by requesting five numbers: *page width, left margin, number of title lines, number of lines,* and *number of columns.* In response to

```
Page width?
```

```
10 REM Forms layout
20 CLS : KEY OFF
30 INPUT "Page width"; PWIDTH
40 INPUT "Left margin"; LMARGIN
50 IF LMARGIN >= 0 THEN MFLAG = 0 ELSE MFLAG = 1 : LMARGIN = 0
60 INPUT "Number of title lines"; NTITLES
70 INPUT "Number of lines"; NLINES
80 INPUT "Number of columns"; NCOLS
90 PRINT
100 DIM FWIDTH(NLINES, NCOLS), TWIDTH(NTITLES, 3)
110 DIM CWIDTH(NCOLS), LJUST(NLINES, NCOLS)
120 DIM FSPACES(NLINES, NCOLS + 1), TSPACES(NTITLES, 4)
130 PRINT : PRINT "Enter title widths--"
140 PRINT
150 PRINT , "Left", "Center", "Right"
160 PRINT
170 FOR I = 1 TO NTITLES
180     PRINT "Title line"; I;
190     FOR J = 1 TO 3
200         PRINT TAB(14*J); : INPUT; "   ", TWIDTH(I, J)
210     NEXT
220     PRINT
230 NEXT
240 PRINT
250 PRINT : PRINT "Enter field widths--"
260 PRINT
270 PRINT "Columns: ";
280 FOR J = 1 TO NCOLS : PRINT TAB(6*J + 6); J; : NEXT : PRINT
290 PRINT
300 FOR I = 1 TO NLINES
310     PRINT "Line"; I;
320     FOR J = 1 TO NCOLS
330         PRINT TAB(6*J + 6); : INPUT; " ", FWIDTH(I, J)
340         LJUST(I, J) = (FWIDTH(I, J) < 0)
350         FWIDTH(I, J) = ABS(FWIDTH(I, J))
360     NEXT
370     PRINT
380 NEXT
390 FOR J = 1 TO NCOLS
400     CWIDTH(J) = FWIDTH(1, J)
410     FOR I = 2 TO NLINES
420         IF FWIDTH(I, J) > CWIDTH(J) THEN CWIDTH(J) = FWIDTH(I, J)
430     NEXT
440 NEXT
450 CSPACE = PWIDTH - 2*LMARGIN
460 FOR J = 1 TO NCOLS : CSPACE = CSPACE - CWIDTH(J) : NEXT
470 CSPACE = CSPACE / (NCOLS + 2*MFLAG - 1)
480 IF MFLAG THEN LMARGIN = CSPACE
490 RMARGIN = PWIDTH
```

*Figure C.1*   This BASIC program calculates the spacings between printed items needed to produce a neatly formatted report.

enter the maximum number of characters that can be printed on each line. In response to

    Left margin?

enter the number of spaces to appear to the left of the print area. If you enter a positive number, the program will use the left margin that you specify. If you enter a negative

```
500 FOR I = 1 TO NLINES
510     PBLANK = 0 : PCOL = LMARGIN
520     FOR J = 1 TO NCOLS
530         PFIELD = INT(PCOL)
540         IF NOT LJUST(I, J) THEN
                PFIELD = PFIELD + INT((CWIDTH(J) - FWIDTH(I, J))/2)
550         FSPACES(I, J) = PFIELD - PBLANK
560         PBLANK = PFIELD + FWIDTH(I, J)
570         PCOL = PCOL + CWIDTH(J) + CSPACE
580     NEXT
590     FSPACES(I, NCOLS + 1) = PWIDTH - PBLANK
600     IF FSPACES(I, NCOLS + 1) < RMARGIN THEN RMARGIN = FSPACES(I, NCOLS + 1)
610 NEXT
620 LMARGIN = INT(LMARGIN)
630 FOR I = 1 TO NTITLES
640     TSPACES(I, 1) = LMARGIN : TSPACES(I, 4) = RMARGIN
650     LS = INT((PWIDTH - TWIDTH(I, 2))/2)
660     RS = PWIDTH - LS - TWIDTH(I, 2)
670     TSPACES(I, 2) = LS - LMARGIN - TWIDTH(I, 1)
680     TSPACES(I, 3) = RS - RMARGIN - TWIDTH(I, 3)
690 NEXT
700 PRINT : PRINT : PRINT "Title spacings--"
710 PRINT
720 PRINT , SPC(5); "Left", SPC(4); "Center", SPC(5); "Right"
730 PRINT
740 FOR I = 1 TO NTITLES
750     PRINT "Title line"; I;
760     FOR J = 1 TO 4
770         PRINT TAB(14*J); TSPACES(I, J);
780     NEXT
790     PRINT
800 NEXT
810 PRINT : PRINT : PRINT "Field spacings--"
820 PRINT
830 PRINT "Columns: ";
840 FOR J = 1 TO NCOLS : PRINT TAB(6*J + 9); J; : NEXT : PRINT
850 PRINT
860 FOR I = 1 TO NLINES
870     PRINT "Line"; I;
880     FOR J = 1 TO NCOLS + 1
890         PRINT TAB(6*J + 6); FSPACES(I, J);
900     NEXT
910     PRINT
920 NEXT
```

*Figure C.1 (continued)*

number, however, the program will choose a left margin approximately equal to the spacing between the columns of the report.

The next three prompts are

```
Number of title lines?
Number of lines?
Number of columns?
```

The title lines are the identifying lines at the top of a report that are not aligned with the columns of data. The footing lines that appear at the bottom of a report can also usually be treated as title lines when using this program. *Number of lines* is the number of lines of column headings plus one for the detail line. (Although many detail lines will be printed on each page of the report, we deal with only one representative detail line when doing the layout.) *Number of columns* is the number of columns into which the printed data is to be arranged.

Each title line has a *left part,* which begins at the left margin, a *center part,* which is centered horizontally, and a *right part,* which ends at the right margin. The program now asks you to enter the widths of the left, center, and right parts for each title line. If one of these parts does not appear in a particular title line, enter 0 for the width of the missing part.

The widths are entered as entries in a table. The program displays the column headings Left, Center, and Right. It then types Title line 1 and positions the cursor in the Left column. At this point, you enter the width of the left part of title line 1 and press the Enter key. The program then moves the cursor to the Center column, after which you enter the width of the center part of title line 1 and press Enter. After you have entered the widths of all three parts of title line 1, the program goes on to title line 2, and so on. Remember always to press Enter (rather than Tab or the space bar) after typing each width. The program will automatically move the cursor to the proper position in the table for entering the next width.

The final data that the program needs is the width of each field in each column. The fields can be column headings or data fields in the detail line (as mentioned, the latter are represented by their COBOL pictures). The field widths are also entered in tabular form. The program sets up a table with one column in the table for each column in the report. For each line, the program moves the cursor from column to column as you enter the width of each column heading or detail item. Again, remember to press Enter after typing each field width.

If, on the line for which you are entering data, no column heading occurs in a particular column, enter 0 for the width of the missing column heading. The program will normally center printed items in their columns. But some items, such as column headings for a column containing variable-length alphanumeric items, are best left-justified—printed at the left edge of the column. To get an item left-justified, enter its field width as a negative number. For example, if the width of a 10-character item is entered as 10, the item will be centered. If the width is entered as -10, the item will be left justified.

After you have entered all the field widths, the program takes a few moments to do its calculations and then prints out the spacings between the printed items. The item spacings are printed in the form of tables similar to the ones in which you entered the title part and field widths. Note, however, that the spacings are not aligned with the column headings of the tables. Instead, the item spacings appear to the left of the first column, between columns, and to the right of the last column, just as the corresponding spaces are positioned with respect to the columns in the printed report.

The item spacings can be used directly to write COBOL record descriptions for the various printed lines. (For instance, see the example in Chapter 3.) For your information, the program gives the space following the last printed item on each line, although this space does not usually have to be included in COBOL record descriptions.

# Appendix D

## Assembly Language Subroutines

This appendix describes briefly how to write assembly language subroutines that can be called from COBOL programs. Knowledge of assembly language is assumed; information on assembly language programming can be found in the Macro Assembler reference manual as well as in books on programming the 8086 and 8088 microprocessors. Note that material on programming the 8086 also applies to the 8088 used in the IBM Personal Computer.

A subroutine must be given access to the parameters specified in the USING list of the CALL statement. For example, if the subroutine SUBR is called by

```
CALL "SUBR" USING PARM1, PARM2, PARM3,
```

then SUBR must be given access to the memory areas corresponding to PARM1, PARM2, and PARM3. In COBOL, this is done by passing the addresses of the parameters to the subroutine. When SUBR begins execution, the DS register will point to the data segment containing the parameter values, and the addresses of the parameters (more precisely, their offsets in the data segment pointed to by DS) will be on the stack.

The calling program pushes the addresses of the parameters onto the stack before calling the subroutine. The CALL instruction saves the contents of the CS and IP registers on the stack. When the subroutine begins execution, the top five words of the stack look like this (the SP register points to the top of the stack):

```
SP ---> saved IP contents
        saved CS contents
        address of PARM3
        address of PARM2
        address of PARM1
```

The stack contains a two-word return address—the saved IP and CS values—followed by a one-word address for each parameter. Note that the parameter addresses appear in reverse order: PARM3 first, then PARM2, and finally PARM1.

Values on the stack are addressed using the BP register. The assembly language program begins by saving the current contents of the BP register on the stack, then setting the BP register to point to the top of the stack. The following instructions accomplish this:

```
PUSH    BP
MOV     BP,SP
```

The stack now looks like this:

```
BP ---> saved BP contents
        saved IP contents
        saved CS contents
        address of PARM3
        address of PARM2
        address of PARM1
```

The easiest way to refer locations on the stack is to use an assembly language *structure,* which is similar to a COBOL record. (Structures are available only in the full Macro Assembler—not in the Small Assembler.) The area of the stack used by a subroutine is called a *stack frame.* The following structure describes the stack frame for a program with three parameters:

```
STACKFR STRUC
        DW      ?
        DW      ?
        DW      ?
PARM3   DW      ?
PARM2   DW      ?
PARM1   DW      ?
STACKFR ENDS
```

The first three words of the structure correspond to the saved register values. The next three correspond to the parameter addresses. We can use the labels PARM1, PARM2, and PARM3 to refer to the locations containing the parameter addresses. For example, the instruction

```
MOV        BX,[BP].PARM1
```

moves the address of PARM1 to the BX register.

The addresses obtained from the stack are used to access and manipulate the values of the parameters. The subroutine has no way of determining how many parameters it was passed or the picture and usage of each. Therefore, the documentation for the assembly language subroutine must state how many parameters the subroutine expects and what picture and usage each must have. It is the responsibility of the COBOL programmer to call the subroutine with the proper number of parameters and make sure that each parameter has the required picture and usage.

Numbers are usually passed as COMP-0 values, which are one-word binary values and so can be readily manipulated by the 8088. There is, however, an important difference between the way words are stored in COBOL and by the 8088. The 8088 always stores a word with the least significant byte first. COBOL uses the reverse order: the most significant byte precedes the least significant byte. Because of this difference, we cannot use a word-oriented instruction to load or store the value of a COMP-0 parameter. Instead, the two bytes of the parameter value must be loaded and stored separately.

Note that the program EXAMPLE and the subroutine ADDIT in chapter 10 of the first edition of the COBOL reference manual are highly misleading. ADDIT does not take into account the reversal of the order of bytes for COMP-0 values. Worse yet, the parameter values supplied to ADDIT by EXAMPLE are such that the subroutine works in spite of the error. If, however, the value of PARM1 or PARM2, or the value to be returned for PARM3, is greater than 255 (so that the value occupies more than one byte) ADDIT will not return the correct result.

We can simplify accessing COMP-0 values by describing them with a structure:

```
COMP_0    STRUC
HIBYTE    DB       ?
LOBYTE    DB       ?
COMP_0    ENDS
```

If PARM1 has COMP-0 usage, we can get the value of PARM1 into the AX register as follows:

```
MOV        BX,[BP].PARM1
MOV        AL,[BX].LOBYTE
MOV        AH,[BX].HIBYTE
```

Likewise, if PARM3 has COMP-0 usage, we can store the contents of the AX register as the value of PARM3 as follows:

```
MOV        BX,[BP].PARM3
MOV        [BX].LOBYTE,AL
MOV        [BX].HIBYTE,AH
```

Note that we cannot refer to a COMP-0 parameter value with an arithmetic instruction, because the arithmetic instruction would fetch the bytes in the wrong order. Thus,

```
        MOV       BX,[BP],PARM2
        ADD       AX,[BX]
```

is wrong. Instead, we must move the value of PARM2 into a register before doing the addition:

```
        MOV       BX,[BP],PARM2
        MOV       DL,[BX],LOBYTE
        MOV       DH,[BX],HIBYTE
        ADD       AX,DX
```

An assembly language subroutine must not cause the stack to overflow. A subroutine that makes substantial use of the stack may have to use its own stack area. The SS and SP registers must be restored to their original values before the subroutine returns.

As an example, we will write a subroutine UCASE that converts all the letters in an alphanumeric item to upper case. Such a conversion might be needed before comparing alphanumeric items for alphabetical order. In alphabetizing, we do not wish to distinguish between upper-case and lower-case letters, whereas in the ASCII code all upper-case letters precede all lower-case letters.

Figure D.1 shows a COBOL program, UPPER, which was written to test the subroutine UCASE. In the Working-Storage Section of UPPER, TEST-LINE is the alphanumeric item whose contents are to be converted; TEST-LINE has a picture of X(60) and so contains 60 characters. The subroutine UCASE can handle alphanumeric items of different lengths, but the length of the item to be converted must be passed as a parameter. CHAR-COUNT is a COMP-0 item whose value is 60, the number of characters to be converted. Note that a COMP-0 item is always a one-word binary number, regardless of the picture specified for it.

The Procedure Division begins by prompting the user to type a line, which is accepted as the value of TEST-LINE. UCASE is called to convert the letters in

```
IDENTIFICATION DIVISION.
PROGRAM-ID. UPPER.

ENVIRONMENT DIVISION.

DATA DIVISION.
WORKING-STORAGE SECTION.
01  CHAR-COUNT        PIC 99 COMP-0 VALUE 60.
01  TEST-LINE         PIC X(60).

PROCEDURE DIVISION.
CONVERT.
    DISPLAY (1, 1) ERASE
            (5, 1) "Type line:         ".
    ACCEPT (, ) TEST-LINE WITH PROMPT.
    CALL "UCASE" USING CHAR-COUNT, TEST-LINE.
    DISPLAY (7, 1) "Converted line: " TEST-LINE.
    STOP RUN.
```

*Figure D.1*  This program calls an assembly language subroutine to convert lower-case letter in TEST-LINE to upper-case.

```
        CALL "UCASE" USING CHAR-COUNT, TEST-LINE.
```

The parameter CHAR-COUNT gives the number of characters to be converted; the parameter TEST-LINE contains the characters that are to be converted. After UCASE has been executed, UPPER prints the converted line and terminates.

Figure D.2 shows the assembly language subroutine for UCASE. We begin by declaring the name UCASE as public so it will be made available to the linker and hence to the COBOL program. If the name used in the COBOL program is longer than six characters, only the first six characters should be used in the assembly language subroutine. The reason is that the COBOL compiler truncates all subroutine names to six

```
        PUBLIC  UCASE               ; Called from COBOL with
                                    ; CALL "UCASE" USING COUNT, STRING.

STACKFR STRUC                       ; Stack frame
        DW      ?                   ; Saved contents of BP
        DW      ?                   ; Return address: IP
        DW      ?                   ; Return address: CS
STRING  DW      ?                   ; Address of string
COUNT   DW      ?                   ; Address of character count
STACKFR ENDS

COMP_O  STRUC                       ; COMP-O value
HIBYTE  DB      ?                   ; Most significant byte
LOBYTE  DB      ?                   ; Least significant byte
COMP_O  ENDS

UCSEG   SEGMENT 'CODE'              ; UCSEG will appear as a CODE
        ASSUME  CS:UCSEG            ; segment in the linker map

UCASE   PROC    FAR                 ; Entry point for UCASE
        PUSH    BP                  ; Save caller's BP
        MOV     BP,SP               ; Set BP to point to stack frame
        PUSH    DS                  ; Copy contents of DS ...
        POP     ES                  ; ... into ES (STOSB uses ES)
        MOV     BX,[BP].COUNT       ; Get address of character count
        MOV     CL,[BX].LOBYTE      ; Get low order byte of count
        MOV     CH,[BX].HIBYTE      ; Get high order byte of count
        MOV     SI,[BP].STRING      ; Set SI to point to string
        MOV     DI,[BP].STRING      ; Set DI to point to string
        CLD                         ; Set autoincrement for SI and DI
UC1:    LODSB                       ; Load character into AL
        CMP     AL,'a'              ; Does character precede 'a'?
        JB      UC2                 ; Yes: don't change it
        CMP     AL,'z'              ; Does character follow 'z'?
        JA      UC2                 ; Yes: don't change it
        SUB     AL,32               ; Convert character to upper case
UC2:    STOSB                       ; Store character back in memory
        LOOP    UC1                 ; Repeat until (CX) = 0
        POP     BP                  ; Restore caller's BP
        RET     4                   ; Discard 4 bytes of
UCASE   ENDP                        ; parameters and return

UCSEG   ENDS
        END
```

*Figure D.2*  This assembly language subroutine converts lower-case letters to upper-case.

characters. If the full name is used in the subroutine, the linker will not recognize it as being the same as the truncated name supplied by the COBOL compiler.

As already explained, we use a structure STACKFR to describe the part of the stack used by the subroutine. COUNT corresponds to the parameter CHAR-COUNT in the COBOL program, and STRING correspond to the COBOL parameter TEST-LINE. The structure COMP_0 defines the order of the bytes for a COMP-0 value.

We use a SEGMENT pseudo-op to define the code segment for the subroutine:

```
UCSEG    SEGMENT 'CODE'
```

Giving UCSEG the class 'CODE' causes it to be labeled as a CODE segment and listed with the other CODE segments in the map produced by the linker. The assembler is told to assume that the CS register points to UCSEG:

```
ASSUME   CS:UCSEG
```

The assembler does not have to be told anything about the contents of other segment registers. *We* assume, however, that the DS register points to the segment containing the parameter values.

Since UCASE and the calling program are in different code segments, UCASE is defined as a FAR procedure:

```
UCASE    PROC    FAR
```

UCASE begins by saving the contents of the BP register and setting BP to point to the top of the stack:

```
PUSH     BP
MOV      BP,SP
```

This subroutine contains the STOSB instruction, which uses ES rather than DS for addressing. Therefore, the segment value in DS must be copied into ES:

```
PUSH     DS
POP      ES
```

The COBOL program restores the original value of ES after the subroutine returns; therefore the subroutine can change the contents of ES without saving and restoring its original value.

The value of the COUNT parameter is moved to the CX register, where it will be used to control the number of characters processed:

```
MOV      BX,[BP].COUNT
MOV      CL,[BX].LOBYTE
MOV      CH,[BX].HIBYTE
```

The address of the alphanumeric item to be converted is moved to both the SI and the DI registers:

```
MOV      SI,[BP].STRING
MOV      DI,[BP].STRING
```

The instructions CLD through LOOP convert the letters in the alphanumeric item to upper case by subtracting 32 from their ASCII codes. We will not go into the details of this part of the subroutine, which should be clear to anyone familiar with 8088 assembly language.

When its work is finished, UCASE prepares to return by restoring the saved contents of the BP register:

```
POP       BP
```

It is the responsibility of the subroutine to remove the parameter addresses from the stack. This job will be done by the RET instruction if we tell it the number of bytes to discard. Since each parameter address occupies one word, or two bytes, and the subroutine has two parameters, four bytes of parameter addresses need to be discarded:

```
RET       4
```

# Index